THE SCIENTIFIC
TRAVELER

THE SCIENTIFIC TRAVELER

A Guide to the People, Places, and Institutions of Europe

Charles Tanford

Jacqueline Reynolds

John Wiley & Sons, Inc.

NEW YORK • CHICHESTER • BRISBANE • TORONTO • SINGAPORE

Front cover, photo credits: the background photo is courtesy of the authors; the lower left photo is courtesy of the Swedish Central Board of National Antiquities; and the lower photo is courtesy of the Carlsberg Breweries, Copenhagen.

The maps were prepared by Jackie Taylor and George Dardis (Cambridge, England). Many of the illustrations represent the authors' own photographs. Sources for others are as follows:

Picture Credits: 21, Spanish National Tourist Office, London. 45, Italian State Tourist Office (E.N.I.T.), London. 52, from C. Lyell, *Principles of Geology*, published in 1830. 99, by courtesy of the Director of the Royal Institution. 105, by courtesy of the Jenner Museum, Berkeley. 107, photo provided by the Bowood Estate. 124, with permission of Manchester City Council. 128, with permission of Lincolnshire County Council Recreational Services. 158, from *The Cambridge Encyclopedia of Earth Sciences*. 193, Conservatoire National des Arts et Métiers, Paris. 195, copyright Institut Pasteur, Paris. 199, photo by cliché Loïc-Jahan, Chateauneuf-de-Grasse. A similar photograph has appeared previously in the book *Through France with Berzelius* by C. G. Bernhard. 210, with permission of the Académie Nationale de Médecine, Paris. 211, with permission of Éditions du Castelet, Boulogne, France. 222, with permission of Boerhaave Museum, Leiden. 262, photo, Deutsches Museum, Munich. 265, courtesy Wundt Institut, Leipzig. 266, photo, Deutsches Museum, Munich. 304, photo provided by Carlsberg Breweries, Copenhagen. 317, (left) Swedish Linnaean Society, Uppsala. (right) Photo by Ingmar Holmåsen, Malmköping, Sweden. 319, courtesy Brahe Museum on the Island of Ven.

Text credit: 27, excerpt from letter by Pliny the Younger from *Pliny: A Selection of His Letters* by Clarence Greig (Cambridge: Cambridge University Press, 1978). Reprinted by permission.

Library of Congress Cataloging in Publication Data

Tanford, Charles
   The scientific traveler : a guide to the people, places, and
institutions of Europe / by Charles Tanford and Jacqueline Reynolds.
     p.   cm. — (Wiley science editions)
   Includes indexes.
   ISBN 0-471-57698-0 — ISBN 0-471-55566-5 (paper)
   1. Science—Europe—History—Guidebooks. 2. Research—Europe—
History—Guidebooks. I. Reynolds, Jacqueline A. (Jacqueline Ann),
   II. Title. III. Series
Q127.E8T36 1992
509.4—dc20

Q
127
.E8
T36
1992

92-5489

Printed in the United States of America

10 9 8 7 6 5 4 3 2 1

I have never forgotten the thrill, as a fresh undergraduate at Cambridge, of knowing that I was walking where Newton himself had once trod.
A. P. French, in *Newton's Dream*, McGill-Queen's University Press, 1988

A man who has not been to Italy is always conscious of an inferiority.
Samuel Johnson in 1776, quoted by James Boswell

Preface

When the idea for this book was conceived, we visualized it as an accessory travel guide, a book about interesting places in Europe that are related to the history of scientific discovery. We lectured our friends about the tourist's tendency to wander in and out of art galleries and ancient churches with nary a thought for possible *scientific sites* that might be just around the corner. We sought to rectify the absence of such places from ordinary guidebooks—to find them, to visit them, and to list and describe those we particularly enjoyed and found worthwhile.

We quickly recognized that we did not want to produce a mere list of buildings, cemeteries, and monuments. Travelers do not carry encyclopedias. We needed to provide a framework that would put each particular place into reasonable historical and scientific perspective, to jog the memory of the expert, and to provide some orientation for the novice. What was so intriguing about an individual, his work, the place where it was done, and the state of the world at the time? From this evolved a structure—one chapter per country and a division of each chapter into two parts: a narrative "minitext" (hopefully readable by layman and scientist alike) and a more overtly descriptive section on places to visit.

Now a few words about what this book is not. Despite the partly historical content of our textual summaries, it is in no way a capsule *history* of science, as the scholar in that field would define it. Neither is it a *textbook* laying out the foundations of the various scientific disciplines. We were both teachers for many years and may have occasionally yielded to the urge to lecture a bit, but only where it seemed essential to give substance to our narrative, and even then we have tried to avoid technical jargon.

In the final analysis, this remains a personal book and is certainly not all-inclusive. Our selection of people and places has been based on our own interest and enjoyment; other writers might have made different choices.

Practical Notes

Maps for each country give an overview of the location of places to visit; they are not intended to provide explicit directions for how to get there. We assume that all travelers will carry standard tourist maps for each country they visit; most places we mention can readily be reached by car or public transportation with the help of such maps. However, there are some places that may be more difficult to find—Neandertal in Germany, for example—and in such instances we try to provide reasonably detailed instructions. Automobile service stations or railway information offices are usually reliable sources for additional help if it is needed.

We indicate *approximate* dates and times when museums and the like are open to the public, but have not given detailed information, such as what happens on bank holidays. Details tend to change and travelers are urged to telephone in advance if they are on a tight schedule—we have provided telephone numbers where possible. Most museums require an admission charge, which likewise may be adjusted frequently. We have not listed such charges, nor have we explicitly indicated the exceptional cases where admission is free. The *telephone numbers* we give are for calls within the country of destination. Calls across national boundaries require a country prefix and deletion of the "0" at the beginning of internal dialing codes. Note that telephone numbers are themselves subject to change: for example, all British city codes will add a "1" after the initial "0" in April 1994. Alterations are especially likely in what used to be East Germany and in other formerly communist countries.

Almost all towns have official tourist information offices, and they provide alternative sources of information once one has arrived. Their main purpose may often seem to be to find overnight accommodation for visitors, but it has been our experience that the staff is nearly always knowledgeable about museums and local history and welcomes questions about them. Not infrequently they may know of interesting places to see in addition to the ones that we have listed.

Acknowledgments

We are grateful to numerous colleagues and to custodians of archives and museums, who have provided us with information and guidance and who have encouraged us by their enthusiasm for our undertaking. We are especially grateful to Walter Gratzer for his support over a period of several years and for his many specific suggestions as to content.

An incomplete list of the many others to whom we are indebted includes Walter Alvarez, Matt Cartmill, Toni Dorfer, Derek Gjertsen, Ian Glynn, Gordon Herries-Davies, Adolf Hohenester, Walter Höflechner, Walter Kauzmann, Marc le Maire, Pierre Liénard, P. Pollak, Ben Reynolds, Fred Rosen, Peter Swinbank, Alex Tanford, J. C. Thackray, Christel Wegeleben, Urban

Wråkberg, and Martin Zulauf. Among national offices, the Swedish Tourist Board has been exceptionally helpful.

We thank Cambridge University Press for permission to reproduce a portion of Clarence Greig's translation of Pliny the Younger's letter about his uncle's death at Pompeii following the eruption of Vesuvius. Our account of this event is similar to one that appeared in a previous book by one of us (C.T.), *Ben Franklin Stilled the Waves* (Duke University Press, 1989).

Contents

"MITTELEUROPA"

SCANDINAVIA AND THE BALTIC

THE SCIENTIFIC TRAVELER

INTRODUCTION

1

Our European Heritage

"Science is the cultural activity for which the twentieth century will be preeminently remembered," science writer Walter Gratzer tells us. "Its Golden Age is in full flower." Most of the origins of this golden age are to be found in Europe, in nearly every part of it. Scientists traveling in Europe, whether consciously seeking roots or not, will find records of their predecessors, sometimes in museums or in homes preserved, sometimes in the form of grand monuments or other public tribute. Or the remembrance may be just a simple tombstone, perhaps with flowers on it from an unknown disciple.

Much of this book is an account of our own journey to seek out these remembrances and of the discoveries and reflections that blossomed from it. Science emerges as remarkably international, even centuries ago. New ideas spread almost instantaneously from one end of Europe to the other without respect for national boundaries, unimpeded even by bitter wars across them. Names we all recognize—the classical "greats," if you want to use that term— belong to scientists who came from every corner of the continent, as the map of birthplaces on page 2 demonstrates. This remains true even if we confine ourselves to a single limited topic, a sequence of swiftly following events—from Volta in Italy to Ørsted in Denmark to Ampère in Fiance to Faraday in England, for example, in the understanding and use of electric currents.

(What about the world outside Europe? Should it be included? In a practical sense, in dealing with what we perceive today as the most critical steps forward, there is no need to venture further afield. In the very dim past, going back even before the Greeks, Persia and India were undoubtedly seminal sources of wisdom, and in the *immediate present* science is, of course, totally global. But in between, from Copernicus to Einstein, our roots are almost entirely European.)

In contrast to the transnational essence of questions and ideas, the conduct of the search itself is often *intensely national*. Each country has its own

1

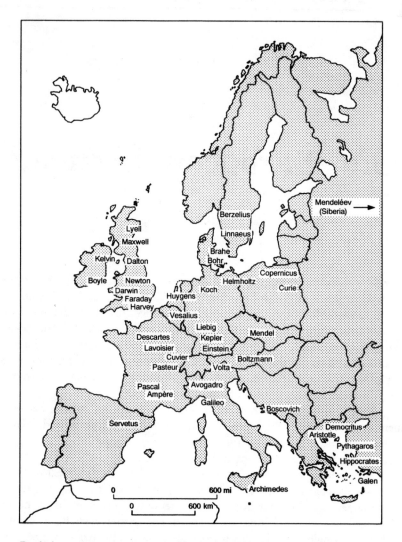

Birthplaces. Names of some of the best-known scientists and the places where they were born.

unique traditions and style in the manner of doing research, extent of public support, personal intervention of monarchs, and so forth. Science is ultimately the product of men and women, conditioned by the countries in which they were educated or subsequently chose to live and by governments that could help or interfere. Scientific ideas can appropriately be called "international," but never the people who created them nor the circumstances in which they were created. The national ethos continues to this day—the celebration of past achievements is muted in some countries, flamboyant in others.

The traveler (as distinct from tourist) comes prepared or even eager to learn, and it needs to be said right from the start that there is much to be learned. Science has not yet been integrated into our culture in quite the same way as art, architecture, literature, or music; even scientists themselves are more often than not abysmally ignorant of the history of their subject. Let us cite, for example, Sidney Brenner, former director of Cambridge's Laboratory of Molecular Biology, who wrote as follows in 1985: "For most young molecular biologists, the history of the subject is divided into two epochs: the last two years and everything else before that. The present and the very recent past are perceived in sharp detail but the rest is swathed in a legendary mist where Crick, Watson, Mendel, Darwin—perhaps even Aristotle—coexist as uneasy contemporaries." It may read like an exaggeration, but it is really quite true, not only for molecular biology, but for all presently highly active fields of science. The entering student or researcher (and, through the popular press, even the mere spectator) is confronted headlong with the immediate problem, with a minimum of background, barely enough to understand the jargon of the particular field, and denied the stimulation that a historical perspective could provide.

Our journey provides this historical perspective. In the people and places described in this book we meet the antecedent era, when what are now textbook fundamentals were first established. We may come away a little humbled.

On "Being There." But we digress, for the sheer pleasure of "being there" is by itself enough to justify the journey. Scholarship is all well and good. The archives filled with it are an essential resource of any civilized society, but there is something special about standing at the actual place where history was made or seeing the actual tool by which the world of nature was forced to yield some of its secrets.

Stones can speak, in a tongue distinct from that of books. All too often they speak of violence and destruction; sometimes they testify to manual or artistic skills. Where we shall take you, they reveal (if you are prepared to listen) the genius of the inquisitive mind.

THE MEDITERRANEAN

2

Ancient Greece

Ancient Greece is the fountainhead, the source from which all later streams of wisdom spring—at least by some accounts. Its history records seven centuries of flourishing philosophy and scientific thought, an enormous period on the time scale by which we now measure scientific progress, longer than all the years from Galileo to the present day. Furthermore, the country was larger then than the country we know today and for much of its golden age encompassed segments of Asia Minor, North Africa, and even parts of Italy. The philosophical center of gravity shifted often, from Pergamum to Athens to Syracuse to Alexandria—"Greece," in the context of our search for scientific roots, is neither a single place nor a specific moment in time.

But was it really "science," in its modern sense, that long ago? Were there laboratories? Were important and exciting discoveries made akin to our twentieth-century unveiling of subatomic particles and the chemical nature of human genes? These experimental aspects of science we know were absent, but we should stop and reflect that modern discoveries come from asking modern questions. That is where the Greeks excelled. They were the first to ask the right kind of questions, and whether their answers were "right" is less important. As G. E. R. Lloyd, the foremost authority on the scientific philosophy of Greece, has put it: "The study of early Greek Science is as much a study of the development and interaction of opinions concerning the nature of inquiry as of the content of the theories put forward."

The Greek tradition of inquiry into the causes of natural phenomena begins (as Aristotle tells us later in a retrospective mood) with Thales of Miletus and his followers in the sixth century B.C. "All things are made of water," Thales said. We may find this laughable today, but the point is that he sought to know what the world is made of, not who made it; he sought answers from within the material world, not from the supernatural without.

4

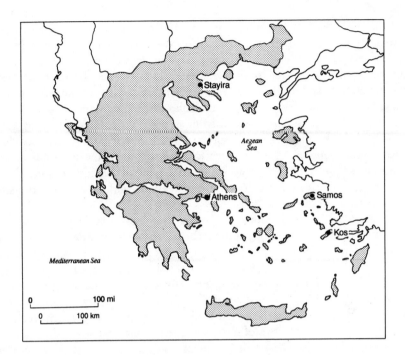

Simultaneously with the Milesians another philosophical school emerged in Samos, led by the redoubtable Pythagoras. Of them, Aristotle wrote: "Therefore, since all other things seemed in their whole nature to be modeled on numbers, and numbers seemed to be the first things in the whole of nature, they supposed the elements of numbers to be the elements of all things, and the whole heaven to be a musical scale and a number." The Pythagoreans were fascinated by the relationships between numbers and the physical world, and we may detect more than a little mysticism in their reported ideas. But again it proves to be the beginning of one of the pivotal concepts of modern scientific philosophy—the need to be quantitative in our observations about nature.

In the fifth century B.C. came Democritus, popularly regarded as the founder of the first atomic theory of matter, and soon after that Athens became the intellectual center of Greece, graced by the presence of the two antithetical giants of Greek philosophy, Plato and Aristotle. Aristotle, the most influential figure that Western science has ever seen, was destined to dominate our thinking for over 2,000 years. Plato, on the other hand, is often viewed historically as anti-science, but that's a harsh view. He did indeed downgrade mere observation in favor of a mentally derived perfection, but idealization is in fact very much a part of today's science, as reflected, for example, in our often idealized mathematical representation of the laws of astronomy and physics.

After Alexander the Great (who, as a boy, had been tutored by Aristotle),

Athens itself became less important and Hellenic science spread to the far corners of what was then the civilized world—to Alexandria in Egypt (where Euclid was), to Syracuse in Sicily (where Archimedes helped resist the Romans), and to some degree even to Rome itself, whence came the poet Lucretius (around 60 B.C.) and his six-volume *De rerum natura*, elegant hexameter verse in praise of the atomic view of matter and the Epicurean philosophy based thereon. But eventually scientific studies waned in all parts of the Graeco-Roman world and Greek works might not have survived at all were it not for Arab scholars, who preserved and extended the great classics we now know and subsequently reintroduced them into our own civilization via the Spanish Moors. Greek influence was in this way reasserted in the Western world many centuries after the texts were originally written.

Aristotle. Aristotle and his followers were known as *Peripatetics* because they walked about the grounds of the Athens Lyceum as they debated the issues of philosophy. It would be absurd to try to elaborate on their discourse here, but it is well to keep in mind the chief elements that create such a big gap between then and now: (1) Aristotle could not conceive of space without matter. (2) Aristotle could not conceive of motion in the absence of a force—the antithesis of Newton's first law. We shall see as we progress through this book that much of the early history of science in every country is a story of the courage and imagination that was needed to break away from these ideas, which had become entrenched. (This, of course, is not to imply that Aristotle's influence was wholly bad. On the contrary, his advocacy and demonstration of the value of empirical investigations can be viewed as a spur for the ultimate overturn of the particulars of his doctrines.)

Hippocrates. Not all contributors to the legacy of early Greek science could afford to spend their hours pacing back and forth in their gardens, debating cause and effect and other abstract subjects. Some of them actually earned an honest living treating the ill and infirm. Thus, from the fifth century B.C., we have a remarkable group of texts, the *Hippocratic Corpus*, named for a physician from the island of Kos. It is unlikely that Hippocrates himself actually wrote any of these treatises. It is also true that they are filled with inaccuracies and false ideas about human biology and illness. Nevertheless, the writers of the *Corpus* made a truly great contribution by separating medicine from superstition and magic spells and introducing instead a kind of empiricism—meticulous observation of human illness, detailed case histories not unlike records found in a physician's office today. The honesty of the recorders is phenomenal—they report a death rate of nearly 60 percent in the typical medical practice, a statistic that few modern doctors would be willing to put into print.

Astronomers. Hellenic science after Aristotle gradually moved from general philosophizing about the world to greater specialization, with mathematics and astronomy in the forefront. In the third century B.C. Aristarchus of Samos put forth a startling hypothesis, namely that the sun and not the earth was the center of the universe, a proposition that was totally rejected by the astronomers of his own time and by all subsequent scientists until Copernicus. Hipparchus (second century B.C.), the first systematic astronomer of whom we have records, carried out extensive surveys of the heavens from the island of Rhodes but never considered the heliocentric theory as a viable model for his observations. The greatest of the astronomers was Ptolemy, who systematized and recorded all extant astronomical data and theories in Alexandria and constructed a complicated, earth-centered model of the universe that persisted and influenced astronomers for centuries. Even when the great arguments about the model for the universe began, they were based for quite some time on Ptolemy's remarkably accurate observational data base.

   Galen. Human biology, influenced in spirit perhaps by the *Hippocratic Corpus*, but certainly not in substance, was to be vastly affected by a much later Greek scholar. Galen, born in Pergamum in 129 A.D., when Roman rule had replaced that of the Greeks, studied medicine at Smyrna, Corinth, and Alexandria and spent most of his career in the service of the Roman army and emperors. He was a prodigious writer (83 of his works are now extant), recording and cataloguing his own anatomical studies of dissected animals as well as collecting earlier work by others. His anatomical observations, frequently carried out on apes and other lower vertebrate species, became the bible of teachers and medical practitioners despite the obvious differences between lower animals and man. We shall see the extraordinary durability of Galenic dogma in later chapters of this book—how cautious the innovators of the fifteenth and sixteenth centuries had to be when they began to undermine the legend of Galen's infallibility. (It is worth noting parenthetically that Galen's writings extended to ethical matters as they related to doctors and patients. "The profit motive is incompatible with a serious devotion to the art [of medicine]," he declared. Sound advice for many civilized societies today?)

PRINCIPAL PLACES TO VISIT

GENERAL COMMENT

Present-day Greece abounds with physical remnants of its days of glory. Ancient monuments, sculpture, and excavated ruins are to be found in practically every nook and cranny of the country. But we cannot actually visit "Ancient Greece" and see the house in which Aristotle worked or the observatory used by Hipparchus; we must be content with a few excavated stumps of formerly massive columns and our own imaginations. By all means, go to modern Greece and see the Acropolis, Delphi, Olympia, the beautiful fishing port of Kavala—

sunbathe on some of the islands if that is your bent. In addition, we give here a few places you might visit to get some feeling of "being there" in relation to the origins of science and scientific philosophy.

ATHENS

What one would like to do in Athens is to relive the spirit of its famous schools, the Academy of Plato and the Lyceum of Aristotle. That is, of course, impossible. Even where ancient structures have been preserved or restored, as on the Acropolis, hordes of tourists with their chattering guides and their buses waiting nearby thwart any attempt to "relive" the distant past. As for the Academy and the Lyceum, here we don't even have buildings to help the imagination.

The inner city of old Athens was actually quite small, an area about 1¼ miles (2 km) in diameter, surrounding the Acropolis, completely enclosed by a double wall with fifteen gates to the outside—a section of wall and ruins of two gates can be seen at the Keramikos archaeological site on the west side of the city. The Academy and the Lyceum were both *outside* the walls, in shady wooded groves away from the hustle and bustle. The Academy lay toward the west and the normal road to it would have been through the Keramikos site. The precise location has been identified and extensively excavated. A signpost "ΑΚΑΔΗΜΙΑΣ ΠΛΑΤΩΝΟΣ" marks the spot, adjacent to the church of Ag.Trifonis, but there are no explanatory plaques and no museum. The excavated areas create little unkempt patches of green in otherwise dismal surroundings. The "groves of académe" are hard to visualize.

The Lyceum was on the opposite side of the city, possibly within the present National Gradens, a well-maintained park and arboretum just a short walk from Syntagma Square. Here we do indeed have tree-lined walks, but they are modern ones, put in by Queen Amalia in Greece's days of monarchy for private use of the royal family. The *precise* location of the Lyceum is still a matter for research. American visitors with friends in the academic world might want to make arrangements to contact someone at the American School of Classical Studies (founded 1882), a thriving establishment in elegant grounds on the lower slopes of the high hill (Likavitos) that stands to the north of the National Gardens. Here one can undoubtedly find the experts who would know the latest scoop on the exact location of the Lyceum and matters of that sort. The British School of Archaeology (founded in 1886) is right next door, in equally elegant quarters, and the French counterpart (originally founded in 1846) is not far away.

An etymological comment is in order. Our word *academy* and the French *lycée* are derived directly from the names of the Athens institutions and personify places of learning, but the names in ancient Greece had in themselves no educational connotation. The Academy was named after the gardens it occupied, which in turn commemorated a legendary hero, Akademos; the Lyceum was named after an epithet describing the god Apollo—Apollo Lyceus, meaning Apollo the protector of flocks, who keeps the wolf away.

Syntagma Square is the center of reference for Athens tourists. The Keramikos site is directly west on Ermou Street. The American and British schools are to the east of the square on Souidias Street. The site of the Academy is best reached by taxi, but the taxi driver will probably not know where it is—the street address is the corner of Alexandrias and Marathonomahon Streets.

ISLAND OF KOS (One of the Dodecanese islands)

The island of Kos was the home of the famous physician, Hippocrates. It is a popular area because of its mild climate and sandy beaches, but has been badly scarred by intemperate eagerness to cater to mass tourism. Roads, hotels, and discos spring up without much regard for how they affect their environment.

After the death of Hippocrates (around 360 B.C.), a temple/sanitarium was built on Kos, dedicated to the god of healing, Asklepios. People came from all over the Mediterranean to seek help by prayer or to be treated by Hippocratic doctors. They continued to come for nearly a thousand years, until a terrible earthquake and subsequent ravages by the Saracens all but destroyed the place. The remains have been excavated and some columns have been re-erected, to create an impressive memorial from which we can get a good picture of what it must have been like in its heyday.

The Asklepieion, as the temple is called, lies in open country on a limestone fold of a hill and is remarkable for its spacious design—three terraces, one above the other, joined by broad stone staircases. Patients were presumably treated by physicians on the lowest level, in "shops" lining a large, open rec-

A section of the excavated Asklepieion on the Island of Kos.

tangular space. They then went on to pray to their gods on the middle and topmost levels. The remains there reflect the continuity of use. The most prominent group of columns, for example, seven in number on the middle level, dates from Roman times, outlining a temple dedicated to Apollo; two thicker Ionic columns on the same level are much earlier. We know from the writer Strabo (who lived in the age of Augustus) that all the temples were filled with artistic treasures, many brought as offerings by the patients themselves. And it is interesting that tributes to Hippocrates continue to this day. The ceremony of the Hippocratic oath is sometimes held here. An International Hippocratic Foundation is housed in modern buildings adjacent to the archaeological area. It serves as a center for professional congresses.

The city of Kos itself has an archaeological museum with a statue of Hippocrates and a mosaic from the second or third century A.D. depicting the physician welcoming the god Asklepios. There is also the so-called Plane Tree of Hippocrates standing next to the medieval fortress overlooking the city's harbor. According to legend, the physician taught and wrote in the shade of this tree, whose outer shell is now more than 30 feet in diameter. Lawrence Durrell once visited this place: "I slept under the tree for two nights," he wrote, "hoping that the spirit of the old god-physician might confer some of his healing powers upon me, but it was winter and all I achieved was a touch of rheumatism."

The Asklepieion is about 2.5 miles (4 km) west of the city of Kos, and bicycles are a popular means for getting there. The archaeological site and the museum are open all year, but closed on Mondays. Telephone 0242–28763 and 0242–28326 respectively.

ISLAND OF SAMOS (Northern Aegean)

This is the island of philosopher/mathematician Pythagoras and of Aristarchus, who lived 300 years later, when Samos was under control of first the Egyptians and later the Syrians; he is famous for being the first proponent of a heliocentric system of planets and stars. The island is physically attractive, with a backbone of mountains reaching to nearly 5,000 feet (1,500 m) above sea level. There are wooded pine forests on the mountain slopes, vineyards below, and sandy coves for bathing at the seashore. The island has been less spoiled by tourism than many others. We can still see islanders tending herds of goats or carting their produce to market on the backs of donkeys.

The ancient capital of Samos, formerly Tigani, was renamed Pythagorio in 1955, in honor of the island's famous native son. There is a tiny museum in the town hall, space shared with the mayor's offices, but nothing within is about Pythagoras—all we have is his bust on a pedestal outside. An adjacent street is named for Aristarchus, but there are no plaques to proclaim his espousal of heliocentricity or to explain how he came to the idea. All we can do is to wander around the island, imagining the astronomer doing likewise, dreaming up new geometrical methods for measuring distances and sizes of the objects he saw in the skies. Strangely enough, our imagination gets some help, for on a hill above Pythagorio is the Tunnel of Eupalinus, 3,385 feet (1,026 m) in length and tall enough for a man to stand within it. It was built during the reign of the island's most ambitious ruler, Polycrates, not long after the time of Pythagoras. It used to have pipes on the floor to carry water to the town from springs on the other side of the hill. The digging was done by two teams of workers, one from each side, and they met properly in the middle. Pretty good geometry for 525 B.C.!

Also relevant to our story is a short drive or taxi ride east from the town of Samos, to the Strait of Mykali, for here we see the Turkish mainland not much over a mile (2 km) away, almost within swimming distance. And at this point we are but 33 miles (50 km) from Miletus, the earliest of all sources of Greek scientific philosophy. Samos may be *formally* an island in the geographic sense, but at the time of Pythagoras it was far from insular in its intellectual life, being always in close communication with the mainland coastal cities. Today we have Greeks on one side of the Strait and Turks on the other, and not much love between them, but back then it was all Greek—the center of Greek civilization, in fact, for the age of Pericles in Athens was still some decades away.

STAGIRA
(65 miles or 100 km east of Thessaloniki)

The Halkadiki Peninsula lies in Macedonia, the northeastern portion of Greece and one of the most attractive parts of the country. The peninsula is studded with small fishing villages along the coast, and inland are thickly wooded hills, high mountain passes, and magnificent views. Three long narrow fingers jut out into the Aegean Sea and on one of them stands Mount Athos, 6,500 feet (2,000 m) high, the center of an incredible medieval relic, a monastic community utterly cut off from the world. Women, children, and eunuchs are forbidden; no roads enter. Male tourists are admitted, gaining access by boat from Ouranoupolis; a beard as proof of maleness is desirable, but no longer the absolute requirement that it used to be.

If you venture to this remote part of Greece, you will find yourself close to Stagira (or Stayira), the place where, in 384 B.C., the great Aristotle was born. The present town of that name, on the road from the coast inland to Arnea, has named a large park and picnic area after Aristotle, with a prominent (modern) white stone statue of the philosopher himself. However, the actual birthplace is not the present town but *ancient Stagira*, which was perched on high bluffs at the edge of the open sea, about 10 miles (15 km) away, just south of the present village of Olimbiada. There are signposts everywhere, beginning on the main coastal highway from Stavros toward Mount Athos, so that the site and the excavations made there cannot be missed.

It is, of course, a long way to come and the ruins *per se* are less rewarding than many other archaeological sites. But can we really pass it by? Can we fail to be moved at least a little by being on the very piece of land that nurtured the man whose thoughts and writings dominated Western academic institutions for so many centuries after he was dead?

In England the association of man with place has always been strong. Aristotle was no exception, as we can see from the following lines of John Dryden—poet and dramatist, but elected to the company of scientists, the fledgling Royal Society, in 1663:

> The longest Tyrrany that ever sway'd
> Was that wherein our Ancestors betray'd
> Their free-born Reason to the *Stagirite*
> And made his Torch their Universal Night.

The exultation he felt over what he saw as the then emerging downfall of Aristotelian dogma comes through loud and clear.

Much further east, beyond Xanthi, a side road off the main highway leads to Abdera, the birthplace of another famous ancient sage, Democritus, father of the atomic theory of matter. Here again signposts direct us to the excavated ruins of the ancient town—the excavated area is more extensive than at Stagira.

3

Spain

Most of us today would be hard put to identify a historic event of scientific importance associated with Spain or to name a Spanish Galileo or Pasteur. Our view of Spain is more artistic or romantic: the country of El Greco, Goya, and Picasso, and of Don Quixote tilting at windmills; the land of flamenco dancers and of sun-washed beaches crowded with tourists escaping from the chills of more northerly latitudes. To an older generation Spain means Hemingway and bull fights, civil war and the International Brigade fighting against fascism.

Which is not to suggest that we deny Spain a certain distinction in the realm of the search, but the search in this case is of a special kind. Spain and its neighbor Portugal are famous—celebrated in popular story and song—for exploration of the world, for their voyages of discovery, conquest, and colonization. That is what adventurous Spaniards were still doing (dismantling indigenous civilizations in favor of their own, for example, in Mexico and Peru) when the rudiments of a more cerebral adventure, the scientific exploration of nature, were beginning to appear in other parts of Europe.

These conventional views of Spain are partly misleading. Spain's role in the history of science is indeed meager after 1500, but a few centuries earlier Spain, in fact, had a golden age of its own, in which it played a crucial role for the ultimate appearance of scientific thought and development in other European countries. For 500 years (around the year 1000), while traditional Western civilization existed in a kind of intellectual amnesia, an Islamic culture was flourishing in Spain and brought with it elegance, education, scholarship, and even science. We speak of Greek philosophy and science as a forerunner of Western science, but tend to forget (or may not even be aware) that Greek learning came to us indirectly, through Arabic translations. Spain was the actual port of entry for eastern scholarship into Europe.

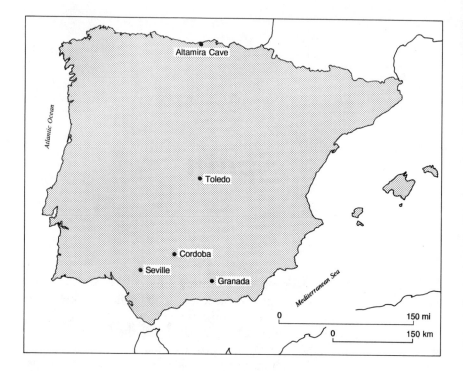

Islamic Science

A popular tourist guide to Spain echoes the conventional view. It has a chronology of the country's history from the centuries before Christ, when Phoenicians, Greeks, and Carthaginians in turn conquered the land, up to the twentieth century and its destructive Civil War—a total of 66 dated items. It is striking that only two dates are given for the Middle Ages: 711, marking the conquest of Spain by the Moors, and 778, the year of Charlemagne's failed invasion from the north. The next dates are 1474 (succession of Isabel to the throne of Castile), 1479 (unification of all Christian Spain under one crown by Ferdinand), and 1492 (reconquest of Granada, the last remaining Moorish territory). Did nothing interesting happen in between? Are the years between 778 and 1474 best forgotten, a period of darkness perhaps, preceding a subsequent Christian flowering of the arts and culture?

As it happens, such implication would be quite wrong, for Spain was actually Europe's intellectual center in the days of the Moors, an island of tolerance and philosophy and the home of the only science there was. If there was a period of darkness at all, it came *after* the Moors were conquered—the infamous Torquemada was appointed Grand Inquisitor in 1483 and most original thought was thereafter banned. It is arguable that even art went into a decline with Christian dominance. What remains of Moorish architecture (in

Granada, for example) has a beauty and a sense of proportion that are altogether lacking in the garish Spanish Gothic that replaced it.

The Moors were a people of mixed Arab and Berber stock who had been converted to Islam in the eighth century. A knowledge of the great Greek classics, in Arabic or sometimes Hebrew translation and usually embellished by commentaries, was part of the cultural tradition they brought with them to Spain. In Spain the process of copying, translating, and improving was continued, and Latin translations began to make their appearance. Some historians have tended to denigrate the contributions of this Moslem era of scholarship—one popular work, for example, has been contemptuously described as "a Latin translation of a Hebrew translation of a commentary made upon an Arabic translation of a Syriac translation of a Greek text." But that's just academic backbiting. The point to be made is that, after a long period of intellectual stagnation, European scholars were made aware of early Greek philosophy, not just as prescribed doctrine, but as something that the scholar could (and should) seek to improve.

Take **Ibn Rushd,** for example, also known by his Spanish name of Averroës and often nicknamed the "Commentator." He was born in Córdoba in 1126 and did most of his work there. He is mostly famous for critical evaluation of the existing works of Aristotle, some of which he was able to discard as spurious. He was so fearless in his opinions that he even managed to upset the normally tolerant authorities toward the end of his life and, as a consequence, his books were burned and the further study of philosophy was briefly forbidden. He soon regained royal favor, however, and died (in 1198) at the court of the ruling monarch in Marrakech, Morocco, which was part of the same "country"—only the Straits of Gibraltar separate Morocco from Spain. (His body was, in fact, brought back to Córdoba for burial there.) Many copies of Ibn Rushd's books survived the burning and many of them were translated into Hebrew, where they caused less offense to the establishment, and it is the texts in that language that proved particularly influential in transmitting the Aristotelian system to later scientists and philosophers. When we talk of Aristotle in relation to the birth of modern science—Galileo sweeping aside the errors of Aristotelian mechanics, for example—we usually mean Aristotle as interpreted by Ibn Rushd.

Among original works created in Spain, we have the first illustrated book on surgery (written by Abu al Qasim in Córdoba around 1000), essentially a medical encyclopedia in 30 parts covering the author's 50 years of experience in medical practice. In the field of chemistry, there was a scholar in Seville who published influential treatises on procedures for purification of chemical compounds—we don't know his name because he tried to boost his sales by writing under the name of a popular earlier author. In the twelfth century, also from Seville, came Al-Bitruji with a controversial textbook of astronomy, critical of Ptolemy, but not much of an improvement. He is cited by Copernicus, 400 years later.

Not all the scholars of this period were Moslems. The Jews lived in relative harmony with the Moors and contributed much to the medieval flowering of Spanish culture. One of the best known is Moses ben Maimon (Maimonides), philosopher and physician, one of the first open critics of Galen's orthodox system of anatomy and medicine. He was born in Córdoba, roughly contemporary with Ibn Rushd; unlike the latter he did not remain there, but moved to Cairo with his family while still a youth. Among the Jewish scholars we also have a popular figure, Abraham Ibn Ezra (Rabbi ben Ezra), born in Toledo around 1090, whose philosophical ideas on man's spiritual development inspired a poem by Robert Browning:

> Grow old along with me!
> The best is yet to be,
> The last of life, for which the first was made.

Also in Toledo, a little later than Ibn Ezra, we reach the peak of activity in translation from Arabic or Hebrew into Latin. Gerard of Cremona (1114–1187), a Christian, was the most famous of them. He moved from his native Italy to Toledo at age twenty-five or thirty and became the most prolific of the translators. His most influential work was a translation of Ptolemy's *Almagest*—that's the version from which most Europeans learned what was to become the officially sanctioned model for the motion of the heavenly bodies. He was only one of many foreigners, however. Many others came to learn Arabic and to study the famous texts for themselves.

(The most useful Islamic transmission was perhaps the Eastern method of writing numbers, originally Hindu, what we now call "Arabic" numerals. A trailblazer here was Leonardo Fibonacci of Pisa. His father was a businessman and sent his son to North Africa for the specific purpose of learning the new system, as applied to the calculation of business costs and profits. Leonardo ended up as a distinguished mathematician, preferring scholarship to commerce.)

The golden period in Iberia came to an end with the reconquest by Catholic sovereigns from the north. By the end of the fifteenth century, all Jews and Moslems who refused baptism in the Roman faith were expelled from the country, and, in the words of one writer, "Spain became the champion of a reactionary, introverted church, closed to all ideas and influences which were not impeccably orthodox."

Mixing Religion and Science Can Be Bad for One's Health

From this new Spain, dominated by a religious fanaticism that is difficult to imagine today, came a rebellious young man called **Michael Servetus**. He was born near Huesca in Upper Aragon, just south of the Pyrenées, in 1511, and he may have attended the University of Saragossa not far from his home. He left Spain at an early age to study at the University of Toulouse and soon became infamous for a theological heresy: He claimed to find no mention of the Trinity in the Bible and advocated abandonment of Trinitarian doctrine. This was unfortunately an issue on which the new Protestant reformers and the established Church of Rome were united and his writings on the subject brought down on him the wrath of both. For a while he stayed out of serious mischief by studying medicine at the University of Paris and becoming an accomplished physician and expert at human dissection. (At Paris he was a contemporary or near-contemporary of a much more subtle and successful rebel, Andreas Vesalius, whose rebellion against established opinion was strictly confined to the anatomical doctrine of Galen.)

During this period as physician, Servetus earned (very much posthumously) an imperishable place in the history of science for being the first person in the Western world to recognize the lesser (pulmonary) circulation of the blood. He realized that the fundamental change from venous to arterial blood must take place in the lungs when air is mixed with the blood and that all blood ultimately destined for the tissues must first pass from the right side of the heart, through the lungs, and then back to the left side. It was his misfortune, and that of later scientists, that he saw his remarkable deduction in the context of a theological problem—how the divine spirit (supposedly alive in the air around us) is introduced into the blood and disseminated to all parts of the body. When he came to publish his scientific work, it was as part of a religious *magnum opus*, which reemphasized his earlier heretical intransigence. Servetus became a hunted man. He tried to hide his identity, but was recognized in Geneva and denounced as a heretic. Geneva, of course, was the bastion of Calvinism, but the Calvinists were not to be outdone by the Catholic Inquisition in their zeal to suppress theological dissent. Servetus was burned at the stake in 1553, his last cry a reaffirmation of his views on the Trinity.

The thousand printed copies of Servetus's book were unremittingly sought out for confiscation and burning. Only three copies remained and it was not realized until 1694 that they contained anything of scientific interest. Even William Harvey was apparently never aware of the work.

Altamira Cave: Prehistoric Art

Four centuries after the last Moors were driven from the country, a discovery was made in a cave close to the Cantabrian coast of Spain. It was destined to have a profound effect on our perception of the antiquity and inherent character of our own species.

The discovery was made by accident in the year 1879. Don Marcelino de Sautuola, local nobleman and landowner, had dug in the floor of Altamira cave many times before, keeping his head down to avoid bumping into the low ceiling, for he had an amateur interest in archaeology. He often found flint tools and charred bones in the ground and collected them at home, curious about the unknown inhabitants of a bygone age who had left them in the cave. On this particular day he was accompanied by his little daughter Maria, who wandered off into a side cave while he was working and, being shorter than her dad, she looked upward as well as down as she explored the cave, lantern in hand. That is how the frescoes were found—Maria saw that the cave's walls and ceilings were covered with remarkable animal paintings.

De Sautuola shrewdly recognized the paintings for what they were, the artistic legacy of a prehistoric people, but expert opinion ridiculed this possibility, and de Sautuola was even accused of having deliberately faked the paintings. The artistry was far too advanced, it was said, to have been executed by the primitive hunters who made the flint knives, and, besides, the caves were dark, of course, and whoever did the painting would have had to have lanterns to provide light. It was all too preposterous for words. It was not until 20 years later, when similar paintings were discovered in the Dordogne region of France, that the validity of de Sautuola's claim began to be accepted, but he was no longer alive by then. It's another example of prejudiced opposition, a discovery not recognized for its true value during the discoverer's lifetime.

What these paintings do is redefine the upper Palaeolithic Age (40,000–10,000 B.C.). We now know that it was a time when a region stretching several hundred kilometers south from the Dordogne area in France and along the north coast of Spain was inhabited by a resourceful people who shared a common way of life, which included a remarkable skill in artistic expression. Their drawings and paintings (mostly of animals) are at the same time beautiful (in the artistic sense) and astonishingly accurate. The artists clearly had a working knowledge of animal anatomy and presumably must have been aware of the similarities between animal and human anatomy.

The painting technique of the artists became very sophisticated toward the end of the palaeolithic period (the so-called Magdalenian period, 15,000 to 12,000 B.C.). The painters first engraved outlines of their subjects in the rock, then filled in the cut with black paste, and finally colored the outlined space with pigments that were complex mixtures of natural pigments (chiefly ochre), carbon black, blood, and other materials. Cavities and depressions in the rock surface were used to obtain three-dimensional effects, to depict the swelling muscles in running animals, for example. Despite its complexity, the technique (and its evolution) is essentially the same throughout the entire region. The location of the paintings is also similar everywhere—they are always in caves that were not used as living quarters but purposely set apart for their special use. These latter features bring out the most important scientific aspect of these paintings, creating a seminal chapter in the development of anthropology. They are evidence suggesting art for the sake of decoration and they indicate that artistic skills were a *learned tradition*, transmitted from one family to another and from one region to another. These were not the primitive cavemen of the popular comics, but representatives of a sophisticated culture with sensitivity for artistic expression that is comparable to our own.

PRINCIPAL PLACES TO VISIT

ALTAMIRA CAVE (near Santillana del Mar)

Altamira Cave, about 1.3 miles (2 km) from the Cantabrian village of Santillana del Mar, lies in tranquil, rolling country, quite different from the cave art area in the Dordogne, where the caves are set in steep limestone cliffs. The paintings in the cave date from about 15,000 to 12,000 B.C. The spectacular ceiling frescoes show remarkably realistic full-color representations of bison in various poses (asleep, running, and so forth), wild boar, primitive horses, and reindeer. They provide excellent examples of the three-dimensional effect achieved by taking advantage of undulations in the rock surface. Access to the cave is through a visitor center and, unfortunately, conservation measures require that only a handful of people can be admitted each day, the precise number depending on outside humidity and temperature. Even with this restriction there are signs of some surface deterioration, so that, to be realistic, one must be prepared for the possibility that the cave may some day be closed to the public altogether. At the present time appointments for viewing must be made in writing at least six months in advance. Coming without reservation one can camp on the doorstep, hoping that some visitors with permission will not show up, in which case one may be admitted if the guards are in a charitable mood.

If one succeeds in getting in, then the caves will be found to be an unforgettable sight, a humbling experience in a way for those who vaguely think of artistic creation as something that began in Italy in the Renaissance. The Altamira caves are more spacious than the caves built into the cliffs in the Dordogne area in France and the size of each viewing group is limited to only five people, which makes for a more relaxed visit and greater opportunity to examine the pictures in detail.

For those who fail to be admitted, there is a museum and a videotaped film. The latter is badly produced and cannot be recommended as a substitute for the real thing. We recommend instead the realistic reproduction of the Altamira ceiling which can be seen at the Le Thot Center of Prehistory in the Dordogne (see under "France"), as part of a visit to the cave art in that area. There is also a reproduction of the Altamira ceiling in the Museo Arqueològico Nacional in Madrid—we have not seen it and therefore cannot comment on it.

It should be noted that Santillana del Mar itself is an extraordinary little place, well worth a visit. It has cobbled streets, old village houses still shared by the owners with their livestock, churches, fountains, and so on, all astonishingly well preserved from Santillana's fifteenth-century heyday.

For admission to the cave apply in writing to Jefe de las Cuevas de Altamira, Santillana del Mar.

REMNANTS OF THE MOORS

The Moors established universities and libraries in Córdoba, Seville, Toledo, Granada, Murcia, Almeria, Valencia, and Cadiz. They had a famous hospital and medical school in Córdoba, reputed to be equal to those of Cairo and Baghdad. Curricula at the universities included algebra, physics, astronomy, and medicine. The Hindu (Arabic) number system was introduced and eventually came to replace the Roman numerals throughout Europe.

Unfortunately, little in the way of bricks and mortar is left today to remind us directly of the former scientific glory. We do, however, recommend a visit to Spain. Go view the remnants of Moorish civilization found in Toledo, Granada, Córdoba, or Seville and contemplate the time when these places housed scholars who preserved ancient learning for the Western world.

CÓRDOBA

In Córdoba we can feel closer than in any other Spanish city to erstwhile Islamic intellectual activity. For one thing, the city was the birthplace of the two greatest philosophers of the twelfth century, Ibn Rushd (who remained here for most of his life) and Maimonides (who moved to Cairo as a youth). For another, the *Mezquita*, the great mosque, has been preserved in all its grandeur—unfortunately with a garish Christian church built within its walls, making for a truly bizarre combination of architectural styles. And the mosque is undoubtedly where teachers and pupils would gather for discussion and where scribes would make their copies, for classrooms and libraries lay normally within the precincts of mosques.

Adjacent to the *Mezquita* is the old Jewish quarter (*Juderia*), with narrow streets filled with lively crowds and, on summer evenings, the gay sound of guitars and flamenco dancers. There is a Plaza de Maimonides here and a statue of Maimonides in the Plaza de Tiberiades. There is a statue of Averroës (Ibn Rushd) in the *Zoco*, where craftsmen now have their stalls. There is also a municipal museum, but don't expect any reverence there for the golden years of yore—the museum is devoted almost exclusively to bullfighting and to Córdoba's famous matadors.

The Mezquita (mosque) at Córdoba. The design, lacking the strong *unidirectional* focus of a Christian church, fosters multipurpose utilization of space—not just for prayer, but also for teaching students and for research into ancient texts.

GRANADA

Córdoba was taken by the Christians in 1236, but Granada remained in Moorish hands until 1492, a refuge for artists and others who had been driven out of Córdoba, Seville, and elsewhere. Granada contains the most brilliant of all the products of Moorish architecture, the elaborate, intricately decorated Alhambra, with its gardens, courtyards, galleries, and statues—one of the artistic wonders of Europe. At one time Granada also had an acclaimed medical center and, at the time of the great plague, emissaries came here from all over Europe to consult (unsuccessfully) with local physicians. Where was the former medical center and have any of its buildings survived? There are no plaques or signs to tell us.

TOLEDO

Toledo stands in a loop of the Tagus (Tajo) River, on a site of unsurpassed beauty. An unforgettable view of the town, with brilliant blue Castilian sky in the background, is obtained from the *Parador Conde de Orgaz*, a state-owned hotel on the steep hills of the southern river bank. Toledo was "liberated" by

Christian forces at an early stage of the wars to wrest control from the Muslims, even earlier than Córdoba, but its Castilian rulers were first tolerant and encouraged intermingling of the races, so that Moorish traditions of education and culture continued for some time. In the twelfth century Toledo was probably the most important Jewish town in all of Europe; Rabbi ben Ezra lived here during that period. In fact, the realization that there used to be close intermingling of Jewish and Islamic intellectuals is an important lesson to be learned from a visit here—the beautiful *El Transito* synagogue, built in the fourteenth century, has been recently restored. Nearby is the El Greco museum, commemorating the great artist from Crete who came to live and paint in Toledo at the invitation of Philip II in 1585. Many of his paintings may be seen in a gallery in Toledo's cathedral.

4

Italy

Italy is perhaps the ideal place to begin a journey through scientific Europe. Not only does it have a continuity of creative effort from the third century B.C. to the present, but it adds to that a national pride in the past, a conscious effort to blend it with the present, to let us see the land as a mosaic of ancient and modern. We notice it most readily in the preservation of old buildings—in Italy, when ideologies change or tyrants are overthrown, the new rulers don't go on a rampage of destruction—but it applies to people as well. It is a land that prizes the individual and makes every effort to preserve his or her memory and achievements. One gets the feeling that the Italians would really like to erect an ornate monument to every individual who ever lived there, to make sure that no one is forgotten. Scientists tend to be neglected in many countries in comparison with artists or generals, but in Italy there is always some narrow back street or corner in a cathedral or villa on a lake where some evidence in stone or bronze is provided to say that so-and-so is not merely an entry in a textbook, but that he was an actual person who lived and loved and worked in a specific place.

That Italy should have continuity in its contributions to scientific progress is in itself somewhat surprising, for political circumstances would seem to have been unfavorable. It did indeed have its time of greatness, centuries on end when all the world that was important belonged to Rome, but, unexpectedly, that was not a period noted for scientific excellence. (Have those who try to relate science to sociology ever commented on that anomaly?) Much later, when Italy was a fragmented land of independent and contentious city-states—its battle towers still preserved in many smaller towns—and when it was invaded by the French and then the Spaniards and the Austrians and then the French once more, that's when the Italian spirit of original scientific inquiry seems to have asserted itself most prominently.

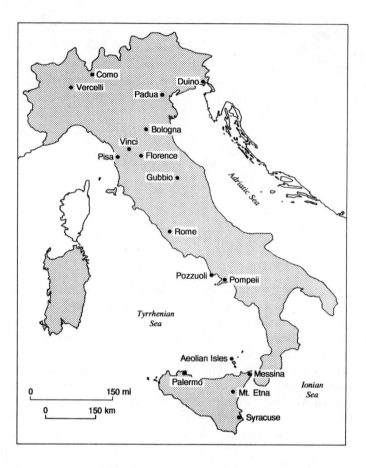

Greeks and Romans

Archimedes of Syracuse. Archimedes (287 to 212 B.C.) belongs to the Greek tradition and indeed, though born in Syracuse, visited the great Greek center of learning in Alexandria as part of his education at a time when Euclid may still have been alive. However, we know more about Archimedes as a person than we do about most other Greek scientists because of Plutarch, the Roman storyteller and biographer (the source of inspiration for *Julius Caesar* and other Shakespearean plays). Archimedes appears in Plutarch's biography of Marcus Claudius Marcellus, whose conquest of southern Italy in the third century B.C. was frustrated by three years of resistance at Syracuse, masterminded, it is said, by the inventive genius of Archimedes, who designed a famous catapult and other weapons for Syracuse's ruler Hiero II. Thus, though Euclid, Hippocrates, and even Aristotle come to us as little more than names attached to texts, their personal lives largely nebulous, we get through Plutarch an actual glimpse of Archimedes the man and of the time in which he lived.

Plutarch pictures Archimedes as single-mindedly immersed in his work, ever intent on solving problems, often with the aid of geometrical figures drawn with a stick in the sand, forgetful even about meals and his daily visit to the baths—his servants sometimes had to drag him there forcibly, it is said. One oft-repeated tale relates to Archimedes' sudden insight into the concept of specific gravity and how to measure it. Hiero had had a golden crown made for himself, but suspected the goldsmith of having adulterated the pure gold he had been given with a baser metal. Hiero asked Archimedes to devise a method for testing its purity, a difficult problem at the time. Archimedes is said to have had the inspiration for its solution while he was in the bath. His body displaced water, which flowed out over the sides of the bath. It occurred to him that all solid objects do the same thing but that the volume of water for a given weight would be different for every substance, depending on what we now call its density—and that this provided a way to distinguish gold from other metals. He was so excited that he is reported to have jumped out of the bath and run naked down the street to his home shouting, "Eureka" ("I have found it").

A sadder anecdote relates to Archimedes' death. When Marcellus finally prevailed against the defenses of Syracuse, he gave strict orders that Archimedes' house and life be spared, but Archimedes was so deep in some calculation he was making that he did not notice the Romans storming through the town until the shadow of a soldier fell across his diagram in the dust. When challenged by the soldier, he failed to respond properly and the soldier ran him through with a sword. Archimedes was seventy-five years old and perhaps he was a little hard of hearing by then as well as absent-minded. (Three hundred years later, the great Roman orator Marcus Tullius Cicero was stationed in Sicily as quaestor. He sought out Archimedes' tomb and finding it overgrown with thorns and briars, lamented on how soon our men of genius are forgotten.)

Archimedes was a remarkably modern scientist—original, imaginative, and usually seen in retrospect to have been right at least in the methods he employed in his work. His first love was mathematics. His best-known treatise is called *The Sand Reckoner,* and in it he set himself the task of calculating the number of grains of sand that the universe would hold on the basis of the then conventional ideas about cosmic dimensions—this being chiefly intended as an exercise in how to handle large numbers at a time, we must remember, when no decimal system yet existed. (The result of the calculation, in modern terms, was 10^{63} grains.) Geometrical achievements of Archimedes include an accurate determination of the ratio of the circumference of a circle to its diameter, in modern parlance the value of π. The calculation was based on the principle that the sum of the edges of a circumscribed polygon, tangential to the circle, must always exceed the circle's circumference, whereas the edges of an inscribed polygon, vertices touching the circle, must always be less than the circumference. Both sums approach the circumference as the number of sides of the polygons increase—an early application of the concept of asymptotic approach to a limit.

Archimedes' mechanical inventions were all related to geometry and involved the principle of what we now call mechanical leverage. "Give me a place to stand on, and I will move the Earth," is a famous quotation, which illustrates the breadth of his comprehension of the subject. He derived formulas for the mechanical action of wedges, inclined planes, capstans, and screws. He invented a device still known as *Archimedes' Screw*—a spiral passage in an inclined cylinder—for raising water to high levels. As we have already indicated, he developed ingenious military machines to help in the defense of Syracuse.

Archimedes' most important contribution to the future growth of science remains, however, his discovery of the principles of specific gravity and buoyancy. There is much more to this than a basis for an amusing anecdote; it was a truly profound intellectual advance and provided the essential foundation for the work of Galileo who recognized from Archimedes' work that general rules about falling bodies can't be made without taking differences in density into account. Altogether, Galileo cited Archimedes more than 100 times in his published works.

Related Place to Visit: Syracuse.

Pliny the Elder and the Great Eruption of Vesuvius. Pliny the Elder was born at Lake Como in the reign of Tiberius, and he died in Pompeii in the eruption of Vesuvius in A.D. 79. He was an indefatigable reader and prolific writer, who needed little sleep, had a slave read to him even during rubdowns after his bath, and had a secretary perpetually at his side to take dictation. He produced a remarkable 37-volume *Natural History*, an outpouring of all reports about the natural world that he could find in the works of over 500 earlier Greek and Roman writers, with added comments from his own experience. Historians of science have severely criticized the work, and one of them calls Pliny "scientifically far inferior to his sources." There is truth in the criticism, and much of *Natural History* is undoubtedly shallow, misleading, and often wrong. But has the historical judgment perhaps been a little too harsh? Encyclopedias can never be more than entry ports into the world of knowledge. We hope that their contents have been filtered, doors leading into false trails closed off, but this is never entirely true, even in modern encyclopedias written by massive teams of experts. We can hardly expect it from a work by a single individual from the first century A.D. Rather than criticize, we should perhaps marvel that such a work exists at all, identifying all there is to know: lists of towns and rivers and all the different races of man; the physical universe—cosmology, astronomy, meteorology, geology; all the trees and all the animals; a volume on diseases and what to do about them; and a mention of all the known "miracles" of nature. Benjamin Franklin read the works of Pliny in his youth, and later confirmed one of the "miracles" for himself, the one about oil smoothing the waves on water in a storm. Where else could Franklin and other youths of his time have had their imaginations fired by the immensity of what there is to know?

Whatever his scientific shortcomings, Pliny is a memorable figure in

Western history because he is one of very few scientists on record who died a hero's death in quest for knowledge. Pliny was in the Bay of Naples at the time of the great eruption of Vesuvius in 79 A.D. and, instead of beating a prudent retreat, rushed to shore at Pompeii to observe the eruption more closely. The story, told by his nephew Pliny the Younger, then eighteen years old, is a literary classic:

> My uncle was in charge of the Roman fleet at Misenum. About two o'clock on August 24th my mother showed me a cloud which was very big and looked odd. My uncle had spent his day as usual. He had been sunbathing, had taken a cold bath and had his lunch. He was now studying, when he heard about the cloud. He called a slave to fetch his shoes, climbed up a hill and got the best view he could of the mystery.
>
> The cloud was getting bigger and it had a flat head, like a Mediterranean Pine tree. It was carried up into the air on a very long trunk which broke into branches. The trunk was made by the blast from the volcano pushing up hard. As it got higher into the atmosphere, the blast was less strong and the ash got heavier and began to fan out. The cloud sometimes glowed white hot, sometimes the earth and ash in it made it dirty and blotchy. For a long time we did not know which mountain it was coming from. It was only later we found it was Vesuvius.
>
> My uncle, who was a great scholar, just could not keep away. He ordered all the warships to be launched and he went on one himself. . . . He sailed right into the middle of the danger.
>
> As he sailed to the town, he made careful observations. He took notes of everything that was going on. You can see how unafraid he was. When they got near Pompeii, the ashes were hotter and fell more thickly. They were also hit by pumice and stones. These had been burned black and broken into pieces by the fires. All of a sudden they sailed into the shallows, which were full of debris from the volcano. For a moment my uncle stopped and thought he might turn back. When the helmsman said he should, he replied, "Fortune favors the fearless. Sail round to the villa of Pomponianus!"

And sail they did, but, once there, they could not escape because the wind was strong and from the wrong direction. The younger Pliny, of course, was still at Misenum, and what follows must be strongly flavored by his imagination, but it is worthwhile to quote some of it:

> In every part of the world it was day. In Pompeii it was the blackest of black nights. Those who were left in the city, only got rid of the dark by torches and all sorts of lamps.
>
> My uncle decided to go out onto the shore and see for himself if the sea would let them sail. But it was still angry and against them. His slaves put down a sheet for him to lie on and he demanded and drank one or two cups of cold water. Then the flames and the smell of sulphur, which always tells you the flames are coming, made the others run away. These flames made him wake up. He stood up, leaning on two young slaves, but he fell down straight away. I suppose the thick fumes had blocked his windpipe and closed his gullet which was always weak and giving him trouble. When they found his body in the light two days later, there was not a mark on it.

Pliny the Elder was fifty-six years old when he died.

Geological Postscript. Volcanic eruptions are classified according to the amount of debris ejected into the atmosphere. The most potent type is to this day called *Plinian,* and is characterized by an eruptive column more than 19 miles (30 km) in height, depositing rock and ashes over an area of 390 square miles (1,000 km^2) or more. The cloud with a flat head, "like a Mediterranean Pine tree" in the younger Pliny's account, is the distinguishing hallmark. (Sticky, viscous magma is the underlying cause of such violent eruptions—it resists escape of subterranean gases until the pressure becomes very high.)

Related Places to Visit: Pompeii, Como.

The Fifteenth Century: Emerging from the Middle Ages

Europe's First Universities. A momentous event, affecting all of Western civilization, took place in Bologna in the twelfth century with the founding of Europe's first university in the modern sense, with professors who gave lectures and students who earned degrees. Different sources give different dates for the foundation, but it was certainly no later than 1156—preceding the vaunted Italian artistic renaissance by more than a century! As many as 10,000 students flocked to Bologna from all over Europe to attended its classes in the thirteenth century, a phenomenal number testifying to the intense thirst for knowledge as Christian Europe began to follow Islam out of the darkness of the Middle Ages.

Other Italian cities soon followed Bologna's lead—Modena, Padua, Vicenza, Naples, and so forth—and the movement spread quickly to other countries as well. The Italian universities were at first intended chiefly for the study of jurisprudence, a subject of great importance in a period when commerce was expanding and opportunities for huge profits and disastrous losses required an orderly system of laws to adjudicate rival claims. But subject matter expanded quickly to satisfy the demands of inquisitive minds; theology, philosophy, and medicine became important parts of the curriculum. Bologna in particular soon became famous (or notorious, depending on one's point of view) for its anatomy courses—Bologna was the first city in the Christian era where dissection of human corpses was legally sanctioned.

Bologna had another distinction, that of having female professors on its faculty as early as the fourteenth century. One of them, Novella d'Andrea, is said to have been so beautiful that she distracted the students (presumably almost entirely male) and took to presenting her lectures from behind a screen. Much later, but still long before women graced the lecture podium anywhere else in Europe, Laura Bassi (1711–1778) was a Bologna science professor for over 30 years. She inspired many students, the most famous being Lazzaro Spallanzani, who was sent to Bologna by his father to study law, but eventually abandoned that subject in favor of science and, during a long career, did much influential research in biology, including a painstaking study confuting earlier proposals that some living animals spring to life entirely spontaneously. (This study was carried out 100 years after the experiments of Nicholas Steno in Florence, which we describe below, but belief in the spontaneous generation of life from inanimate matter was hard to stamp out. Steno had disproved it for flies in a flask; Spallanzini had to do it all over again for microscopic *animalcules*.)

In the context of our search for the roots of science, the university at Padua (founded in 1222) is especially important. Two early literary students here are worth mentioning, their writings and careers being not entirely irrelevant to our story. One of them, Dante Alighieri, the first great writer in the Italian language, was a student in Padua around 1285. In his great literary masterpiece, the *Divine Comedy*, he recounts his journey through the realms of the dead, guided in turn through Inferno, Purgatory, and Paradise. He lingered longest, of course, in Hell, with its forbidding motto, "All hope abandon, ye who enter here," inscribed over the entrance portal, and he found a considerable population of former Florentine residents within. Dante's work provides us (apart from its literary merit) with a fascinating insight into the medieval picture of the world, with physics, philosophy, and theology merged into a unitary whole almost without perceptible dividing lines. The physical part of the picture comes straight out of Ptolemy's *Almagest*, with its concentric spheres for the sun, planets, and stars and the earth at the center. In the thirteenth and fourteenth centuries (before Galileo and others started raising questions) this would have been an intrinsic part of popular culture because of the universal belief in astrology at the time.

The other Paduan literary giant (35 years after Dante) was the poet Petrarch, composer of sonnets inspired by his love for "Laura." He was an ambitious man ("upwardly mobile" we might call him today) and traveled a great deal. He first saw his Laura in church in Avignon in 1327; he owned a house in Parma; he was crowned "Prince of Poets" at the Capitol in Rome in 1341, in consequence, it is said, of a conniving tête-à-tête with the King of Naples. Seen through his eyes, Italy has an unexpected unity. It is said of Petrarch that the popularity of his romantic poetry unified all Italy in spirit way back then, in spite of the political disunity that persisted for another 500 years.

In 1405 Padua became part of the Republic of Venice, and it was to remain under its domination for 400 years, until the conquest of Italy by Napoleon. In the midst of this Venetian period, Padua became what one might call the first international center for science in the modern sense, with students and researchers flocking there from all over Europe to be trained in the new way of thinking about the world, in the new philosophy that replaced the old scholasticism with a more experimental approach. Copernicus came from Poland to study here from 1501 to 1503, following an initial year of education at Bologna. Vesalius came from Belgium (via Paris) in 1536 and became the first of a succession of great professors of anatomy. John Caius (founder of Caius College in Cambridge) was a Padua student from 1539 to 1541, and William Harvey, sometimes called the father of physiology, followed in his footsteps from 1599 to 1602. Meanwhile, in physics, there was Galileo, Padua professor for 18 years, from 1592 to 1610. It was here that Galileo first looked through a telescope, and it was here that he put together the text for his *Siderius Nuncius*, published in 1610. Even royalty came—Gustavus Adolphus of Sweden attended the university while Galileo was there. Was there ever another time when the seeds for so many diverse sciences were planted in a single fertile piece of land?

Padua may even earlier have been immeasurably important for English science, the catalyst for England's later sustained prominence in the field. Thomas Linacre (1460–1524), a fellow of All Souls' College in Oxford, took a degree of Doctor of Medicine at Padua around 1490, and then returned to England, imbued with the spirit of the Renaissance. He brought knowledge of the Greek language and awareness of Greek science to England; he taught and influenced the great philosopher Erasmus and Henry VIII's "man for all seasons," Sir Thomas More; he influenced Henry VIII himself by becoming his personal physician; he became the chief instrument in the grant of a royal charter for creation of the Royal College of Physicians in London.

Related Places to Visit: Bologna, Padua.

Leonardo da Vinci. Here, lest we exaggerate the praise of academia, comes Leonardo, from an in-between period, after the founding of the universities but before they came to full flower. But he himself was never at a university, which raises questions perennial to the academic common room. Must one be a scholarly academic to be classified as scientist? Can engineering and technology qualify as science, and if so, under what circumstances?

Leonardo (1452–1519) was the epitome of the "Renaissance man." He was one of the great painters of all time, and also an architect, engineer, designer of futuristic mechanical contrivances, a man with apparently inexhaustible knowledge of practically everything. He was a generation ahead of Copernicus, lived before Columbus discovered America, a full century before Galileo. How to define the words *science* and *scientist* at that time is not easy to decide. Leonardo was never a professor of natural philosophy and never struggled to develop and publish theoretical concepts about how the world works. Yet he wanted to know for himself how certain things work and, to judge from his notebooks, he did in fact have practical understanding of much that we might call science today—forces, levers, and winches, for example, and even the mechanics of flight. He clearly knew a thing or two about physics—at this pre-Galilean point in time, he probably knew more than the professors.

A curious fact about Leonardo is his undaunted left-handedness. His notebooks are written backwards (from right to left) in mirror image script.

Related Places to Visit: Vinci, Amboise (France).

The Scientific Renaissance: Zenith of Italian Science

Sixteenth Century: Lessons in Anatomy. The year 1543 was a year of decision, a watershed. Before then science looked backward to the Greek masters, to Aristotle, to Ptolemy, to Galen. Even progressive, innovative people—artists inventing new formulas for mixing paint, Guelphs and Ghibellines finding more effective tactics to fight one another in battle, physicians struggling for new ways to combat the ravages of the great plagues—based their forward-looking practical ideas on a scientific and philosophical framework that was sacrosanct and had not varied for centuries. Then, within the single year of 1543, two books were published, quite independently and in opposite corners of Europe, that changed all that and heralded a new forward-looking age for science itself. They were *De revolutionibus orbium coelestium* by Nicolaus Copernicus, turning point for physical science, and *De humani corporis fabrica* (fabric of the human body) by Andreas Vesalius, a similar landmark for biological sciences. These books were not revolutionary manifestos, nor did they intentionally advocate new methods for thinking about nature, as Francis Bacon and René Descartes were to do more than 50 years later. Their influence was more by way of example, the authors permitting themselves a relaxation of reverence for old doctrine, but by no means implying a lack of respect. (There were no provocative acts, such as the public burning of Galen's texts by Paracelsus, which so infuriated the physicians of Basel in 1527.)

Andreas Vesalius was born in Brussels in 1514 and studied medicine in Louvain and Paris before coming to Padua. The anatomy courses in his curriculum would have been based reverentially on Galen's work. The gross errors in Galen's texts (arising partly from studying animals rather than humans) were perpetuated even by scholars who knew that humans and lower animals are different, and even by the early dissectors of human cadavers (when that practice began to be tolerated) who could see with their own eyes that what Galen described was not to be seen. "This must be a poor specimen," they tended to say by way of excuse to their students—such was the power of Galen's word.

Vesalius was only in his early twenties on his appointment as a Padua professor and the revolution he wrought began innocently enough with an alteration in the standard procedure for teaching anatomy to medical students. He actually carried out dissections himself rather than following the custom of allowing a barber-surgeon to manipulate the cadaver while the professor sat in a chair lecturing to the students—in other words, reading Galen's text to them. Vesalius then made drawings of what he saw and woodcuts were made from the drawings to obtain the multiple copies needed for the *Fabrica*. It was the first real textbook of human anatomy and, curiously, the very presence of its accurate illustrations managed to upset some of Vesalius's colleagues. Galen's descriptions had been purely verbal and gave a lecturer more scope for imaginative interpretation of what a dissection revealed. (There is a fascinating link here between art and science. Galen had no access to the kind of artistic talent that was commonplace in Renaissance Italy—some experts believe that Vesalius's woodcuts were prepared in the studio of the Venetian painter Titian.)

Vesalius did not remain long in Padua, for he left the academic scene soon after publication of *Fabrica*. His family had a long record of medical service to royalty and he returned to that tradition, becoming court physician to the King of Spain, Charles V, and later to his son, Philip II. He subsequently tired of this and wanted to resume a teaching career, but resignation from royal service was difficult. There are apocryphal stories about his final years, one being that he fell afoul of the Inquisition for performing unpermitted human dissections and was ordered to make a pilgrimage to Jerusalem to expiate his sins. In any event, go to Jerusalem he did, and he died on the return voyage on the Greek Ionian island of Zakynthos (also called Zante) under unexplained circumstances.

As for the Galenic misconceptions that fell prey to Vesalius's meticulously documented observations, we can give only a couple of examples. The idea of hollow nerves, supposed to contain fluid that carried messages to and from the brain, was one of them. The "bone of Luz" was another—it was a bone, supposedly at the base of the spine, from which the body was thought to be regenerated on Judgment Day. Vesalius himself never went beyond exposure of such errors and never saw (or, at least, never drew attention to) structures that Galen had not mentioned at all. But he prepared the ground for innovation by inspiring those who followed him at Padua—he founded what we now call a "school," a group of anatomists who bit by bit filled in the missing pieces that had been absent altogether in Galen's account. Here are some selected names:

Realdo Colombo (1510–1559), Vesalius's immediate successor as professor of anatomy, discovered the separate vascular pathway for blood to and from the lungs.

The Spaniard, Michael Servetus (1511–1553), never actually in Padua, but influenced by Vesalius as a fellow-student in Paris, went beyond this and recognized that the fundamental change from venous to arterial blood takes place *in the lungs* when air is mixed with the blood. (Servetus made the mistake of linking anatomical structure to Christian doctrine and suffered accordingly— we have given a brief account in the preceding chapter.)

Girolamo Fabrici or Fabricius (1537–1619) discovered the valves in the veins, but without appreciating their significance. He was a Vesalius student who taught at Padua for 64 years, and it was for him that the Doge of Venice authorized the building of the Padua anatomical theater around 1590. Fabrici was held locally in extraordinary esteem—given the privilege of wearing the same purple and gold robe as the university's rector and awarded the Golden Collar of the Order of St. Mark when he retired.

Bartolomeo Eustachi (1505–1574) wrote a definitive treatise on the ear and discovered the *Eustachian tubes*, which connect the middle ear to the pharynx and thereby provide access for air to regulate the pressure within the ear. (They are also, of course, the cause of many an earache when they become blocked.)

Gabriele Fallopio (1523-1562) concentrated on the reproductive system. He described the *Fallopian tubes* which carry mammalian ova from the ovary to the uterus. He also disproved the notion, popular at the time, that the penis penetrates into the uterus during coition.

What an era of revelation it was about the workings of the human body! It was not just the structure or anatomy that was revealed, but also function—the description of what each organ does in the machinery of life. For in those days the word *function* did not yet imply, as it tends to do nowadays, a detailed chemical explanation, but rather the first glimmering of actual mechanical design, and new insight into function invariably went hand in hand with the discovery of new structures. The most dramatic example is provided by William Harvey, who discovered the *circulation* of the blood, as distinct from the then prevailing notion that blood was a nutrient, flowing one way to the body's peripheries. Harvey's work was done in England, but he had received his training and initial knowledge of the anatomy of the cardiovascular system as a student in Padua, instructed by the celebrated Girolamo Fabrici.

Related Place to Visit: Padua.

Galileo Galilei. The Birth of the Modern Age of Science. Galileo (1564–1642) was short and stocky, with red hair and a graying beard. He had an intense, cold look in his eyes. He was mean in spirit, according to some sources, and was not well-liked. But what a place he holds in history! He is the symbol for the beginning of the modern age of science, the age within which we still live today.

Why is it that we hold him in such high regard? He recognized the fallacy of Aristotelian doctrines of motion, of course, but he was not the first to do so, and that is not the main reason. What really counts is that Galileo swept away the very foundations of the old philosophy and changed the way people think. The Greeks and the medieval world after them were forever seeking *causes*. They wondered *why* an object falls to the ground and analyzed the question in terms of an ingenious hierarchy of *movers*. Galileo, by contrast, asked *how* an object falls—he used purposefully designed experiments to give an exact description, using his pulse to measure time, for example, for there were as yet no accurate clocks. He found that the velocity of motion is directly proportional to the time elapsed since the start of a fall and that the total distance traversed is proportional to the square of that time. He set physics on the path it has followed ever since—mathematical description must precede explanation (causes, forces). Galileo never progressed to (or even attempted) a comprehensive understanding of the laws of motion, as was done a century later by Isaac Newton, but he sowed the first seeds.

Galileo's story begins in Pisa. He was born there, studied at Pisa University, and then held the post of professor of mathematics there from 1589 until he moved to Padua in 1592. And, as everyone knows, Pisa's famous Leaning Tower figures prominently in the popular Galileo legend, skepticism from historians notwithstanding. Pisa is also the place where Galileo's close relationship with the great Dukes of Tuscany (the Medici) began. In his day the Tuscan court and all its retinue moved from Florence to Pisa each year from Christmas to Easter, and the Dukes always took a keen interest in the university and its scholars. Galileo thus came early to their notice, and they eventually became his active patrons. When he began to run into trouble with the Church in Rome, the Medici interceded for him and protected him from the worst of the orthodox wrath. After Galileo's conviction by the Inquisition, he stayed in Siena in the custody of Tuscan Archbishop Ascanio Piccolomini for six months, but was then allowed to return (under severe restrictions) to his own villa just outside Florence. He lived there, effectively under house arrest, for the last ten years of his life, and it was here that his last great work, *Two New Sciences*, was written.

As events transpired, it was his observations of the sky (not his terrestial mechanics) that made Galileo a public figure. He was not the inventor of the telescope, but he built the first models with good optical sharpness and he was the first to use them for astronomical observation, in 1609 and 1610, while he was a professor at Padua. A more practical use was for Venice's shipping companies to recognize incoming ships when they were still half a day's sail from the port—that's how Galileo obtained what modern terminology would call the necessary "funding" for his research.

Using his telescope, Galileo studied the uneven surface of the moon and demonstrated the existence of valleys, craters, and mountains. The shadows cast by the latter enabled him to calculate that some of them must be about four miles high. He showed that the Milky Way is composed of a multitude of individual stars, and he observed the existence of sunspots, from whose motion he concluded that the sun must be in continuous rotation. The most sensational discovery were the moons of Jupiter, one of the great events in astronomical history, the first addition to the solar system since antiquity. It was a triumph for the experimental method, too, because the obvious explanation at first view was that these were new fixed stars, made visible by the power of the telescope. But Galileo plotted their positions relative to Jupiter on a day-by-day basis, and found them alternating regularly between east and west. No stars could behave that way; they had to be small satellites in rapid rotation about their planet. These observations effectively destroyed Ptolemy's geocentric model of the universe and cried out for acceptance of the modestly made suggestion of Copernicus that the motions of the planets, as observed from Earth, were most simply explained if all of them (including the Earth) orbit about the Sun. Galileo found that Venus as seen from Earth has phases just like the moon and that was the crowning blow—it was predictable from the Copernican model and was confirmed by an experiment deliberately done to test the prediction.

All of this caused furor among the philosophers and concern in the established Church. The roughness of the moon's surface (which would seem to us to be a relatively innocuous part of the results) particularly incensed the philosophers because "perfection of the heavens" was central to their philosophical dogma. Absurd rationalizations of Galileo's result were proposed by some; others believed that the lenses distorted what they saw. The leading philosophy professors at the University of Padua refused to look through the telescope at all, despite repeated invitations from Galileo, unwilling to even entertain the possibility that anything seen through new-fangled "spectacles" could affect the age-old wisdom of profound scholars. Galileo wrote about this in a letter to Kepler: "What shall we make of all this? Shall we laugh or shall we cry?"

Related Places to Visit: Florence, Pisa, Padua, Middelburg (Netherlands).

Science of the Grand Dukes. Florence is one of the great places in the history of modern civilization, testimony to the benevolent patronage of the Medici family, who caused the arts to flourish. But the Medici, late in their history, patronized science as well and created the Accademia del Cimento, an institution housed in their family mansion, the Pitti Palace, with Leopoldo de Medici, brother of the Duke, an actual active participant. There was a glorious period of about ten years (1657–1667) when this ambitiously conceived institution produced major works of scientific research. There are two reasons for its early demise: One (a typically Italian happening) is that Leopoldo was appointed a cardinal in 1667 and became preoccupied with the duties of that position. The second reason (more thought-provoking with respect to the motivations for scientific discovery) is that a rule of anonymity had been adopted—research results were published in the name of the Accademia as a whole, without the names of individual contributors. That just didn't work. The individuals submerged by this rule found themselves unable to live with denial of due public credit, and they gradually drifted away.

The projects of the Accademia reached far and wide. They set up weather stations all over Europe (probably inspired by Torricelli's invention of the atmospheric barometer a few years earlier). They accurately measured the speed of sound. Two of its members, **Francesco Redi** and **Nicolaus Steno,** made such outstanding individual contributions in biology and geology that their names inevitably emerged in spite of the rule of anonymity.

Francesco Redi (1626–1698) made the first convincing attack on the doctrine of spontaneous generation inherited from Aristotle and still almost universally accepted at the time. According to this doctrine insects and other low forms of life arise *spontaneously* from decaying animal and plant matter, without need for the seeds or eggs or sperm that higher forms of life require. Redi demonstrated the fallacy of this by very simple experiments. He put dead snakes, fish, and so on into wide-mouthed flasks, some of which were sealed and some kept open. The open flasks soon became infested with maggots, but the closed ones did not, though the meat within them became putrid and smelly. In those days, of course, no attempts were made to exclude flies from daily life, and Redi observed that the maggots in the open flasks developed into flies just like the ones that hovered all around. The conclusion was obvious—flies lay eggs, the eggs generate new organisms of the identical species, the putrifying matter simply provides nourishment for their growth. To guard against the possibility that lack of air in the sealed flasks was the determining factor, Redi repeated the experiment (with the same result) using unsealed flasks covered with a fine gauze through which air could flow, but which flies could not penetrate. The precise scientific logic is astonishing for a work of biology at such an early date.

Nicolaus Steno (1638–1686) made his name through his book *Prodromus*, one of the earliest attempts at a systematic account of the geological history of the earth. On the basis of the geological strata in the Tuscan landscape around him, Steno postulated six successive stages: first the rock layers as originally created, then subsurface cavities eaten out by water or fire, then collapse, and so forth. It was very sophisticated for the time, and Steno assumed that what he could see in Tuscany would probably apply over much of the earth. Steno's theory would seem to imply a longer than conventional time scale for the earth's existence, but Steno alluded to this only vaguely in *Prodromus*, and preferred to leave the impression that he adhered confidently to the biblical chronology. He was in fact a deeply religious man. He was actually Danish, born in Copenhagen, the name by which he is known being a latinized version of his Danish name, Niels Stensen. Florence converted him from his native Lutheranism to Catholicism, and in 1675 he became a Catholic priest and gave up his scientific research.

Related Place to Visit: Florence.

Electricity on the Move

Galvani, Volta, and Napoleon. The eighteenth century was not a happy one for Italy. The French ruled the northwestern Piedmont and the Austrians held Lombardy and within it the rich Duchy of Milan. When the last of the Medicis died in 1737, Florence and Tuscany also acquired an Austrian ruler. Venice retained its independence, but not its greatness, for the main ports of commerce had moved further west to Spain, England, and the Netherlands.

Then, however, in 1796 and 1797, came a new force—Napoleon Bonaparte invaded from the north and carried all before him. He created the Cisalpine and Ligurian republics, followed in 1805 by a "Kingdom" of Italy, with Napoleon personally wearing the iron crown of the Lombards. He was a conqueror, but also (at least in the north) something of a hero, a proverbial breath of fresh air compared to the previously dominant heavy-handed Austrians. (After Napoleon's final defeat in 1815, the Austrians regained hegemony, but this time all Italy joined in rebellion to drive them out and to move toward a politically united nation.)

The century's scientific highlight in Italy was the discovery of electric currents. The story begins with Luigi Galvani (1737–1798), a medical professor in Bologna, a rather mediocre scientist, but one whose name has become permanently incorporated into the English language, both in technical terminology (galvanometer) and in everyday speech (galvanize). He was experimenting with disembodied nerve/muscle preparations (legs, spinal cord, and connecting nerves), making them twitch in response to electrical stimulation of the spinal cord, when he made a startling observation. He had a row of his frog remains mounted to an iron railing in his garden, fastened by brass hooks, when he saw them begin to twitch spontaneously even without an applied stimulus. Galvani was fired with excitement and had a vision of "animal electricity," an internal electrical fluid, supposedly generated in the brain, then passed along a nerve to the muscle, and stored there (condenser-like), ready for practical use. This kind of sensational discovery, hinting at some mysterious powerful force, always attracts universal attention. (A few years earlier, a claimed psychic force, "animal magnetism," had been the rage of fashionable society in Paris.) Galvani instantly became front page news.

Enter now Alessandro Volta (1745–1827), a physicist from Como and professor of physics at the University of Pavia, a humble man at the time, who (in his youth) had come close to taking holy orders. He was angered by the publicity given to Galvani's discovery. He had earlier in his career dabbled a little in static and atmospheric electricity (though he was by this time working on something quite different) and his first reaction to Galvani's reports was total disbelief—he had a low opinion of physicians and found it hard to believe that any of them could do anything sensible in the field of electricity, a sentiment to which some modern physicists might still subscribe. Volta, in fact, confirmed Galvani's actual observation for himself, but soon disproved the "animal electricity" explanation. Mere contact between brass and iron (with a little moisture) generates electricity—frogs are not necessary and had in effect been only a detecting device in Galvani's experiments. Volta might well have rested on his laurels then, but Galvani had an enthusiastic following, who persisted for years in defending the original interpretation. A tooth and toenail battle with them kept Volta at the bench!

It quickly became apparent that the kind of electricity produced by wet bimetallic contacts is different from the then familiar form, the discharge of static electricity from a Leyden jar. The electric tension that could be obtained was much lower and no sparks were generated, but (more than compensating) the bimetallic system proved to be a continuous source of electric current, whereas a Leyden jar must be recharged after each discharge. Furthermore it was soon found that the tension (which we now appropriately call *voltage*) could be increased by linking many bimetallic pairs in series, with paper strips saturated with salt water in between, forming the famous Voltaic pile. In short, the electric battery was born and its use spread rapidly all over Europe. Within a year it was used in England to generate sufficient voltage for the decomposition of water into gaseous hydrogen and oxygen.

It was, of course, a revolution. Before Volta, electricity had been a serious subject for scholars, but for the general public it was mostly a plaything. Sparks and electric shocks were ingredients of electrical entertainments, but what else were they good for? Volta's batteries led the way to a previously undreamed of source of useful power.

Galvani and Volta fared very differently under the French conquerors. Galvani refused to swear allegiance to the newly created Cisalpine Republic and consequently lost his job at the University of Bologna. He died in poverty and sorrow. But Volta (though initially hostile to the French) quickly came to realize that the French were more genuine supporters of education and research than the Austrians had ever been, and he became an ardent Napoleon enthusiast. The Emperor reciprocated. Volta, on a trip to Paris as a representative of the University of Pavia, demonstrated his current-generating pile to the Paris Academy, at sessions attended by Napoleon himself. Napoleon immediately grasped its enormous practical potential and presented Volta with a gold medal and a pension and even made him a senator of the kingdom of Italy. He also authorized an annual award for whoever "makes a contribution to electricity and galvanism comparable to Franklin's and Volta's," an award subsequently won quite appropriately by Humphry Davy, who worked out the correct chemical explanation for how a battery works, something that Volta had not managed to do.

Alessandro Volta himself eventually retired to his birthplace in Como, where he died at age eighty-two, Como's most honored citizen.

Related Places to Visit: Bologna, Como.

The Nineteenth Century

Clear Thinking about Molecules—and Some Not So Clear. We turn to chemistry and to **Amedeo Avogadro,** one of the best remembered names in the history of that science. He came from the Piedmont area, where his family had been pillars of society for more than six centuries—in the country-wide thirteenth century struggles between the Guelphs and the Ghibellines, it was the Avogadros who had carried the Guelph banner (in support of the papacy) in Vercelli. Amedeo himself was less affected by Napoleon's invasion than Galvani or Volta, because the Piedmont had already been dominated by the French for some time before Napoleon arrived on the scene. He was a teacher of natural philosophy at the Royal College of Vercelli in 1811 when the work at the heart of our story was published. (Our story begins, however, much later, in the year 1860, and at that time features another Italian, a patriotic Sicilian, an active participant—an artillery officer—in the revolt of Sicily against its Bourbon rulers and a member of Sicily's temporary ruling council when that revolt eventually succeeded.)

In September 1860 some of the leading chemists of the day met in Karlsruhe (Germany) for an extraordinary three-day conference. They sought (predictably in vain) to settle a most vexing problem, one that had plagued the science of chemistry ever since John Dalton had created the modern atomic theory in 1808: "What are the relative weights of the atoms?" By 1860 the number of known distinct atoms had risen to about 60, but that crucial question remained unresolved. Everyone agreed that 8 grams of oxygen combine with 1 gram of hydrogen to form 9 grams of water, or conversely, when water is split up, that it yields oxygen and hydrogen in the weight ratio of 8 to 1. But does that mean, as Dalton had supposed, that the relative atomic weights are also 8:1, an oxygen atom (O) weighing eight times as much as a hydrogen atom (H)? If so, it would mean that a water molecule contains one atom of each kind and has a molecular formula of HO. But there were alternative possibilities, including the one we now know to be true—the relative weights are O/H = 16, and the formula for water is H_2O. How do we choose? We need more information than is given by the combining weights alone, some other somehow elusive principle.

One of the participants in the Karlsruhe conference was the Italian Stanislao Cannizzaro, a Sicilian native and patriot, but a professor at the University of Genoa at the time. He brought a simple message, telling the conference that his countryman Amedeo Avogadro, now dead (he had died at age eighty in 1856), had solved their problem way back in 1811, just three years after publication of Dalton's theory. Avogadro, while at the Royal College in Vercelli, had indeed accomplished that, using common sense and avoiding the kind of preconceived notions that (we now realize) blinded the two generations of chemists that came after him. But Vercelli was then (and remains) somewhat off the beaten track and Avogadro was a rather solitary and unassuming man. His message never quite managed to penetrate to the forefront of chemical thinking.

The conference listened politely to Cannizzaro, but without enthusiasm. The name of Avogadro was not unknown to them, but they all knew that his ideas had been rejected out of hand by none other than Jöns Jakob Berzelius, also now dead, but still revered as one of the great father figures of chemical science. Most of the chemical community had acquiesced in Berzelius's rejection. We can't guess how many of those at Karlsruhe remembered the reason for the rejection, but they were clearly reluctant to go back to a 50-year-old paper, preferring to stick to more recent ideas, some of which were truly bizarre. For example, the senior man at the conference, Jean-Baptiste Dumas from France, wanted everyone to believe that inorganic chemistry and organic chemistry must be irreconcilable systems with different laws of combination, and that the atoms common to both (carbon, hydrogen, oxygen, nitrogen) have different relative weights in each system. The meeting ended on a dismal note. Scientific questions can't be decided by vote, they concluded, and every chemist should be allowed full freedom to use whatever system of atomic weights he preferred.

Avogadro's solution to the problem had been very simple. It applied only to gaseous reactions, where gas volumes could be measured to supplement combining weights. It rested on the simple hypothesis, not actually original with him but given scholarly justification in his publications, that equal volumes of gas or vapor, at the same temperature and pressure, contain the same number of *particles*. Measurements were again easy to make. Using oxygen and hydrogen and water again for purpose of illustration, the result was that when water vapor (steam) is dissociated two volumes of water produce two volumes of hydrogen and one volume of oxygen. By Avogadro's hypothesis this means two particles of water yield two particles of hydrogen and one particle of oxygen. It was this result that created the trouble (not the underlying assumption on which it was based) for it conflicted with orthodox preconceived notions about atoms and molecules—an accepted one-to-one correspondence between atoms and elements—which leads to the prediction that the ultimate *particles* of a gas must be molecules in the case of compounds and single atoms in the case of elements.

If the experimental result had been that one volume of water gives two of hydrogen and one of oxygen, then there would have been no objection. It would have meant that dissociation of one water molecule yields two atoms of H and one of O (i.e., water is H_2O and not HO). But two water molecules yielding one *atom* of oxygen makes no sense. In fact Avogadro's results as a whole can't make sense at all unless the then existing dogma about atoms and molecules is discarded and we allow an element to have molecules of more than one atom, such as O_2, H_2, and even P_4 in the case of phosphorus vapor. Avogadro took that conclusion in his stride. The ultimate particles in gases of some of the elements could not be single atoms; there is no way to circumvent this. No law of physics prevents it, so why not?

As so often happens, cherished dogmas were a stronger force than reasoned arguments. Berzelius had been especially adamant. He thought he knew how molecules must be held together—by electrical attraction, individual atoms being intrinsically either positive or negative. Identical atoms would have the same electrical polarity and would repel each other. They could never combine pairwise as required by Avogadro's data.

Cannizzaro left the Karlsruhe conference as soon as it was over, probably with a sense of failure. But, as it happened, failure turned overnight to success. Cannizzaro was a dedicated teacher and had prepared a set of lectures for his students, lectures that were models of clarity and precise logic. They were easier to follow and more insistent than Avogadro's original papers, leaving no doubt that the intuitively attractive orthodox dogma was untenable. Cannizzaro had brought printed copies of the lectures with him to Karslruhe and another Italian at the meeting (a friend from the University of Pavia) distributed them after he left to anyone who wanted one. Among the latter was young Lothar Meyer, a new assistant professor at the University of Breslau, soon to become one of the shining lights of German chemistry. What happened next has become legend. In Meyer's own words: "I too got a copy, which I put in my pocket to read on my long journey home. I read it again and again and was astonished at the light which the writing threw on the most important points at issue. The scales fell from my eyes, doubt vanished, and a sense of the calmest certainty took its place." Meyer's enthusiasm proved infective, and soon one wondered how controversy could ever have existed.

Once the relative weights of the commonest atoms were definitely established, the remainder fell quickly into place and the now familiar periodicity in their properties, when arranged in order of increasing mass, became apparent almost immediately thereafter. Many years later, when chemists and physicists began to be concerned about the *absolute* mass of an atom, infinitely smaller than the *relative* weights we have been discussing, Amedeo Avogadro was paid a fitting tribute when his name was given to the number that links the two scales. Avogadro's Number, represented by capital N, equal to 6.02×10^{23}, is probably the single most important numerical bit of information in all of chemistry. Every student of chemistry is required to engrave it in his memory, but few probably learn the full story behind it.

Related Places to Visit: Vercelli, Palermo.

The Grand Tour: Lyell in Italy. We noted earlier that many Englishmen traveled to Italy in the fifteenth and sixteenth centuries for an education, chiefly to the University of Padua. Soon afterwards an even greater influx of English visitors began to all the cities of Italy, more relaxed and without a formal educational mission—the "Grand Tour" had come into existence, a *sine qua non* for the rich, the fashionable, and the literate. John Milton traveled in Italy in 1638 and 1639 and visited Galileo at Arcetri, and streams of other poets followed. Keats died in Rome of the fever in 1821, Shelley was drowned in a boating accident in the Bay of Spezia in 1822. Scientists were not immune to the lure of foreign lands. Robert Boyle, only sixteen at the time and not yet even dreaming about a career, was in Italy in 1641 and 1642 with his older brother Francis and their French tutor—the party was wintering in Florence when Galileo died and Boyle wrote about the event in his diaries.

In the nineteenth century we have one such traveling scientist who merits special mention, the restless geologist Charles Lyell (see under "England"). He first came to Italy about the time of Keats and Shelley, on the Grand Tour with his parents in a private coach pulled by hired horses, with excursions on foot where coaches could not travel. The family crossed France, wandered all around Switzerland, and climbed the Simplon Pass (eight horses were required) to enter Italy, going south as far as Florence. But it is a less luxurious trip, ten years later, traversing the full length of the country, that was to make geological history. The shores, rocks, and volcanoes of Italy became the proving ground for Lyell's far-reaching theoretical views of geological phenomena, which would soon become the dominant doctrine in the field.

Related Places to Visit: Pozzuoli, Mount Etna.

Starfish on the Beach: Cells That Fight Intruders. Elie Metchnikoff (1845–1916) had twice attempted suicide. The first time was in 1873 when his first wife died of tuberculosis; the second time was in 1880 when political unrest and student uprisings made life at the University of Odessa (where he was a professor) very difficult and, on top of that, his second wife, Olga, almost died of typhoid fever. A little later the situation in Odessa became so bad that Metchnikoff could stand it no longer and resigned. This time he found a healthier response to stress: He moved with his family to the opposite end of Europe, to Messina in Sicily, where life was tranquil, the weather was benign, and vast opportunity existed to study invertebrate animals, which were Metchnikoff's research interest at the time. Olga's family had lots of money, so the Metchnikoffs were able to lead a full life without financial worries.

One day the family was at the circus, watching performing apes, and Metchnikoff himself was at home, looking through his microscope at transparent larvae of starfish, a common invertebrate from the beaches of the Straits of Messina. He could see mobile cells within the larval body and got the idea that they might be there as a defense against intruding foreign bodies, a theory he quickly tested by pricking larvae with thorns from a rose bush in his garden. The mobile cells rushed to surround the intruding thorn! Perhaps vertebrate animals had similar cells to fight bacterial invasion and the like? As he said later, "Thus it was in Messina that the great event of my scientific life took place. A zoologist until then, I suddenly became a pathologist."

Metchnikoff first gave the name *Fresszellen* (eating cells) to cells of this kind, but soon switched to the more polite Greek equivalent, *phagocyte*. He went on to show that the white blood corpuscles of higher animals and man have a similar beneficial function, taking up bacteria and other invading particles, preventing them from their often hostile mission. (In doing so he disproved an old dogma, which held that white blood cells are deleterious, helping to spread infection throughout the body.) Years later, in 1908, Metchnikoff won part of the Nobel Prize for his discoveries.

Related Place to Visit: Messina/Taormina in Sicily.

The Twentieth Century

Twentieth-century Italy cannot match some of the other large European countries in their investment in scientific research, but there has been continued contribution to progress on a more modest scale. Several Italians have won Nobel prizes, in physics, in chemistry, and in medical science. The work we describe here, one of the most fascinating pieces of research of the past several decades, was actually done by an international team, collaborating with Italians and using an Italian geological site.

Problem of the 1980s: What Killed the Dinosaurs? Every school child is taught today about the dinosaurs and the giant flying reptiles and marine reptiles that existed about the same time. Their fossil remains are found all over the world, but about 65 million years ago they abruptly became extinct. Why did they die? The problem has fascinated scientists for many years. Many solutions have been suggested, but none before 1980 offered a convincing explanation. An acceptable solution must account for two puzzling facts: One is that the disaster struck simultaneously all over the world, and the other is that the dinosaurs did not die alone—their demise is part of a *mass extinction*, in which as many as half the then living species may have perished.

The probably correct solution to the problem (satisfactorily accounting for both the above facts) has come from analysis of stratified rocks, specifically from the walls of Bottaccione Gorge on the outskirts of the Umbrian town of Gubbio. The explanation is dramatic. It was an object from outer space that did it, collision of the earth with a small asteroid!

The evidence was provided by a research team headed by an American physicist and his geologist son—Luis Alvarez, winner of the Nobel Prize in physics in 1968 for unrelated work, and Walter Alvarez, a geology professor at the University of California. The basis for their conclusion is what has become known as the *iridium anomaly*. Iridium is a chemical element that is exceptionally rare in the outer mantle of the earth, but more abundant in extraterrestial matter, and the Alvarez team set out to exploit this by doing an analysis for the relative abundance of iridum and other atomic species in sedimentary rock that could be accurately dated. The Bottaccione Gorge is ideal for this purpose. Its successive strata of sediment are exceptionally well defined and had been previously used for other geological studies so that there was no problem with assignment of dates. The critical Cretaceous-Tertiary boundary (the technical name for where the fossil record changes abruptly) is clearly marked by a 1-centimeter layer of clay.

The results were unambiguous. Twenty-eight elements were measured, and samples taken at intervals over the height of the Bottaccione wall revealed only small fluctuations for 27 of them. Iridium alone was anomalous, with a sharp additional peak precisely at the boundary layer, sure indication that material from outer space had become mixed with the normal sediment. (It needs to be appreciated that the incredibly tiny iridium content of the samples required an exotic analytical method—analysis of gamma rays released after bombardment with neutrons. Previous subnuclear physics expertise of Alvarez père undoubtedly contributed here.)

How could impact with a small asteroid trigger a massive extinction? That is not hard to imagine. An object colliding with the earth would become pulverized on impact and would at the same time pulverize an even larger section of the earth's crust at the impact site. Much of the resulting debris would be thrown high into the atmosphere and would end up as stratospheric dust, which would then take several years to settle. During this period the access of sunlight to the earth's surface would be sharply reduced, the growth of vegetation would be drastically impeded, and giant creatures wholly dependent on plant food would not be able to survive. Extinction could have been complete in just a few years, a time incredibly short by geological standards. The principle is the same as for the effect of volcanic eruptions on our weather, but on a more massive scale. Note also the parallel with the dire prediction of a nuclear winter—a future disaster that might follow a nuclear war.

The asteroid size required to account for the observed iridium enrichment is only 6.5 miles (10 km). The explanation, of course, requires that the iridium anomaly be found worldwide, and the Alvarez team indeed confirmed this with analyses of sedimentary rocks in Denmark and New Zealand. One would also like to be able to identify the impact crater left by the event, but this has so far been unsuccessful, though possible candidates are beginning to emerge in the 1990s literature. There is of course no reason why the impact site should be anywhere near Gubbio, and it could even be on the bottom of an ocean.

Related Places to Visit: Gubbio, Stevns Klint (Denmark).

PRINCIPAL PLACES TO VISIT

Mainland Italy

BOLOGNA

Bologna itself is an impressive city, with broad arcaded streets, many closed to private cars. It is the site of the first real university in Europe, which, politics and pestilence notwithstanding, has flourished more or less uninterruptedly to the present day. The university began as a community of professors and scholars without a permanent home (despite the presence of as many as 10,000 students), but a regular building was eventually constructed in 1563. The university remained there until 1803, when the move to its present site outside the city center was made.

The old university is in the Palazzo Archiginnasio, located on the Piazza Galvani behind the Basilica San Petronio. Escutcheons of former rectors and professors densely cover the courtyard, surrounding vestibules and staircases. Most of the building is now occupied by a modern library, but the historical parts have been restored to their original state and are open to the public. The most interesting part is the anatomical theater, originally built in 1637, leading off a gallery overlooking the courtyard. It is a spacious rectangular room, built entirely of wood, with only three tiers of seats. Statues of Hippocrates, Galen, and other doctors/anatomists of antiquity line the wall, and there are busts of prominent local physicians. A centerpiece of the room is the lecture podium with an impressive canopy supported by statues of skinless human bodies in which the musculature is clearly exposed to view. The visitor should apply to the Porter's lodge for admission.

Luigi Galvani and Guglielmo Marconi (*see* p. 115) are well-remembered Bolognesi. There is a statue of Galvani in the piazza named after him.

COMO

Como is beautifully situated at the foot of Lake Como, with high mountains behind. In Roman times it was important as the southern terminus for trans-alpine passes, which, of course, it remains today [except that, for most traffic, the St. Gotthard pass has been replaced by a 10-mile (16 km) tunnel]. In the time of Alessandro Volta, Como was under irksome Austrian domination.

No other city in the world pays as splendid a tribute to a scientist as Como does to Alessandro Volta. The most spectacular memorial is the Tempio Voltiano, a neoclassical rotunda—like a temple to an old Roman god—which juts out into the lake, the centerpiece of Como's lakefront. The building contains an excellent museum, one of the best in Europe devoted to a single individual and his work. We see Volta's "piles" in all stages of development, the original "tower" of disks, a later "corona" of beakers connected by wires, and a "pile of troughs" that looks not unlike a modern automobile battery. There are paintings of Volta demonstrating electric currents to an eager-to-learn Napoleon Bonaparte. An upstairs gallery has an impressive collection of books that Volta used either in his own training or as a professor at the University of Pavia. Many of them, including, for example, Joseph Priestley's famous *History of Electricity* (1767), are in English. Most of the electrical apparatus in the Tempio actually consists of faithful reproductions. The city of Como mounted an exhibit of every genuine

The Tempio Voltiano on the lakefront of the city of Como.

Volta pile it could find on the occasion of the 1899 centenary of the first discovery—unfortunately, a disastrous fire destroyed the lot.

Como also has a piazza named after Volta with a prominent statue of him, and a street, the Viale Alessandro Volta, which contains (at number 62) the grand townhouse where he was born. The high school where he first taught physics (the Liceo A. Volta) and the church where he was married are other places on the official Volta itinerary, as is the Torre di Porta Nuovo at the corner of Viale Verese and Viale C. Cattaneo. This tower is part of the surviving segment of the ancient city walls, and from 1783 to 1806 it was used as a physics laboratory by Volta's friend Canon Gattoni. It is here that Volta actually carried out all of his experiments. Today (somewhat ironically) it houses an electric power relay station, and nothing of the old interior remains. Finally, at Camnago Volta, three kilometers from Como, we can see Volta's former summer house and the mausoleum where he was buried.

The city of Como also remembers Pliny the Elder and his nephew and chronicler, Pliny the Younger. Interestingly, it does not do so in the form of some nineteenth- or twentieth-century move to give belated recognition, but by means of monuments dating back to about 1480. The two famous native sons grace the left and right of the main doorway of the Como Cathedral, a splendid edifice built entirely of marble. (A few kilometers northeast, near Torno, is the much visited *Villa Pliniana*, occupying the site of a former country mansion of the younger Pliny.)

The Volta temple is open daily except Monday. Telephone (tourist office) 031–262091.

DUINO (near Trieste)

Trieste and the adjacent Istrian peninsula (now in Croatia) were part of Austria for many years until the end of World War I. This was Austria's outlet to the sea, for commerce and for seaside holidays. Duino, 16 miles (25 km) north of Trieste, lies in this region, a quiet fishing village in a spectacular setting in the midst of sheer vertical cliffs. The famous Austrian physicist Ludwig Boltzmann came here for a holiday near the end of the summer in 1906 to try to relax from overwork, illness, and mental depression. It did not work and he hanged himself the day before he was supposed to return to Vienna. (We have given an account of Boltzmann's work and the hostile reception it received from some of his peers under "Austria.")

A cliff-top footpath (named after the German poet Rainer Maria Rilke, who lived in Duino from 1910 to 1914) joins Duino to the nearby resort of Sistiana. A walk along the path puts one in a reflective mood—the peaceful beauty, so different from the noisy clamor of Italian cities; the historical vicissitudes of national ownership of the area; and reflection about Boltzmann himself, driven to irrational suicide in spite of his brilliant creative mind. He must have walked this way often, and there even used to be a false story that he died by throwing himself off one of the cliffs.

FLORENCE

Florence is one of the showplaces for the European tourist. Art and architecture are, of course, preeminent and emphasized by most guidebooks, but there is much to admire for the traveling scientist as well, reflecting the legacy of Galileo and the patronage of the Medici.

The successive residences used by the Medici over the centuries are part of the normal tourist itinerary. The Pitti Palace, one of the great sites of Florence, with a collection of 11 Raphael paintings and many other masterpieces of art, is the place where the Accademia del Cimento held its meetings around 1660. The original rooms used for meetings, glass manufacture, and so on can no longer be identified, but the royal apartments from a later date are open for public view, and they are lavishly decorated indeed. Has scientific research ever again been conducted in such opulent quarters?

The Museo di Storia della Scienza is an exceptionally well organized museum. Among its contents are mathematical instruments, telescopes, barometers and other meteorological instruments, and models of the celestial spheres, including a particularly impressive one, three meters high, built between 1588 and 1593 by Antonio Santucci. One room is dedicated to Galileo's instruments and includes a working model of the kind of inclined plane he used to demonstrate that the rate of fall of bodies under gravity is independent of their mass. One room contains both artistic and scientific glass pieces. The grand dukes had imported Venetian glassmakers into Florence long before the days of the Accademia, and they continued to use them afterwards for decorative as well as useful glassware. Another room contains microscopes and some of Francesco Redi's drawings of insect reproductive systems, results of microscopic observations which he published in 1668 to supplement his flask-based disproof of the notion of spontaneous generation. The museum also contains portraits of scientists associated with the Medici and a painting of the Accademia in session. Only nine people are seen; there were never more than a handful of senior members.

Italy's greatest monument to Galileo is in the Church of Santa Croce. Galileo had ordered in his will that he was to be buried here, in a vault where other members of his family were interred. The city fathers (never seriously influenced by the verdict of the Inquisition) at once voted money for a marble memorial in Santa Croce, but the Holy Office in Rome intervened—such public recognition was deemed inappropriate for someone who during his life had "caused scandal to all Christendom by his false and damnable doctrine." Galileo's family and friends accordingly had to be satisifed with a modest private burial in an adjacent chapel. But the banishment did not last too long. Galileo's

Galileo's tomb in the church of Santa Croce in
Florence.

former pupil and subsequent biographer, Vincenzio Viviani, charged his own
heirs with the erection of a proper monument. He died in 1703 and his will was
carried out in 1737. The tomb then built in Santa Croce is splendid in all
respects. It has a prominent location close to the entrance to the church,
directly opposite the tomb of Florence's greatest artist and architect, Michelangelo Buonarroti. "He gave his all to geometry, astronomy and philosophy," the inscription on Galileo's tomb proclaims, "no others of his time were
comparable."

The house of Galileo's confinement after the Inquisition, Il Gioiello, is in
the suburb of Arcetri, about 2 miles (3 km) from the center of Florence. Galileo
had previously chosen this place for his residence because it was adjacent to the
Convent of San Matteo, where his two daughters were nuns. The house is
owned by the state, but it is not in good condition and is at present closed to the
public.

The museum is open daily except Sundays. Telephone: 055-293493.

GUBBIO

Gubbio is an out-of-the-way place, about 25 miles (40 km) from Perugia. It is an ancient town, built in parallel terraces on a steep mountainside and famous for its pottery, which is sold in many little shops. Legend has it that St. Francis of Assisi came here in the thirteenth century to save the town from a gigantic wolf that was terrorizing the neighborhood. St. Francis is said to have gone fearlessly to the wolf's lair to reproach him for his misdeeds, whereupon the wolf is said to have become penitent and promised never to hurt another soul. He became Gubbio's friendly mascot and was buried on consecrated soil.

The geological site related to the discovery of the iridium anomaly is in the Bottaccione Gorge, directly north of the town, on the road toward Scheggia. The cutting of this road is what created the site, laying bare for the researcher (and today's visitor) the 1,320 foot (400 m) high stratified surface, which corresponds to a time span of deposit (from what was once overlying ocean) of over 100 million years.

The area of interest begins 0.6 miles (1 km) from the edge of the town, at the Ristorante Bottaccione, and extends about 1,650 feet (500 m) to the north. A walk along this stretch provides a unique opportunity for the layman to see geological research in action. One is unlikely to see actual explorations in progress, but all previous explorers have left indelible marks of their work—the rock face is literally honeycombed with drill holes from which rock samples were taken. Different sections are identified with metal signs, labeled "Gubbio Paleomagnetic Section" and assigned zone numbers. The whole scene is at road level and no climbing or other exertion is needed. Drill holes become particularly dense near the point where an aqueduct crosses the road, which is the general vicinity from which samples for iridium and other metal analysis were taken.

We note as we walk along that the rock face is covered in many places by metal screen, but this is to protect the road from falling rock and is not related to geological exploration. It will also be noted that the rock strata are generally tilted relative to the road level, but that is an unimportant feature, the more important factor being that the strata are continuous, without major breaks or faults. In many places a gross boundary between red and white limestone is clearly evident even to the untutored eye. The actual scientific boundary is a 1 centimeter thick layer of soft clay between the red and the white, which one can see if one looks very carefully. Note that the word *paleomagnetic* in the identifying labels refers to the earlier intensive use of the area by geologists from many different countries, who came here to study a quite separate problem, namely how the earth's magnetic field must have changed through the ages—a fascinating phenomenon, with intermittent dramatic reversals of the field, which represents another puzzle for modern science, as yet without explanation.

PADUA

Padua, the town of arcaded streets, is one of the birthplaces of modern science. Galileo discovered the moons of Jupiter here and Vesalius and his followers destroyed the scholastic traditions in biology and medicine. The university is known as *il Bo* (meaning *the ox*), after the name of an inn on whose site it stands. Its showpiece is the *Teatro Anatomico*, built in 1594 to the design of the anatomist Fabricius and preserved in its original state. It brilliantly evokes the intensity with which the very earliest public dissections of human corpses must have been attended by eager medical students. The theater has an oval shape, with a very small diameter, but there is room (*standing* room) for more than 200 students, in six wooden tiered galleries around the edge. There is a dissecting table in the center, with a hole in the floor under it, presumably for rapid disposal of dissected items—the room must have been hot and the smell horrendous.

A distinctive feature of the university in general is the multitude of escutcheons, which seem to cover all available wall surface and even some areas of the ceiling. They are the emblems of all the professors who taught at Padua, from about 1550 to 1700, when the practice of installing escutcheons was discontinued.

Padua's famous law courts (*Palazzo del Ragione*) are close by. Some of the early interest in anatomical investigations was stimulated by the demands of the legal profession for expert evidence in trials for violent crimes.

Guided tours of *il Bo* are provided daily except Sunday. Telephone (tourist office): 049–875–0655.

PISA

Pisa has one of the great piazzas of Italy, the Piazza del Duomo, on which stands the bright marble cathedral, the famous *campanile* (the Leaning Tower) and the baptistery. The spacious open areas in between are not paved, but set to green lawns, giving the whole an almost rural setting.

Both the cathedral and the Leaning Tower are linked to Galileo's early awareness of the physical laws of motion. One popular anecdote tells us that he dropped unequal weights from the Leaning Tower to disprove Aristotle's dictum that the rate of the natural fall of bodies toward the earth's surface is proportional to body weight. A second anecdote has him deducing the law of the pendulum from watching the oscillations of the great chandelier opposite the altar in the cathedral. Both stories have been ridiculed by many scholars, but the definitive scientific biography of Galileo by Stillman Drake tends to support at least the first. It is true that Galileo used inclined planes for his *experiments* on Aristotle's law, so as to slow down the rate of fall (he used his pulse to measure time), but, once he knew what the answer was, he made use of the Leaning Tower as a more effective way to *demonstrate* the result qualitatively to others.

As for the cathedral lamp, we are snidely told by the scrupulous historians that it was not installed until 1587, whereas the observation of isochronism is supposed to have happened in 1583. But surely there was a lamp there before the present one and surely it obeyed the same laws of physics? One can see the new chandelier today. The rope that holds it to the ceiling is many meters long and the lamp would undoubtedly be set swinging back and forth, even by miniscule air currents, if the authorities did not prudently prevent it by tying the lamp laterally to firm supports.

The area of Pisa University lies just south of the Duomo. Much of it has remained externally unchanged since Galileo's time, and, indeed, students still come to have their lunch or to bask in the sunshine on the grass of the piazza, and they still outnumber the tourists when the university is in session. How many of them stop to think that Galileo, too, may have come here to relax 400 years before them and perhaps have dreamed in the sunshine of future glory?

There is a small museum in the *Comus Galilaeana*, a house at 26 Via Santa Maria, where Galileo once lived. It is open daily, mornings only.

POMPEII

Follow the crowd to Pompeii! It is one of the greatest historical sites of Europe and tourists flock there from all over the world. The town was buried by a rain of molten lava and cinders to a depth of several feet. The lava solidified to a crust of volcanic rock, preserving for posterity all that was buried, except the roofs of the buildings, which collapsed under the weight. The ruins were rediscovered in the seventeenth century and systematic excavations began 100 years later. The whole town is laid bare for us to see: The Forum, official buildings, shops, residences, the public baths. The streets have high pavements at the sides for pedestrians and a broader roadway in the center for horses and wagons, where chariot wheels have left deep ruts. The private homes are luxurious villas, often with gardens and fountains—Pliny must have lived in just such a villa in his home in Miseno across the bay. It is a moving experience to be surrounded by all the evidence for a thriving city, full of busy life, and to know that it was all extinguished in just a few hours. (And Vesuvius is still there to see, one of the few still active volcanoes on the European Continent. Could disaster strike again some day?)

POZZUOLI (near Naples)

The Temple of Serapis (*Tempio di Serapide*) made an enormous impression on Charles Lyell, the English geologist. He used his sketch of it as the frontispiece for the first volume of his *Principles of Geology*, and the three columns of the temple appear again on one side of the Lyell Medal, first struck in 1873. Lyell shows the foundations of the Temple rising from the sea with a background of

Surviving columns of the Temple of Serapis at Pozzuoli, as
sketched by Charles Lyell in 1829. The remains stand
today in the midst of a noisy polluted city, but the bands of
encrusted shells are still clearly seen.

park-like countryside, a fine mansion on a hill, a bit of old Roman aqueduct. The
lowest ten feet of the three columns had a smooth exterior and so had the top
half, but in between lay a segment over ten feet in height that was encrusted
with distinctive marine mollusks and therefore must have been for many years
submerged below sea level.

The key factor in interpretion is that it has been only 2,000 years since the
monument was built, far too short a time for any significant change in the actual
sea level. It is the *ground level* that must have changed here, first sinking by more
than 20 feet to allow the sea to reach halfway up the columns and then rising
again many years later to let the entire columns stand free once more. Earthquakes, a frequent occurrence in Pozzuoli, must of course have been the cause,
and what gave Lyell food for thought is that 2,000 years is but an instant on the
geological time scale. If earthquakes can cause this much visible change in so
short a time, imagine what they can accomplish over a longer geological period!
Here was the solid evidence for Lyell's trademark—uniformitarianism, continuity, the explanation of former changes of the earth's surface *by reference to causes
now in operation.* No one-time disaster (such as Noah's flood) could possibly leave
a record such as this.

Today's visitor, regrettably, will not see the Temple in Lyell's pastoral
environs, but in a fenced-off enclosure in the busiest, noisiest, dirtiest part of
Pozzuoli, near the fish market and ferry terminal, jammed with traffic and

people. However, one can still clearly see the telltale bands of encrustation, to almost halfway up the columns, where marine mollusks glued themselves to the stone in layer after layer, over many years of submersion. The evidence here is indisputable: The ground level fell, then rose again, then fell again, shaking, but not completely destroying, the Temple.

ROME

Galen, the great anatomist of antiquity, lived at the time when the Roman Empire was at its zenith and all of the Mediterranean lay within the imperial realm. Galen himself moved from his native Pergamum to Rome in the year 161 A.D. and established a medical practice there. He shuttled back and forth thereafter between the two cities. He was personal physician (and personal friend) of the Emperor Marcus Aurelius, whose equestrian statue stands in the Piazza del Campidoglio, on the Capitoline hill, and of the emperors who followed him, Commodus and Septimus Severus. The triumphal arch erected in honor of the latter in 203 A.D. is one of the most impressive structures within the area of the restored Republican forum. Galen's own quarters appear to have been in the Temple of Peace, which no longer stands, but it is known to have been located below the forum of Augustus, close to the present public entrance to the Republican forum. A serious fire in 192 A.D. destroyed a large part of Galen's library.

VERCELLI

Vercelli was a town of great note in the early thirteenth century. That is when the Basilica Sant'Andrea was built (completed in 1227) and when a university was founded, the first large scientific institution in all of Piedmont. Then, 100 years later, came the struggles between the Guelphs and the Ghibellines—part of a country-wide conflict—with the Avogadros carrying the Guelph banner and the Tizzonis in opposition. Here the Tizzonis won and Vercelli went downhill, the university closed down and there followed (in the words of the municipal brochure) "grievous times, . . . military occupations, epidemics and famines" without implication that the victorous Ghibellines were to blame. Vercelli today is best known as the center of the largest rice-producing area in Europe. The town itself is old-fashioned, with tree-lined avenues, virtually untouched by the blight of tourism.

We know of course, that the Avogadros survived despite defeat. Vercelli is, in fact, where Amedeo Avogadro spent his most productive years as a professor at the local college. The town is proud of him and pays its tribute with a prominent statue between the railway station and the Basilica Sant'Andea (also a survivor, little changed in 700 years). There Avogadro stands, his narrow face drawing attention, like a painting from El Greco. The statue was erected in 1956 on the 100th anniversary of Avogadro's death. (The college itself no longer

TRA GLI ANNI 1809 E 1819
MENTRE INSEGNAVA FISICA
NEL REALE COLLEGIO
DI VERCELLI
AMEDEO AVOGADRO
DI QUAREGNA
ELABORÒ LA LEGGE
CHE PORTA IL SUO NOME
FONDAMENTO MIRABILE
PER LE SCIENZE
FISICHE E CHIMICHE

Amedeo Avogadro, across from
the train station in Vercelli.

exists. Its former quarters at Via Alessandro Manzoni 11 have been considerably altered and now house the Vercelli provincial archives.)

The Avogadro family headquarters is actually in the village of Quarenga, a few kilometers north of Vercelli. There is a mausoleum there where Amedeo Avogadro and his wife are buried. The statue by the railway station acknowledges this. It is inscribed "Amedeo Avogadro di Quarenga."

VINCI

The setting of this village, the birthplace of Leonardo, is exquisite—pellucid light, silver-green olive trees, terraced fields, all against a background of distant hills. The *Museo Vinciano* occupies a castle in a hilltop location. It is filled with models based on Leonardo's drawings, sometimes accompanied by copies of the drawings themselves, all tastefully arranged and clearly labeled in English as well as Italian. There are some unexpected items, including a drawing of a bicycle, which was a purely imaginary means of transportation at the time. This drawing was done by one of Leonardo's pupils and does not come from Leonardo's own notebooks. There is also a copy of one of Leonardo's much publicized sketches of "flying machines," often cited as evidence for his prophetic imagination. On close inspection, his ideas prove to be disappointing, demonstrating that Leonardo had in fact failed, despite much thought on the subject, to gain even a rudimentary understanding of the problems involved in the production of aerodynamic lift.

(Leonardo was obsessed with the idea that human-powered flight should mimic the flight of birds and all his models involve *beating* wings. He seems not to have appreciated that human muscle power in relation to body weight is nowhere close to what it is in birds; he also misunderstood the actual mechanics of a bird wing's power stroke. Leonardo had a better understanding of bird soaring and steering, but apparently gave no thought to the possibility of developing a *fixed* wing aircraft on that basis.)

Higher up on the hill, 1.3 miles (2 km) to the north, is the hamlet of Anchiano, where Leonardo was born.

The museum is open every day. Telephone: 0571–56055.

Sicily

Sicily is the "America" of ancient times, whither the Phoenicians, the Dorians, and the Ionians ventured in turn across the sea to found colonies, to find breathing space, fertile ground for crops, and empty shorelines for new cities to house those who sought freedom from the constraints of overcrowded homelands.

AEOLIAN ISLES

This group of seven volcanic islands is part of a line of volcanoes reaching from Vesuvius to Etna, a feature of geological history that has played an important role in theories on changes to the earth's surface. The entire archipelago is readily accessed by a complicated series of boats running from Milazzo on the mainland to Lipari and Vulcano and between the smaller islands. We strongly recommend a visit to Lipari and a taxi ride around the circular road from which (when the weather is good) you can see the whole chain of islands including the famous, still-smoking Stromboli. Note particularly en route the naturally occurring obsidian—a glazed, black volcanic stone—which made a better knife edge than flint and used to be traded far and wide. In more recent times, pumice has been a major export.

There is a museum of prehistoric archaeological exhibits in the old Bishop's Palace on the Acropolis in the city of Lipari which is well worth a visit, if only for the view.

MESSINA/TAORMINA

The Sicilian coast between Messina and Taormina is heavily touristed at all times of the year, its beauty marred to some degree by hotels built wherever there is sufficient access to the sea. Bright, dark red, five-limbed starfish such as those studied by Metchnikoff are abundant here, living in shallow coastal waters. They are easily spotted by the casual beach stroller.

MOUNT ETNA

Charles Lyell completed his Italian tour in Sicily, where Mount Etna stands as Europe's most spectacular volcano. It has had more than 100 recorded eruptions and continues to have them right up to the present—the effects of eruptions in 1983 and 1985 are clearly seen on the south side. It was here that Lyell first applied the technique of judging the age of fossil deposits by the degree of correspondence of fossil species with existing ones. Commonly, around England and France for example, 80 or 90 percent of fossil species are extinct, but around Etna Lyell found rocks high up on the mountain slopes, overlying relatively old volcanic deposits, that reflected less than 5 percent extinction—more than 95 percent of the species were identical with present-day Mediterranean species. How swift the uplift had been here!

The standard tour of Etna today proceeds from Catania through Nicolosi to Casa Cantoniera at a height of 6,600 feet (2,000 m), about two-thirds of the way to the top. From this point a minibus is available to take the visitor close to the summit—the *funivia* (cable car) being out of commission, seemingly permanently. The car park at Casa Cantoniera is complete with all the standard tourist trappings, such as fast food and souvenirs, but the view is magnificent. A less spectacular panorama is available from the north side of Etna, which is approached from Linguaglossa. Here the area is fertile and green and provides picnic areas and reasonable solitude, unlike the south side, which is stark and devoid of vegetation.

PALERMO

Stanislao Cannizzaro, the hero of the 1860 Karlsruhe conference on atomic weights, was born in Palermo, but lived in Rome after 1871. He was a hero of the revolutions as well and his body was brought back to his native city in 1926, the centenary of his birth, and reburied with due honor in the Palermo Pantheon (i.e., the church of San Doménico). This seventeenth-century building is not one of the great architectural experiences but does have an interesting history in that the rebellious Sicilian parliament of 1848 was convened within its walls. The church is thus a fit resting place for the political heroes of Sicilian history.

Cannizzaro was deeply involved in the battles to drive out the Bourbon rulers of the Kingdom of the Two Sicilies (which extended as far north as the city of Naples) and was appointed a member of the ruling council of Sicily per se after Garibaldi and his famous red-shirted "Thousand" succeeded in capturing the island in 1860. (And for that reason he had to leave the Karslruhe conference earlier than he had intended.) He was also appointed professor of chemistry at the University of Palermo and he made it for a while the foremost center for chemical education in all of Italy. After moving to Rome, Cannizzaro became a senator of the newly unified kingdom of Italy, but continued at the same time to teach chemistry and do research.

SYRACUSE

The old city of Syracuse lies on Ortygia island, connected to the mainland by a short bridge. Here is where the first colonizers settled and where the tyrants of Syracuse's heyday held court. (The word *tyrant* indicates possession of absolute central power, and lacks the unsavory connotation that the term carries today.) Archimedes was a friend, perhaps even a kinsman, of one of the last tyrants, Hiero II, who died in 215 B.C. In today's old city the Piazza Archimede is the center of city life, graced by the ever-present sidewalk cafes. Not far away is the nineteenth-century Arethusa fountain, fed by a freshwater spring that is the legendary cradle of the city. On the mainland, nearest to Ortygia, is Akradina, also part of the ancient city of Syracuse but today somewhat delapidated and scruffy.

The ridge cutting across the northern edge of present-day Syracuse is a feature of the landscape that cannot be missed. It marks the historic northern boundary of the city and contains a line of quarries used as a source of building stone since time immemorial. The archaeological area is here, including what tourist guides may identify as the tomb of Archimedes, but it's in the wrong place for that—Cicero gave the correct location, but even then the site was overgrown.

Eight miles north of Syracuse lies the Castle of Euryalus, the remains of a great fortress from the period of Greek occupation. It is here that Archimedes is said to have set fire to an invading Roman fleet by concentrating the sun's rays through a series of lenses and mirrors.

WESTERN EUROPE

5

England

England has a proud record for innovation and discovery—in the thick of it right from the time of the scientific Renaissance, when Thomas Linacre brought the good news of exciting intellectual stirrings from Padua to the court of King Henry VIII. Over the years since then English scientists have been among the leaders in nearly every new advance, the source of a steady flow of books, research, and new ideas, coming from all corners of the land and often laying the foundations of what would prove to be (and still are) principal fields of knowledge in the overall domain of natural science. These scientific achievements have had a unique English slant, being often the product of the deeds of quite independent individual scientists (even amateurs) and of self-governing institutions, like the Royal Society of London. Direct involvement of kings or national governments has been less than in many other countries.

(And there are suggestions of scientific enterprise long before Linacre, evidenced by the great stone circles that dot the west side of Britain. Scotland is a better place than England to muse about the significance of these monuments and we have therefore discussed the subject under "Scotland," in the following chapter. Stonehenge and Avebury are popular examples that one can visit in England.)

Early Lights

William Gilbert and the "High and Splendid Power" of Magnetism. Gilbert (1544–1602) laid the foundations of magnetism as a science with his book *De magnete*, published in 1600. The phenomena of magnetism was already well known—the magnetic compass was used at sea and as early as the thirteenth century Peter Peregrinus had published a handbook, *Letter on the Magnet*. But the accepted explanation for magnetic orientation was still based on the heavenly spheres of the Greek model of the world. The magnet (called the *lodestone*,

the stone that leads the way) was thought to align itself with the "poles" of the outer fixed celestial spheres. Gilbert postulated that the earth was itself a giant lodestone. He demonstrated the plausibility of this view by making a small, spherical, permanent magnet out of ordinary magnetic material and showing that tiny magnetic needles placed on the surface of this sphere (which he named a *terrella*) behave just like lodestones on the earth's surface. A particularly striking result was that the experimental needles on the terrella mimic declination, the familiar dipping of a compass out of the horizontal plane as one moves from the earth's equator toward the poles. "It has been settled by nature," Gilbert concluded, ". . . that in the pole itself shall be the seat, the throne as it were, of a high and splendid power."

William Gilbert (or Gilberd, as he signed his own name) was born in Colchester (Essex) into a reasonably well-to-do middle class family. His principal profession was that of physician with a fashionable medical practice in London. Magnetism was his hobby, indulged in with his own funds and in the time he could spare from his many professional duties. He was appointed physician to Queen Elizabeth in 1600 and continued in that post for James I, but Gilbert himself died in 1603, presumably from the plague. He never married and lived in London in Wingfield House, a dwelling originally belonging to his stepmother's family. He wrote many works other than *De magnete*, but they were not published during his lifetime.

Seen through modern eyes, Gilbert was truly an experimentalist, altogether brilliant for the time. He did not just speculate on the nature of things as was so common in his day, but actually did experiments, and the invention of the terrella has to be seen as a real stroke of genius. And it should be noted that his book, *De magnete*, was published earlier than Galileo's books and several years ahead of Francis Bacon's philosophically persuasive advocacy of the experimental method. Unfortunately our knowledge of what motivated this remarkable man is limited by lack of historical documents. In his will Gilbert left his books, instruments, and magnetic paraphernalia to the library of the Royal College of Physicians, but the College and its library were destroyed in the Great Fire of London in 1666. Wingfield House, which might have contained letters and other documents, was destroyed in the same disaster.

Related Place to Visit: Colchester.

William Harvey and the Circulation of the Blood. Harvey (1578–1657) said it all in a slim volume of 72 pages, *De motu cordis et sanguinis*, and part of that was dedication (to King Charles I) and preface. The blood circulates, he reported, the same blood is used over and over again. It goes from the left side of the heart to all parts of the body far and near, then returns to the right side of the heart. It goes from there to the lungs for contact with freshly breathed air and then back from the lungs to the left side of the heart and there the cycle begins anew. These simple words were enough for a revolution, for they destroyed a tangled web of unbelievable misinformation—"incongruous, obscure, impossible" in Harvey's own words—and they exerted an influence far beyond Harvey's cardiovascular system. Almost all of animal physiology converges on the circulation of the blood, and wild confusion about the latter inevitably engenders distorted ideas about everything else.

Most of the doctrine about blood circulation taught before Harvey was based on the writings attributed to Galen. Distinction was made between the thicker, denser, muddier venous blood and the thinner, lighter, purer, bright red arterial blood, and everyone assumed they had separate functions. Venous blood was thought to be *nourishment* intended for one-time use, made in the liver from digested food and distributed by the veins to other parts of the body. All the major organs were thought to be made and kept in repair by use of the actual substance of the blood. Only a part of the venous blood was thought to go to the heart and from there to the arterial system and to the lungs, to be infused with life's *vital spirit*, somehow produced from the air we inhale. (Some authorities believed that the arteries contain nothing but air.) Harvey's Padua teacher, Fabrici, had actually observed the tiny valves in the veins of human limbs, which in fact make a shambles of the Galenic doctrine because they face the wrong way, forcing the venous blood to move *inward*, away from all the organs, but Fabrici was blinded by doctrinal prejudice and decided that they only delayed outward flow. He saw the valves as instruments for *fair distribution* of nutritive elements.

Harvey had no special skills or special tools to demolish the false doctrine and to chart the true course of the flow of blood, simply accurate observations that anyone else could have made, coupled to a refreshingly open mind. The heart was clearly acting as a pump. The left ventricle contracts with each heartbeat to force the blood into the arteries and the latter, *not the veins*, send it to the peripheries of the body—"the pulse which we feel in the arteries is nothing but the inthrust of blood into them from the heart." He confirmed the pathway he traced by experiments in which he clamped various blood vessels and watched what swelled and what drained. Only one thing was missing—Harvey was unable to find the connecting links at the periphery by which blood can pass from arteries to veins, though he was convinced they must be there because the rest of the evidence was too strong. Malpighi in Bologna found the blood capillaries a little later, in 1661; it took a microscope to see them and Harvey had had only a weak magnifying lens.

To clinch it all, Harvey supported his observational conclusions with a devastating numerical calculation. The capacity of the left ventricle is about two ounces, and the heart beats about 72 times a minute. That means as much as 144 ounces (9 pounds) of blood might be ejected into the arteries per minute. Even if we suppose that only as little as one-eighth of the contents of the ventricle is actually discharged at each contraction, we are still talking about astronomical figures, 60 pounds of blood per hour! Where can all this blood come from? Where is it going? There is only one possible answer—it must be the same blood, used again and again.

Harvey was born in Kent to a relatively prosperous family and was educated at Cambridge and in Padua, where he studied under the famous anatomist, Fabrici (see under "Italy"). When he returned to England he went to London to set up a medical practice. He was very short in stature (often referred to as "Little Dr. Harvey") but strong in spirit, personality, and character, and he rose quickly to national prominence. In London he became a fellow of the College of Physicians and took an active part in its affairs; he became physician of St. Bartholomew's Hospital in 1609 and continued in that position for 35 years; and he served as personal physician to the king, in the course of which he lived through the turbulent period of England's civil wars and the execution of one of the royal masters he served. (When did he have time for research? His *De motu cordis et sanguinis* was in fact not published until 1628, when he was fifty years old, though he had given lectures and demonstrations about the circulation of blood for ten years before that.)

As royal physician, Harvey was with King James I during his terminal illness (though he was not James's primary doctor) and afterwards had the difficult and possibly dangerous task of being an expert witness into official inquiries into the possibility that the Duke of Buckingham may have done something to hasten the king's death. He did become primary physician for Charles I, and he and the king developed friendship and genuine affection for one another. When civil war came, Harvey left London as part of the king's retinue. At the first major battle of the war, the battle of Edgehill in 1642, the king's own sons (the future Charles II and James II) were still in the royal entourage and were put in Harvey's charge as they watched the battle from the sidelines. After 1646 the king became a prisoner of the victorious Puritans and was no longer allowed choice of his own physician or other visitors, and Harvey probably saw him for the last time that year. The king's execution in Whitehall in January 1649 must have been shocking and sickening for his medical friend— Harvey was seventy years old at the time.

Related Places to Visit: Hempstead, Folkestone, Canterbury, London (St. Bartholomew's).

The 1639 Transit of Venus: A Miracle of Genius. Here we have **Jeremiah Horrocks** (1618–1641), a genius, a prodigy. How he came to reveal his skill in a remote village just north of Manchester and at the time he did is something we shall never be able to explain, for he died at age twenty-three without leaving any clues. He had a friend, William Crabtree, who lived on the outskirts of Manchester and who died himself three years after Horrocks, but survived long enough to preserve some of Horrocks's letters and astronomical records. Without them we would not have known that Horrocks had lived at all. As events actually transpired, his work became known (thanks to Crabtree) to Isaac Newton and to John Flamsteed, England's first Astronomer Royal, and they eagerly made use of it, discussing it and making it part of the body of astronomical knowledge.

Horrocks's historic achievement is his observation of the transit of Venus across the face of the sun on the 24th of November (old style) of 1639, using a telescope he had bought the year before for half a crown. He had mounted it in the window to project the solar image onto a screen in his darkened room. What was so momentous about that? First of all, we have to understand that transits of Venus are extremely rare. There have been only four of them since Horrocks: in 1761, 1769, 1874, and 1882, and the next one is not due till the year 2004!

Secondly, Johannes Kepler's justly celebrated *Rudolphine Tables* (published in 1627), while they predicted with an error of only two days the expected transit of 1761, did not predict the one of 1639 at all. But Horrocks, calculating planetary positions as a sort of hobby, made the prediction, thought he knew exactly when to expect the transit and alerted his friend Crabtree in advance (by letter) to look for it. Horrocks was particularly interested to measure the planet's *diameter* (relative to the sun)—he expected Kepler's estimate to be nearly ten times too large, as indeed it proved to be.

Horrocks was a curate at St. Michael's Church in Hoole, and this presented some difficulties for him in arranging to look for his predicted astronomical event. The day of the transit was a Sunday, and the curate was busy with church duties most of the day. He had to take Holy Communion and Evensong, occupying much of the early afternoon and leaving only a small window of time before sunset. But he managed in spite of this. In his own words

The Sun's distinct image exactly filled the circle, and I watched carefully and unceasingly for any dark body that might enter upon the disk of light; and tho' I could not expect the planet to enter upon the Sun's disk before three o'clock on the afternoon of the 24th, from my own corrected numbers, upon which I chiefly relied; yet I observed the Sun on the 23rd, but more particularly on the 24th; for on the 24th I observed the Sun from the time of its rising to 9 o'clock and again, from a little before ten until noon; and at one in the afternoon, being called in the interval to business of the highest moment, which for these ornamental pursuits I could not with decency neglect. But in all these times I saw nothing on the Sun's face except one small and common spot, which I had seen on the preceding day and which also I afterwards saw on some of the following days.

But at 3h 15m in the afternoon, when I was again at liberty to continue my labours, . . . I beheld a most agreeable sight, a *spot*, which had been the object of my most sanguine wishes, of an unusual size, and of a perfectly circular shape, just wholly entered upon the Sun's disk on the left side, so that the limbs of the *Sun* and *Venus* exactly coincided in the very point of contact. I was immediately sensible that this round spot was the planet *Venus*, and applied myself with the utmost care to prosecute my observations.

Crabtree, too, got a glimpse, though there were clouds over Manchester until 3h 35m. No one else in the world could possibly have seen the spectacle, and those familiar with the vagaries of English weather might well be astonished at the near miraculous nature of a clear sky on the west coast of the midlands at all. Horrocks and Crabtree, incidentally, kept in touch during this period only by letter. And they did not meet in person in the months that followed, though they were making plans to do so just before Horrocks died. Hoole and Manchester are only 30 miles apart, but for Horrocks and Crabtree and their primitive telescopes the 93 million miles through space to the sun (26 million to Venus) were more easily managed than the short journey over land.

Related Places to Visit: Much Hoole, Manchester.

Civil War and Restoration

Public protest and general obstructionism have always been part of the English political scene, but a real revolution occurred in the seventeenth century that culminated in the public execution of Charles I in 1649. A decade of republican government followed, the only nonmonarchic period in England's history, but the republic was a failure, its leader Oliver Cromwell even more arbitrary than Charles I had been, and the monarchy was restored (legally, by free election) in 1660 with Charles II on the throne. Viewed superficially, the Commonwealth had had little permanent effect, but in terms of intellectual values the revolution was a real turning point. An age of pragmatism and individualism emerged, fertile soil for the scholars that were to come.

For science the reign of Charles II was a period of glorious years. Two of England's greatest institutions were founded then: the Royal Society of London (charter granted by Charles II in 1662) and the Royal Observatory at Greenwich (set up by the king in 1675 to make astronomical observations "in a royal manner"). And with them came a succession of memorable Astronomers Royal (such as Edmond Halley) and famous Fellows of the Society (Robert Boyle and Robert Hooke, for example). And, to top it all, there was Isaac Newton, who made the transition from student to fellow at Trinity College, Cambridge, in 1669.

On the negative side, the Commonwealth's noble ideal of universal education was scrapped by the Restoration, a regression that had a lasting effect—for a long time afterward, education remained the privilege of an elite. And religious restrictions appeared, excluding puritans, Roman Catholics, and other dissidents from all types of public office. Schoolmasters and college fellows were among the civil servants affected; dons at Oxford and Cambridge were required to become actual ordained clergy, fully obeisant to Church of England doctrine. But if these restrictive acts were detrimental to scientific scholarship, it was only a short-term effect. The English are an ungovernable people, as Christopher Hill has said, and the response to imposing religious uniformity on the scholars of the day was a proliferation of dissident academies, independent of state support. A decentralization of scientific power followed, an ultimately healthy spreading of research and philosophy away from London, Oxford, and Cambridge to the provinces.

(An interesting footnote is that, even within its own established framework, the state did not want to go so far as to lose the services of Isaac Newton. He was made exempt of the restrictive laws, not *ad hominem*, which would have been considered an unacceptable precedent, but by the device of royal decree, which exempted the position of Lucasian Professor that Newton by then held, not just for him, but for all his successors, too.)

Invention of "Species." One notable scientist who may have profited directly from the religious Act of Uniformity was **John Ray** (1627–1705). He seemed quite comfortable and not overly ambitious as a Cambridge fellow

(Trinity College again, as it happens) but was stirred to action when required to take an oath he found morally repugnant. He quit his teaching job and embarked on a new career of naturalist, becoming perhaps England's greatest ever of that ilk. Another Trinity Fellow, Francis Willughby, was a confederate in Ray's rebellion. Unlike Ray, he was rich and able to bestow an annual grant on his friend. The two of them formed the grandiose plan of publishing a comprehensive *flora* and *fauna*, Ray covering the plants and Willughby the animals, and they traveled together all over Europe to achieve their goal. Willughby unfortunately died young (at age 37), but he had made provision in his will for continuance of his beneficence to Ray. Ray actually moved into the Willughby's house and edited and published (under Willughby's name) treaties on birds and fishes that his friend had almost completed. He went on to survey insects, serpents, and other animals, in addition to continuing his own previously begun catalog of plants.

Seeing before him the uncountable *specimens* that nature presents to the acute observer, Ray recognized that they represented not a continuum, but discrete types, able to give rise, through reproduction, to individuals just like themselves—in short, he recognized the existence of *species*. He was the essential forerunner of Linnaeus, who taught us how to name the species and how to arrange them into logical groups, and of Darwin, who taught us how they evolved from one another. (Ray, of course, believed species to be fixed, as did Linnaeus.)

Related Places to Visit: Black Notley, Cambridge.

The Royal Society of London. The jewel in the crown of Good King Charles's reign is The Royal Society of London for Improving Natural Knowledge, the oldest scholarly society in England and the most influential of all of Europe's science academies. It was started informally at Oxford, then moved to London where it was officially constituted with the blessing of Charles II. The King himself and the Duke of York (the future James II) were among the early fellows—though only to symbolize royal approval, with no suggestion of active participation or support from the royal purse. The society held weekly meetings for philosophical discussion, provided for experiments to be done for the benefit of the membership, and started a library and a museum. In 1664 it began to publish its *Philosophical Transactions,* one of the greatest science periodicals of all time. The front page of each issue, for a century thereafter, proclaimed its noble purpose, to publicize "the present undertakings, studies, and labours of the INGENIOUS, in many considerable parts of the world."

John Wilkins, later to become the Bishop of Chester, was in a sense the founding father. He was Warden of Wadham College, Oxford (1648 to 1659), and was a guiding spirit in the creation of the seminal "invisible college," a little group that met weekly to learn and discuss the new scientific philosophy, the direct forerunner of the Royal Society as such. Wilkins was the author of a curious book, *The Discovery of a World in the Moon,* with an appendix on "The possibility of a passage thither." Pleasure and profit will be as great, he claimed, as the pleasure and profit derived from the discovery of America. (The Duchess of Newcastle asked where to rest her horses if she undertook the journey. "Use your castles in the air," Wilkins is said to have replied.)

Wilkins typifies the early days of the RS, as we shall call it here, which reflect a unique *voluntary* effort, an inner-directed enthusiasm for science and its prospects by rank amateurs as well as by persons whom we would today consider professionals in the sense that science was their full-time occupation. Christopher Wren, architect of St. Paul's and other fine churches, was a Wadham student and one of the twelve founding members of the RS (and president from 1680 to 1682). Samuel Pepys, the brilliant and earthy diarist, was president from 1684 to 1686. Robert Boyle, one of the key figures in the *intellectual* history of science, whose life and work we discuss under "Ireland," was another of the twelve original founders. Henry Oldenburg, a German who originally came to England as a lobbyist for the trading interests of his native city of Bremen, caught the fever and stayed on as part of the RS's company. Though never a practicing scientist himself, he was the RS secretary for 14 years, an indefatigable arbiter of disputes, author of a voluminous correspondence, originator of the tradition of direct interaction between the RS and foreign scientists. Many modern historians credit him with doing more to shape the future of the RS than any other early member. (More than Isaac Newton, for instance, who was president for 24 years, from 1703 to 1727, but whose institutional influence is not generally regarded as enduring.)

From an earlier period, a century before, it is not inappropriate to mention Thomas Gresham (1519–1579), he of the famous law about bad money and good. He was not, of course, directly involved with the RS in any way, but he had some of the same qualities as the actual founders—desire for knowledge, the confidence to build what proved to be lasting organizations, an attitude of personal responsibility—and he played a crucial indirect role in the creation of the RS, via the college he brought into being in London. Gresham, a financier and founder of the Royal Exchange, left instructions in his will for the erection of a college on property he himself had owned, and provision of stipends for seven professors to give lectures—one each day of the week—on astronomy, geometry, physics, law, divinity, rhetoric, and music. His legacy, Gresham College, was where the RS held its weekly meetings for the first 50 years of its existence. Christopher Wren was a Gresham professor and so was the RS's experimentalist, Robert Hooke, who had his lodgings at the college and did all his experiments there. London was a crowded city, and (in the absence of direct royal patronage) the lack of a congenial or even a tolerable headquarters might well have nipped the RS in the bud.

Robert Hooke (1635–1702) stands above all, perhaps, as the RS's experimental arm. Could the RS have survived without him? Hooke, the son of an impecunious parish vicar from the Isle of Wight, came to Oxford (Christ Church college) as a student in 1653, joined the circle of the "invisible college," and was soon hired by Robert Boyle as his laboratory assistant. He helped Boyle construct the first modern air pump and assisted in the experiments that led to the formulation of "Boyle's Law" for gas volume as a function of pressure. Through Boyle's influence, Hooke was given the salaried post of curator of experiments when the RS was formally founded. He was himself elected a fellow in 1663 and served as secretary from 1677 to 1682. He was appointed Professor of Geometry at Gresham College in 1665 and lived in the lodgings that came with that position for the rest of his life.

Hooke became one of the most highly regarded scientists of the period, eclipsed (according to modern judgment) only by Newton. His most lasting contributions are his microscopic observations. He first named the biological cell, for example, to designate the neat subdivisions of the fabric that he observed in cork and similar vegetable substances. (His Micrographia, published in 1665, are available today in reprinted facsimile form.) He became interested in clocks and the springs that powered them, which led to a theory of elasticity—"Hooke's law" is still elasticity's basic principle. He proposed a cyclic theory for the history of the earth (100 years ahead of Hutton) and had original ideas (which proved to be incorrect) on earthquakes and subterranean eruptions. But he rarely pursued a single problem for very long—for example, he never pursued the suggestive observations of cells at all—and was described in later years as one who "originated much but perfected little."

Original research was, of course, not Hooke's only function at the RS—his greatest value may have come from use of his experimental skills as a kind of referee. For example, when van Leeuwenhoek communicated his first microscopic observations of animalcules to the RS in 1676, they caused great sensation and, at first, disbelief. The RS instructed Hooke to see if he could repeat the observations and gave full credence to them only after he was indeed able to do so. (The fact that van Leeuwenhoek chose to publicize his work through the RS is a striking illustration of how rapidly the RS attained international status. A large share of the credit for this undoubtedly belongs to Henry Oldenburg.)

Much has been written about Hooke as a person or personality, none of it complimentary. No portrait has survived (which is very unusual), but verbal descriptions are explicit: "in person but despicable, being crooked and low in stature, and as he grew older more and more deformed" and in temper "melancholy, mistrustful, and jealous." Hooke was quarrelsome to an extraordinary degree and engaged in bitter priority disputes with almost everybody who was anybody—especially with Newton. But Dutch scientist Huygens, the English astronomer Oldenburg, and even his biographer Richard Waller were also among the many targets of his venom. Only Robert Boyle, to whom Hooke was beholden as teacher and early sponsor, seems to have been spared. (Hooke's avidity for medical remedies is of interest in this connection, testing out all sorts of medicines and purges—a not surprising eccentricity, perhaps, in a man with scientific brilliance who was nevertheless personally embittered and afflicted with a morbid jealousy of his colleagues.)

Postscript: The Royal Society Today. The RS still flourishes, the *Transactions* are still published. But the organization has grown as science itself has grown and it has become unwieldy in the process. Its official duties today include giving scientific advice to the government and its principal role in the scholarly community has been reduced to that of an honor society. It is a mark of scientific prestige to be "FRS" (*Fellow* of the Royal Society); an embarrassment for otherwise prominent scientists to remain excluded as they approach the end of their career. It is sadly no longer a place for discussion of fundamental truths. Can you imagine any present member of the RS (or its American equivalent, the National Academy of Sciences) setting up a laboratory experiment at a meeting in order to demonstrate his latest finding to his colleagues? Or a modern membership committee repeating experiments at its sessions to decide whether some foreign researcher merits admission?

Related Places to Visit: Oxford, Isle of Wight, London.

The Royal Greenwich Observatory, the other great institution founded (in 1674) by Charles II, also still flourishes, though it has moved away from its old Greenwich site, which is now the National Maritime Museum. Over the years this venerable institution has given us the prime meridian of the world, the zero of longitude, relative to which all others are measured, and Greenwich Mean Time (GMT), the standard by which all other times are calibrated. It has also given us (in the post of Astronomer Royal) a steady succession of distinguished astronomers. The first was John Flamsteed (1646–1719), who served for 44 years. The best remembered is **Edmond Halley** (1656–1742).

Halley had already had a long and productive career before he was appointed Astronomer Royal at the age of sixty-four—cataloging stars of the southern hemisphere; observing a new comet and calculating its orbit, accurately predicting its return 77 years later; sailing the world to measure magnetic deviations. But it is sometimes argued that his most influential act came as a quite young man, when he proved to be the moving force behind the publication of Newton's *Principia.* It was 1684 and Halley, Hooke, and Wren (at a Royal Society meeting) were discussing the problem of how to derive Kepler's laws of planetary motion, but they couldn't arrive at a consensus. Hooke, as usual, claimed he had solved the problem, but refused to reveal how. Halley was in Cambridge shortly thereafter and posed essentially that question to Newton, who, to Halley's amazement, told him without hesitation how it had to be done. "How do you know it?" Halley asked. "Why, I have calculated it," Newton replied. When Halley wanted to see the calculation, Newton was not able to find it among his papers, but promised to repeat the calculation. When he did so, he found he had made an error—the revision made for Halley was the first correct version. Halley then persuaded Newton to publish the entire *Principia* and not only served as editor but saw the manuscript through the tedious publication process.

Related Place to Visit: Greenwich Observatory.

Isaac Newton and After

If science were like sports and demanded the ranking of all-time greats in an absolute order, then **Isaac Newton** (1642–1727) would be a likely choice for "number one." And he was popularly recognized as such. In the words of Alexander Pope (contemporary of Newton's later years):

> Nature and Nature's laws
>   lay hid in night;
> GOD said "let NEWTON be"
>   and all was light.

Though as a person, it must be said, he was not attractive. He was an unsociable child with few human ties and grew into a difficult and irascible adult. He never married. In the words of the biographer Richard Westfall, he was "ravished by the desire to know." He sat silently at the college table, "as isolated in his private world as though he had not come." "A mind forever voyaging through strange seas of thought, alone," as Wordsworth put it. In later life he feuded bitterly with many of his contemporaries.

Newton's intellectual brilliance illuminated many fields. As a mathematician early in his career he invented the calculus, in effect creating a new mathematical language that allowed rigorous expression of dynamic concepts in science, such as velocity, force, and acceleration. In this particular historical tour de force, Newton was matched (in Germany) by Gottfried Leibniz, who somewhat later and independently invented a form of calculus. It is Leibniz's symbols (dy/dx) that we use today.

In the field of optics, it was Newton who discovered that sunlight is a mixture of all colors of the spectrum, which initially was not such a plausible concept even though Newton's experiments did not really permit any other explanation. He went on to express the view that light consists of small corpuscles, subject to the same laws as other bodies. This particulate view of light, however, ran into difficulties. It was opposed at the time by Christiaan Huygens in the Netherlands, who believed that light was a wave, and it was eventually disproved by Thomas Young in England and Auguste Fresnel in France, who showed unequivocally the wave-like properties of light rays. But then in the twentieth century Newton's light corpuscles came back into their own and the two theories were merged. Both were right, and the questions that Newton himself could not answer about the behavior of light were resolved by the new physics of quantum mechanics.

But the monumental work of Newton's lifetime was his *Principia* ("Mathematical Principles of Natural Philosophy"), one of the great enduring classics in all of science. Despite being written in Latin, it created a popular revolution, the extent of which it is almost impossible to imagine today. For 2,000 years philosophers and laymen alike had been convinced of the irreconcilability of heaven and earth—the natural laws in one place different from those in the other. This principle was, of course, buttressed by religion, but there was solid physical evidence as well: The apple falls to the ground, but the great big moon hangs in the sky forever. Newton liberated us from this dichotomy by showing that the motion of the planets (Kepler's laws) and motion on earth were governed by exactly the same principles. Central to this thesis was Newton's *Universal Law of Gravitation*, stating that the force of attraction between bodies of different mass is proportional to the product of the masses and varies inversely as the square of the distance between the masses. This same intrinsic force applies on earth and in the heavens, and the bodies in the sky do not collapse into one another because the gravitational force is balanced by the inertial force generated by their orbital motion.

In the later part of his life, Newton turned to the study of alchemy, theology, and history, as well as serving as warden of the Mint in London; he was president of the Royal Society for more than 20 years; he was knighted by Queen Anne, who came herself to Cambridge to confer the honor. Sir Isaac lived to be eighty-five and was buried with much pomp and circumstance in Westminster Abbey.

Related Places to Visit: Woolsthorpe and Grantham, Cambridge, Upminster, London.

Eighteenth-Century Eccentrics. The eighteenth century was the century of the Enlightenment in France, a period to which the French look back with particular pride. Scotland, too, had a similar movement, smaller in numbers but equally intense. For English science, however, it was a relatively modest century—possibly a reaction to the genius of Newton, the hero worshipper's feeling that emulation would be hopeless. Whatever the cause, we cannot in this century match the exuberance of King Charles's time, nor the brilliance of the nineteenth century to come. There were quite a few noteworthy names and productive individuals, but they were relatively minor figures, who did not shake the world in the sense that Newton, Faraday, or Charles Darwin did. A common characteristic is that all of them were eccentrics, unorthodox, not rooted in the established centers. Many of them belonged to clubs and societies in urban centers, which met regularly for exchange of books and ideas and even to do experiments. The most influential of these clubs was the **Lunar Society** of Birmingham, so called because the club met at the time of the full moon, to provide light for safe journey between the members' homes where the meetings were held.

One of the co-founders of the Lunar Society was **Erasmus Darwin** (1731–1802), Charles Darwin's grandfather. He had a successful medical practice in Lichfield, a few miles north of Birmingham, but was at the same time a tireless inventor, an experimenter, and even a writer of poetry. He was an early exponent of the idea of evolution, though he had the details wrong, à la Lamarck. His greatest contemporary influence was through his championing of Linnaeus's system for the classification of plants, which is based on the sexual parts of the flowers. The system was still being criticized at the time and Erasmus consciously set out to promote it, driven by the conviction that sexual reproduction is the basic foundation for all of life, obviously so for animals, but equally so (even if less obviously) for plants. He popularized the idea, following Linnaeus in his manner of stressing sexuality. Here is a typical extract from his poetic book, *The Loves of the Plants*, giving Darwin's description of *Lychnis*, the scarlet campion of the meadows around him:

> Each wanton beauty, trick'd in all her grace,
> Shakes the bright dew-drops from her blushing face;
> In gay undress displays her rival charms,
> And calls her wondering lovers to her arms.

At the foot of the page, in fine print, the botanical facts are set forth in more conventional prose: *Lychnis* has distinct male and female flowers, with either ten males, or five females, and so forth. The reader can see why we use the term *eccentric*, for none of this would have gone over well in Oxford or Cambridge.

The most eccentric of all, perhaps was **Joseph Priestley** (1733–1804), archdissenter, who obstinately insisted, or so it seems today, on taking the unpopular side in any argument. He is best known for his discovery of oxygen, which he stubbornly persisted in *refusing* to recognize for what it actually was. He was equally well known in his time for his provocative views on religion—his denial of the Holy Trinity was much stronger than mere dissent and was repugnant to many nonconformists as well as to the conservatives.

Priestley was the son of a cloth dresser, born in a small town near Leeds. He was educated as a minister at a "dissenting academy" at Daventry, and for six years he taught literature and language at another such school in Warrington. He gravitated to London for intellectual stimulation, became friends with John Canton and Benjamin Franklin, and wrote an influential work, *The History and Present State of Electricity*, which included some of his own experiments and earned him election to the Royal Society. In 1773 he received an attractive offer to enter the service of the politically ambitious Earl of Shelburne, formally as librarian, but actually as an aide of broader usefulness, a sort of resident intellectual. It was during this period that Priestley did most of his chemical work. He chemically defined not only oxygen, but also ammonia, hydrogen chloride, hydrogen sulfide, and several other new gases. (Furthermore, he demonstrated quantitatively that oxygen is four or five times as effective as ordinary air for sustaining life and in purely chemical processes as well. But he was a stubborn adherent of the phlogiston theory (see p. 167) and refused to accept Lavoisier's logical explanation for his discovery—that air is a mixture and that oxygen is its active component—even after Lavoisier had convinced almost everybody else, even long after Lavoisier was dead.)

Priestley eventually left the Earl's service and returned to the ministry in Birmingham. There his theological views became increasingly radical, and in

1791 he even expressed support for the French Revolution (implicitly favoring an end to monarchy in Britain, too?). With this he provoked mob violence. His home and the New Meeting House, where he was minister, were destroyed, and his personal safety was threatened. On the advice of his friends he moved to the New World, to the now independent United States of America. His polemic writing continued from there, and one of his detractors commented that "the Government of Heaven itself, should he ever get there, will, in his opinion, want reformation."

From the opposite end of the social spectrum we have **Henry Cavendish** (1731–1810), a member of the immensely rich family of the Dukes of Devonshire, who divorced himself from that family's normal public life to become an ascetic loner in the quest for scientific knowledge. He regularly attended meetings of the Royal Society and of the dining club composed of some of its members, but was almost a recluse otherwise, taking great pains to avoid most kinds of human contact. He gave his orders for dinner by leaving notes on the hall table and his women servants were instructed to keep out of his sight on pain of dismissal. Like Priestley, Cavendish was chiefly a gas chemist, who in 1766 discovered "combustible air" (hydrogen) and demonstrated that it could be combined with a portion of "ordinary air" to form water. This was an event of equal importance with Priestley's discovery of oxygen and occurred several years earlier.

Cavendish published only a part of his scientific work. Much of it was stored in sealed packages, which were not opened until the 1870s when the seventh Duke of Devonshire provided the endowment for the Cavendish Physical Laboratory at Cambridge University and persuaded James Clerk Maxwell, first Cavendish professor, to edit the papers for publication. They revealed a more versatile scientist than had been realized before, one who anticipated many modern theoretical concepts—the recognition of heat as molecular motion, for example.

Finally there are two representatives from the industrial sector, **James Watt** (1736–1819) and **Josiah Wedgwood** (1730–1795). Watt, as nearly everybody knows, was the inventive genius behind the development of the modern steam engine. He was actually a Scotsman, in a sense a product of the Scottish Enlightenment, though never an intellectual participant in it. He was ambitious for worldly success and left Scotland when he recognized the more lucrative market for his skills in the commercial city of Birmingham. There he went into partnership with Matthew Boulton (originally a manufacturer of buckles) to mass-produce and sell his famous engine, which became the backbone for the mushrooming factories and prosperity of Victorian England. Today we might not classify this sort of thing as science, but at the time the steam engine was a phenomenon that excited scientists as much as a natural phenomenon would have done and was just as important to the development of the physics of heat and energy. Watt was a Fellow of the Royal Society and an active participant in the lively discussions of the Birmingham Lunar Society.

Wedgwood was a pottery designer and manufacturer, founder of the Staffordshire factories that still bear his name. He was another active member of the Lunar Society and generously supplied fellow Lunarite Joseph Priestley with crucibles and other ceramic ware for his research. He himself took a scientific approach to pottery making and invented a pyrometer for measuring the high temperatures in firing ovens, which earned him membership in the Royal Society. On a more personal note, Wedgwood was a progenitor of Charles Darwin. His daughter Suzannah married Erasmus Darwin's son and eventually became Charles Darwin's mother. And when Charles himself came to take a wife, he married his first cousin Emma, also a granddaughter of Josiah Wedgwood.

Related Places to Visit: Birmingham, Leeds, Calne, Chatsworth, Lichfield, Maer, and Barlaston.

Colonials and Outsiders. Two eccentrics outside the normal roster of English scientists illustrate the deep penetration of scientific curiosity, across the ocean to the colonies and across social boundaries to a simple seafaring man. They testify to the continuing enlightened spirit of the Royal Society, for both were welcomed into the fellowship of the Society and published their papers in its *Philosophical Transactions.*

One was **Benjamin Franklin** (1706–1790), whom we don't usually think of as English. Wasn't he one of the founders of the United States? Indeed he was, but he was by then seventy years old. For most of his life the American colonies were an extension of England and the colonial residents were English citizens. In the early years of his life Franklin thought of himself as English and was proud of the fact. His father had been born in Northamptonshire and his cousins still lived there. Franklin himself went to London in 1724 to procure the tools that would enable him to become a printer in Philadelphia. When, like many another English gentleman, he became an amateur scientist and made important discoveries about electricity, he turned to the Royal Society to have them published. He was soon nominated to become a Fellow and even won the coveted Copley Medal in 1754. Later he was sent to London by the colony of Pennsylvania as a petitioner (not in any sense as a threatening separatist), and he lived there from 1757 to 1762 and again from 1765 to 1775. He was a fully accepted member of the scientific community, an active participant in Royal Society meetings, and member of many of its committees. He continued to do experiments of his own, such as the well-known wave-stilling experiment on Clapham Common.

Unlike Benjamin Franklin, **James Cook** (1728–1779) was, of course, a proper Englishman, a Yorkshireman, in fact, and what could be more English than that? But we normally think of him as an explorer—a naval man—not as a scientist. And explorer he was, but a major goal of his first expedition was scientific—observation of the transit of Venus across the sun (only the second since the one observed by Horrocks in 1639), which was expected to occur in

1769 and to be visible from the Pacific. Moreover Joseph Banks (subsequently one of our foremost botanists and president of the Royal Society) came along as the expedition's naturalist, bringing with him a sizable personal staff, which caused some inconvenience for Cook. Nevertheless, Cook took great interest in (and contributed to) Banks's doings and eventually became a Fellow of the Royal Society.

Cook made his own unique and well-known contribution to science by providing one of the first explicit testaments to the relation between diet and health, almost twentieth century-like in its emphasis on *vegetable* foods. On one of his trips Cook sailed south and east from the Cape of Good Hope to circumnavigate the world, in the process of destroying the popular notion of the existence of a great southern continent. The total travel time was three years and the remarkable and unprecedented medical fact about it was that *not a single man was lost to scurvy!* One died of a lingering illness, two were drowned, and one was killed by a fall, but the dread disease of sailors, scurvy—marked by weakened capillaries and hemorrhaging skin and gums—claimed not a single victim. All the rest came home with health intact. Cook wrote a paper for the *Philosophical Transactions* to explain how he accomplished this by dint of careful attention to cleanliness, availability of fresh water, and by his choice of what was fed to his crew. "Sour Krout" was a prominent component, "not only a wholesome vegetable food, but, in my judgment, high antiscorbutic." "Rob of lemons and oranges" ("rob" meaning condensed juice or syrup) was also mentioned as valuable, though expensive, and "sweet-wort," a presumably alcoholic malt liquor, was thought as possibly the most important of all and dished out at the rate of two to three pints per man per day.

As we all know, the critical dietary factor is vitamin C (first chemically isolated in 1928). Retrospective judgment would question sweet-wort as a source for the vitamin, and it must be said to his credit that Cook himself actually waffles a bit on this particular drink, not altogether convinced that it would cure advanced cases of scurvy.

Related Places to Visit: Ecton, Whitby and environs.

From Bath to Manchester: Western Initiative

At the end of the century, from the west of England (more testimony to the vitality of England's provinces), came two discoveries that were more substantial. They were still the work of isolated individuals, far from a university or research institute—one a musician who made astronomy his hobby and the other, a country doctor with an alert mind—but they were far-reaching in their effect and indeed propelled the discoverers into the international scientific limelight. (In addition, a woman slips into the story, one of the earliest female scientists in England.)

And equally innovative genius flowered soon after in the industrial city of Manchester.

Discovery of the Planet Uranus. In 1781 the city of Bath, a fashionable health resort without academic pretensions, witnessed the discovery of the planet Uranus, the first new planet since antiquity. The other planets known at the time (Mercury, Venus, Mars, Jupiter, Saturn) are clearly visible to the naked eye and their vagabond motions against the distant stars had been studied and recorded since time immemorial. There had been centuries of debate about their actual sizes, distances between them, and so forth, but the observational data had always remained the same, not significantly changed from what had been recorded by Ptolemy in Alexandria around 140 A.D. Needless to say, the discovery of a new planet—1.8 *billion* miles from the sun, compared to the earth's 93 *million*—created a sensation, and the discoverer, **William Herschel** (1738–1822) acquired great fame.

Herschel came from Germany, where he had been an oboist in the band of the Hanoverian guards. He continued to play music in England, first in Leeds and then as organist of the posh Octagon Chapel in Bath. Settled in the latter city, he found time to pursue a long-held private obsession with astronomy. He proved to be a skilled craftsman and learned to make reflecting telescopes of unequalled light-gathering power, grinding and polishing his own mirrors. In 1772 he brought his sister **Caroline Herschel** (1750–1848) from Hanover to join him and, with her aid, set himself the task of systematically scanning the sky and cataloguing special features, such as double stars and nebulae. Caroline kept track of comets.

It was during his second multi-year scan, in 1781, that Herschel encountered his new object in the sky, clearly not a star, but also not one of the known planets—what could it be? Herschel, lacking theoretical training, did not know how to calculate an orbit for his object and rather lamely decided it must be a comet; it was other astronomers (at the Royal Society in London), with better theoretical knowledge than Herschel, who decided that the object must be a planet circulating the sun. In spite of his misinterpretation, it was Herschel who seems to have gained the major share of the credit. He was also politically astute, for he named his discovery *Georgium Sidus*, in honor of fellow Hanoverian King George III. The name, we know, didn't stick, but it did bring its reward in the form of a royal pension of £200 a year, with an extra stipend of £50 for his sister. Herschel was required to live near Windsor Castle to earn his stipend and to allow the king to look through his telescope occasionally and to explain to him what he saw.

Herschel went on to make many other contributions to our knowledge of the sky and in 1800, experimenting with the use of a thermometer to sense the impact of radiation, he made the important discovery of *infrared light*. He found that the thermometer responded to invisible rays beyond the end of the visible spectrum, and that these invisible rays obeyed the same laws of refraction as ordinary light. But Herschel's theoretical or speculative views continued to be shaky, as they had been when he first proposed that Uranus was a comet. He was personally convinced, for example, that there is "great probability, not to say almost absolute certainty" that the moon is inhabited.

Caroline eventually conducted her own independent research, discovered eight new comets, was the author of a revision of the standard catalog of stars, and received numerous honors, including in 1828 (at age 78) the gold medal of the Royal Astronomical Society. (But she did not make it into the Royal Society! It was 1945 before the first women were admitted into that august body. This is shamefully late, given the Royal Society's traditionally liberal policy in the election of male fellows.)

Related Place to Visit: Bath.

Milkmaids Don't Get Smallpox. Here we have a romantic tale: a country doctor in a sleepy little town, well-educated, to be sure, but inclined to gentle pursuits—writing poetry, playing the flute, observing local natural history. He makes a momentous discovery, and it catapults him into the public spotlight, bringing him worldwide acclaim and modest fortune. But he never quite takes to the public life, and at the end of his days we find him still peacefully in Berkeley, serving as a justice of the peace. In his last (posthumous) paper he is again an observer of nature, describing the enlarged ovaries and testes of birds that migrate to England to nest and reproduce.

Edward Jenner (1749–1823) was the son of the vicar of Berkeley. He was orphaned at the age of five, but his elder brother Stephen saw to it that he had an excellent education—apprenticeship to a local surgeon at age fourteen and then several years in London with the prominent surgeon and anatomist, John Hunter. While in London, Jenner also worked with Sir Joseph Banks, Captain Cook's naturalist. Jenner's job was to preserve and arrange zoological specimens brought back from Cook's first voyage.

Jenner started medical practice in his native Berkeley in 1773, and we must suppose that he approached it with the same intelligent curiosity that he applied to his observations of cuckoos and hedgehogs, the topics of his first two published papers. His famous work was on the more serious subject of smallpox, one of the great scourges of the time. An almost modern kind of preventive treatment against it was already known, brought to England more than 50 years earlier by Lady Mary Wortley Montague, wife of the ambassador to Turkey. The treatment (used in Turkey and neighboring countries) took the form of inoculating healthy individuals with *live infectious material* obtained from pustules of infected patients. While this procedure conferred lifelong immunity, it was hazardous and sometimes lethal. People were willing to subject themselves to it only because a more massive infection during an epidemic seemed the greater risk.

Jenner was intrigued by the immunity of milkmen and milkmaids to smallpox, a resistance seemingly related to previous contraction of a pox disease of the teats of milk cows that was communicable to human beings. He reasoned that it might be possible to protect anyone from smallpox by deliberately infecting them with the less virulent cowpox. Twenty years of meticulous study lay ahead before he summoned the courage to perform the crucial experiment, but then it proved a huge success. A young boy inoculated with extract from a cowpox pustule proved immune to subsequent inoculation with a similar extract from a smallpox victim.

Jenner published his results in a small volume at his own expense, and worldwide reaction was instantaneous. The *vaccine* (so named after the Latin word for cow) could be preserved as a dry powder, and soon Jenner was busy sending samples to all corners of the globe. He was voted large grants by the British parliament, and a national program of vaccination was begun. Though Britain and France were at war, Napoleon had a medal struck in honor of Jenner and made vaccination compulsory in the French army. Other national programs followed and smallpox has recently been declared eradicated, even from the remotest corner of the earth.

Subsequent leaders in immunology have sometimes been ungenerous in their recognition of Jenner's achievement, and have felt the need to demonstrate their own superior wisdom. Louis Pasteur, for example, is reported to have said (with respect to his own work on chicken cholera), "In this case I have demonstrated a thing that Jenner never could do in smallpox—and that is, that the microbe that kills is the same one that guards the animal from death." Jenner's infectious agent, of course, wasn't a microbe, but a filterable virus, an essentially molecular entity and not a living bacterium. It was also not the *same* virus in this case, but a related virus (cowpox versus smallpox). Jenner's work is the forerunner of modern immunology, which recognizes that the immune response is not to the whole infectious agent, but only to some surface segment. Much work goes today into creating artificially attenuated viruses, where the critical surface segment is retained, but the site of virulence is changed. In the case of cowpox, nature has handed us such a thing on a platter.

Related Place to Visit: Berkeley.

Atoms and Energy: Manchester Science. Smokestacks belching noxious fumes into ever-murky skies above—that was till recently the popular image of the city of Manchester. The city is a product of the industrial revolution and for most of its existence has been true to this picture of grim pollution, coupled with gross social inequality—wealthy barons of industry on the one hand, masses of underpaid workers in unsanitary housing on the other. As late as 1890, the life expectancy in Manchester was six years below the average for England and Wales.

But there is another side to Manchester, which has received less publicity. For nearly two centuries it has nurtured a tradition for scientific research and discovery—not, as might have been expected, *industrial* science tied to the smoky factories, but *pure* and *fundamental* science. Three of the great highlights of physical science originated in Manchester, tied to the work of three brilliant thinkers and experimenters, John Dalton (1766–1844), James Prescott Joule (1818–1889), and Ernest Rutherford (1871–1937). Dalton created the working model of the atom here, pretty much the way that laboratory chemists think of it to this day, little spherical bodies, combining with each other in specific integral ratios to form molecules. Joule did more than anyone else to establish the concept of a universal thing called energy, demolishing decades of misconceptions about the separate identities of heat, electrical energy, and so forth. Rutherford is the father of the "modern" atom, explaining in a sense how Dalton's atoms work when they combine, but also going beyond that in providing one of the opening chapters for our current world of subatomic particles and megabuck accelerators to study them. No other provincial city in Europe can rival Manchester in the record of providing so many of the basic milestones for our understanding of the material world around us.

John Dalton was born in the tiny and remote village of Eaglesfield in Cumbria, the son of a poor cotton weaver. William Wordsworth, the poet, was born (in 1770) in the larger town of Cockermouth, just two miles away. Poet and scientist both knew the blind philosopher and local sage, John Gough, who lived in nearby Keswick. Wordsworth wrote about him in his poem *The Excursion:* "Methinks I see him now, his eyeballs roll'd beneath his ample brow." For Dalton he was a source of educational guidance and was responsible (in 1793) for getting him a teaching job in Manchester.

Dalton became interested in what one might call systematics of science before he came to Manchester and in that city found kindred spirits to encourage his pursuits. He never married and for more than a quarter century shared a humble dwelling in George Street with a friend. The Manchester Literary and Philosophical Society was the center of his scientific world. He contributed 116 papers to its proceedings and was its president from 1819 until his death. He was invited to lecture at the then newly founded Royal Institution in London in 1804 and again in 1809 and made other occasional trips to the capital; he once made a short visit to Paris; once a year he took a holiday in the Lake District; but most of the time he was in Manchester, gradually becoming one of its most respected citizens.

Dalton's great classic, *A New System of Chemical Philosophy*, was published in Manchester in several volumes, the first appearing in 1808. The atomic theory of chemical combination was only a part of the book, but it was soon recognized as the vital part. Atoms are seen as tiny (invisible) spherical bodies of fixed mass; each different *chemical element* has its own distinct kind of atom; atoms combine in *definite proportions* to form molecules (which Dalton called *compound atoms*). Dalton's measurements of relative combining weights were crude and his assumption that simple molecules have a 1:1 stoichiometry (water = HO) distorted his figures for relative atomic masses, but those are trivial faults. What counts is Dalton's conceptual revolution—he established the model that chemists have used ever since to visualize and think about what goes on in their reaction flasks. Derek Gjertsen quotes a nineteenth century student's answer to an examination question: "Atoms are blocks of wood, painted in various colors, invented by Dr. Dalton." The only difference today is that the blocks are made of plastic.

James Prescott Joule came from a family who owned a brewery, which, not surprisingly, prospered with the multiplication of Manchester's factories and population. Both James and his elder brother Benjamin were given a good education by private tutors, including none other than John Dalton, then about seventy years old, who taught the boys natural philosophy, mathematics, and some chemistry. Both brothers were financially independent for many years, so that they could afford the luxury of ambitious careers outside the world of industry or commerce. Brother Benjamin (presumably less inspired by Dalton than James) chose music and James chose science, setting up his experiments in the homes where he lived and occasionally in the family brewery.

Joule's fame rests on his establishment of the equivalence between the then entirely separate notions of mechanical energy (mechanical work done) and heat (the poorly defined "something" that could raise the temperature of matter). He measured the temperature change induced in water when mechanical work was done, which is equivalent to measuring the heat produced, and determined the ratio between the two quantities in the distinct units then used for them. He used a paddle-wheel, turning against friction in water in a vessel with baffles designed to maximize that friction. He did the same experiment, with mercury in the vessel instead of water. In another experiment he forcibly rotated a small electromagnet in water between the poles of another magnet, working this time against the magnetic force that would by itself keep the electromagnet in fixed orientation. In other experiments he measured the heat produced by metal grinding against metal and by current flowing in wire. The experiments were done with what was for the time an awesome precision, with meticulous awareness of and correction for possible sources of error—leakage of heat from his apparatus into the surroundings and that sort of thing. His result was always the same, regardless of the manner of work being done, 772 foot-pounds of work produced one British Thermal Unit (BTU) of heat, a BTU being the amount of heat needed to raise the temperature of one pound of water by one degree Fahrenheit.

These were among the most extraordinary experiments ever done in classical physics. They contain the germ of the law of conservation of energy, for example, formally stated a little later by Heinrich Helmholtz in Germany, but clearly recognized by Joule in essence. He expressed it as the indestructibility and self-sufficiency of natural powers—only God can destroy (or create) the agents of nature.

Equally important, Joule's results settled the vexing controversy about the intrinsic nature of heat. The classical conception was that heat is a substance ("caloric"), much like a chemical element. Lavoisier had said that in 1789. Carnot had assumed it (almost thought he had proved it) in his seminal 1824 experiments on the conversion of heat into useful work. The contrary idea that heat is energy, the energy inherent in molecular motion, was recognized as plausible, but there were deemed to be no compelling arguments in its favor. Joule's results left no room for doubt. The same paddle wheel could be used over and over again, heat was produced every time that work was done, nothing emanated from the substance of the wheel or from the liquid in which it turned.

Joule was remarkably provincial, rarely leaving the city of Manchester and certainly unappreciated by his London contemporaries. He did, however, attend meetings of the British Association for the Advancement of Science which had a deliberate policy of spreading science to the provinces and generally met in places remote from London, such as York, Plymouth, Liverpool, and so on. Joule read his paper on heat and work to the Association's 1847 meeting in Oxford and it proved to be a fateful occasion, for young William Thomson (later Lord Kelvin) was in the audience and immediately recognized the importance of what Joule had done. This encounter led directly to Thomson's subsequent preoccupation with thermodynamics, as well as to collaboration between the two men. They arranged to meet in Switzerland to measure the rise in the water temperature when a mountain torrent falls from a great height.

A *Final Comment on Manchester:* We should emphasize that Dalton and Joule were no flash in the pan—Manchester was still the "atomic city" par excellence in the early twentieth century. In addition to Ernest Rutherford (already mentioned) there was J. J. Thomson, discoverer of the electron a decade before Rutherford, who was educated at Manchester's Owens College, precursor of the present University.

Related Places to Visit: Eaglesfield, Manchester.

The Nineteenth Century: Michael Faraday

"Oh London Town's a fine town, and London sights are rare,
And London ale is right ale, and brisk's the London air."—John Masefield, *London Town*

London, pretty much in eclipse (for us) since the death of Newton, came back into its own in the early nineteenth century. The spearhead was a typical private English enterprise, the **Royal Institution,** a marvellous establishment that retains to this day the brisk air of innovation with which it began. The Institution was the brainchild of Benjamin Thompson (Count Rumford), American-born adventurer, scientist, and crusader for the use of science as a social tool. A specific mandate at the beginning was "Bettering the Condition and Increasing the Comforts of the Poor." It was to be supported by private subscription—it was too early for the welfare state—and unconventional means were created to encourage the rich to part with their money, popular lectures to which *ladies* were admitted being particularly successful. Competent scientists were to become salaried employees—the beginning of the end for amateurs and eccentrics!

The first regular lecturer was **Thomas Young** (1773–1829), son of a Somerset merchant and banker and one of the most versatile and brilliant men that English science has ever seen, but a dilettante, who himself later admitted that his work had often consisted of "acute suggestions," rather than fully documented airtight proofs. The spread of his interests is virtually incomprehensible in today's specialized world. He was a practicing physician and published medical treatises; he effectively proved the wave theory of light (at the expense of Newton's corpuscular theory); he was the first to explain the phenomenon of surface tension at a liquid surface; he generated theories of elasticity and of ocean tides; he was the genius who worked out the key to the Rosetta stone, the first Egyptian hieroglyphics to be deciphered. But none of it was ever quite finished. The credit for the *ultimate* decipherment of hieroglyphics, for example, is generally given to the Frenchman, Jean Champollion, and not to Young.

Young's course of lectures at the Royal Institution was eventually published, and Lord Rayleigh, when he became professor and lecturer 80 years later, found them inspiring and, in fact, did much to promote Young's stature in the history books. But at the time they were much too erudite for his audience. Young lacked the common touch that was needed to maintain a large fee-paying audience and soon had to resign. His successor, Humphry Davy, however, was an instant success as lecturer and managed thereby to attract the financial support that was needed to stabilize the Royal Institution and set up an ambitious research program, which proved to be just as successful as the lectures. (The "poor" seem to have been largely forgotten.)

Humphry Davy (1778–1829) came from Cornwall, from a family of unpretentious yeoman stock. He was largely self-educated, and it is said that he may have been spurred on to a career in science by Gregory Watt, the rather sickly son of James Watt, who sought the winter warmth of Cornwall for the sake of his health and had found lodgings with the Davy family. In any event, young Davy soon found science-related employment at Thomas Beddoes' Pneumatic Institution in Clifton (close to Bristol) and there discovered the anesthetic properties of nitrous oxide (laughing gas). It did not become (as he had hoped it might) a widely used medical agent, but it did bring him fame by a different and unexpected route—sniffing the gas became a popular rage. While in Clifton, Davy also became a member of the local literary circles and started to write poetry himself. Here he met the poets Coleridge and Southey, who became his lifelong friends.

Davy's most important work at the Royal Institution was inspired by Alessandro Volta's sensational discovery of the voltaic pile. The continuous source of electricity that it provided could be used to disrupt chemical compounds (e.g., H_2O into oxygen and hydrogen), and Davy enthusiastically poured his energies into exploration of the new possibilities thereby created. He found that he could use the pile to decompose the previous intractable "earths," producing thereby shiny, quicksilver-like globules of a whole range of new metals—sodium from soda, potassium from potash, calcium from lime, and several others. It was a discovery of the first magnitude, deliberately sought, based on a kind of comprehension of what chemistry was all about that would have been unthinkable even a decade earlier. Davy, when he first saw the metal break through the earthy crust, is reported to have danced about the room in ecstasy. Napoleon gave Davy a medal for the work and Davy went to France to collect it in person, despite the fact that England and France were engaged in a bitter war. Davy was subjected to some criticism for his breach of the battle lines but swept it aside: "The two countries or governments are at war," he said, "the men of science are not"—a noble sentiment which today's world might not be inclined to accept with tolerance.

Michael Faraday, the Incomparable. After Davy came Michael Faraday (1791–1867), the shining star in the Institution's history and one of the genuine wonders in the history of all of science. In his laboratory, in the basement of the Royal Institution, he carried out, mostly with his own hands, a body of experimental investigations that have perhaps no equal in their scope and brilliance and in the direct impact they had on human society. (And he was a great lecturer as well. He instituted the regular Friday Evening Discourses and the ever popular annual Children's Christmas Lectures. He himself gave the children's lectures nineteen times, at a guinea per head for adults and half that price per child.)

In chemistry Faraday discovered the rules of electrolysis and electrochemical deposition. He introduced the words *electrode, anode, cathode, electrolyte, dielectric,* and many others. In the realm of physics, Faraday used iron filings to map the lines of force associated with a magnet, and, lo and behold, the lines were *curved,* and how do you reconcile that with Newtonian mechanics, where forces act in straight lines between two bodies? Faraday (lacking formal theoretical training) was not halted by this momentous question (as some of his contemporaries were) but instead forged ahead. He established that not only iron but many other substances respond in some way to a magnetic force. Even light was affected, he found—magnetic force alters the direction of polarization of light.

The crowning achievement was in electromagnetism, Faraday's reversal of Ørsted's effect, his production of electricity from a changing magnetic field instead of vice versa. What a revolution that caused! Generation of a magnetic field from an electric current was scientifically fascinating but without great practical value, but ability to generate electricity *de novo* is an entirely different matter. Electricity is our most versatile source of power and Faraday suddenly made it readily available, simply by rotating a magnet, without the chemicals that batteries require. Faraday invented electrical induction, the electrical transformer, the dynamo, the first electric motor. *All generation of electricity to this day,* whether derived from burning coal or water power or nuclear reaction, is produced by means of the dynamo and is based on the principles that Faraday recognized and demonstrated in experiments he carried out between August and December of 1831.

In the wealth of these purely experimental discoveries, it is easy to miss Faraday's intellectual insight and the guidance it provided for his successors (and which, of course, guided himself to doing the right experiments). All biographers cite the fact that Faraday, by his own admission, was a mathematical illiterate. Nevertheless his mind worked in *theoretical mode* to complement his experimental skill, and everyone agrees that it was Faraday who created the idea of a physical field of force, even if he didn't write the equations for it. As the German physicist Hermann Helmholtz put it, "Faraday performed in his brain the work of a great mathematician without using a single mathematical formula."

The marvel of it is that it is difficult to imagine anyone less likely, by dint of birth or early education, to reach such heights of success. Faraday's father had been a poor blacksmith in the wilds of the high moors of the Pennines and had moved to London only shortly before Michael's birth, to find a better paying job, unsuccessfully by all accounts—the Faradays remained as poor in the big city as they had been up north. There were no decent schools then for the likes of young Michael and his knowledge of reading, writing, and arithmetic was, as he himself later said, only "rudimentary." At age thirteen, like many a poor boy after him, he took a job delivering newspapers. It was pure luck that his master was also a bookbinder and took him on as apprentice, where he was able to educate himself by devouring a wide variety of the material that came through the shop. It was luck again when one of the shop's customers gave him some tickets to Humphry Davy's lectures at the Royal Institution. Faraday was so enthralled that he took the bold step of writing to Davy to ask for a job, and it was luck once more than Davy had a vacancy and could hire Faraday as his assistant. Shortly thereafter Davy was knighted, and then he married a wealthy bluestocking lady and set off with his bride on an 18-month grand tour of Europe. Faraday was asked to come along as secretary and scientific assistant, which, of course, he did—he had never traveled more than a dozen miles from London before! He met Ampère, Cuvier, Volta, Gay-Lussac, and other eminent European scientists and, in between visits, he and Sir Humphry talked. All of chemistry and physics must have been discussed and debated. Faraday's education became complete.

Faraday remained at the Royal Institution for nearly 50 years. He had his residence in the building, as part of the compensation for his assistantship, and never seemed to yearn for grander quarters. Initially he had only two rooms. Two more were added after he himself became married, but that was all. Faraday was invited to become President of the Royal Society in 1857, but turned down the honor. He effectively retired from the Institution in 1862 and moved to a house at Hampton Court, provided for him by Queen Victoria. After his death he was buried in a simple grave in Highgate cemetery, but there is also a commemorative plaque in Westminster, close to a similar plaque for Maxwell.

Related Places to Visit: London (Royal Institution, British Museum, Westminster Abbey), Penzance.

Dinosaurs and Relics of the Flood. Digging for fossils goes back a long way in England, a manifestation of the buoyant amateur enthusiasm for science, particularly a science that unlike astronomy was very inexpensive to carry out. One of the earliest diggers was the physician John Woodward (1665–1728), who had a fanatic's mission to prove the literal truth of the Biblical story of Noah's flood. (His fossil collection is still on view in Cambridge.) A century later, another amateur paleontologist, James Parkinson (1755–1824), published a book entitled *Organic Remains of a Former World.* The frontispiece shows Noah's Ark, with some ammonites and trilobites that had missed the boat lying nearby waiting to be fossilized. (Parkinson was a physician who also wrote a celebrated *Essay of Shaking Palsy* in 1817, describing what we now call Parkinson's Disease.) An even later and more authoritative voice was that of **William Buckland** (1784–1856), Oxford's most famous (or should one say notorious?) professor of geology, who searched far and wide for what he considered relics of the Deluge. His popular *Reliquiae Diluvianae* was published in 1823, subtitled "Observations on the organic remains contained in caves, fissures, and diluvial gravel, and on other geological phenomena, attesting the action of an universal deluge." Ironically, Charles Lyell, who swept away all notions of diluvianism in the 1830s, had been an enthusiastic student of Buckland's from 1816 to 1818.

Of greater long-range significance was the discovery about this time of giant skeletons, attesting to the former presence on earth of animals of incredible size and bizarre shapes—the dinosaurs (fearsome lizards) and their marine analogues, the ichthyosaurs. The first such skeleton (of the marine variety) was found in 1812 by a young girl, Mary Anning, in Lyme Regis. She was soon "adopted" by William Buckland and the two of them became a common sight, wading in search of fossils in the shallow waters off the rocky Lyme Regis shore. The first proper description of one of the spectacular terrestrial dinosaurs was given by Gideon Mantell (1790–1852), based on remains he found in Tilgate Forest, about halfway between London and Brighton.

Dinosaur fossils were soon discovered in all parts of the world, attesting to widespread distribution, and they were never associated with human remains, indicative of an early period in terrestrial history when man did *not* exist, but giant creatures, *now extinct,* dominated the whole globe. The question of whether these findings could be made compatible (by those who wished it) with the Biblical story of creation is not really important. The important point is that the dinosaurs gripped the imagination of the British public as no other scientific discovery had ever done. Models were built for the great Crystal Palace Exhibition of 1851; books about them were avidly read. The influence on the popular awareness of biological science must have been enormous. Surely this prepared the ground for the later ready acceptance of evolution.

Related Places to Visit: Cambridge (Sedgwick Museum), Kirbymoorside, Lyme Regis.

Peripatetic Geologist. **Charles Lyell** (1797–1875) wrote the "textbook" of geology, establishing the framework that molded the thoughts of teachers and students for 50 years or more. It was 1830, geology was in its infancy, and exponents of every wild speculation about the history of the earth were hawking their wares in London and Paris, the two centers of the burgeoning science. William Buckland, Lyell's teacher at Oxford, was still preaching the literal biblical story; John Playfair's *Illustrations of the Huttonian Theory*, on the other hand, was making a persuasive case for Hutton's everlasting earth, without beginning or end. The president of London's Geological Society was a Werner student, a Neptunist; the French, contrariwise, were Vulcanists.

Lyell's *Principles of Geology* was first published in a four-volume edition between 1830 and 1833 and an astonishing eleven subsequent editions (some with extensive revisions) were produced during Lyell's lifetime. The reason for the book's success and the reason for Lyell's enormous influence was that *Principles of Geology* was not (in the modern fashion) an inoffensive balanced account of existing ideas—Lyell unambiguously threw out what seemed to him to be absurd and made decisive choices between what was left. Above all, he was an indefatigable and purposeful traveler, continually subjecting his ideas to test. To call it experimental testing would be perhaps too strong a term, but he could not or would not believe any assertion of fact or inference without going to see for himself, questioning the original proponent and anyone else who might have been an informed bystander. He went on long arduous trips, virtually every year of his life, no matter what other duties he might have. Wherever he went he sought out scientists of whom he knew, but he sought out knowledgeable people even if there were no affirmed experts. His friend Roderick Murchison had given him good advice—every village includes a naturalist, he had told him, and to find that person, start by asking at the chemist's shop.

Lyell's textbook opted for what is essentially Hutton's theory of the earth. "An attempt to explain the former changes in the earth's surface by reference to causes now in operation," is how he says it in the subtitle of the book. But he pushed Hutton's doctrine to an extreme. Hutton supposed that the same kind of forces keep operating over and over again, but Lyell believed in addition that the *rate of change* had always been the same and that put him into direct conflict with the *catastrophism* theory, i.e., Cuvier's view of geological history as indicating periods of little change, punctuated by natural disasters. The term *uniformitarianism* is generally used to describe Lyell's point of view, an ungainly word invented not by Lyell, but by the prominent Cambridge scholar William Whewell in a review written in 1832.

The fossil record was an important factor in Lyell's thinking, and he interpreted it as providing a firm and convincing foundation for slow and gradual change. Lyell (in collaboration with the French paleontologist Paul Deshayes) made a major original contribution by statistical comparison of mollusk fossils as a function of where they were found. There was a high proportion of still-living species near the top of the present surface of the earth's crust, but a progressive increase in extinct species in lower deposits. On the basis of these results Lyell subdivided the Tertiary Era in geological stratigraphy (the period beginning about 60 million years ago) into the still standard subdivisions of Eocene, Miocene, Plicene, and Pleistocene periods. (The root *cene*, incidentally, means *recent*—the entire Tertiary Era is recent on the geological time scale.)

Almost everyone knows that Charles Darwin took the first volume of Lyell's *Principles* with him to read on the historic voyage of the Beagle (Volume 2 caught up with him in Montevideo a year later), that the two scientists became good friends after Darwin returned to London in 1837, and that Lyell played an important and skillful role in the first public announcement of the theory of natural selection in 1858. What is less well known is that Lyell's dictum of uniform change made him at first a vocal opponent of the idea of evolution. He believed that living species were fixed and that newly *created* species took the place of the old when the latter became extinct by virtue of lack of adaptability. His conversion to the Darwinian theory was appropriately slow and gradual.

Related Places to Visit: Kirriemuir (Scotland), Pozzuoli and Mount Etna (Italy).

The Golden Age of Science

Since the middle of the nineteenth century it has been a golden age for science. At the start, "evolution" transformed biology and Cambridge transformed physics. The momentum gained went on to transform our lives, leading to the now familiar (and costly) role of science in all our affairs.

Charles Darwin and Alfred Wallace: The Origin of Species. It has been said that Darwin was to the nineteenth century what Galileo and Newton had been to the seventeenth, creator of a previously unimaginable revolution in our conception of the natural world. The statement itself is surely indisputable. Darwin was as devastating a force in history as any military man.

However, in deference to historical accuracy with respect to the scientific ideas per se (as opposed, shall we say, to *popular* influence), it is not quite fair to use the name Darwin by itself, without the acknowledgment that Wallace had the same idea independently at about the same time. Both men received their inspiration from the same source—overseas journeys away from England, in this case far beyond the now familiar European scene to virtually unexplored terrain in South America and/or Malaysia.

Charles Darwin (1809–1882), the man we have just called a "devastating force" in history, was by no means a conquering hero. He sounded no trumpets, he beat no drums. He was a lifelong hypochondriac, an indecisive ditherer. It would be wrong to label him as reluctant to *reveal* his theory of the origin of species, for he wrote it all down in a 230-page manuscript in 1844, and described and discussed it freely in his correspondence. But formal publication was another matter. Imagine yourself in his position, having just upset the applecart of conventional opinion about creation and the smug certainty of man's position at its apex. What would you have done? What Darwin did was to devote the following eight years of his working life to the taxonomy of barnacles! It was not until June 1858, when the bombshell of Alfred Wallace's paper with the same theory arrived by post at Down House, that Darwin finally got down to the task of publication. Even then considerable persuasion by Darwin's friends, Charles Lyell and Joseph Hooker, was necessary.

Darwin's faltering sense of resolution is evident from his earliest days. His father, a successful physician, sent him to Edinburgh to study medicine, but that enterprise failed and he was shipped off to Cambridge to become a clergyman instead. Darwin began his beetle collection there, but had little enthusiasm for the prescribed studies. By his own admission, he went to very few lectures and had little interest in most subjects. He did form a decisive friendship in Cambridge with the botanist John Stevens Henslow, and it was the latter who recommended him for the position of unpaid naturalist on the Royal Navy's surveying ship, HMS *Beagle*. Darwin was twenty-two years old when the five-year journey began, regarded himself (correctly) as better prepared to survey geology than flora and fauna, and took along the just published first volume of Lyell's *Principles of Geology* as reading matter. His geological observations and a new hypothesis about the origin of oceanic islands and coral reefs were the first things he published after his return to England in 1836. Darwin was secretary of the Geological Society in London from 1838 to 1841; a book, *Structure and Distribution of Coral Reefs*, came out in 1842.

Darwin, now ensconced at Down House, with no further thought of travel, next turned to the acute observations of birds and other animals that he had made on his voyage and to the theory which had gradually crystallized in his mind. Evolution itself was nothing new, contrary to much present popular opinion. Darwin himself, in an introduction to *The Origin of Species*, lists 24 scientists who had proposed evolutionary ideas, beginning with Lamarck in 1809 and even including Richard Owen, who was soon to become Darwin's bitter opponent in the arena of public acceptance. The uniqueness in Darwin's proposal was a plausible *natural mechanism* for evolution, i.e., natural selection, survival of the fittest.

The Origin of Species, when finally published, became an immediate sensation, and was ultimately translated into 29 languages. Not everyone was enthusiastic, of course, and we all know that there are still vociferous detractors today. Politicians at the time must have had not a little discomfort, for Darwin was never offered the knighthood he had every right to expect. (Three of his ten children were knighted after his death.)

Alfred Russel Wallace (1823–1913) had the idea of natural selection *independently* of Darwin. But he was a much younger man and lacked Darwin's status— no illustrious grandparents, no university degree—and he is perhaps given less than his fair share of the credit for the discovery. On the other hand, there is no doubt that Darwin had the concept in his mind (even though it was unpublished) several years before Wallace set out on his first journey of exploration.

Wallace was the eighth of nine children of a West Country family beset by constant economic woes. His urge for travel to remote places was first aroused by reading the works of Alexander von Humboldt and others in the 1840s, including Darwin's journal of the *Beagle* voyage. He and a friend (Henry Walter Bates) decided to take off on a bold trip of their own to the Amazon basin, without sponsors or financial support, hoping to make money from the sale of exotic specimens at home. Wallace unfortunately lost most of his materials (and almost his life) when his ship sank on the return voyage, but he managed to publish a book about his trip, and, undaunted by the previous disaster, set off on another journey, this time to the Malay archipelago. Evolution of species had been on his mind right from the start of his first journey, and he wrote his first paper on his hypothesis in 1855, without apparently attracting much attention. The "bombshell" paper mailed to Darwin from Malaysia in 1858 was his second (and clearly more fruitful) account.

Wallace, despite his many years of experience in collecting and classifying, was only thirty-five years old in 1858, fifteen years younger than Darwin. He went on to live to the ripe old age of ninety and became a popular and respected figure in the world of natural history—despite some adventurous excursions into spiritualism, socialism, and the like, which diminished his reputation in some quarters.

Richard Owen (1804–1892) and **Thomas Huxley** (1825–1895): We cannot leave the subject of evolution without mention of these two prominent Victorian naturalists, whose bitter warfare pro and con helped enormously to sharpen public awareness of the subject.

Richard Owen, lacking private wealth, had to work for a living and did so as a museum man. He became supervisor of the natural history collections at the British Museum and in this job acquired an enviable national reputation. He was a proponent of evolution of a sort, but apparently not Darwin's kind, for, after publication of *The Origin of Species*, he became Darwin's bitter enemy—purely out of jealousy is what Darwin himself believed.

Huxley, on the other hand, was another upper-class figure. He had been in the Navy, and he too went on his voyage of exploration (on HMS *Rattlesnake*), but no notable discoveries resulted. Huxley's fame comes, in fact, from his tireless efforts as writer, public lecturer, and, above all, crusader for Darwin and his message. He wrote the obituary notice for Darwin in the magazine *Nature*, expressing a judgment that he himself helped to bring about: "He found a great truth, trodden under foot, reviled by bigots, and ridiculed by all the world; he lived long enough to see it . . . established in science, inseparably incorporated with the common thoughts of men."

There was a final twist to the rivalry between Owen and Huxley. Late in Owen's life he saw the natural history collection of the British Museum achieve independent status, and he presided proudly over its move to new buildings in South Kensington, the site it still occupies, Huxley, over Owen's strenuous opposition, contrived to have a statue of Darwin placed on the museum's main staircase. But it didn't last long. It was eventually replaced by a statue of Owen, in his memory as the museum's virtual creator, and Owen stands there to this day.

Related Places to Visit: Downe (near London), London (Westminster Abbey, Museum of Natural History).

Physics to the Fore in Cambridge. An event of great importance for British science, and indeed for the future development of all physics, was the founding of the **Cavendish Laboratory** at Cambridge University in 1871 and the simultaneous creation of the Cavendish professorship for experimental physics. The necessary endowment was provided by William Cavendish, seventh Duke of Devonshire, who was Chancellor of the University at the time. The laboratory provided unprecedented opportunity for hands-on experiments by students (as distinct from demonstration) as well as great facilities for faculty research.

James Clerk Maxwell (see under "Scotland") was the first Cavendish Professor, and he personally supervised the construction of the laboratory and the purchase of equipment. In effect, he set the tone for the future, making the Cavendish one of the best equipped physics laboratories in the world. Lord Rayleigh came next after Maxwell's early death, but his enthusiasm for the job was not great. He resigned after only five years and, in fact, carried out all his own research at his home in Terling where he had converted one wing into a laboratory filled with equipment purchased with his own money. (He was the last polymath, delving into a huge variety of problems. To cite just a few examples, he wrote an authoritative treatise on sound, he figured out why the sky is blue, he was codiscoverer of argon.)

With the advent of Rayleigh we move into the modern era of the Nobel Prize as a sort of public proclaimer (not necessarily infallible) of each year's champion researchers. Rayleigh in 1904 won one of the first physics prizes to be awarded, given for the discovery of argon. (Codiscoverer William Ramsay won a separate prize in chemistry the same year.) Each of the next three Cavendish professors, J. J. Thomson, Ernest Rutherford, and Lawrence Bragg, were likewise Nobel Prize winners, though only Thomson's 1906 prize was for work actually done at the Cavendish—his discovery of the electron. Rutherford and Bragg, who came to Cambridge in 1919 and 1938, respectively, had received their awards years earlier.

Closely associated with the Cavendish Laboratory is **Trinity College,** which has been Cambridge's favorite college for scientists ever since Newton was there as a student and fellow in the seventeenth century. All the Cavendish professors we have mentioned were Trinity men, for example. Trinity is unique among Oxford and Cambridge colleges in another way, by having its master appointed by the Crown (instead of the normal procedure of election by the fellows), which makes the position one of unusual honor in the English academic world— J. J. Thomson and Alan Hodgkin have been among scientists who have held the position. One of Trinity's earlier Victorian masters, **William Whewell,** a man of mighty strength and frame (as well as mind), was enormously influential in promoting the study and teaching of science, though (like his later counterpart of Oxford's Balliol College, Benjamin Jowett) he aspired to be and was generally regarded as being omniscient, knowing all there is to know. Whewell wrote many books about science and coined many now familiar words: e.g., *scientist, physicist*. Charles Lyell consulted Whewell when it came to assigning names (Eocene, Miocene, etc.) to the geological ages he defined on the basis of fossil content.

Colleges like Trinity were the important entities at both Oxford and Cambridge through most of their histories—the university as such was largely a paper institution. But this is rapidly changing. In the words of the historian G. M. Trevelyan (another Trinity man): "The vast growth of physical science with its laboratories and its endowments has greatly increased the importance of the University as such, diverting wealth and functions that under the old system would have gone to the Colleges."

Related Places to Visit: Cambridge (Cavendish Laboratory, Trinity College).

Inside the Atom. The Cavendish Laboratory is inextricably part of the revolution in physics that took place at the turn of the century. The "new physics," as it used to be called when we were young, had two distinct parts—one theoretical and mathematical (quantum theory, relativity), the other experimental (dismemberment of the atom, transmutation of elements). British science was in the lead in the experimental part, but had little to do with the theoretical one, which flourished mainly on the Continent, in Denmark (Niels Bohr), in Germany (Max Planck), and in Switzerland (Albert Einstein). Theory and experiment combined when Niels Bohr went to work with Ernest Rutherford in Manchester, as we shall see.

J. J. Thomson led the experimental dismemberment of the atom by his work on electrons. Many people had been studying the negative particles given off in cathode ray tubes, but these particles were generally believed to be of atomic size. Thomson actually measured their mass (strictly speaking, the ratio of mass to electric charge) and showed they were more than 1,000 times smaller than the smallest known atom!

Enter **Ernest Rutherford** (1871–1937), a student of Thomson's and a native New Zealander. Under Thomson's direction he set about studying the "emanations" that came from atoms bombarded with ultraviolet light and the newly discovered x-rays. He continued these studies in his new professorship at McGill University in Canada in 1898 and later at the University of Manchester in 1907. It was at McGill and Manchester that he discovered the atomic nucleus and alpha particles (a helium nucleus carrying two positive charges), identified beta rays as electrons, detected gamma rays as x-ray-like emanations, and most importantly, predicted the existence of the then unknown neutron. With the knowledge of these particles, Rutherford proposed his planetary model for atoms, with a heavy positive nucleus at the center and the electrons arranged in shells around it. This is where the aforementioned link with the new theoretical physics came in, for Rutherford's model was theoretically impossible without the quantum theory—classically the negative electrons should have collapsed into the positive nucleus—and this is the vital input that Niels Bohr supplied.

In 1919 Rutherford began a new phase of atomic research, the reversal of atomic disintegration. Can we bombard an atom with the normally emitted rays, he wondered, and get something different? He did indeed. He hit a nitrogen atom with an alpha particle and created oxygen-17 and a proton. Transmutation of the elements—the goal of alchemists far back in time—was realized! That same year Rutherford succeeded his old mentor, Thomson, as director of the Cavendish Laboratory in Cambridge where he continued to work until his death. His influence on modern physics extended far beyond his own discoveries through the generation of physicists whose careers began in Rutherford's laboratory—Niels Bohr, already mentioned, James Chadwick, who finally discovered the elusive but predicted neutron in 1932, John Cockcroft, and E. T. S. Walton, who built the first particle accelerator, to name only a few.

Related Places to Visit: Cambridge, Manchester, Copenhagen (Denmark).

The Piltdown Hoax. Where there's gold, there's fraud, as the world of science has been forcefully reminded in recent years. But the Piltdown fraud, one of the most notorious, took place long ago, before there was any possibility of monetary reward.

Post-Darwinian debasement prepared the ground, for it was at first rather humiliating for men to think that they were descended directly from the beasts. Honor was deemed to be preserved by the dogma that brain size created a sharp demarcation, but fossils to suggest the stepwise evolution of a large brain were lacking, until (in 1912) a skull and jawbone discovered on Piltdown Common in Sussex obligingly filled the gap, providing an ape-like jaw associated with a huge (almost human) cranial cavity, in an early Pleistocene environment, probably close to a million years old. Most of the experts accepted it at face value, vying with each other in reconstructing models of the whole body of this "missing link."

The unraveling of the plot took several decades, initially spurred by the discovery of other skulls of equal antiquity all over the world, none of which suggested that brain size had led the way in the evolution of early man—the Piltdown skull simply didn't fit. It eventually turned out to be a modern human skull, only 2,000 years old, and the jawbone was practically yesterday's, subsequently identified by anatomists as coming from an orangutan. All the bones had been carefully stained to give the superficial appearance of great antiquity.

Who was the culprit? Nobody knows for certain. Many theories have been proposed, and almost everyone concerned has been implicated by one or another of them. The most recent book, *Piltdown: A Scientific Forgery* by F. Spencer, points the finger of guilt at Sir Arthur Keith (one of the reconstructors), who would have had ready access to both orangutan and human remains and is said to have been driven by insane ambition for a leading place in the world of science. (If true, is there a parallel with modern fraud—fame rather than fortune as the underlying motive?)

Related Place to Visit: Piltdown.

The Recent Past and Present

Watson and Crick: The Birth of Molecular Biology. The elucidation in 1953 of the molecular structure of DNA, the celebrated "double helix," was surely the greatest biological discovery of the twentieth century. Curiously, it happened in Cambridge's Cavendish Laboratory, the very same place where so much history was made in pure physics. This was no accident but the result of the conviction of many individuals, especially Lawrence Bragg, then director of the Cavendish, that a blending of the methods of structural physics with biological insight would produce proud results. That notion must have been coupled with indulgent flexibility by the managers of Britain's relatively meager postwar resources, for there cannot initially have been much hope of success for such a far-out project. The detailed story of the actual progress on this problem, and toward related discoveries that were made in Cambridge about the same time, has a uniquely English flavor—an important factor was obligatory afternoon tea in the common room and the exchange of ideas that went along with it. (Two successful popular books have been written about the discovery by the protagonists themselves: *What Mad Pursuits* by Francis Crick and *The Double Helix* by James Watson. Read them both to get two very different pictures of genius in the laboratory.)

The DNA problem goes to the core of the basis of life. The genetic information carried by the DNA of a single cell contains billions of bits of information, the blueprint for how an organism is built and how it functions. It only takes a difference of about 1 bit per 1,000 to mark one individual human being as distinct from another; differences of the order of 1/100 take us from one animal species to another; differences in the order of 1/10 from an animal to a plant. A single mutation (only one bit altered) at a critical spot can be lethal. How does DNA code this information? How are true error-free copies made over and over again when cells divide? How is the paternal and maternal mix of characteristics achieved in sexual reproduction? How is the information within DNA expressed? (We now know that proteins, not DNA, are the *working molecules* of living cells that determine what a cell is capable of doing. The last question in the foregoing list can thus be paraphrased: How can DNA dictate the primary structures of proteins that a cell actually synthesizes?)

The bold step taken in answering these questions—the genius, if you like, of Watson and Crick and the underlying Cambridge philosophy—was to go directly to the three dimensional atomic structure of DNA, bypassing all kinds of unsolved problems that still lined the road between genetics and chemistry.

Watson and Crick did not themselves do the experimental x-ray diffraction studies that formed the basis of the structure determination, but they did the interpreting of the photographic array of spots that the diffracted x-rays produce, and they did it with their minds and pencil and .paper, for the computer programs one would now use had not yet been written. The double helix was the result, and, as it happens, this particular structure by itself virtually solves the problem of how genetic material replicates itself. The mutual alignment of the two helices leaves very little to the imagination.

Once this problem was solved, a whole army of scientists all over the world was able to work out how DNA code is translated into the structure of proteins, how DNA is damaged and repaired, and how it can be mutated—all the processes necessary for survival of living organisms. This is a true example of the old adage "a picture is worth a thousand words." The helical structure allows the scientist to ask his questions in an entirely new way and to design problem-solving experiments that he could never have thought of without the picture before him.

Viruses, Muscles, and Nerves. Cambridge continues to stand in the forefront of research in molecular biology, which of course now has its own buildings and budget, quite separate from the Cavendish Laboratory. Atomic arrangements within the molecules of viruses are gradually being elucidated. The molecules involved in muscle contraction are being identified and studied. The processes of nerve stimulation and conduction are gradually becoming understood. "Structure" is still the key word and x-rays are still a primary experimental tool. But no other biological molecule has ever been found to yield its secrets as readily as DNA did—the simplicity of the double helical structure was a unique result.

Related Place to Visit: Cambridge.

PRINCIPAL PLACES TO VISIT

London and Environs

The city of London is less emotional about its heroes than some other capital cities and this urban restraint extends to its scientists and their discoveries. There is not much glorification here, apart from the one official catchall shrine of honor, Westminster Abbey. It is particularly unfortunate that some of the early sites we would like to visit no longer exist. The Royal College of Physicians, for example, founded in 1518 by Thomas Linacre and subsequently the scientific base for William Gilbert and William Harvey, was destroyed by the Great Fire of London in 1666. (There is a plaque at Warwick Lane, between St. Paul's and the Old Bailey, to indicate a former location, but that refers to its second home, occupied from 1674 to 1825.) The original Gresham College was also damaged in the Great Fire, but was repaired and back in use by 1674—only to fall victim to commercial urban developments later on. The outskirts of London have fared a little better. The Greenwich Observatory is preserved.

BRITISH MUSEUM (Great Russell St. WC1)

This is one of greatest museums of the world, but mainly dedicated to the arts and civilizations of past ages.

One science-related item is the Rosetta stone, displayed in the Egyptian Sculpture Gallery on the ground floor. It contains the trilingual text—hieroglyphic, demotic, and Greek—of a decree issued on the first anniversary of the coronation of Ptolemy V, King of Egypt. The text, finely chiseled on a slab of black basalt, is still clearly legible except where the surface itself has been damaged. Posters mounted beside the stone give an account of its history and the Anglo-French rivalry that was part of it. Officers of the French army made the discovery and recognized its importance, but the stone came to England as one of the spoils of war. Thomas Young, the great polymath of British science around 1800, vied with the Frenchman Jean Champollion in the decipherment of the hieroglyphics. Young was the first to recognize that some hieroglyphics were alphabetical characters in spite of their pictorial appearance. He published all his evidence for this conclusion, but Champollion stuck for some time with the more conventional view that they were all pictographs. Young, in turn, was wrong in many of his specific assignments and Champollion, eventually won over to the alphabetical theory, is credited with the definitive transliteration of the text. (However, it took a new bilingual text, discovered later in another place, to convince Champollion and set him off in the right direction—he never acknowledged Young's priority for the basic underlying *idea.*)

The British Museum is open seven days a week. Telephone 071-636-1555.

DOWNE (near Farnborough, Kent, 14 miles south of central London)

Charles Darwin's search for a suitable home, as described in his autobiography, strikes a familiar note: "After several fruitless searches in Surrey and elsewhere, we found this house and purchased it." The house was Down House, a secluded property at the edge of the village of Downe, and it was to remain Darwin's home from 1842 until his death in 1882. Almost the entire body of his work originated here. The preservation of the house as a national memorial is due to the benevolence of a London surgeon, Sir George Buckston Browne, who stepped in to prevent its sale in 1927. It is now partially restored as it was in Darwin's

Down House, where Darwin wrote *The Origin of Species.*

lifetime and its spacious grounds, too, are being maintained, so that the visitor can walk in the same gardens that served as rest and inspiration for the originator of the theory of evolution. (The house itself was and still is rather ordinary in external features. Darwin added the bay windows in the back as soon as he moved in and the veranda in 1874.)

The ground floor of Down House serves as a museum. The drawing room and the "Old Study," are furnished more or less exactly as they were when Darwin lived here. The study was his daily workplace for 35 years and we can see the chair by the window where he did his writing, with a cloth-covered lapboard on which to rest the paper; his microscope rests on the ledge of the other window. The study is in the front of the house and the windows face the public lane which runs alongside. Darwin had the road level lowered and put in the wall we now see in order to gain more privacy, but passers-by on horseback could still look in.

The most interesting part of the visit is the "Charles Darwin Room," formerly the dining room, now a display room for paintings, photographs, and showcases of memorabilia. It contains a model of HMS *Beagle*, for example. Another room is devoted to manuscripts and books of grandfather Erasmus Darwin, and the "New Study" (Darwin's workplace after 1877) houses a rather superficial exhibit on evolution, from when the earth was "a mass of whirling gases" until the appearance of modern man.

Down House is open afternoons from March to December 15, but closed on Mondays and Tuesdays. Telephone 0689-859119. The upper floors are presently occupied by private tenants, but there are plans afoot to convert the entire building to a Darwin study center.

GEOLOGICAL SOCIETY OF LONDON
(off Piccadilly)

The creation of this society in 1807 was controversial, perceived by many as an unwarranted intrusion on traditional turf of the Royal Society. It has an intriguing meeting room with opposing benches, as in the House of Commons, rather than the standard auditorium structure—quite appropriate in view of the many huge professional arguments that have taken place here. There is a bust of Charles Lyell in the library and pictures of other famous geologists hang on the walls. One painting on the staircase is a depiction of some of the principal figures in the Piltdown case in the process of examining the famous skull. This building is not open to the general public, but anyone with even a remote professional interest can walk in and at least see the library.

GREENWICH
(7 miles east of the center of London)

The construction of the Royal Observatory was ordered in 1674 by King Charles II to solve the problem of determining longitude for ships at sea. He said "let it be done in royal fashion"; he wanted none of his shipowners and sailors deprived of any help the heavens could supply. As it turned out, the problem of making sufficiently accurate astronomical observations from the unsteady deck of a ship proved too difficult, and eventually it was an alternative method based on precise time-keeping that won out. The scientific basis for the latter is the familiar difference in time between two places, which is in direct proportion to the difference in longitude. Local time on board ship is easy to measure by using sunrise or sunset to calibrate one's watch, but where does one get an *accurate* reference time with which to compare it? Parliament offered a prize of £20,000 for the solution to the problem in 1714, but the prize was not awarded until 1773, when a Yorkshireman, John Harrison, proved able to construct a chronometer that would not deviate for weeks on end from the chosen reference time, which we now call *Greenwich time*.

The smoke and street lights of the city have forced the working Greenwich Observatory to move away into the countryside, but happily the historic buildings have been preserved and now constitute a part of the National Maritime Museum, which is arguably the single most spectacular scientific tourist destination in all of England. As expected, the major emphasis is on the reading of celestial position and on accurate clocks.

One of the old buildings is Flamsteed House, which was designed by Christopher Wren for the first Astronomer Royal and has been authentically restored. (Its ground floor and basement served as residence for successive Astronomers Royal until 1948.) Of equal interest is the Meridian House added later. The Greenwich meridian is *formally defined* by the center of the astronomical transit instrument in this building. We actually see two meridians marked on the ground, one corresponding to the transit instrument of James Bradley (used

Flamsteed House, designed by Sir Christopher Wren "for the observator's habitation and a little for pomp." The ball on the turret (red in color) was added in 1833. It was the world's first visual time signal, and it is still raised and dropped at precisely 1 P.M. each day. The line running across the picture from left to right is the Greenwich meridian.

from 1750 to 1850) and the other to the instrument installed in 1851 by George Airy, the seventh Astronomer Royal. The lines are 19 feet apart, which is equivalent to 0.02 seconds of transit time—then too small to be significant. Within the building we have a collection of astrolabes and other astronomical tools. The most impressive are the huge protractor-like calibrated devices for measuring elevation above the horizon (quadrants, sectants, octants). Historical plaques are everywhere—their reports of the quarrels between Flamsteed and Halley are especially interesting.

The principal building of the Maritime Museum is actually a few minutes walk away from the old observatory, housed in an architectural masterpiece, the Queen's House, designed by Inigo Jones and completed in 1635 before the observatory was even contemplated. It houses ship models, navigational instruments, and sea charts—and, most important, clocks, providing a fascinating visual history of the improvement in chronometry. The prize-winning chronometer of John Harrison, still in working order, is included. There are also many items on display relating to the explorations of Captain Cook.

The museum and old observatory are open seven days a week. Telephone 081-858-4422.

NATURAL HISTORY MUSEUM
(Cromwell Rd., SW7)

The Natural History Museum and the Geological Museum used to be separate entities but are now combined. The main building is a fantastic architectural structure, well worth viewing for its own sake. The principal exhibits in the

Natural History Museum include dinosaurs and their living relatives, man's place in evolution, human biology, and living and fossil mammals. The museum has recently undergone a major administrative reorganization and now leans toward "trendy" presentations, ostensibly to lure an otherwise uninterested public.

The formerly separate Geological Museum has a good exhibit called *Story of the Earth*, but without names of people or any reference to the titanic struggles that often took place to establish individual chapters of the story. This is a pity because many of the controversies make fascinating stories. The exhibit does, however, accurately present the current views on the origin of sun, earth, and moon, describes the inner core of the earth, the surrounding mantle and the outer crust; it has up-to-date accounts of very modern topics, such as reversal of magnetic field and plate tectonics.

A fascinating organization in the museum's "back rooms" is the International Commission on Zoological Nomenclature, the body responsible for keeping track of the scientific names of all species of the animal kingdom (fossils as well as alive) and for assigning names to new species—15,000 new species names are added to the zoological literature each year! The commission's quarters are not open to the public, but visitors with any legitimate interest are warmly received. (The "back rooms" of the museum have recently been subjected to controversial administrative changes with the objective of diminishing scholarly activities. The future is somewhat uncertain.)

A statue commemorating Richard Owen, founder of the museum but also resolute opponent of Darwinism, stands impressively on the staircase. The story of its erection (at the expense of a statue of Charles Darwin) is told on p. 88.

The museum is open seven days a week. Telephone 071-725-7866 or 071-589-6323.

ROYAL INSTITUTION
(Albemarle St., off Piccadilly)

The Royal Institution is famous for its unique public lectures, its chemical and physical researches, and, above all, as the home and laboratory of Michael Faraday. The Faraday Museum (in the basement) includes Faraday's magnetic laboratory, restored to its original size and condition, and all manner of Faraday apparatus. Especially prominent is the giant electromagnet that Faraday built to demonstrate the weak diamagnetism of substances previously thought to be nonmagnetic. An upstairs gallery displays equipment used by other institute scientists, such as Humphry Davy. The lecture hall and paintings of famous lecturers in action are regrettably in parts of the institute not open to the public.

A statue of Faraday stands in the entrance vestibule, at the foot of the staircase. It was commissioned by a group of public-spirited citizens (chaired by the Prince of Wales), who wanted to erect a suitable memorial in Westminster Abbey. But the family was adamant that no statue should exist in a church that Faraday would never have entered himself, and so it came to rest here at the

Michael Faraday giving the Christmas lecture at the Royal Institution in 1856. Prince Albert is in the front row with the future King Edward VII beside him.

Royal Institution. A small plaque was eventually placed in Westminster Abbey in 1931.

The museum is open afternoons, Tuesday and Thursday only. Telephone 071-409-2992.

ROYAL SOCIETY

The original meeting place for the Royal Society was at Gresham College (destroyed in the great fire of 1666). It has, subsequently, had a number of homes: Arundel House in the Strand, a building on Crane Court (off Fleet Street), then Burlington House off Piccadilly, and now on Carlton House Terrace, above "The Mall" leading out from Buckingham Palace. The Crane Court house was used during Newton's presidency. On May 2, 1715, Newton, Halley, and other notable figures observed a total eclipse of the sun from the roof of the building. The time of the eclipse had been accurately predicted by Halley. (Crane Court today is lined by law offices, but it retains the narrow seclusion of the days of yore. There is no plaque.)

ST. BARTHOLOMEW'S HOSPITAL (Holborn, EC1)

William Harvey was chief physician here from 1609 to 1643. A clinical ward and a small building are named after him but none of the actual buildings in which he worked remains. St. Bartholomew the Great, the City's oldest and perhaps most interesting church, is close by.

SCIENCE MUSEUM
(Exhibition Road, South Kensington, SW7)

The Science Museum has a remarkably comprehensive scope. Its full name is "The National Museum of Science and Industry" and it of course includes the eye-catching products of technology that every museum of this kind must show: Stephenson's locomotive, a 1905 Rolls-Royce, a reconstruction of the Apollo 10 command module and lunar lander, for example. But the overall collection, augmented by dioramas and posters, manages also to give an encyclopedic kind of overview of pure science: all fields are represented, virtually every advance or discovery mentioned in our book makes its brief appearance here with a few words and a picture or two. It is all too much to take in on a single visit, and we note that multiple visits are encouraged by a very modest price for an annual pass as compared to the one-time entrance fee.

Specific items include (on the ground floor) a modern version of Foucault's pendulum, less impressive than the original because of a quite small amplitude of pendulous swing. The second floor has a good exhibit on nuclear physics, the atom bomb, and useful nuclear energy, including, for example, a picture of the Hahn and Meitner apparatus in the German Museum in Munich and an explanation of why Hahn did not at first appreciate what he had wrought (see under "Germany" for our account). The chemistry rooms on the same floor show atomic models from Dalton's wooden spheres to the most modern representations. The third floor has more on physics—heat and thermodynamics, electricity and magnetism, optics, and so on.

Biochemistry and cell biology are well represented (on the second floor) with a large display on "Living Molecules"—DNA, proteins, antibodies, muscle filaments, and so on. An unusual item is a Svedberg ultracentrifuge, a huge instrument in which solutions containing large molecules are exposed to very high centrifugal fields in cells in which the resulting outward sedimentation can be followed by optical methods. (The characterization of macromolecules that can be obtained by this means has loomed large in the biophysical research done by the authors of this book during their days in the laboratory. We admit to some nostalgia on seeing Svedberg's original design.)

The fourth and fifth floors of the museum, smaller in area than the others, house the Wellcome Museum of the History of Medicine. It includes 40 tableaux giving glimpses of medical history from neolithic times to the present. It shows a model of the Padua anatomy theater, for example, and such scenes as Joseph Lister having disinfectant sprayed around his operating table. An upper gallery has a somewhat more systematic historical orientation, with successive periods (Tribal Society, Oriental, Mesopotamia and Egypt, etc.) each given its own specific section.

. Special exhibits often supplement the more permanent ones and may cause some inconvenience to the visitor. In 1991 a large display of Japanese robotics caused some minor problems in finding one's way around, and a section devoted exclusively to Faraday on the bicentenary of his birth proved to be in poor taste, with garishly colored lights and a gigantic statue of the scientist activating all types of electrical devices, including kitchen mixers and electrical saws—there was even an attendant dressed to resemble Faraday in person.

The museum is open seven days a week. Telephone 071-589-3456 or 071-938-8111.

UPMINSTER
(Essex, 19 miles east of central London)

William Derham (1657–1735) was Rector of Upminister for nearly 50 years from 1689 until his death. He was a Fellow of the Royal Society, delivered the Boyle lectures at the Royal Society in 1711 and 1712, and wrote books about John Ray, Robert Hooke, and their work. His best known exploit is the measurement of the velocity of sound in 1705, which led to what is now regarded as a black mark on the record of Isaac Newton. Newton had made a crude measurement in the Great Court at Trinity College, leading to a value of 968 feet/second (293m/sec) whereas Derham made a much more accurate measurement of 1,142 feet/second (346 m/sec). The Derham measurement involved prearranged firing of cannon at half-hour intervals by a gunnery unit stationed at Blackheath 12.5 miles (20 km) away. Derham could see the flash from the tower of the Upminster church and then could hear the sound a little later. His published report is an exemplary model of a careful experiment, including all manner of controls on the validity of the research, e.g., barrels of the gun were pointed toward Upminster in some firings but in the opposite direction in others without effect on the result.

No blame, of course, attaches to Newton's inaccurate experiment, based, as it was, on a very short travel path in comparison with Derham's 12.5 miles. What gives Newton a black mark is that he theoretically *predicted* a value near 968 feet/second in the first edition of *Principia*, and then deliberately manipulated some of the parameters in the *prediction* in a later edition in order to arrive precisely at Derham's result. (It wasn't really dishonest, because the parameters were what we now call "guesstimates," but it was distinctly self-serving.)

St. Laurence church in Upminster is still the parish church, standing close to the business center of the town. The building is quite unremarkable, except for the crucial tower, which dates from the thirteenth century. It has a wooden pointed top, high enough to stand out over all the surrounding buildings. We didn't check to see whether Blackheath is still visible from it. There is a tablet on the wall inside the church at the base of the tower, listing all the rectors from 1336 onward. A modest framed notice beneath it draws attention to the life and deeds of William Derham, without specifically mentioning the measurement of the velocity of sound. One of the utilitarian outbuildings of the church is named Derham Hall and carries a similar explanatory inscription.

Upminster is served both by Underground and British Rail. The station is close to the church.

WESTMINSTER ABBEY

There are no "two cultures" in this place of national remembrance—scientists and other celebrities are memorialized side-by-side. Isaac Newton's tomb is one of the grandest in the Abbey. Lord Kelvin is buried at his side and also has a huge window in his honor. Altogether about 30 scientists are represented. Some, like Newton and Kelvin, were actually buried here; others have memorials in the Abbey but are buried elsewhere. One scientist, geologist William Buckland (memorial in the South Aisle), was actually Dean of Westminster from 1845 to 1856. Few of the memorials attempt an account of the basis for honorable recognition. James Prescott Joule is an exception, described as "establishing the Law of the Conservation of Energy," and Charles Lyell is another, cited for "deciphering the fragmentary records of the earth's history."

Some Abbey funerals are noteworthy. Irish Archbishop James Ussher, not a scientist by modern standards, perhaps, but judged to be one in his time, was buried here in 1656 (in the Chapel of St. Paul). It was the time of the Puritan Commonwealth, but Oliver Cromwell ordered that the Anglican funeral service, then normally forbidden, should be used in deference to Ussher's status. Newton's funeral in 1727 was attended by Voltaire and has been described by him—the body lay in state in the Jerusalem Chamber (public access through the Deanery) and was followed to its grave by all of the Fellows of the Royal Society. The 1912 funeral service for surgeon Lord Lister (memorial in the North Choir aisle) has been described by Sir William Osler—the Abbey was packed to the door with nurses, students, and doctors, and there were reserved seats for representatives from all over Europe. We know of no scientist who was refused admission, as Lord Byron was when his funeral cortège reached the door in 1824—poetic genius eventually won out over moral objections, and a memorial was erected for him in 1969.

Visitors should remember that the Abbey is a church and will not admit sightseers when a service is in progress. Note also that there is an admission charge to pass beyond the nave, which one must do to see the famous poets' corner and the majority of the scientists' memorials. The *Official Guide*, available from the shop outside the Abbey, is indispensable for anyone seeking to locate a particular person.

Plaques and Other Miscellany in the City of London. London has many plaques marking the homes (or sites of homes) of previous illustrious residents. A recent book, *The Blue Plaques of London*, includes Henry Cavendish, 11 Bedford Square, WC1; Charles Darwin, Biological Science Building, University College,

110 Gower Street, WC1; Michael Faraday, 48 Blandford Street, W1; Benjamin Franklin, 36 Craven Street, WC2; Joseph Lister, 12 Park Crescent, NW1; Charles Lyell, 73 Harley Street, W1; and Isaac Newton, 87 Jermyn Street, SW1. One plaque not listed in the book is on the house occupied by James Clerk Maxwell (of Scotland) when he was professor at King's College (1860–1866)—it is at 16 Palace Gardens Terrace, W8, just west of Kensington Gardens.

Michael Faraday is buried in Highgate Cemetery because his religious convictions forbade the ostentation of Westminster Abbey. The grave is in the relatively neglected western section of the cemetery, not as freely accessible as the eastern section, where Karl Marx and some popular literary figures are interred.

There are few outdoor statues in London, but there is one of Sigmund Freud (a strange choice?) outside the public library at Swiss Cottage (South Hampstead, NW8). The **National Portrait Gallery** (off Trafalgar Square) has portraits of practically everybody, from royalty to entrepreneurs. Rooms 6, 7, and 14 are devoted to scientists and engineers.

South and West England

AVEBURY (near Marlborough, Wiltshire)

We find here the largest prehistoric earthwork and stone circle in Britain, so large that much of the village of Avebury and the highway that runs through it lie within the circle. Unlike Stonehenge, this is not an isolated monument but part of an area rich with other remains, attesting to continuous occupation from 3500 B.C., much earlier than the circle itself. Peripheral places of interest include a stone-lined avenue leading to a burial site a mile away. A museum contains pottery, tools, stone axes, and the like and explains the local history. We are told that the people who lived here did not yet have the use of the wheel, which makes their grand construction projects all the more remarkable.

(Avebury was first recognized for what it is by John Aubrey, one of the earliest fellows of the Royal Society, who surveyed the area for Charles II. Aubrey is best known for his book, *Brief Lives*, which contains crisp character sketches of several of his Royal Society colleagues.)

The site is visitor-friendly, with well-marked footpaths, large car parks, and pubs for food and drink. Everything is open all year.

BATH (Avon)

Bath was a spa resort at the time of the Roman occupation of England and has ever since remained a fashionable place to live or visit. The celebrated Royal Crescent (built 1767–1774) is one of the most graceful and beautiful examples of domestic architecture in all of England. Bath's perhaps unexpected association with science stems from the presence here of William and Caroline Herschel, who actually came to Bath as musicians, William as organist of the fashionable Octagon Chapel and Caroline as a vocalist. But they started to build telescopes and map the skies and eventually acquired fame and royal patronage as astronomers. They left in 1782 at the King's command to take up residence and set up their telescopes close to Windsor Castle.

Herschel's house at 19 New King Street, where he lived and worked from 1777 to 1782 (and where the planet Uranus was discovered) is now a museum, located close to the city's main tourist sights. The telescopes, built with the help of another brother, Alexander, were the reflecting kind, with about the best resolving power of any instruments of his day. William cast the mirrors himself, using the special alloy *speculum*, and Alexander built the bodies out of wood. Brightly varnished, they are beautiful to behold. There is a replica in the museum on the ground floor. Visitors may be intrigued by a picture on the wall, showing practically everybody in the world of science around 1800, supposedly assembled together for discussion at the Royal Institution in London. Herschel is there, of course, together with Cavendish, Dalton, Jenner, Rumford, Watt, and many others. This picture actually represents an imaginary scene, painted in 1862—no such assembly ever took place.

The work rooms where the telescopes were built are in the basement of the museum and they are more or less intact—old tools and lenses are present. Upstairs is a reconstructed music room, furnished to give an idea of what it might have looked like in Herschel's day. It has an old pianoforte and the organ keyboard rescued from the old Octagon Chapel when it was converted to other use. (The Chapel is on Milsom Street and now houses the National Center of Photography.)

The museum is open daily from March to October. Telephone 0225–336228. Other places where Herschel telescopes may be seen include the Whipple Museum in Cambridge and the Teylers Museum in Haarlem, the Netherlands.

BERKELEY (Gloucestershire)

Berkeley, about halfway between Gloucester and Bristol, is far enough away from the main road to have remained a quiet little market town. Teashops outnumber service stations. Little old ladies wander around the town, visiting the historic castle and the ancient church of St. Mary-the-Virgin. Edward Jenner's father (Stephen) was vicar of the church from 1729 to 1755, and Edward was born in the vicarage. Later on, when he could afford it, he purchased the Chantry, a fine mansion adjacent to the church, which remained his home for the rest of his life. It now houses the Jenner Museum (established in 1985).

The museum contains all kinds of memorabilia and includes a picture of the humble old vicarage where Jenner was born. (The Chantry itself served as home of the vicars of Berkeley from 1885 to 1980.) The exhibits include papers dating from the days when Jenner was a naturalist, including one on the unfriendly nesting habits of the cuckoo and another on bird migration. Jenner's old study is preserved and contains some nineteenth century surgical instruments, including one of the multi-pointed devices (for penetration below skin surface) that were used for vaccinations from his day until well into modern times. There is a separate "all about smallpox" room, with a gruesome picture of someone ill with smallpox, covered densely from head to toe with huge ugly pustules. All of Jenner's medals and honors are here and copies of contemporary humorous cartoons.

Another room is dedicated to the World Health Organization. Short films are shown here on the nature and course of smallpox and on its worldwide eradication by the WHO-sponsored vaccination program. One film detailing Jenner's life and work is done in cartoon form for children. On the outside are pretty gardens and tucked away in a corner is a little thatched hut, the *Temple of Vaccinia*. It was built for Jenner by an eccentric friend and poor people came there to be vaccinated free of charge. Inside are the shoulder blade and scapula of a whale, reputedly dissected by Jenner in 1788.

Next to the Chantry is the Church of St. Mary-the-Virgin, parts of which date back to the twelfth century. The chancel of the church, at the east end, is where Jenner and members of his family are buried. The stained glass east window of the church was put in explicitly in honor of Edward Jenner in 1873. It shows scenes from the Bible of Jesus healing the sick, mostly by the laying on of hands. There is nothing that has to do specifically with smallpox or Jenner. (It is

The Temple of Vaccinia, where Jenner gave free vaccinations for those who could not afford to pay.

quite different in that respect from the Pasteur mausoleum in Paris, where the decorations are exclusively in praise of Louis Pasteur!) Other local celebrities are buried inside the Berkeley church, including Thomas, Lord of Berkeley (1326–1361), who was the lord of the castle at the time when Edward II was murdered there in 1327.

The museum is open from April to September and on Sundays in October. Telephone 0453-810631.

BLACK NOTLEY (near Braintree, Essex)

This is a tranquil village in the midst of farming country. John Ray was born here in 1627, the son of a poor blacksmith. He first set out to be a theologian, but the wonder of the flowers of the countryside drove him to botany instead. He became an academic, close to home in Cambridge. He explored much of Britain and the European Continent with his friend Francis Willughby. After the latter's early death Ray lived for a while in Willughby's Warwickshire manor house, but eventually he came back here, and it was here that much of his published work was actually written. We can see "John Ray Cottage," his father's forge, where he was born. The village also has a "John Ray Garden" with a little formal maze.

Ray is buried in the graveyard of the church of St. Peter and Paul, which stands well outside the modern village, opposite an immense farmyard with a large sixteenth-century wooden barn. The location suggests that the church was once part of an old estate and manor house. Ray's grave is identified by a tall tombstone next to the church entrance. The original Latin inscriptions on its sides are badly worn and difficult to read, but a modern inscription and plaque were put on by the Ray Society in 1984. (An English translation of the original was put up inside the church at the same time.) Note that there is also a fine monument to Ray in the city of Braintree, just a few miles from Black Notley.

CALNE (near Chippenham, Wiltshire)

Joseph Priestley was in the service of the politically ambitious Earl of Shelburne from 1773 to 1780, formally as librarian, but actually as an aide of broader usefulness, a sort of resident intellectual. Bowood House, about two miles (3.2 km) west of Calne, was (and still is) the country home of the Shelburnes, and Priestley used to spend his summers here and his winters at the Earl's London house. Shelburne encouraged and financed Priestley's scientific work. The studies of gases, summarized in the famous book *Experiments and Observations on Different Kinds of Air*, were mostly done during this period, the discovery of oxygen being made at Bowood House on August 1, 1774, in a small room set aside specifically as a laboratory for Priestley. These were courtly surroundings indeed, for a man who championed proletarian revolution.

Bowood House, where Priestley discovered oxygen.

A leaflet for visitors explains that the estate has "been added to or reduced, reflecting social changes and family fortunes, like the continual movement of the tides." In fact, what used to be the "big house" was demolished in 1955. The orangery and its attendant pavilions remain, and they contain the Shelburne library, Priestley's laboratory next door to it, a chapel, a sculpture gallery, a picture gallery, and plenty of space for the family residence and servant quarters. The laboratory has none of Priestley's equipment, but it contains original letters from Priestley to the Earl about Priestley's scientific work and his supervision of the education of the Earl's children. The adjacent library is decorated by 16 huge black basalt vases with so-called "Etruscan" designs, which were made for the family in 1813 by Josiah Wedgwood II, but represent a style popularized much earlier by the first Josiah Wedgwood. As the main text explains, the latter provided Priestley with much of his scientific ceramic ware—presumably lacking "Etruscan" adornments.

The Bowood grounds (100 acres) are elegantly landscaped and include a lake with a Doric temple on its banks, terraced gardens leading up to the main house entrance, an arboretum, and much more. To aid the family fortunes there is now a commercial garden center with "pick-your-own" fields, an adventure playground for children, a licensed restaurant, and a tea room.

The house and grounds are open daily from April to early November. Telephone 0249–812102.

CAMBRIDGE

Where else can we find so much of the history of British science?

Trinity College heads the list, one of the group of splendid colleges whose green lawns back onto the river Cam. Its Great Court, entered from Trinity

Street through the main portal, is the largest of its kind—with central fountain, ancient sundial, the college chapel on the north side, the colorful great gate, and the clocktower adjacent to it, it is one of the most impressive sights in the town. The clock, incidentally, strikes the hours twice in succession, first in deep bass and then in a lighter tone.

The appearance of the college has changed remarkably little since Newton came here as a student in 1661 for what would prove to be his residence for more than 30 years. His rooms (for the last half of his stay) were in front, above the porter's lodge, between the main portal and the chapel. He had his own steps (now gone) leading down to a little garden below and on to Trinity Street. The chapel has a rather large vestibule, which today contains a statue of Newton alongside other distinguished Trinity Fellows: Francis Bacon (long before Newton); Isaac Barrow, Newton's predecessor as Lucasian Professor, who was the first to recognize Newton's genius and nominated him as successor when he himself resigned in 1669; William Whewell, the "name-giver"—his statue gives a good idea of the man's rugged physical frame, to which reference is often made. Stones in the ante-chapel floor and plaques on the wall commemorate other Trinitarian celebrities (by no means all scientists): philosopher Bertrand Russell, mathematicians G. H. Hardy and A. N. Whitehead, poet A. E. Housman, to name only a few.

On the west side of the court is the Hall (the college dining area), where Queen Anne came to dine in 1705 before conferring knighthood on Newton. Behind the Hall (access through its foyer) is a separate smaller court with the college library, a dignified classical building designed by Christopher Wren. It contains busts of John Ray and Francis Willughby at the entrance and numerous busts on the bookcases—Newton is there, but most of them are popular celebrities unrelated to the college, such as Shakespeare and Julius Caesar. The library is, of course, in constant use and only open to the public during the lunch period. Even then part of it is roped off for the sole use of readers and this part contains the library's greatest treasure, nearly a thousand volumes of Newton's personal collection. He is known to have had more than 1,750 books in his personal library, a prodigious number considering the date: There were about as many on alchemy and chemistry as on physics and mathematics.

Adjacent to Trinity is **Caius College,** where William Harvey was an undergraduate in the 1590s, and next to that is **King's College,** with its famous chapel. Not all the colleges are along the river. **Christ's College,** for example, is near the city center. It was the college attended by Charles Darwin.

Cambridge college precincts, chapels, and so forth, are normally open to the public for at least part of each day. Trinity College Library is open from 12 to 2 P.M., Monday to Friday. One must apply in writing to the Librarian to see Newton's books.

The *Cavendish Laboratory,* a historical shrine for physicists, as well as the place where Watson and Crick ushered in the modern era of molecular biology in 1953, was on Free School Lane, a narrow street just a couple of hundred yards

The old Cavendish Laboratory on Free School Lane.

from King's College. The site was abandoned for more modern quarters in 1974, and the building is now the home of a miscellany of minor university acitivities. A plaque reminds us of its days of greatness, and the Maxwell lecture theater remains still the locale for undergraduate physics lectures. The new Cavendish Laboratory is about a mile and a half to the west, on Madingley Road, on a lovely site, with its own pond and adjacent to open fields. It has a small museum in the middle one of its three buildings (the Bragg building), which contains Maxwell's handwritten list of the original equipment, Lord Rutherford's desk, apparatus old and new, many photographs, and other memorabilia. Current research is particularly strong in radioastronomy and superconductivity.

Cambridge Museums. Also on Free School Lane is the **Whipple Museum** for the history of science, small, but well planned and worth a visit. Navigational devices, chronometers, mensuration tools, and calculating machines of a previous age are well displayed, accompanied by explanations in lay language of exactly how each device was used and its importance to man's social or economic well-being. Of particular interest is the display of Napier's Bones, a calculating device John Napier invented before he thought of logarithms (see under "Scotland").

Around the corner on Pembroke Street is the **Sedgwick Museum** for geology, named after Adam Sedgwick (1785–1873), who was Woodwardian Professor of Geology for more than 50 years, from 1818 until his death. Sedgwick had been a tutor at Trinity College without any training in geology when the Woodwardian chair became vacant. Bored with his job of drilling students for the mathematics tripos, he applied for it and was accepted. Field trips at once began to take the place of dreary tutorials and an outstanding career was on its way.

John Woodward (1665–1728), for whom this endowed chair is named, provided the nucleus for the museum's collection of fossils, which are still to be seen in their original cabinets. Woodward had considered the fossils as testimony in support of the Biblical story of Noah's flood, a view that was, of course, no longer held in Sedgwick's time. The present museum has a vast display of everything from giant dinosaur skeletons to tiny mollusks. One of the best exhibits, formed by specimens collected just a few miles from Cambridge, gives a grand notion of the local fauna 120,000 years ago during the last interglacial period—hippopotamus, lion, elephant, rhinoceros, hyena, and so forth—just like central Africa today!

The Sedgwick Museum is open throughout the year, Monday to Friday and Saturday mornings. Telephone 0223-333456. The Whipple Museum is open weekday afternoons, but may be closed outside term time. Telephone 0223-334540.

CANTERBURY (Kent)

When you make your pilgrimage to the celebrated cathedral, don't fail to visit the King's School, lying within the cathedral precincts on the north side, one of the oldest schools in Britain. Thomas Linacre was an early scientific student

The King's School behind Canterbury Cathedral. No girls were admitted in Harvey's time.

here around 1475, while the school was still a monastic institution. Henry VIII established the present secular grammar school in 1541 after he had confiscated the monastic properties; Richard Boyle, the father of Robert Boyle, and William Harvey were among the subsequently famous boys in the 1580s. The school has always been (and still is) a most rigorous school, its statutes calling for expulsion of any boy "remarkable for extraordinary slowness and dullness or for a disposition repugnant to learning" in order that "he may not like a drone devour the honey of the bees." Is this where the often crude and rapacious Earl of Cork (Richard Boyle) received the germ of inspiration for better things, resulting in his sending his sons Robert and Francis to Europe for an expensive and rigorous education?

Today's school retains the high standards of those days, but of course admits girls as well as boys. It has 700 pupils and an annual fee around £10,000 per pupil. One difference from the old days is the absence of choristers, members of the cathedral choir, subject to less stringent educational requirements than the rest. They actually persisted until after World War II, when a separate choir school was created for them.

Note: For foreign visitors King's School may be a particularly convenient way to see an English "Public School" in action. Access is easy—just continue north beyond the infirmary cloisters in the cathedral precincts. The school has recently expanded across Broad Street into what used to be a training college for monks and the stream of students crossing the street from one class to the next provides an alternative signpost to the main part of the campus. Note that the pupils wear uniforms, including the obligatory wing collar for boys. Purple robes designate prefects, the peer group guardians of law and order at all such institutions. Classes are held mostly in the mornings, afternoons being devoted to other activities: organized sports on some days and socially relevant projects on others—the latter a truly modern touch.

COLCHESTER (Essex)

In Colchester they spell Gilbert's name with a "*d*"—William Gilberd—and his modern descendants use the same spelling. *Tymperleys*, the fine Elizabethan timbered house where he was born, still stands on Trinity Street, added to and remodeled many times, but in its present state meticulously faithful to the original design. The property was purchased in 1956 (and saved from destruction) by a Colchester businessman, who used it to display his collection of clocks—the building is in fact now an official clock museum. (And it gives us another insight into the history of science, unrelated to Gilbert. Christiaan Huygens's invention of the pendulum clock in the Netherlands swiftly spurred the creation of a clock-building industry all over Europe. The Huygens design was brought to England in 1658 by Ahaseurus Fromantel, a Dutchman whose family had settled in Colchester in the previous century to escape religious discrimination, and Colchester thereby became England's center for the clock industry.)

Gilbert died in London in 1603, possibly of the plague. His body was brought to Colchester by his brothers for burial in the chancel of Holy Trinity

Church, across the street from Tymperleys. The church building is now a museum dedicated to Colchester's history—its famous oyster beds and such—but the memorial erected by the brothers over Gilbert's tomb is still in place. Its inscription is in Latin and unusually explicit about the interred's career. Here are excerpts in English translation:

> This eldest son of Jerome Gilberd, gentleman, was born in the town of Colchester, studied the art of medicine at Cambridge, practised the same for more than 30 years at London with singular success, . . . He composed a book celebrated amongst foreigners concerning the magnet, for nautical science. He died the year of human redemption 1603, the last day of November.

The memorial has a decorative border bearing the coats of arms of William himself and numerous other members of the family.

ECTON (near Northampton)

Ecton is a period village (its High Street an official conservation area) somehow left dangling on the hillside when the major road below was improved. (The turn to the village is easily missed.) It was for centuries the home of the Franklin family and we visit here to remind ourselves that America was part of Britain at the time and that Josiah Franklin's move across the ocean in 1683 was not a move to a foreign land. Benjamin Franklin visited here in 1758 to search for his family roots, but the last of the local line, his uncle Thomas, had died in 1702, and no close relatives remained.

The Franklins had been the Ecton blacksmiths, and their smithy was at the back of what is now the Three Horseshoes Inn. The old family home, on the opposite side of the street, has an inscription above the door. Uncle Thomas and his wife, Eleanor, are buried in the yard of St. Mary Magdalene church (near the north door), and there is a tablet to indicate the connection to their American nephew.

FOLKESTONE (Kent)

William Harvey, born in Folkestone in 1578, is celebrated by a fine statue on The Leas, Folkestone's grand upper esplanade, parallel to the sea front on top of the cliffs. The church of St. Mary and St. Eanswith, tucked away into a quiet area at the east end of The Leas, has a Harvey Aisle and a window in his honor. It is interesting that Folkestone, though an important port and center of commerce, did not have any regular school at the time. Harvey presumably received the rudiments of an education at home or church, for he could not otherwise have qualified for entry, at age nine or ten, to Kings School in Canterbury.

The church is open part of every day. Telephone at the Vicarage: 0303–52947.

HEMPSTEAD (near Saffron Walden, Essex)

William Harvey lies buried here in this village, about 15 miles (24 km) south of Cambridge. He probably never lived here himself, but came to be buried here because he was for the last ten years of his long life effectively a member of the families of his brothers Daniel and Eliab, successful merchants and traders, with substantial homes in London. Eliab, perhaps imbued with a sense of history, decided to establish a country residence in Hempstead and at the same time created the chapel in St. Andrew's Church and a vault beneath it for the burial of Harveys present and future. Sadly, the first two to be interred were two young daughters of Eliab, Sarah and Elizabeth, who died aged thirteen and nine, respectively, in 1655 and 1656. William Harvey, who had no children of his own, had been very fond of them, as he was of all his nephews and nieces. When William died in 1657 (in London) the family vault was the natural place for his burial, undoubtedly agreed upon between the brothers beforehand. A large delegation from the College of Physicians came from London to attend the funeral—it was at the time an arduous two-day trip from the city.

The chapel is in the northeast corner of the church. There is a slab in the floor (with inlaid figures and coats of arms) for access to the vault. One can peer inside from a grating on the outside of the church to get a glimpse of the coffins within. A marble bust, sculpted shortly after Harvey's death, adorns the wall of the chapel and is considered an excellent likeness. The most impressive monument, however, is a splendid large marble sarcophagus, perhaps too large to be appropriate for a man who has been described as "short of stature." The sarcophagus was installed in 1883 by the Royal College of Physicians, and Harvey's remains were moved to it from the vault.

The coffins of Eliab and many later Harveys are in the vault, with appropriate wall memorials in the chapel above. They include another Eliab, an admiral who commanded one of the ships under Nelson at the battle of Trafalgar, and his son, Captain Edward Harvey of the Coldstream Guards, who fell (aged twenty-two) at the battle of Burgos in 1812.

ISLE OF WIGHT

The Isle of Wight illustrates a maxim that applies (probably uniquely) to English science. No matter where you may go for sightseeing or recreation, no matter how seemingly remote from present centers of commerce or transport, you will almost inevitably find that the place has had an unexpected role in the history of science. In addition to the tourist attraction that may have led you there (the Cowes sailing races, for example, in the Isle of Wight, or the house where Queen Victoria died), less publicized sites of considerable interest may lie just around the corner.

Freshwater, near the western tip of the Isle of Wight, is of interest to us because it is the birthplace of Robert Hooke. His father was a curate at All

Saints Church, in the heart of old Freshwater village, by the saltings of the river Yar. The location is lovely, hardly changed at least in recent centuries, at the top of a hill now called Hooke Hill. At the foot of the hill is a stone memorial, with the message: "Robert Hooke. Born nearby 1635. Physicist, scientist, architect & inventor." Many ancient cottages line the road up the hill and one of them was probably the Hooke family home, but it is not known which one. Note that Robert's father was only a curate, an underling to the rector (whose name was George Warburton). Robert Hooke remained conscious of the stigma of his social inferiority all through his life. It was very likely the cause of his notorious belligerence toward Newton and others.

Freshwater also enjoys some note for having been the principal home of the poet Lord Tennyson after he became poet laureate. He bought Farringford, a magnificent mansion, for his residence. It is now a plush hotel, with its own nine-hole golf course and other amenities; the room that used to be Tennyson's library has been kept intact and is essentially a small museum. Even this poetic shrine has connection with the history of science, for Tennyson was of the Victorian period when scientists and *literati* mixed to some extent. Lord Kelvin was a particular friend, one of twelve pallbearers when Tennyson was buried in Westminster Abbey in 1892. The Kelvins in fact continued to be friends of the family after the poet's death; Lord and Lady Kelvin were visitors at Farringford in June 1898 when they were taken to see the nearby Marconi Station for wireless telegraphy. Kelvin, who had many years earlier been the prime mover of cable telegraphy, sent a wireless message to George Stokes in Cambridge, described in a famous letter in which he expressed his pleasure at being able to send this message "through the ether" instead of along wires. A chance remark like this sometimes reveals more than a page of text—denial of the existence of the ether would have been inconceivable to Kelvin and most of his colleagues, although the failed experiment to demonstrate its existence was by then a decade old. (Einstein eventually abolished the idea as "superfluous.")

Every visitor to the Isle of Wight should take the walk to the Needles Headland on Alum Bay—an extension of the Tennyson trail from Freshwater, if one wants to make a long excursion of it. It is where the Marconi transmitting station was located, and it is arguably the most spectacular bit of scenery on the island. (Later on, when transatlantic telegraphy became the goal, Marconi's operation was moved to another beauty spot, this time in Cornwall, described immediately below.)

THE LIZARD (Cornwall)

The Lizard is England's most southerly point, made especially attractive by a spectacular segment of the Cornish Coast Path along the tops of the cliffs all around the peninsula. Six miles (10 km) northwest of the point itself, accessible from Poldhu Cove, is the Marconi Memorial, a granite obelisk erected to mark the site of transmission of the first transatlantic wireless telegraph message. The message, consisting of the Morse code letter S (three dots), repeated at preset intervals so that it could be readily identified as a deliberate human signal, was sent out from here by staff of the Marconi Company in December 1901, Marconi himself being at the receiving end in Newfoundland. On the other side of the Lizard, on the Coast Path around Bass Point, a plaque indicates the site of a building (the signal station) where Marconi prepared and tested his equipment prior to the event. The peninsula is still today a major radiotelecommunication center. Goonhilly Downs, inland from Lizard Point or Poldhu Cove, is a virtual forest of skyward-pointing dishes.

How did Marconi, an Italian (and an avid patriot), happen to do his work in England? The ultimate reason is that his mother was Irish, a member of the Jameson family of Irish whiskey fame. When Marconi (initially inspired by Hertz's experiments with electromagnetic waves) was unable to interest the Italian government in the practical potential of his work, he appealed to his Irish cousins for help. One of them turned out to be influential in the London business world and able to find investors to finance Marconi's projects.

LYME REGIS (Dorset)

The cliffs around Lyme Regis and nearby Charmouth have been a paradise for fossil seekers for 200 years and remain so today. They rise steeply from the beach.

The cliffs at Lyme Regis.

They are subject to a complex of rotational slides, sand runs, mud flows and slides, and rock falls—land movements that continually alter the precise shape and character of the seaward edge. And in so doing they spew forth the fossilized remains of the life forms of millions of years ago. It was here in 1811 that a young girl, Mary Anning, discovered the first complete fossilized skeleton of one of the great giant lizards—that of a 180 million-year-old marine lizard *icthyosaurus*—which she sold to the British Museum for £25. Mary Anning later became great friends with Oxford geologist William Buckland (who was a native of this region born in nearby Axminster) and found many more unique specimens—among them a new species of *Pterodactyl*.

For the uninitiated, which before our visit here included the present writers, it should be pointed out that the term *dinosaur* refers exclusively to terrestrial giant reptiles; *icthyosaurs* have a marine origin and *pterodactyls* were flying species. It should also be noted that Mary Anning's find occurred after a violent storm, which caused tons of rock to break away from the cliffs, and that even moderate storms still cause rock to break away today. Fossils can then be found by the diligent searcher on the beach; no hammering at the rock face is needed. Beautiful large ammonites are quite common and even *icthyosaurus* backbone vertebrae still appear a few times each year. Caution is necessary, however. The rocks are steep and the beach at their base disappears at high tide, making it easy to be trapped without a way of escape.

Mary Anning's father (Richard Anning) was a carpenter by trade, but he also sold fossils to Lyme Regis holiday makers, who, just like today's visitors, loved to take home souvenirs. Mary and her brother Joseph had gone beachcombing for fossils even as children. They were experienced collectors and immediately able to recognize a new find when it appeared. They are buried in the graveyard of the church of St. Michael the Archangel, with a single tombstone for both. Mary is also commemorated by a stained glass window in the church, erected in her memory by the vicar of Lyme and by members of the Geological Society of London, with an appropriate tribute inscribed in the glass. The window itself pictures the several corporal works of mercy—feeding the hungry and so on—without direct link to fossils. (The church is interesting in its own right, with a sloping floor and a Norman vestibule.)

There is a small museum not far from the church, much of which focuses on fossils and on Mary Anning. It contains an *icthyosaurus* skeleton similar to that found in 1811. There is considerable evidence that the house in which the Anning family lived was on the site now occupied by the museum. (There is another fine *icthyosaurus* specimen in the Sedgwick Museum in Cambridge. Adam Sedgwick bought it from Mary Anning in 1835 for £50.)

The Lyme Regis museum is open daily from April to October. Telephone 02974-3370.

OXFORD

Oxford was the hub of scientific activity in England at the time of the restoration of the monarchy in 1660. Robert Boyle lived from 1655 to 1668 in the house of apothecary John Crosse on the High Street, next door to University College, and his assistant Robert Hooke lived with him. There were no separate work places for use as laboratories in those days; Boyle did his best known experiments right in this building and Boyle's Law for gaseous expansion was discovered here. Boyle also wrote *The Sceptical Chymist* during this period. The site where the house once stood is marked by a plaque.

Wadham College is where the group that proved to be the embryo of the Royal Society was founded in 1648. John Wilkins, the head of the college, was the guiding spirit, and Christopher Wren was a Wadham student and part of the founding group. The Royal Society has created a research professorship at Oxford in commemoration of its birthplace, and the appointee is by statute a fellow of Wadham.

Since those early days Oxford has never been the equal of Cambridge in scientific activity—Edmund Halley and William Buckland are the best known residents of the intervening 300 years. Halley was Savilian Professor of Geometry from 1703 to 1742 and his house and observatory at 7 New College Lane bears a commemorative plaque.

A distinctive feature of Oxford life are the Rhodes scholars (created under the will of Cecil Rhodes), most of whom come from the United States. They may join any college of their choice, but they also have a building of their own, for special dinners and the like, on South Parks Road.

PENZANCE (Cornwall)

Penzance, virtually the end of the world for England—the literal Land's End is just a few miles away—is a delightfully situated seaport, at the center of what was once a thriving mining area. It was the world's premier supplier of tin for almost 2,000 years and (more briefly, in the nineteenth century) a source of copper. Humphry Davy, one of England's greatest chemists, was born here in 1778. Penzance celebrates the fact with a statue at the top of Market Jew Street, which rises steeply from the harbor to the Market House. The statue is elevated on a pedestal, augmenting the dominance of its position, and bears a plaque with a scientifically accurate summary of Davy's career.

It is appropriate to advise the tourist to avoid Land's End, the unique position of which has been shamefully exploited for commercial profit. On the other hand, we recommend a visit to Cape Cornwall, only five miles (8 km) away, with a good view of Land's End and situated in an area rich in abandoned tin mines, whose brick smokestacks stick out into the air all around us. It should

Humphry Davy on a pedestal in the
marketplace in Penzance.

be remembered that Humphry Davy, aside from his purely scientific accomplishments, was the inventor of the miner's safety lamp, a device not needed in a tin
mine, but possibly inspired by his origins in a mining area.

PILTDOWN (near Uckfield, Sussex)

The sites of anthropological discoveries are sometimes huge gashes in the earth,
created by quarrying or road construction, or spectacular deep caves, their
entrances long hidden from sight. The Piltdown site at Barkham Manor is more
prosaic, a place in a field near a ditch, where there used to be a gravel pit in
which amateur diggers had found bones and tools in the past. It is part of what
used to be an extensive diversified manorial estate, but has recently been
converted into an ambitious 26-acre vineyard, complete with modern wine
making equipment, and a great barn and shop where refreshments can be
purchased and the wines tasted. Two white wines were about to be put on the
market when we visited in 1989, one called *Barkham Manor* and the other
Piltdown Man. There is a pub, also called *Piltdown Man*, near the point where the
side road to the vineyard leads off from the A272 highway.

A self-guiding trail (explanatory leaflet provided) takes visitors through
fields planted with different grape varieties and through the winery buildings.
The place where the skull was found is one of the numbered spots on this trail,

marked by two monuments. One, a proud stone monument, was obviously erected before the hoax was discovered. The inscription reads:

> Here in the old river gravel Mr. Charles Dawson, F.S.A., found the fossil skull of Piltdown Man 1912–1913. The discovery was described by Mr. Charles Dawson and Sir Arthur Smith Woodward in the Quarterly Journal of the Geological Society 1913–1915.

An adjacent plaque, more factual and put up many years later, explains that the remains were a deliberate hoax. It states that the first announcement came December 18, 1912, identifies Dawson as a local solicitor and amateur archaeologist and Woodward as "keeper of geology" at the British Museum. It also tells us that Woodward and Dawson returned to the site in 1913 with the French Jesuit, Teilhard de Chardin. The latter, digging around some more, uncovered a tooth, subsequently identified as of canine origin. The proof of the hoax is correctly ascribed to Dr. K. P. Oakley.

The vineyard and buildings are open to the public daily except Mondays. Telephone 0825-722103.

STONEHENGE (near Amesbury, Wiltshire)

Here we have Britain's most famous prehistoric monument, but it is perpetually jammed with tour buses and visitors and sometimes even "occupied" by the forces of undesirable cults. The Stone Age circles in Avebury and on the Scottish offshore islands may be more rewarding for the thoughtful visitor.

Midlands and North

BIRMINGHAM

Birmingham's leading position in England's industrial midlands was originally based firmly on James Watt's steam engine. The Museum of Science and Industry on Newhall Street (in its James Watt Building) has one of the oldest working models extant, the Smethwick engine erected in 1779 to Watt's design. It is a monstrous engine, two floors high, which functioned to cycle water in and out of the locks of the adjacent canal. It still works and on the first and third Wednesday of every month the museum staff gets up steam and have it running!

The city is also commendably cognizant of its place in the more general history of science. Chamberlain Square, the local rendezvous for a bit of sun at lunchtime, has a Gothic fountain at its center and James Watt and Joseph Priestley on pedestals at the top of a flight of steps, overlooking the scene. (The back of Queen Victoria can be seen if we look in the direction of adjacent Victoria Square.) The town hall, council house, central library, and the museum and art gallery line the square. The museum is principally dedicated to art, but it has a "Local History Gallery" on its lowest floor. The gallery is well designed and informative and includes a panel on the Lunar Society, the little scientific discussion group that was founded by Erasmus Darwin and met in the members' houses by the light of the moon so as to be able to find their way back home late at night. Pictures of 12 of its 14 members are shown, including Priestley, Watt, and the latter's industrialist partner, Matthew Boulton.

Another panel describes the 1791 riots in which Priestley's house and laboratory were destroyed. The riots were provoked when a group of Birmigham dissenters arranged a dinner for July 14, 1791, the second anniversary of the storming of the Bastille, to celebrate and glorify the French Revolution. Printed announcements publicized the event at five shillings per head, including the cost of wine. An angry mob formed. Claiming that church and king were threatened by the dissenters, the mob rioted for five days, attacking meeting houses (the dissenters' places of Sunday worship) and private dwellings. There is a vivid picture of the mob swarming over Priestley's house on Fair Hill and smashing it to pieces. And a fine house it was, as shown by another picture of it dating from an earlier day. (Until recently Birmingham's principal Unitarian church continued to occupy the site of the New Meeting House where Priestley was minister, but in 1978 the entire area was razed to make room for the city's International Convention Center.)

Both museums are open seven days a week. Telephone 021–235–2834 for the Chamberlain Square museum and 021–236–1022 for the Museum of Science and Industry.

CHATSWORTH (near Chesterfield, Derbyshire)

The Cavendish family (the Dukes of Devonshire) has been exceptionally prominent in the history of science in England. Henry Cavendish, the eccentric discoverer of hydrogen, was one of them, and his father (Charles) is in the record books as the inventor of the maximum-minimum thermometer. The mightiest deed was the creation of the Cavendish Laboratory in Cambridge by William Cavendish, the seventh Duke of Devonshire.

Chatsworth, the grandest of English country houses, has been the principal seat of the family since 1688 and has become one of England's most popular tourist attractions. The interior houses an unparalleled collection of art and sculpture; the celebrated gardens contain an orangery, a multitude of fountains, and a huge cascade. How big is the mansion? According to the current Duchess in a recent interview: "They say there are 175 rooms, but I've never counted them. It's fairly meaningless, because some are as big as squash courts and others smaller than laundry baskets." Henry Cavendish's surviving manuscripts are held in one of the rooms and can be seen by appointment.

Chatsworth is open daily, April to October. Telephone 0246–582204.

EAGLESFIELD (near Cockermouth, Cumbria)

One never ceases to be amazed at the lack of intellectual backwaters in the England of earlier centuries. Scholars and literary figures turn up no matter how far we stray from the main road. The tiny village of Eaglesfield, in an idyllic setting at the edge of the Lake District, is a good example, for it is the birthplace of John Dalton. The former Dalton house, a whitewashed bungalow, still stands and bears the commemorative inscription "John Dalton DCL.LLD—The Discoverer of the Atomic Theory—was born here Sept. 5 1766, died at Manchester July 27 1844." The house is still a private residence and not open to the public.

The poet William Wordsworth was born in 1770 in Cockermouth, just a couple of miles away. His father was business manager for Sir James Lowther and the Wordsworth home, rented from Sir James, is a more substantial house than Dalton's. It is now a National Trust property, retains the original staircase and fireplaces, and is open for public view. Both Dalton and Wordsworth retained a lifelong love for the Lake District. Dalton returned to the area each year for his summer holiday and Wordsworth came to live there permanently (at Grasmere, further south) and even wrote a travel guide to the lakes.

KIRBYMOORSIDE (North Yorkshire)

Kirkdale cave, where William Buckland in 1821 identified the bones of all sorts of exotic species—lions, elephants, hyenas, and so on—is on a byroad west of Kirbymoorside, at the point where the road fords *Hodge Beck*, a normally dry stream with its main course underground. The cave opening is now well above-ground (but easily accessible) in a limestone cliff, and one can look through the opening to see the spacious interior, going back 20 or 30 yards into the rock. The entrance is only 3 feet high, which led Buckland to conclude that the cave must once have been a den for hyenas, who dragged in remains of larger animals piecemeal for food. Buckland accepted these finds as *prima facie* evidence for the Biblical narrative of the Flood; they were a major stimulus for his best-selling *Reliquiae Diluvianae*, published in 1823.

(The best public display of fossils from the interglacial period when these exotic animals roamed the English countryside is at the Sedgwick Museum in Cambridge, but the specimens there, from the Cambridge vicinity, were collected more than 50 years later. Kirkdale cave was the eye-opening site.)

LEEDS (West Yorkshire):
Joseph Priestley twixt church and brewery

Joseph Priestley was born in Birstal Fieldhead, a few miles southwest of Leeds, and returned to his home area in 1767 as the practicing minister of Mill Hill

Chapel. The chapel (rebuilt since Priestley's day) is centrally located on City Square and is now formally designated as Unitarian, disbelief in the Holy Trinity being no longer the defiant gesture it once was. It has a "Priestley Hall" in back for church functions.

The City Square itself is a likeable place, designed to be both commemorative (for Priestley, of course, among others) and decorative. It has an impressive equestrian statue of Edward, the Black Prince, the "flower of English chivalry," and around him are statues of Priestley, James Watt, and two other local worthies—but to balance their weighty masculinity, we also have eight scantily clad nymphs, four labeled *Morn* and four labeled *Even*. Next to the square we have a thoroughly modern office building, "Priestley House," which is said to be on the site of the house that Priestley occupied when he was minister of the adjoining chapel.

What is not told on the explanatory plaque is that there used to be a brewery on the other side of Priestley's house and that Priestley found it (though not necessarily its commercial product) just as interesting as his church. The gas above the fermentation vats was carbon dioxide, unable to maintain the burning of a candle, but clearly the same gas that was present in the various mineral waters that people drank for the sake of real or imagined benefits to their health. Priestley got the initial ideas here that led to his later invention of artificially carbonated water—which earned him the Royal Society's Copley Medal—and to his subsequent research on gases in general.

LICHFIELD (Staffordshire, 16 miles [26 km] north of Birmingham)

Lichfield is a pleasant place to visit, with a rather unusual cathedral, a fine park near the town center, and many monuments to Samuel Johnson, who was born here in 1709. (And even a statue to James Boswell, the publicizer of Johnson's life and deeds.) Perhaps surprisingly, the town also makes quite a little fuss over Erasmus Darwin, who had his medical practice here for 25 years, during the period when he was one of the pillars of Birmingham's Lunar Society. His imposing residence at the edge of Cathedral Close still stands and is marked by a plaque. The cathedral, which is crowded with many monuments, has a brass plate in Darwin's memory in the aisle of the south choir. Lichfield's Science and Engineering Society sponsors an Erasmus Darwin Memorial Lecture and other local groups have laid out the *Darwin Walk*, a 10-mile (16-km) trail around the town which is supposed to recreate the flora and fauna of 200 years ago. (Different towns have different styles: Shrewsbury, Charles Darwin's birthplace, is much more niggardly in the celebration of the Darwin name than Lichfield, although Erasmus was a lesser figure than his grandson and only a transient resident here.)

MAER and BARLASTON
(near Stoke-on-Trent, Staffordshire)

Josiah Wedgwood was born in Burslem, the Mother of Potteries, on the northern outskirts of Stoke, where the first Wedgwood factories were located. From 1769 to 1950 the manufacturing was done in nearby Etruria, but the present site is about 5 miles (8 km) south of Stoke, on a picturesque estate near the village of Barlaston. There is an impressive Wedgwood Visitor Center there, attracting busloads of tourists, who (it is hoped) will not leave without a piece or two of the famous pottery in their shopping bags. The center has an excellent museum, devoted mostly to pottery making and design—the ornamental black or blue vases and urns of Josiah's days are truly delightful. The first room of the museum, however, stresses Josiah's scientific interests and his friendship with Joseph Priestley and others, for whom he supplied ceramic chemical laboratory ware. (There is only one small showcase containing actual samples.)

Maer Hall, in the village of the same name about 10 miles (16 km) southwest of Stoke, though viewed only from the outside, may be more interesting to the scientifically oriented visitor because of its intimate connection with Charles Darwin. It was the home of Josiah Wedgwood II, the elder Josiah's son and Charles Darwin's father-in-law. The Hall (which has passed through several owners) and the gorgeous estate on which it sits have changed little since the Wedgwood days, except that much of the surrounding land now no longer belongs to the owners of the manor. Seen from the chuchyard on the hill across the street it gives an impression of enormous wealth and good living, testimony to the highly privileged segment of society from which Charles Darwin derived. Charles himself writes about his visits to Maer as a teenager. He loved the shooting and the family atmosphere:

> In the summer the whole family used often to sit on the steps of the old portico, with the flower garden in front, and with the steep wooded bank, opposite to the house, reflected in the lake, with here and there a fish rising or a water-bird paddling about. Nothing has left a more vivid picture on my mind than those evenings at Maer.

Charles presumably first became acquainted with Emma Wedgwood (his mother's cousin) at this time. They were married about ten years later in 1839 (after the voyage of the *Beagle*) in the Parish Church of St. Peter. The hill on which it stands is connected to the Hall by a stone bridge across the road. The marriage certificate is reproduced in a historical pamphlet that can be purchased in the church.

The Wedgwood Visitor Center is open daily in the summer, six days a week in the winter. Telephone 0782-204141 or 0782-204218.

MANCHESTER

In the center of Manchester stands the Town Hall, a massive Victorian Gothic structure with an extravagantly spacious interior and a proud clock and bell tower to catch the eye from the outside. It was built in 1877 and it proclaims in no uncertain fashion that "Manchester has arrived," with remarkable emphasis on science as integral to the city's history. We see it right from the start, as we enter the building from Albert Square, with statues of John Dalton and James Prescott Joule just inside the door, one on the left and one on the right. Even more impressive is the Great Hall upstairs, which is adorned with 12 mural paintings by the celebrated pre-Raphaelite painter Ford Madox Brown. They took 15 years to complete and give a panorama of the city's history—the building of a Roman fort at *Mancenion*, the expulsion of the Danes in the tenth century, the foundation of the textile industry by Flemish weavers, and so forth. Two of the 12 panels deal with pure science. One shows William Crabtree observing the transit of Venus across the sun in 1639, the other shows John Dalton collecting marsh-fire gas, watched by a group of children and a cow peering curiously across a fence.

James Prescott Joule was still alive when Ford Madox Brown was doing his work, so that Joule's contribution to Mancunian science was too recent to be recognized in the retrospective view of the paintings. His experimental apparatus and other relics are held today in a basement of Manchester's Museum of Science and Industry, where they can be seen by visitors if advance application is made. The museum per se, despite its name, bears little relation to science— "Thrill to the sounds of industry," "Wonder at the miracle of flight" are typical museum themes. Joule's first public presentation of his experiments on heat and work in 1847 was given in the reading room of St. Ann's Church, which stands

John Dalton collecting marsh-fire gas. A mural painting by Ford Madox Brown in the Manchester Town Hall.

on the square of the same name. Historians of science often refer to the lecture as the "St. Ann's Church Lecture."

The organization that played so great a role in the cultural history of Manchester—the intellectual home of both Dalton and Joule—is the Manchester Literary and Philosophical Society, popularly known as the "Lit and Phil." Founded in 1781, it still flourishes, still publishes its *Memoirs*, still holds weekly meetings to widen "public appreciation of any form of literature, science, the arts and public affairs" (party politics explicitly excluded). It is completely independent, relying entirely on subscriptions and other private support, and is run from a small, quite ordinary office. Many of its meetings have for decades been regularly held in the Portico Library, another independent relic of the time of Dalton and Joule, both of whom were members. Its single large room, surmounted by a Georgian dome, has recently been restored and is open to the public. Note the shelves and their inscribed designations, e.g., "Polite Literature," "Voyages and Travels." It is a great place to imbibe the Victorian atmosphere, like something out of a Dickens novel, but in three dimensions.

About a mile south of the city center, on Oxford Street, is **Manchester University.** Ernest Rutherford was professor of physics here from 1907 to 1919. It is where the modern picture of the inside of an atom first emerged and where the seeds of purposeful atomic disintegration were planted. The physics laboratories have moved to new quarters since that time, but Rutherford's laboratory still exists in the basement of the present psychology building—boarded up, no sign to indicate its former illustrious inhabitants. (The porter will show you where it is.) There is a plaque on the main road nearby, at the corner of Coupland Street and Oxford Street.

The Great Hall in the Town Hall is used for banquets and other functions and may be closed to the public at unpredictable times. Telephone 061–236–3377, extension 309/310. The Portico Library is at the corner of Mosley and Charlotte Streets and is open Monday to Friday. Telephone 061–236–6785. A booklet entitled *Men and Women of Manchester* is for sale in the Tourist Office. It lists houses where Dalton and Joule lived and their places of burial.

MUCH HOOLE (near Preston, Lancashire)

In 1639, the year that Jeremiah Horrocks observed the transit of Venus across the face of the sun, he was here in Hoole as curate (or curate-in-training), to conduct services at St. Michael's Church. He had been brought in by John Stones, who had built himself a fine mansion (Carr House) nearby and had then set about revitalizing and rebuilding the church. Horrocks lived at Carr House and may have served as tutor for the Stones' children. He had a south-facing first-floor room directly over the porch, and that is where he actually made his observations. On the fateful Sunday we must imagine him shuttling back and

St. Michael's Church at Much Hoole has memorials for
Horrocks inside and out. The porch dates from Horrocks's
time, but all else (including the sundial) is relatively recent.

forth between the house and chapel, to look at the sun whenever the heavy
schedule of his spiritual duties allowed it.

More than 200 years later one Robert Brickell was appointed rector of St.
Michael's and became fascinated with the Horrocks story. He wrote a small book
entitled *A Chapter of Romance in Science,* and set about the task of providing a
proper memorial for its hero. The results are there for us to see today. The east
window is particularly prominent, full of references to the great event—the
astronomical sign for Venus, depiction of the sun with the planetary circle upon
it, and the artist's impression of Horrocks himself in the act of observation. The
present rector, when we visited, was a little embarrassed by the window's
location, right behind the altar, with the person of Horrocks superimposed upon
the cross in the line of sight of the congregation. He clearly would have preferred
a more traditional figure there. Other church memorials include a marble tablet
(dated 1859), which, among other information, tells us about Horrocks that
"loving science much, he loved religion more." There is a prominent vertical
sundial over the south door with the motto, *Sine sole sileo* ("Without the sun I am
silent"), and a more modern clock dedicated to Horrocks on the north side of the
tower.

The church is at the south edge of Much Hoole, about half a mile from the southern
turnoff to the village off route A59. Carr House sits at the road junction itself, and
amazingly, has been preserved almost unchanged in external appearance—still a grand
sight. It is a private residence, not open to the public, but is easily seen from the road.
The church is normally kept locked when not in use. Telephone (Rectory) 0772–
612267.

SHREWSBURY (Shropshire)

Shrewsbury, as seen by the visitor, is a constricted town, with most of the old parts squeezed into a loop of the River Severn. Charles Darwin was born here in 1809, and there is a bronze statue of him near the castle, in front of the town library. The library used to house Shrewsbury School, where Darwin received his education to age sixteen, when he left to study medicine in Edinburgh. Earlier famous students included Judge Jeffreys, the hanging judge of the reign of Charles II. Darwin House ("The Mount"), where Charles was born and where his father practiced medicine, is outside the Severn loop across Welsh Bridge and is now an office building, with the gates closed outside office hours. Darwin's father and mother are both buried at Montford, about five miles (8 km) to the west. Shrewsbury's pride in its famous son is on the whole rather muted. Do not be misled by signs pointing to "Charles Darwin Center"—that's a small shopping center off the main shopping street.

WHITBY (North Yorkshire)
and MIDDLESBROUGH (Cleveland)

Marton, three miles (5 km) south of Middlesbrough, is where James Cook was born in 1728. Great Ayton, a few miles further south, is where he spent his boyhood and went to school. Whitby, on the coast, is where he learned his trade and learned to love the sea and where the ships of his voyages were built. And all these places are part of Yorkshire, new-fangled names for the counties notwithstanding.

Whitby is the prime attraction, a picturesque, old, red-tiled whaling port where the river Esk enters the open water between high cliffs. Cook learned the seafaring trade here, first as an apprentice and then as an employee of John Walker, Whitby shipowner. He lived in an attic in Walker's house on Grape Lane, which is now the Captain Cook Memorial Museum. It contains authentic charts, manuscripts, furniture, and so forth, and it stands right at the waterside, where we can see across the river Esk to the shipyards where Cook's ships were built. The town is still relatively unspoilt here, and this is the spot where we can get the best feeling for why Cook might have yearned for the sea itself, in spite of the security of his job on shore. Above the harbour on West Cliff stands a bronze statue of Cook, with a stone carving of the ship *Resolution* on the back of the pedestal. There is a truly spectacular view from here, of the harbour, Whitby Abbey, and the open sea beyond.

There is another Captain Cook museum in Stewart Park, Marton, close to the site where the simple thatched cottage of Cook's birth had once stood. It portrays Cook's early life in the area. In the city of Middlesbrough itself, in the indoor shopping center on the north side, we have another ship model, a replica of the *Endeavour,* above our heads, suspended from the ceiling. In Great Ayton the family cottage of Cook's boyhood is marked by an obelisk from Australia. The cottage itself was removed in 1934 and sent to Australia, where it now stands in Fitzroy Gardens, Melbourne.

The Whitby museum is open daily, April to October. Telephone (tourist office) 0947–602674. The Marton museum is open all year, closed Mondays. Telephone 0642–311211.

WOOLSTHORPE and GRANTHAM (Lincolnshire)

Isaac Newton was born on Christmas Day in 1642, at Woolsthorpe Manor, a few miles south of Grantham, now preserved as a monument by the National Trust. He was educated at King's School in the city of Grantham, a very old grammar school founded in 1328.

Woolsthorpe is not in any sense a museum, but simply a house—a farmhouse really, for manor is too grand a name—that has been preserved. It does, however, contain a replica of Newton's device for producing the colored spectrum from white light, an electric candle replacing the sunlight that he himself used. The house has some interest for its own sake: There is an owl hole under the eaves, for example, to provide a nesting place for owls, with the intent that they should keep the place clear of mice and other vermin.

One must remember when one visits that this is not merely Newton's place of birth, for he returned to Woolsthorpe to live with his widowed mother after his graduation from Cambridge. It was the time of the Great Plague throughout

Newton's birthplace, Woolsthorpe Manor, from a painting by J. C. Barrow in 1799. The house is now a National Trust property.

Europe (31,000 people perished in London alone over a two-year period), and Cambridge was badly affected, not a healthy place to be. Newton thus spent 1665 to 1667 in virtual seclusion at Woolsthorpe, during which time he formulated the binomial theorem of mathematics, developed calculus, studied decomposition of white light into its spectral colors by means of a prism, and began his study of mechanics, including the universal law of gravitation. Surely two of the most productive years ever spent by a single scientist, notwithstanding the fact that none of the work was published until later, some of it *much* later—Newton's fear of adverse criticism is well known.

Newtons's only near-contemporary rival in the field of physics (if, that is, he had one at all) was the Dutchman Christiaan Huygens and a fascinating contrast emerges if one can combine a visit to Woolsthorpe with a visit to the Huygens family summer home "Hofwijck" on the outskirts of Den Haag—or, at least, if one can remember one when one visits the other. For Christiaan Huygens had a truly aristocratic family background, with a grandfather who had been secretary to the Dutch national hero, William I of Orange. The old summer home (now the official Huygens museum) is an appropriately elegant house, set among orchards and decorative canals, with fine furnishings, clearly designed for elegant garden parties and musical soirées, attended by well-dressed gentlemen and ladies with long dresses and delicate slippers. The Newtons were not poor. They were country squires and their family home in Woolsthorpe was substantial. But their house was clearly a farmhouse, designed for people who work all day with muddy boots.

Woolsthorpe is open to the public from March to October, afternoons only, and closed Thursdays and Fridays. Telephone: 0476-860338.

City of Grantham. Celebration of the Newton connection in Grantham is not impressive. An undistinguished statue stands on St. Peter's Hill, a small park at the center of the town. The Old Schoolroom of King's School, where Newton actually attended classes from 1654 to 1660, is still in use as the school library and a plaque commemorating Newton's presence there was put up in 1960. Other local pride in Newton is regrettably vulgar. "Filet of pork Isaac Newton" was a dinner menu item at the George Inn when we were there. There is an "Isaac Newton shopping center" with a large and hideous plastic apple over the main entrance from the car park.

6

Scotland

The name *Scotland* will conjure up for some the vision of a land till recently uncivilized, the home of disunited barbaric tribes, exhorted to battle by wailing bagpipes. Surely no science could have penetrated into this land of cold and rugged highland glens! Could the natives even read and write?

Such a view of the Scots would be grossly incorrect. They have had, in fact, a traditional fervor for education and at least as much enthusiasm for science and philosophy as their English neighbors to the south. In the eighteenth century, in particular, Scotland had a productive period of Enlightenment, rivaling the French movement of the same name, and it undoubtedly became the intellectual center of the English-speaking world for a considerable period. "If there was an English enlightenment (as distinct from the Scottish)," it has been said, "it was an enlightenment of the practical mind." But even the practical mind owed much to Scotland. James Watt, perhaps the most famous of the practical men, who developed the first useful steam engine in England, was in fact born and educated in the Glasgow area and obtained his first steam engine patent there.

The bagpipes, of course, remain an inconsistency for some of us, an unexplained vestige of earlier primitive traditions.

Stone Age Astronomy?

For primitive man in northern latitudes, the frightening changes in the seasons, from 20 hours or more of sunlight in summer to almost perpetual night in winter, must have been a powerful stimulus to set the mind to thinking, not only about cause and effect, but also about practical matters, like being able to measure one's progress through the familiar cycle of seasonal change. One would know from past experience that night never completely swallows the sun—we are not doomed to end our lives in darkness, slowly freezing to death. But when will the

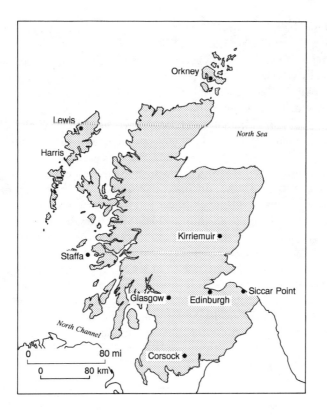

long-awaited turnaround come? Can we be sure that the proper day has not already passed, that we haven't somehow been missed this year? Some kind of calendar, some reliable way to keep records from year to year is needed. Some way for the priest or other figure in authority to reassure those who are frightened.

Ideally one would like a permanent scale, against which the long-term movements of the sun can be measured. Mountain peaks east or west of one's dwelling (or the local temple) can serve this purpose and can be used to watch sunrise and sunset move from peak to peak and back again with the passing seasons. Where the land is flat one can erect an artificial line of peaks with wooden poles or upright stones to serve the same purpose, but in this case, where the distance to the marker line is short, parallax becomes a problem and a firmly positioned auxiliary point must be established to provide a fixed viewing position. Perhaps every village built an appropriate structure, where the villagers could gather each morning as midwinter (or midsummer) approached, waiting for the actual turnaround and ready to celebrate when it came. (It is not essential that the sun itself be used as the signal. In ancient Egypt, with its relatively sophisticated society, the rising and/or setting of the bright star Sirius was used to predict arrival of Nile floods.)

Along the west coast of Britain, from Orkney down to Cornwall, there are hundreds of stone circles or archaeological remains of stone circles, claimed by some to represent such Stone Age calendar clocks, deliberately built, with stones intentionally placed in specified positions for unique recognition of midsummer day, for example. But this claim is controversial and there are others who argue that the circles had a more general ceremonial function, even if (as in the case of mountain peaks) they might secondarily have been used as the community calendars. Stonehenge, west of London, is the grandest and most famous of these circles, but what we see there is a late version, probably tampered with for decorative purposes, a massive monument standing alone, without other traces of the community that it may originally have served. Scotland has more authen-tic examples, such as the Ring of Brogar and the nearby Stenness Stones on the island of Orkney. They are among the oldest such relics, built between 2500 and 3000 B.C., as compared to about 1600 B.C. for Stonehenge, and they are set in an area rich in other Stone Age sites. Perhaps the best advantage is that one rarely sees more than a dozen sightseers here at a time, in contrast to the busloads at Stonhenge, and one can let one's imagination wander to the time when the structures were built, before man knew about metals, before he knew how to write—and one can try to decide for oneself the riddle of their origin. The official sign posts, erected at the sites by the authorities, are neutral. They indicate that the circles had ceremonial function, without specifying exactly what that function was.

Related Places to Visit: Orkney and Lewis and Harris.

John Napier, Laird of Merchiston: Inventor of Logarithms

Long before the official Enlightenment we have the remarkable John Napier (1560–1617), eighth Laird of Merchiston. He was a landowner, lord of a manor with a good income from his crops and cattle. He was active in local and national affairs and a vigorous protagonist for the Protestants against the Papists. It was enough to keep him busy, one would think, but Napier also had a hobby, mathematics (especially as applied to numerical computation), and his hobby gained him a prominent place in history. He not only invented logarithms, but undertook the laborious task of computing the world's first table of logarithms, something that required more than 20 years of his life. Adaptations of Napier's logarithms became the universal tool for numerical calculations from the day of first publication (in 1614) until the advent of calculating machines and elec-tronic computers in the twentieth century.

Napier had even earlier developed a neat device for simple multiplication, called "Napier's Bones," which greatly facilitated the carrying over from one column to the next. And he played a large part in defining the columns themselves, the decimal notation we now use, with a point or comma after the integer. Decimals per se had been in use in the East for centuries before this, and they were first used in the West by the Flemish mathematician Simon Stevin in 1585, but Stevin's notation was extremely awkward—Napier's notation is the one we use today.

The generation now growing up, familiar with computers from their earliest days in school, may never be able to appreciate the indispensability of logarithms and slide rules—the latter being just logarithmic scales etched on wood or metal. They were the only calculating aids available to most scientists for more than 300 years. There were actually two kinds of logarithms in all the tabulations, Napierian (or "natural") and Briggsian. The latter were the ones we used the most, being based on the decimal system ($\log 10 = 1$, $\log 100 = 2$, etc.) and thus more convenient to use for multiplication and division. But the difference is a trivial matter of scale. Henry Briggs, the originator of the decimal system and professor of geometry at Gresham College in London, never claimed great originality for himself. He twice visited Edinburgh—no casual jaunt in 1625—to discuss his proposal personally with Napier.

Related Places to Visit: Edinburgh (Merchiston castle), Cambridge (Whipple museum).

The Scottish Enlightenment

In the eighteenth century Scotland could boast a host of brilliant men. There was Adam Smith, author of *The Wealth of Nations*, justly called the founder of scientific economics. There was Joseph Black, the first person to recognize carbon dioxide as a chemically distinct gas, thereby opening up the field of pneumatics and laying the groundwork for Joseph Priestley and others who followed him. In medicine, there was John Pringle, who first made his name on the field of battle and went on to become physician to the English monarchy and president of the Royal Society of London. In geology, there was James Hutton. And the philosophical tone, so to speak, was set by David Hume, the no-nonsense rationalist philosopher. Outside science and philosophy, there were brilliant architects, jurists, and the like. A "hotbed of genius," the Edinburgh of the time has been called.

James Hutton (1726–1797) was a personification of the Scottish Enlightenment, curious about everything—not just geology, but also medicine, farming, philosophy, chemistry, and economics—and ever ready to do experiments to test his ideas. Joseph Black, the chemist, was his best friend, but both of them were part of a much wider circle of other intellectuals. Neither one ever married, nor did their contemporaries, David Hume and Adam Smith, but there is no suggestion that any of them considered bachelorhood an element of being enlightened. Most likely they just never had the time for matrimony. Hutton, unlike the others, held no academic appointment, but did attract devoted followers, who went with him on his geological explorations and (after his death) enthusiastically promoted his ideas. One of them was John Clerk of Eldin, a great-granduncle of James Clerk Maxwell, who accompanied Hutton on many excursions and made drawings of what they had seen. He left a portfolio of the drawings in the Clerk homestead, but they went unrecognized for what they were until 1968.

In his revolutionary *Theory of the Earth*, first made public at two meetings of the Royal Society of Edinburgh in 1785, Hutton proposed a "steady state" earth, in which geological processes act continuously at a uniform and slow rate to generate what is seen around us. Water erodes rocks, washing them into the sea, where their debris is deposited, layer after layer, and often exposed to view when the sea recedes. These deposits become heated under the enormous pressure of the weight above them and eventually melt and are thrust up in molten form through the crust of the earth, where they resolidify, ready for erosion to begin again. The sensational aspect is the apparent cyclic nature of the changes in the earth's surface and the implication that the earth must be very old. Up to that time most people had taken the biblical story of the Creation more or less on faith and with it an estimate of about 6,000 years for the age of the earth. Hutton's proposal was not to change this by a mere factor of 10 or 100. He proposed that the earth had been here virtually forever. His famous dictum, "no vestige of a beginning, no prospect of an end," utterly changed the way we think about ourselves and the globe we inhabit.

Hutton's key innovation was his interpretation of hard rocks (such as granite), which lack the marine fossils of sedimentary rock. Everybody thought that they must be part of the original surface of the earth, unchanged since the day of Creation, but Hutton knew that erosion indiscriminately attacks all kinds of rocks, and could not accept the implied immunity of these particular ones. On the other hand, he found evidence in support of his own cyclic theory in many places, in the form of unconformities in geological sections, *vertical* layers of rock below the more common horizontal strata, indicative of folding and upthrust from the depths below.

A self-renewing world of enormous antiquity was naturally an uncomfortable idea for pious Bible-reading Christians, but Hutton was deemed less of a threat to established religion than David Hume's skeptical philosophy. Hutton himself vigorously denied impiety. He saw "divine wisdom and order" everywhere in the plan of the earth. The writings in the Bible, he said, record the history of man on earth; the account of the Creation was to record that God made all things in a certain order; it was absurd to give the word *day* in that account its literal meaning.

Hutton's ideas were not accepted immediately, partly because he lacked the skill of easy-to-read writing. His *Theory of the Earth* became widely disseminated only after John Playfair (one of Hutton's devoted followers) wrote a clear and concise account of it in 1802, five years after Hutton's death. One intransigent foe remained long after that, Robert Jameson, professor of natural philosophy at Edinburgh University and an avid Neptunist who believed that all rocks originated as deposits from a once-overlying sea. Charles Darwin attended

Jameson's lectures as an Edinburgh student in 1826. He found the lectures incredibly dull and gives an account of Jameson sneering at people who believed that rocks could be injected from below in molten condition.

Related Places to Visit: Edinburgh, Siccar Point.

The Nineteenth Century

In 1871, when Cambridge created its new Cavendish Laboratory for experimental physics, where did they go to find a director and professor? To Scotland! Their first choice was William Thomson from Glasgow, but he declined. They then turned to Germany, to Hermann Helmholtz, but he also declined. So back to Scotland they went, to James Clerk Maxwell, and he took the job, leading the Cavendish Laboratory to its latter-day glory. Thomson (later Lord Kelvin) and Maxwell were the pride of nineteenth-century Scottish physics and remain today on the list of the all-time greats in the world. (And Scotland was up front in nineteenth century medical science, too, as we shall see.)

Heat and Thermodynamics. **William Thomson** (1824–1907) later to become Lord Kelvin, belongs wholly to Glasgow. He lived at a time when Glasgow had become distinctly provincial—far from the mainstream of culture—and indeed he went to Cambridge for his education. But it's not a case of his being the Glasgow boy who went out into the world and made good and is therefore remembered with pride—he made good in Glasgow itself and stayed there. He returned home after his degree, became professor of natural philosophy at the University of Glasgow at the early age of twenty-two, and held that position for an incredible term of 54 years. When Queen Victoria raised William Thomson to the peerage in 1892, he continued to honor his association with Glasgow, choosing the name "Kelvin," after the stream that runs alongside the university campus.

Kelvin's great contribution to pure science is in the field of thermodynamics. He didn't invent the electric refrigerator, but he founded the branch of physics that one has to know in order to design such a device. His main achievement can be formally described by saying that he established an *absolute* temperature scale, independent of the stuff we use to measure hotness in ordinary thermometers. Ordinary thermometric substances all have somewhat individual responses to hotness and therefore tend to disagree with one another except over very narrow ranges, and the absolute scale (appropriately named the "Kelvin" scale) removes such ambiguity. Its importance, however, lies not in that, for ambiguity in measurement could have been removed by international agreement. What Kelvin did was to provide an entirely new concept of what temperature is—to make it an intrinsic physical property of all matter, which exists even if no one is interested in the actual measurement of it. The definition is based on Carnot's theoretical analysis of the conversion of heat to work (as in a steam engine), which showed that useful work could be done only if heat could fall in the process from a higher to a lower temperature. The basis for Kelvin's temperature scale is this implicit potential capacity to convert heat into work. A provocative consequence of the definition is the existence of an *absolute zero* of temperature, a never quite attainable lower limit to how cold matter could become if all the resources of the universe were devoted to refrigerating a tiny little segment of it.

All this is heady stuff (because it's rather abstract), but there is a more tangible side to the story. Carnot interpreted his law of the heat engine in light of the dogma of his time, which viewed heat as an element (called "caloric"), which was always conserved. He regarded the spontaneous flow of heat from high to low temperature as analogous to the spontaneous fall of solid bodies in the gravitational field of the earth. By Kelvin's time, however, it had become apparent that heat is not a separate substance, but a manifestation of the motion of the particles of which all matter is composed. Absolute temperature then becomes a measure of the intensity of that motion, a truly fundamental component of our understanding of how the universe works. And the beauty of it is how well *absolute zero* fits into the picture, becoming effectively the temperature at which all molecular motion has stopped.

Kelvin was equally famous in his time for his work on public projects, most prominently the laying of the transatlantic cable for telegraphic transmission between England and the United States, in which he played a pivotal role. But he is also *infamous* for his outrageous opposition to new ideas when they were not in the immediate area of his own work. Best known is his adamant refusal to accept a reasonably long age for the earth—whereby he seriously impeded the work of geologists and evolutionists. When radioactivity was discovered, it provided a new source of terrestial heat, which should have removed the basis for his earlier objections, but Kelvin dismissed the new evidence out of hand— "The disintegration of the radium atom is wantonly nonsensical," he said. None of this interfered with Kelvin's burial in Westminster Abbey, where he has an ostentatious memorial at the feet of Isaac Newton.

Related Places to Visit: Glasgow, London (Westminster Abbey).

James Clerk Maxwell: The Unified Electromagnetic Field. Maxwell (1831–1879) is rated by present-day physicists as one of their legendary figures, comparable to Isaac Newton and Albert Einstein. In 1931, at the celebration of Maxwell's centenary, Einstein himself called Maxwell's contribution "the most fruitful that physics has experienced since the time of Newton." The work for which Maxwell merits such extravagant praise is his comprehensive theory of electromagnetism and the field associated with it. Most of the work was done at his home ("Glenlair") where he wrote his definitive and celebrated *Treatise on Electricity and Magnetism* during three years of relative seclusion after his withdrawal from academia in 1868 following a less than illustrious teaching career. He returned to the academic world in 1871 to become the first professor of experimental physics at Cambridge University and the first director of the subsequently famous Cavendish Laboratory.

Maxwell, though lacking a title, was born into the landed gentry and never lacked the means for a comfortable life. He was actually not a Maxwell at all, but belonged to the Clerk family, from Penicuik near Edinburgh. His father, John Clerk, had to adopt the surname of Maxwell (for complex legal reasons) when he inherited an estate in "Maxwell territory," near Dumfries, and took up his residence there. Glenlair is where Maxwell grew up and it remained his home for most of his life. Even when he was on the faculty of King's College in London (where he developed his initial ideas on electromagnetism), he invariably spent at least four months of each year at Glenlair. When Maxwell died of cancer in 1879, at the early age of forty-eight, he was in Cambridge, but his body was returned for burial to the Scotland he loved.

Despite the brevity of his career, Maxwell made brilliant contributions to a remarkable variety of subjects: the composition of Saturn's rings, geometrical optics, an explanation of color vision, and more. He was especially appreciated by his contemporaries for his work on the statistical molecular theory of heat and matter, showing how to deal with myriads of gas molecules all together, with molecular velocities statistically distributed about a mean, instead of trying to cope with the essentially impossible task of specifying positions and velocities for each individual molecule. In this he was the first scientist to introduce a probabilistic (basically indeterministic) factor into our view of matter—a subject subsequently developed more fully by Ludwig Boltzmann in Austria and Willard Gibbs in the United States and now known as statistical mechanics.

It is the electromagnetic field, however, that is Maxwell's crowning legacy. The work was highly mathematical—essentially Faraday's rudimentary qualitative ideas put into mathematical form, and extended into a complete theory, with equations by which all interactions between electricity and magnetism could be expressed and understood. But this was not merely an *ex post facto* unification of things already known, for it led directly to one of the momentous scientific discoveries of all time, the discovery that ordinary light, the subject of so much controversy through the preceding centuries, must be a form of electromagnetic radiation. The discovery came about because the velocity with which electromagnetic waves are propagated through space, though not directly measurable at the time, could be readily *calculated* by means of Maxwell's equations from other factors, quantitative relations between electric currents and the magnetic fields they generate, such as had been first measured by Ampère in France. The calculated result was a very large number, a velocity of 3×10^{10} cm/sec or 186,000 miles per hour. More important than the number itself, the result turns out to be identical to the till then seemingly unrelated *measured* speed of light. What a revelation! "Great guns," Maxwell called it in a letter, with uncharacteristic lack of modesty.

Related Places to Visit: Edinburgh, Corsock and Parton, and Cambridge (England).

Antiseptic Surgery. Joseph Lister (1827–1912), son of a London wine dealer, is one of the great figures in the history of medicine. He pioneered the introduction of antiseptic practices into surgery, doing so in the face of strong opposition and ridicule. This may at first seem remote from basic science, but in fact the contrary is true because the germ theory of disease was at the heart of the matter. It was Louis Pasteur who convinced the world that microorganisms exist and cause fermentation and putrefaction, but Lister was one of the first to recognize microbes as a cause of disease, an idea which his professional colleagues were initially unable to accept. The underlying cause for dispute was the great despot of German chemistry, Justus Liebig, who died in 1873, but whose rejection of any hint of *vitalism* in what he thought to be purely chemical processes (putrefaction among them) retained an influence for several years after his death.

Lister received his medical degree in London in 1852 and then went to Edinburgh to spend a month with James Syme, then considered the most original surgeon of his day. As it happened, Syme and Lister took an instant liking to each other and Lister married Syme's oldest daughter Agnes and remained in Scotland for over 20 years, first in Glasgow and then in Edinburgh as Syme's successor. Mortality rates of surgical patients were appallingly high at this time, even for simple amputations. Patients died like flies from blood poisoning and the especially dreaded hospital gangrene. The standard explanation was (à la Liebig) that chemical oxidative degradations were responsible and scrupulous avoidance of contact with air was the advocated preventive measure.

In 1865, Thomas Anderson, professor of chemistry at Glasgow, drew Lister's attention to Pasteur's work on fermentation and his demonstration that living microorganisms (microbes) and not chemical oxidation were the cause of rotting in meat. About the same time Lister learned about the use of carbolic acid (phenol) in the treatment of sewage, to render it odorless and less likely to infect cattle grazing on sewage-fertilized fields. He put two and two together. The battle against decomposition in wounds should not be fought by excluding air, but by carbolic acid dressings that could destroy microorganisms. The new procedure was phenomenally successful, at least in Lister's hands, and one would have thought that its use would spread like wildfire through the medical profession. In fact, it did not do so immediately, for many of Lister's colleagues were not equipped for the preparative precision that was needed for success—enough antiseptic to kill the bugs but not enough to burn the patient—and they often could not reproduce his results.

Truth eventually prevailed, of course. Lister returned to London in 1877— the capital city was then still a backwater in surgical practice and needed his reforming zeal. International recognition came about the same time and Lister received all kinds of awards. What he may have cherished most was being the guest of honor at the Jubilee of Louis Pasteur at the Sorbonne in Paris in 1892.

There is a famous picture of the two together, which can be seen at the Pasteur museum in Paris.

Related Place to Visit: Edinburgh.

PRINCIPAL PLACES TO VISIT

CORSOCK and PARTON (near Dumfries)

This is perhaps the most scenic place of any in this book. For miles around we have green pasture land, patches of trees, scattered farms, seemingly unchanged for centuries—all on rolling, hilly terrain with many picturesque views of the Urr River or Loch Ken below us. The Maxwell estate covered about 6,000 acres, including tenant farms. Glenlair itself is at Nether Corsock, on a marked side road off route B794. It was built according to the design of Maxwell's father, a grand stone mansion by modern standards though relatively modest for the times. The house sadly was gutted by fire in 1929 and has never been repaired. The walls are still there, though, almost to the roof top, enough to recreate for today's visitor the bygone manorial atmosphere. The family that now owns the home farm of the original estate lives in the former servant quarters just a few steps from the ruins. They maintain the access lane, but do nothing about the

The shell of Maxwell's house Glenlair, destroyed by fire in 1929. Maxwell wrote his celebrated *Treatise on Electricity and Magnetism* here, during three years of relative seclusion between 1868 and 1871.

main house itself and there appear to be no plans to preserve it nor to convert it to some modern habitation.

Glenlair is about five miles from the village of Parton, where the Maxwells regularly attended church. Maxwell's remains were moved to Parton after he died in Cambridge, and he is buried in the churchyard of Parton Kirk, in the ruins of an old chapel (the "Old Kirk"). The polished granite tombstone lists Maxwell's father and mother and his widow as buried in the same place. A brass plate was installed at the entrance to the churchyard in June 1989—it calls Maxwell "a good man, full of humor and wisdom." A booklet published in 1979 by the community as a tribute to Maxwell on the centenary of his death is for sale at the Parton post office.

The village of Corsock is even closer to Glenlair than Parton, and the church here, too, can claim close connections with the Maxwells. It was built in 1839 through the influence and exertion of Maxwell's father, and both father and son were among the church elders. The church contains an impressive stained glass window, installed in Maxwell's honor. The motif of the window is the Magi following a brilliant Star of Bethlehem and a Greek inscription is embedded in the glass:

"ΠΑΣΑ.ΔΟΣΙΣ.ΑΓΑΘΗ.ΚΑΙ.ΠΑΝ.ΔΩΡΗΜΑ.ΤΕΛΕΙΟΝ"

Loosely translated, it means "All good giving and every perfect gift"—undoubtedly a reference to the Epistle of James from the New Testament "All good giving and every perfect gift comes from above, *from the Father of the lights of heaven.*" A plaque placed next to the window testifies to "a genius that discovered the kinship between electricity and light and was led through the mystery of Nature to the fuller knowledge of God."

EDINBURGH

Charlotte Square. After 1870, Joseph Lister lived in a town house at 9 Charlotte Square, at the west end of George Street, in the heart of Edinburgh's "New Town." The house is intact and Lister's residence is marked by a plaque. New Town in general and Charlotte Square in particular are areas of beautiful and dignified urban design—fine residences for the affluent in the Georgian and Victorian years, worth a stroll today at the end of a busy day. Besides Lister, Alexander Graham Bell lived here (another Edinburgh product, though he moved to America in middle age) and so did Lord Haig, British field marshal in World War I.

Greyfriars Churchyard. At the south end of George IV Bridge, close to the Royal Scottish Museum, is a sacred spot in Scottish religious history, Greyfriars Church. Here in 1638 the National Covenant was signed to uphold the Presbyterian form of worship. The Covenant was later renounced by Charles II and many bloody rebellions followed. Twelve hundred Covenanters were taken prisoner in a famous battle and then were kept penned up for five months in Greyfriars Churchyard. James Hutton is buried here within the area of the Covenanters Prison, at the south corner of the cemetery. The grave was un- marked when located in recent times. A stone was placed in the wall on the occasion of the 150th anniversary of Hutton's death (1947), with the insciption, "Father of Modern Geology."

Maxwell in Edinburgh. Maxwell attended school at Edinburgh Academy (a school still active today). He was even born in Edinburgh because his parents had come here to assure the best possible medical care during his mother's confinement—she was forty years old, and an earlier child had survived only a few months. Those who want to follow in Maxwell's Edinburgh footsteps can see the house where he was born on India Street (marked by a plaque). Maxwell lodged at 31 Heriot Row, just around the corner, while he was attending school. Edinburgh Academy itself is about half a mile further north, on Henderson Row.

Merchiston Castle. The official residence of the Lairds was Merchiston Castle, which is now a part of Napier Technical College, on Colinton Road, a little over a mile south of the city center. The college is a large modern concrete structure built in 1964, but the castle was left intact and has been most tastefully incorporated into the modern buildings around it. The old gateway to the grounds of the castle has also been left intact. It will be noted that the castle is quite small. John Napier didn't actually live there until after his father died and he himself succeeded to the title in 1608. Two families in the building would have been a crowd. (We visited on a Sunday, and the combination of old and new was perhaps particularly attractive because it was also tranquil—there were no students in evidence.)

Merchiston Castle at Napier Technical College.

There is also a formal memorial to Napier in the center of Edinburgh, in the vestibule of West Kirk (now Church of St. Cuthbert) at the west end of Princes Street Gardens. It is quite modest, but in a way a singular tribute because the church is small and the congregation must walk right by the memorial at every service.

Royal Infirmary. The former surgical hospital where Lister worked, which used to be part of the Royal Infirmary, is now a classroom and office building of Edinburgh University. It is a dour grey stone building (identified by a plaque), typical of much of Edinburgh, at the foot of Infirmary Street, right across South Bridge Street from Chambers Street and the Royal Museum. The present Royal Infirmary surgical wards are in a fascinating old building of Scottish Baronial style on Lauriston Place, a few hundred yards to the west. The vestibule walls are covered by tablets recording royal visits and the names of donors who gave substantial gifts. Some of the donors go back to the 1700s, their names having been transferred from the Old Infirmary in 1881.

Royal Museum of Scotland. The Royal Museum of Scotland on Chambers Street is a national institution, housed in one of the finest Victorian buildings in the country. It is a comprehensive museum, serving both the arts and the sciences. The sculptured heads above the entrance (Queen Victoria, Prince Albert, James Watt, Charles Darwin, Michelangelo, and Isaac Netwon) symbolize its origin and its scope. The spacious main hall is a splendid example of Victorian design, with fountains, ponds, and comfortable seating, which sets a note of cheerful enjoyment for the museum as a whole. The museum was

Plaque in honor of Joseph Lister and his mentor and father-in-law, James Syme, outside the Old Infirmary in Edinburgh.

originally opened as "The Industrial Museum of Scotland," and the scientific exhibits still tend to emphasize technology. But there is a good exhibit on evolution and also a fine "zoo" of large stuffed mammals. From the Enlightenment period there is a nice collection of chemical glassware used by Joseph Black.

Salisbury Crags and Arthur's Seat. Hutton lived on St. John's Hill, on the eastern side of the present Edinburgh University campus. It is instructive to walk around here for a few minutes and to see the good view one gets of Salisbury Crags, a spectacular line of cliffs at the edge of Arthur's Seat, an 800-foot ancient volcano (erupted 325 million years ago) lying within Holyrood Park. Geology was always there for Hutton to look upon, practically in his own backyard.

Hutton and his friends unambiguously identified intrusions of molten rock at Salisbury Crags, pushed into the predominant (and softer) sedimentary rocks, not lying passively at the base where the primeval hard rock was supposed to be. It is possible to drive along the perimeter of the crags (Queens Drive), but it is better to climb to Radical Road, a footpath at the base of the upper cliffs. The best part of the cliff for observation is directly across from the Park Road gate to Holyrood Park and it is known as "Hutton's Section."

The Royal Museum is open daily, afternoons only on Sunday. Telephone 031–225–7534. Edinburgh has held an annual Science Festival each April since 1989, with some events at the museum. A geological guide to the Edinburgh area is available for a nominal fee from the Edinburgh Geological Society (Edinburgh EH9 3LA). Note that Greyfriars churchyard is closed on Saturday afternoons.

GLASGOW

Glasgow abounds with "Kelvin this" and "Kelvin that," but they are generally named for the Kelvin River, not for His Lordship. Our interest here is in the university, which Kelvin honored for so long by his presence and which pays him eloquent tribute in return.

Glasgow University. The university (Britain's fourth oldest) was founded in 1451, but moved to its present site only in 1870, during Kelvin's life time. The principal building is a grandiose Victorian Gothic edifice on the south side of University Avenue and includes two quadrangles, lecture rooms and university offices. On the second floor is the Hunterian Museum, named after William Hunter, a famous anatomist and physician, who was a Glasgow student in the 1730s. The museum has small collections of objects and pictures related to several Scottish scientists, including, of course, Lord Kelvin. A showcase in the general exhibit hall is devoted to him, and there are two smaller cases on the stairs leading to the museum. They show photographs of Kelvin's laboratories and some of the instruments he designed or invented, such as the marine compass which contributed greatly to Kelvin's wealth.

The old Natural Philosophy building nearby (now prosaically renamed "Physics and Astronomy") houses the Kelvin Lecture Theater, a grand old hall which was indeed named for the man and not the river and contains a fine photograph of him in old age. A modern addition to the building has more Kelvin apparatus on exhibit. The Kelvin Museum, used for conferences, is not normally open to the public.

Between the physics building and the Victorian edifice is Professor's Square, former housing for distinguished faculty. Kelvin lived in Number 11, an enormous residence, which Kelvin continued to occupy when in Glasgow, even after he built his own palatial home at Netherhall (near Largs). It must have been enormously expensive to heat—professors were expected to rent out rooms to students to help pay for this and other maintenance costs.

The museum is open all day Monday to Friday, mornings only on Saturday. Telephone 041-330-4221.

The Kelvin River. We must not fail to see the celebrated river. It is actually below the foregoing buildings (down a broad flight of steps) in Kelvingrove Park, Glasgow's prime outdoor summer center. There are two large statues on the university side, one of Kelvin and one of the surgeon Joseph Lister, who began to develop his antiseptic surgical procedures in Glasgow before he moved to Edinburgh.

KIRRIEMUIR: Knighthood for Charles Lyell

Charles Lyell was born on the grand estate of Kinnordy on the outskirts of Kirriemuir. The family moved to southern England when Lyell was only one year old, but his father eventually came back to spend his old age here, and Charles Lyell himself visited frequently and made several geological field trips in the surrounding area. The estate (with manor house intact) is now a wildlife refuge of the Royal Society for the Protection of Birds, but the present Lady Lyell still resides on the outskirts.

Lyell was here in 1848 (his father was then eighty-one years old) when a letter arrived to tell him that he had been recommended for knighthood and that Queen Victoria had approved and was ready to confer this honor upon him. Originally, of course, knighthood had been for soldiers and a man would be dubbed a knight on the field of battle as reward for some feat of bravery. In fact, there was a special word of contempt, "carpet knight," for those who received the honor in the royal chambers. But by the nineteenth century the award was for any meritorious service to the nation, though the sword was still used for the dubbing ceremony as it still is today. When Charles Lyell received his letter, Queen Victoria was at Balmoral Castle, 30 miles (50 km) north of Kirriemuir, and Lyell rode there on horseback to receive the award in a personal ceremony just for himself—up Glen Clova along the southern Esk river, across the high hills around Lochnagar, and then down to the castle through Balmoral Forest. We can retrace at least half of this journey comfortably for ourselves, on the paved road (B955) that follows Glen Clova and terminates at a youth hostel.

Beyond that there are only bridle trails. (It should be noted that Glen Clova, an impressive narrow valley with steep rocky sides, was one of Lyell's favorite field trip destinations in the area.)

The RSPB refuge (Loch of Kinnordy) is open all year round. Telephone 0575-72665 (Lyell estate) or 0575-74097 (tourist office, summers only).

LEWIS AND HARRIS: Archaeological Enigma

The joined islands of Lewis and Harris are the most northerly of the Outer Hebrides. They are often visited for their isolation and scenery or, in the case of Harris, because it is the home of famous Harris Tweed. A tour of Lewis and Harris can be combined with tours of other islands, such as the Isle of Skye or the more remote islands in the Outer Hebrides chain.

When in Lewis and Harris for any reason, a visit to the stone circle at Callanish should not be missed. Like the stone circles on Orkney, it engenders a sense of mystery and seems to invite speculation. Who lived here? What have I in common with these forebears of mine? Physically, however, Callanish bears little resemblance to the Orkney circles. It is much smaller (diameter only 12 meters), contains a chambered tomb *within* the circle, and has impressive long stone-lined avenues leading up to it. A huge stone stands over the burial site, but it is not at the circle's true center. It has been asserted by some that Callanish may be another lunar and stellar site, capable of refined astronomical observations; others have envisaged it as a sacred ceremonial site. Professional archaeologists have been rather taciturn, seeing it as an enigma not easily solved. Enjoy it and add your musings to theirs!

ORKNEY ISLANDS

The Orkney islands are a fascinating place to visit, with unique physical beauty, and quite different in terrain, people, and history from the Scottish mainland just a few miles away across Pentland Firth. The Ring of Brogar and the Standing Stones of Stenness are on the main island, about 0.6 miles (1 km) apart, not far from the town of Stromness. The Ring of Brogar is large, 104 meters in diameter (compared to 91 meters at Stonehenge), and most of its original 60 stones remain intact. Astronomical calendar advocates believe that Brogar was a lunar observatory, and an external stone, called the Comet stone, 137 meters to the southeast, has been proposed as the viewing stone, from which the changing position of the moon could be observed. The Standing Stones of Stenness are the remains of a smaller circle, 31 meters in diameter. Radiocarbon dating of animal bones or wood from holes or ditches associated with the circles suggest that Stenness is older than Brogar by perhaps 500 years. The proposed viewing stone in this case (a very tall stone called the Watch Stone) is directly north of the circle, consistent with the possibility that Stenness might have been used to observe the seasonal changes in the position of the sun.

The Ring of Brogar on the island of Orkney.

To the untutored observer (like the authors of this book) the huge differences in geometrical dimensions and compass orientations among the stone circles generate skepticism about the idea that astronomical observations were the primary purpose of these structures. It's not just that Brogar and Stenness are different, but also Stonehenge in England and Callanish on the island of Lewis—no two of them seem to be alike. Another question, given the huge investment of labor needed for them: Why erect the Ring of Brogar when the Stones of Stenness were already standing nearby, just as they do now? Whatever their true function, Stone Age man certainly went to a lot of trouble to erect these places. Some of the stones weigh close to 100 tons and were moved to their present location from quite large distances away. Presumably mechanical devices had to be invented to set them in upright positions.

Orkney has many other Stone Age monuments. Maes Howe, described as the "supreme example of a neolithic chambered tomb in Great Britain" is just a few hundred meters from Stenness. Archaeologists have assigned it the same approximate date as the Standing Stones, close to 3000 B.C. The excavated settlement of Skara Brae, on the Orkney coast about 6 miles (10 km) to the northwest, dates from the same period. There was a thriving community here, contemporary with the early great dynasties of Egypt, but, as far as is known, in no way connected with them.

Altogether there are 15 monuments on the main Orkney island in the custody of the Ancient Monuments section of the British Department of the Environment and another 17 on some of the smaller islands of the Orkney group. The Midhowe chambered tomb on the island of Rousay is well worth a visit—it is very large and exceptionally well presented for public viewing. Not all the sites stem from the Stone Age. The Orkneys were settled by Norsemen around 800 A.D., and some of the monuments are from that period. (The Orkneys actually remained Norwegian territory until 1468.)

An added dividend to an Orkney visit is the magnificent bird life that can be seen along the rocky coastline. This is a breeding ground for kittiwakes, puffins, gulls, terns; all types of sea birds can be seen nesting in the cliffs in early summer. Use caution in approaching nesting terns—they tend to be nasty, swooping and diving at intruders.

SICCAR POINT (near Cockburnspath)

James Hutton studied geological formations in many parts of Scotland in the course of developing his *Theory of the Earth*. Siccar Point, 35 miles (56 km) south of Edinburgh, has the most striking and most easily accessible example of unconformity, as well as providing a fine panorama of several miles of coastline. We can see multiple horizontal layers of pink sandstone sediment here, near the water line and partly washed away by the sea, and *vertical* strata of harder rock underneath. In many places the vertical strata thrust through the overlying sandstone. In no way could this formation represent sequential sediments from the sea. The vertical strata must be intrusions from deep in the earth, thrust into the softer rocks after melting, recrystallization, and folding, illustrative of Hutton's perpetual recycling of the earth's crust.

Hutton was in an offshore rowboat in the company of John Playfair and Sir James Hall when he found this showpiece in the rock. The latter made a much copied sketch, and Playfair wrote eloquent prose about the occasion: "On us who saw these phenomena for the first time, the impression made will not easily be forgotten."

Siccar Point is about a mile south of the village of Cockburnspath and is approached through Old Cambus Quarry, no longer a quarry, but a group of warehouses with huge parking spaces for trucks. The access road to the quarry (off route A1107) is signposted. To go to the point we proceed on foot from the parking area in a roughly northeasterly direction, through a wooden gate, up a hill to the left, and then across a field to the tops of the cliffs where the unconformity lies directly below at the base of the cliffs. Total distance walked is about 300 yards (270 m). The quarry gates are open only during business hours, but it adds no more than half a mile (0.8 km) to the walking distance if the car is left at the gate.

STAFFA (uninhabited island)

Spectacular basaltic columns of volcanic origin and Fingal's Cave are the attraction here. They are important for the history of geology as well as having been the inspiration for Mendelssohn's music.

Boat trips around Staffa originate from the island of Mull. Telephone (tourist office at Tobermory) 0688-2182.

7

Jreland

Ireland is dearly loved by the literary tourist. In Dublin he or she can retrace the steps of Leopold Bloom on June 16, 1904, as recounted in James Joyce's mammoth novel *Ulysses*, or visit the haunts of James Joyce himself, as described in his autobiographical works. Up north in Sligo county a pilgrimage can be made to the Lake Isle of Innisfree and other sites associated with the poet William Butler Yeats. Back in Dublin there is that medieval masterpiece, the illuminated *Book of Kells*, displayed for public view in the library of Trinity College. But Ireland has a modest scientific heritage, too, as we shall see, with seventeenth-century Robert Boyle in the forefront.

Inevitably, and particularly in regard to Boyle, there arises a question— what constitutes an Irishman? The question is contentious, as is all else connected with this troubled country. Extremists would deny the label "Irish" to anyone not espousing the Roman Catholic religion, and some might label all English colonizers and their progeny as intruders, even if they moved to Ireland as long ago as the sixteenth century, initially at the behest of Queen Elizabeth, to protect her against possible Irish support for the Spaniards. But such a narrow definition is scarcely tenable, for it is among the so-called Anglo-Irish, the minority within what is still a predominantly Catholic country, that we find the most noteworthy Irish scientists—and not only the scientists, but the *literati* as well. Yeats and Swift, the playwrights Synge and O'Casey, they were all Protestants. And so was Arthur Guinness, the founder of the famous brewery!

Richard Boyle, the first Earl of Cork, the father of Robert Boyle, is the example par excellence of the Elizabethan immigrant. He was born in Canterbury, but set out for Ireland to make his fortune. For a paltry sum he purchased the properties in Cork, Waterford, and Tipperary, which Queen Elizabeth had originally bestowed on Sir Walter Raleigh, and he went on to develop this land (which Raleigh never did), building roads and bridges, creating farms and mines.

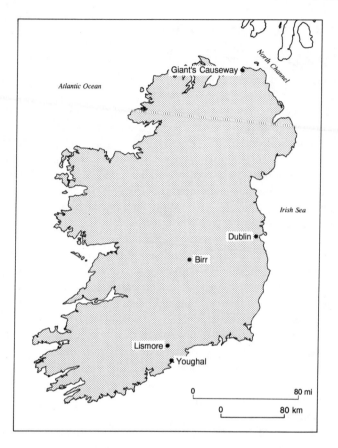

He brought in other English settlers, did his bit for queen and country in keeping down the native population, and was ultimately rewarded by James I with his Earldom. For a time he was probably the richest man in all of Britain. He was in many ways a coarse character, but he was good for Ireland, a builder who has left his mark throughout the southern land. The Earl's independence and adventurous spirit are undoubtedly reflected in son Robert. A purely English upbringing might well have nipped it in the bud.

Northern Ireland. A visit to Ireland quickly makes apparent (for those who didn't already know) that the Ulster Protestants so prominent in the news today are progeny of Presbyterians imported from Scotland and bear no relation to the Anglican Protestants mentioned above. One prominent scientist who came from the Ulster group is William Thomson (later Lord Kelvin), who was born in Belfast in 1824. His family, however, moved back to its Scottish roots (to Glasgow) when William was only seven years old. Never during his long life did Thomson ever express affection or allegiance for Ireland, north or south.

James Ussher (1581–1656): The Age of the Earth

James Ussher was an Irishman from far back, descended from an ancestor who accompanied John Plantagenet to Ireland in 1185 in the capacity of usher and adopted the name from his job. The family joined the Tudor Protestant Reformation and had close links with Queen Elizabeth and subsequent English monarchs. James was one of the very first students at Dublin's newly founded Trinity College, entering in 1594 at age thirteen. He was appointed fellow of Trinity College when he completed his studies, and ordained both deacon and priest on the same day—his uncle was archbishop at the time and undoubtedly made good use of his influence. James himself became archbishop in 1625, of the archdiocese of Armagh, now in Northern Ireland.

Ussher's entry into the annals of science comes from his biblical chronology, which proved to be enormously influential for more than 100 years, a real stumbling block to progress in the field of geology. Ussher's dates were the result of meticulous calculations, based on the genealogies in the books of the Old Testament and supporting manuscripts in Greek, Aramaic, and other languages. (He was regarded as a great scholar because he could read Semitic languages and claimed to be able to distinguish authentic works from those that were merely careless copies.) The first version of the chronology was drawn up, probably in 1597, while Ussher was still a student at Trinity College, but the definitive version was not published until 1654. In this version the origin of the world was dated as the night before October 23 in 4004 B.C.

We must appreciate that no one looked on this calculation as a crackpot clerical tract. It was taken seriously as a product of admirable historical scholarship and hotly debated by other scholars. John Lightfoot, for example, noted Cambridge scholar and vice-chancellor of the university at the time, argued seriously that the correct date and time of the creation should be taken as three days later than Ussher's date, namely October 26, 4004 B.C. at 9:00 A.M. A German astronomer argued for 3963 B.C. as the correct year. Even Isaac Newton took Ussher's dates seriously. He estimated, in his *Principia*, on the basis of the earth's rate of cooling, that it must be at least 50,000 years old, but he was uncomfortable with the result and speculated about latent causes that might have accelerated the cooling process. He did not consider his estimate as a serious denial of Ussher's date.

Ussher (then sixty years old) lost all his lands in the Irish rebellion of 1641 and was forced to live in England thereafter, where he became a trusted supporter of King Charles I and a proponent of the doctrine of the divine rights of kings which he fearlessly expressed in his sermons. He watched the preliminary preparations for the execution of Charles I from the roof of Lady Peterborough's house in St. Martin's Lane (abutting Charing Cross), but the pain became too much for him, and he fainted when the masked executioners began to put up the king's hair to bare his neck in preparation for the sword. Interestingly, his proroyal sentiments seem not to have been resented by Cromwell and his followers. He continued to preach in England during the period of the Commonwealth and was buried in Westminster Abbey by personal order of Cromwell himself.

Note: Ussher's chronologies were actually printed in the margins of bibles from 1701 onwards well into the early twentieth century, and they came to be regarded with the same reverence as the biblical text itself. Here are some of the standard dates: Noah's Flood, 2349 B.C.; exodus from Egypt, 1491 B.C.; accession of King David, 1056 B.C.

Related Place to Visit: Dublin (Trinity College).

Robert Boyle: The "Sceptical Chymist"

Robert Boyle was the youngest son of the Great Earl, born in 1626 in Lismore Castle, when the Earl was sixty years old. Robert in later life candidly acknowledged the good fortune of his birth to high station and wealth, admitting that he could never have even envisaged a life devoted to science without it. He also pointed out the advantage of being the youngest. Had he been an earlier son, the Earl would have obliged him to become involved in political and public affairs, to lead a life that Robert characterized as "a glittering kind of slavery." As it turned out, the Earl could afford to be generous. He sent Robert to Eton College for his basic education and then (at enormous expense) to Geneva and Italy with a private tutor. He was in Florence, studying the works of Galileo, when disaster struck back home—the Irish rebellion of 1641 devastated the Earl's lands and severely depleted the family fortunes. But the rebellion was eventually put down (with the aid of some of Robert's conscripted brothers) and enough of the family fortune was salvaged to keep Robert more or less independent. He never worked at a paying job nor held any university appointment and was even able to hire private assistants for his experiments—Robert Hooke being the most famous— and secretaries for his writing. He lived modestly (Oxford first, then in London with his sister Katharine) and never married, which presumably helped to make ends meet.

Given his firm intention to dedicate his life to science, it was natural that Boyle would want to settle in England, as he did, for a scientific establishment was crystallizing there, curiously encouraged both by the Puritan politicians and the restored royal government that followed it, with underlying visions of the building of a "Brave New World." Boyle became the foremost of these new world builders, leader of the advance guard that paved the way for Isaac Newton and the others who followed a decade or two behind him. He was a versatile man— skilled experimenter, thinking philosopher, socially adept. His achievements read like a catalog of all British science of his time.

He invented (with Robert Hooke's help) the modern air pump and experimented with gases (giving us what we still call "Boyle's Law"). He was a leading dissector of animals. He introduced the use of alcohol as a preservative. He was a member of the "Invisible College," founded by scholars living in Oxford, an organization that was transformed into the Royal Society of London after the Restoration. Boyle became the most influential fellow of the Society in its infant days. Like many of his contemporaries, Boyle was an intensely religious man, and at his death he left a sum of money for the sponsorship of "Boyle Lectures," sermons designed to confute atheism and other heresies. He was urged at one time to enter Holy Orders, with the prospect of becoming Archbishop of Canterbury, it is said, but he preferred science and the good company of the Royal Society.

Most historians believe that Boyle's most important contribution to science was his espousal of a mechanical philosophy, especially with reference to chemistry. Chemistry was an art before Boyle's time, even an *occult* art, completely outside the framework of the world of physics, and that's what Boyle changed. He insisted that chemistry and physics were part and parcel of a single natural philosophy. His famous book, the *Sceptical Chymist*, expresses firm conviction for a particulate theory of matter—in his own words, all matter seems to be "divided into little particles of several sizes and shapes variously moved"— but the book as a whole probably made its impact more by asking the right questions than by providing answers, and by an appeal to quantitative experiment for support or derogation of theoretical ideas. The magic recipes of former chemists, lacking a theoretical basis, were dismissed as unproductive.

Boyle died in 1691 and was buried in the church of St. Martin in the Fields in London. The old church was torn down in 1720 and replaced by the present edifice and, shamefully, no record was made of the disposal of interred remains— Boyle's final resting place is thus unknown. No subsequent memorial was erected either at St. Martin's or at Westminster.

Related Places to Visit: Dublin (St. Patrick's Cathedral), Lismore, Youghal, and Oxford (England).

Nineteenth Century and Beyond

William Rowan Hamilton (1805–1865). "We shall use Hamilton's form of the equations of motion for a system of n degrees of freedom." Thus opens the first chapter of *Elementary Principles in Statistical Mechanics* by J. Willard Gibbs (first published in 1902). Statistical mechanics, the system of rules and equations that makes a working tool out of the conceptual notion that matter consists of myriads of particles in random motion, rests squarely on mathematical innovations developed nearly 70 years earlier by the Irish mathematician. A similar statement can be made about that other twentieth century system, quantum mechanics, which embodies the conceptual notion that energy transfer involves discrete lumps of energy, called *quanta*—Hamiltonian functions are essential for practical application of the idea. This debt of the most powerful methods of modern physics to Irish genius is not always fully appreciated.

Hamilton was a true and proud Irishman all of his life, a prodigy, whose first love was poetry, not science. He was the master of many languages; he was an exuberant extrovert and had a huge capacity for pots of ale. He placed first among 100 candidates when he entered Trinity College and on graduation was immediately appointed professor of astronomy. His two great contributions, the basis for his posthumous fame in modern physics, were made in 1828 and 1843, respectively. One was an innovative general equation of motion for assemblies of many particles; the other was the invention of an equally general mathematical function (of which vectors and tensors are special examples) called *quaternion*. After that, unfortunately, he achieved little more, falling victim to the quest for unattainable grander generalizations in the field of algebra and to a more easily satisfied visceral craving for alcohol.

Related Places to Visit: Dublin (Royal Canal, Trinity College).

William Parsons, Earl of Rosse (1800–1867) was an almost exact contemporary of Hamilton. He built what was then the world's largest telescope on his estate at Birr in central Ireland (improving on the best of the Herschel telescopes), and with it became the first astronomer to see a spiral nebula, the kind that make such spectacular pictures in elementary textbooks. Nebulae of this type are now known to be galaxies, much like our own galaxy. Parsons's achievements are actually quite remarkable because he conscientiously devoted most of his energies to his duties as lord of the manor.

Related Place to Visit: Birr.

An interesting feature of the twentieth century is that **Eamon de Valera,** most intrepid prime minister of the infant Republic of Ireland and the man who kept the country neutral (and largely anti-British) through World War II, was an enthusiast for mathematical and physical science. He set up an Institute for Advanced Studies in Dublin hoping to attract refugees from war-torn Germany, and he did in fact attract the Austrian Nobel Prize winner Erwin Schrödinger who lived in Dublin for 15 years. (Schrödinger's prize had been awarded in 1933 for the creation of wave mechanics, one of the forms of quantum mechanics that depended so intimately on the mathematics of William Hamilton.)

Related Place to Visit: Dublin (Merrion Square).

PRINCIPAL PLACES TO VISIT

BIRR (Offaly)

Birr Castle sits in the midst of a 100-acre demesne, one of the most attractive grounds in all of Ireland. It includes a bit of the Little Brosna River, waterfalls, a lake, formal gardens, and an arboretum. On an open lawn stands the 56-foot outer tube of the Parsons telescope, firmly anchored to two huge gothic stone walls. It was built in 1845 by William Parsons, third Earl of Rosse, entirely by himself with the aid of only local labor. For 75 years it was the largest telescope in the world and astronomers came here from everywhere to see further into space than was possible at home. The Earl discovered and studied spiral nebulae here and some fine pictures of them are exhibited in glass cases on the walls. The castle itself is still the private residence of the Earls of Rosse (and has in fact been in the Parsons family since the 1620s), but the grounds are open to visitors every day of the year. (The original six-foot telescope mirror and a working model of the whole instrument are among the possessions of the Science Museum in London, but are presently not on exhibit.)

DUBLIN

Trinity College, Ireland's most famous educational institution, was founded in the reign of Queen Elizabeth, but the present buildings date from mid-eighteenth century. The most impressive is the Old Library—particularly the Long Room within it, with its high vaulted ceiling, all made of dark wood. The library's most treasured possession, the *Book of Kells* (medieval illuminated gospel) is kept here and some pages are always open for display. The central aisle is lined with busts of famous men, Trinity graduates among them. The graduates include Archbishop Ussher, William Hamilton, and Jonathan Swift. Aristotle, Cicero, Newton, and the Duke of Wellington are some of the honored outsiders.

The College Chapel and the Examination Hall are two much smaller buildings, facing each other across Parliament Square, and both contain prominent tributes to William Ussher. His portrait hangs alongside portraits of Queen Elizabeth and Jonathan Swift in the Examination Hall. In the chapel the central panel of a triptych of stained glass windows is dedicated to his memory. Bishop Berkeley, a famous Trinity-educated cleric a century later than Ussher, with profound views on our perception of nature, is honored similarly to Ussher in both buildings.

The Examination Hall is actually used for examinations, convocations, and other gatherings and is not normally open to the public, though the staff will let you take a peek if it is not in use. The Ussher portrait here is actually a copy, the original being in the Provost's private residence.

St. Patrick's Cathedral is Church of Ireland, on the south side of the River Liffey, the Catholic Cathedral being on the north side. Parts of St. Patrick date from the thirteenth century. All of it has been restored from a state of disrepair with generous financial support from the Guinness brewing family. The cathedral contains a huge number of memorials—a sort of Irish analogue of Westminster Abbey—including a twentieth century window dedicated to William Ussher (a student at the Cathedral choir and grammar school before he entered Trinity College) and the actual tomb of Jonathan Swift. The latter was Dean of the Cathedral and himself composed the Latin epitaph inscribed on his stone, part of which reads "Imitate him, if you dare, this dedicated champion of liberty." Of greatest relevance to this book is the monstrous and vulgar memorial to the family of Richard Boyle, Earl of Cork and father of Robert Boyle, which was erected by the Earl himself for the perpetual glorification of the Boyles. It is 40 feet tall, formally a memorial to his second wife (the one who bore all his children), with effigies of the parents and grandfather of the Countess on upper tiers, the Earl and Countess themselves, recumbent, in the middle (he lying on top of her, it should be noted), and 11 of their children in a row at the base. The infant in the middle of this row is presumably Robert, born in 1627 just before the monument was erected. The artistry is execrable. All the children, including the infant, have old faces and only the figure size indicates chronological age. This structure stood originally next to the high altar, but objections were raised—should the congregation be expected to kneel and pray in front of the Earl of Cork and his wife?—and the monument was moved to the opposite end of the nave. (All of this happened in the Earl's lifetime and he protested vehemently.)

For relief, look at the stairs to the organ loft. They are recent, but artistically in good taste.

Flash of Genius at the Royal Canal. The River Liffey, traversing the center of Dublin from west to east, is the gateway for commerce with Britain. Two canals (built in the eighteenth century) link it to the great River Shannon about 75 miles to the west, and they were the main transport routes inland before the advent of the railways. Both canals retain their towpaths, still providing miles of relatively peaceful but not necessarily scenic walking. The mathematician William Rowan Hamilton used the Royal Canal path to walk to and from the Dunsink Observatory, where he was chief astronomer. In 1843, walking here with his wife, Hamilton had a flash of genius, conjuring up the formulas that essentially define *quaternions*, the complex mathematical functions for which Hamilton is famous. It happened where Brougham Bridge crosses the canal at Broombridge Road in the suburb of Cabra, and Hamilton stopped and scratched the formulas into the stone of the bridge. It sounds like an apocryphal tale, but the evidence for it is strong: Hamilton apparently always had a need to see formulas written out and was well-known for his habitual use of any available surface for his jottings. The inscription has long since moldered away, as Hamilton himself said in a letter written late in life to his son, but there is a plaque on the bridge commemorating the event, with the crucial formula,

$$i^2 = j^2 = k^2 = ijk = -1$$

inscribed upon it. The plaque was put up at the instigation of Eamon de Valera, Ireland's militant Republican premier, who had ambitions in his youth to be a physicist or mathematician and took great pride in Hamilton's achievements.

Brougham Bridge is at what is now an ugly and ill-kempt segment of the Royal Canal. Bus routes 22 and 22A terminate in Cabra near the bridge and provide an alternative means of approach for those who don't want to take the rather long towpath walk. Dunsink Observatory is about 3 miles (5 km) beyond the bridge. Its ancient 12-inch refractor telescope is still in operation and is open for public demonstration on certain Saturday nights. Advance arrangements are required.

Merrion Square. This is one of several attractive squares in Dublin, formerly purely residential, now mostly devoted to offices. Plaques show who lived where. On the south side we have the "Liberator," Daniel O'Connell, at no. 58, W. B. Yeats at no. 82, and the Austrian theoretical physicist, Erwin Schrödinger, at no. 65. His presence in Dublin is a result of prime minister de Valera's interest in physics and mathematics, and the plaque states that he worked in this house from 1940 to 1956. He ventured into a physicist's view of biology while he was here, gave lectures on that subject at Trinity College, and published a book (*What Is Life?*) which is singularly muddled, but is said to have been influential in persuading other physicists to become involved in biological research. Schrödinger himself is actually said to have been more interested in affairs of the heart while in Dublin than in either physics or biology.

LISMORE CASTLE (Waterford)

Lismore Castle, to this day the most grandiose castle in all of Ireland, is where Robert Boyle was born in 1627. The castle was part of Richard Boyle's purchase from Sir Walter Raleigh. It became the property of the Dukes of Devonshire (the Cavendishes) in 1753 by marriage of a Cavendish to a daughter of the fourth Earl of Cork. The gardens are open to the public in the summer months, but the castle itself is a private residence. One can get a fine view of the castle all year round from the road that enters Lismore from Clogheen to the north—a highly scenic road, crossing high moorland, worth taking for its own sake. Another scenic route (quite different in character, mostly wooded) runs south from Lismore to Youghal. Part of the route runs alongside the Blackwater River, which was the main traffic vein of the Boyle "empire" in the olden days. Robert must have traveled it often in his youth. (There is yet another Boyle castle in Ballyduff, a few miles west of Lismore. This one was built by Richard Boyle himself in the 1620s.)

YOUGHAL (County Cork)

Youghal is a narrow ribbon of a town along the edge of the estuary of the Blackwater River, with walls against invaders from the sea. The harbor was built by the Earl of Cork to provide a link to England for his produce.

Youghal was Sir Walter Raleigh's seat during his brief sojourn in Ireland before he sold his lands cheaply to Richard Boyle; the Elizabethan mansion where he lived is still a private residence on spacious grounds adjacent to St. Mary's Church. The church itself (originally dating from 1220) contains another large and vulgar Italian-style monument to the Boyles, erected by the Earl himself, with carvings of the Earl and both his wives, the second (Lady Katherine) in noble ermine, and nine of his fourteen children ranged along the base— but not the yet unborn Robert. The wrought iron railings in this part of the

Details of the Boyle monument in St. Mary's Church in Youghal. The great Earl, recumbent, is above. Some of his 14 children are below. Robert Boyle was not yet born when this monument was erected, but he is included on a similar (equally tasteless) monument in St. Patrick's Cathedral in Dublin.

church bear a score of coats of arms of the Boyles and the families with which they intermarried.

Near the church is New College House, on the site of a medieval college which the Earl acquired with the rest of the land. He put it in the charge of his brother (whom he had made Bishop of Cork) so that most of the collegiate revenues would end up in his own pocket. But let it be noted that the Earl had his generous side as well. He erected six substantial alms houses in 1610 and (as the plaque tells us) "provided £5 apiece yearly for each of ye six old decayed soldiers or Alms Men for ever." The terraced houses are still used for needy widows and were in the process of being converted into apartments when we visited.

In Northern Ireland

GIANT'S CAUSEWAY (near Bushmills, Antrim)

"Ye cliffs and grots where boiling tempests wail." This is a spectacular volcanic site, similar to the one on the Island of Staffa in the Hebrides, but more easily accessible. The sharply sculptured basaltic columns were once the object of furious geological controversy: The Vulcanists saw them as crystallized products of hot molten rocks from the earth's interior; the Neptunists thought they were deposited from receding waters of a globe-encircling flood. The problem was settled in the Auvergne in France, where more modest columns of a similar kind exist in the midst of incontrovertibly volcanic land.

Stones of Contention. Giant's Causeway, from a painting by Susanna Drury in the 1730s.

8

France

French scientists, like their English counterparts, may well have come (by birth) from many different parts of the country, but the *action* in French science has been centered in Paris, where most scientists have held formal, salaried positions paid by the king or other governmental authority. In contrast to England, France has had few scientists from the ranks of the privileged aristocracy; nor were amateurs, eccentrics, and open dissenters ever a significant force.

Certain periods stand out in French intellectual history. The long reign of Louis XIV, the Sun King is an example. He formally ascended the throne at age five, but did not take personal charge until 18 years later in 1661. His reign extended over 50 years after that and was marked by the building of Versailles and the establishment of a brilliant court. He was an enthusiastic patron of writers, artists, and the intelligentsia as a whole.

The Enlightenment followed later in the eighteenth century, a glittering period, but in this case not centered at the court, for Louis XV was weak and ineffective. Its leaders were philosophers—Voltaire, Diderot, Montesquieu, Rousseau—but their philosophies were shaped in large part by the scientific revolution that had preceded them. It was the Age of Reason. Enlightenment meant not *being* enlightened, but *becoming* enlightened by the generation of new ideas through rational thought and open discussion.

Then came the Revolution, an explosion of unprecedented magnitude, a kind of supernova in our social history. Liberal ideas, national education, the metric system, and so forth—we can't count the number of benefits. But it was also a period of strife and turmoil, of unparalleled violence and sickening brutality. Napoleon Bonaparte, at the head of his army, sought to spread the spirit of revolution throughout Europe, successfully in some countries, less so in others. His final defeat left France impotent as a world power, but the ideas of the Revolution (and those of the enlightened philosophes before it) live on!

These successive periods inevitably had enormous impact on the lives of French scientists and their scientific institutions, but the influence on the *substance* of their work is less obvious. A noteworthy aspect of French science is how it flourished unabated right through the Revolution, almost unaffected in terms of its goals. Napoleon Bonaparte, in the wake of the Revolution, was an uncommonly enthusiastic patron of the sciences, but again there is no sign of distortion due to ideology or dreams of conquest. Science, to judge from what went on here, has its own momentum, often only minimally affected by the social ferment around it.

Early Days and Royal Patrons

In the middle of the seventeenth century, still in the infancy of modern science, Galileo scarcely dead and Newton still a baby, France gave us two memorable men, René Descartes and his near contemporary Blaise Pascal, conspicuously different despite their not dissimilar backgrounds. In the same period we see the beginnings of the French Académies and the famous Jardin du Roi.

René Descartes. It is a name almost everyone recognizes. He's a kind of cult figure, a philosopher of untold profundity, reputed to have been of enormous influence on science by virtue of the power of his mind. "I think, therefore I am," he said. There's even an adjective for him ("Cartesian") in the English dictionary. What is this philosophy that gave him so much fame? It is all contained in a single book, Discourse on Method, published in 1637, and one objective historian has summed up its message: If you think hard enough, clearly enough, then you can interpret the world by the unaided powers of your own mind. That would seem to be the antithesis of science rather than a magic formula for arriving at scientific truth, but that is not the way followers of the Cartesian cult see it.

In fact, most of the applications of Descartes' mental power to the real world look rather ridiculous in retrospect. He concluded "without a single doubt" (his own words) that "a vacuum is repugnant to reason." This led to a picture of an infinite universe, full of matter, closely packed with no empty space at all. Whirling vortices, he claimed, created the illusion of discrete solid objects such as the stars and planets in the heavens. In biology Descartes arrived at the "certainty" that man possesses a "soul," which animals lack; he believed (erroneously) that the pineal gland, located in the human brain, is absent in animals and therefore the likely abode of the human soul in the body. (Did he ever read Vesalius? It seems doubtful.)

Away from the real world of matter and animals, Descartes' ideas had greater value and influence. In mathematics, for example, he must be given credit for the fusion of the two fields of algebra and geometry to create what we now call analytical geometry, i.e., the use of equations to describe geometrical lines and figures, an algebraic means of describing any pathway linking positions in space. This was profound for his time because it involves a means of describing space without reference to the matter it contains (or does not contain), thereby sweeping away one of the cherished maxims of Aristotelian authority. But even here, we must insert a slight caveat. Descartes did not recognize the simplicity of a rectangular coordinate system, the now familiar x and y axes of most graphs (and the corresponding x, y, and z axes for three-dimensional space), but resorted to a more complicated geometrical representation. It remained for a later generation of mathematicians to produce the Cartesian coordinate system of today. (Pierre Fermat actually suggested using perpendicular axes at the time, but his work was largely ignored.)

Descartes (1596–1650) was born in the small farming town of La Haye (now called Descartes) and was educated by the Jesuits in their college at La Flèche. His formal schooling ended at the age of sixteen, and he spent the next 17 years or so as a gentleman soldier, fighting in the Netherlands, Bavaria, and in France itself at the siege of La Rochelle. These military years (which ended with his immigration to the Netherlands in 1629) left Descartes much spare time, and it is during this period that he appears to have studied his mathematics and to have cogitated most intensely on philosophical questions. By the end of the 1630s his fame was immense. Queen Christina of Sweden invited him to her court in 1649, but the northern climate proved too severe for him and he died soon after.

Related Places to Visit: Descartes, Paris.

Blaise Pascal (1623–1662). One conspicuous difference between Pascal and Descartes is that the latter, seeking to avoid the contentious character of the French theological and philosophical scene, chose to desert his native land to live in the Netherlands, whereas Pascal lived in France all his life, always close to his family and to whatever controversies were raging. Pascal, in fact, diluted his scientific writing with excursions into unrelated matters and is at least as celebrated in France for his literary skills as for his science and philosophy. His militant religious tract in behalf of Jansenism (against attacks launched by conservative Jesuits), the so-called "provincial letters," is considered a timeless masterpiece of the French language. However, a perhaps more crucial difference between Descartes and Pascal (at least in retrospect) is that Pascal believed in the power of experiment, whereas Descartes relied solely on his thinking.

Pascal was born in Clermont-Ferrand in the mountainous Auvergne, but soon found himself in Paris, where his father had become a tax official. Young Blaise was a genuine child prodigy with a rare gift for mathematics, publishing his first mathematical pamphlets while still in his teens. (He and his equally gifted compatriot, Pierre Fermat, are considered the joint founders of the theory of probability.) He also designed and built one of the first recorded mechanical (gears and wheels) calculating machines, apparently motivated by a wish to assist his father, whose duties as tax collector entailed a huge amount of burdensome arithmetic. Pascal's trailblazing work in this field has been commemorated by the modern computer community. One of the popular languages for mathematical calculation is named after him.

In the context of natural science, it is Pascal's experimental work on vacuum that is the most interesting. It was done between 1646 and 1648 (at the ripe old age of twenty-four), hot on the heels of Evangelista Torricelli's pioneering work in Florence. Torricelli invented the barometer to measure air pressure, asserted that air has weight, and claimed that the empty space above the barometric fluid in a barometer must be devoid of gas, a genuine vacuum. This conclusion flew in the face of the conventional doctrine (and the dictum of Descartes) that nature abhors a vacuum, and Torricelli's observations tended to be explained away—in terms of an emanation from the glass, for example. Pascal's reaction was much more modern in spirit. He asked first whether the observations could be repeated and found that such was the case. He then set out to test the interpretation by thinking up predictions based on it that were susceptible to experimental test. The crucial prediction in this case concerned the effect of external pressure: If Torricelli's analysis were correct, then the liquid column on the closed side of the barometer should fall and the space occupied by vacuum should increase when a barometer is transferred to a lower surrounding pressure, and the change should be reversed when we go back to the original conditions. Pascal tested this at home in Paris with the aid of an air pump, but for a more convincing test, more easily appreciated by the general public, he went back to his roots in Clermont-Ferrand, to the cone-shaped mountain, Puy-de-Dôme, over 1,000 meters in height and just outside the city limits. No pump was needed here. The evacuated space increased and decreased again simply because the weight (pressure) of the overlying air was less on top of the mountain, exactly as predicted.

A triumph for science against Cartesian method? Not quite, for it seems to have been quickly forgotten. France continued for nearly 100 more years to believe in Descartes' filled universe, until the incontestable success of Newton's laws of gravitation finally won the day.

Related Places to Visit: Clermont-Ferrand, Auvergne (Puy-de-Dôme), Paris (St. Jacques Tower, National Technical Museum).

Gardens and Academies. **Le Jardin du Roi** was established in 1626 by order of King Louis XIII, initially for the cultivation and study of medicinal plants. Miraculously it has survived to the present day, unscathed by intervening social and political upheavals. Its name was changed to Le Jardin des Plantes by the Revolution, back again to Jardin du Roi when the monarchy was restored, and once more to Jardin des Plantes when the Republic became permanent. The mission of the institution grew steadily over the years to encompass all of botany, and zoology and geology as well. Museums were added and salaried positions were created. Residences were established within the grounds for the principal administrators. And fortune has favored the enterprise. Vigorous and dedicated men have held the designated positions and lived in the spacious houses. No fewer than three of the important French contributions to science that we have gathered in this chapter were conceived and executed by "jardiniers."

The garden has not, of course, been exempt from the frailties of human nature. Looking at the list of administrators, professors, and other staff, one is struck by the high incidence of nepotism—for example, numerous holders of privileged appointments managed to pass their positions on to their sons when they retired. And anyone who believes that harmony and courteous tolerance are essential fertilizers for the blooming of creative science will not find much supporting evidence here. Conflict and in-house intrigues have been the rule rather than the exception. (The most famous example is the "eulogy" delivered by Georges Cuvier after the death of his colleague Jean-Baptiste Lamarck in 1829. It was so offensive and vitriolic that it was published only after Cuvier himself died in 1832.)

Louis XIII had interests beyond botany—or perhaps his advisor and the real power behind the throne, Cardinal Richelieu, was the true scholar. In any event, Louis was persuaded by Richelieu to officially establish **l'Académie** française in 1635. The original members had been meeting for several years, discussing and criticizing literary contributions, and some say they were less than enthusiastic about their new status and the duties that went with it, such as the charge to produce a dictionary of the French language. This old academy perished (at least by name) in 1793, but resurfaced as a branch of the Institute of France. Membership is limited to 40 persons, commonly known as *immortals*. But real immortality of ideas and writings seems to reside more with scholarly and literary giants who were excluded than with its members. Among the men proposed for membership but denied admission are Descartes, Pascal, Rousseau, Diderot, and Balzac.

L'Académie des sciences, founded in 1666, also owed its official existence to a powerful politician. Colbert, economic genius during the reign of Louis XIV, learned of a loose association between a number of men of science—including Descartes, Gassendi, and Pascal—and persuaded the king to issue a decree to make it official and to provide substantial financial support. This new academy was much more akin to the Royal Society in London (founded 1662) than l'Académie française, not exclusive in its membership, and with the explicit mission of encouraging and sponsoring scientific progress. The state paid lifelong pensions to its members, however, and had more direct influence on its doings than was true in its English sister institution. The academy welcomed foreign members and even sought them out to join its staff. Christiaan Huygens from the Netherlands was an active member. Astronomer Ole Rømer was brought in from Denmark to work at the observatory built by Louis XIV and directed by the Académie. It was here that Rømer made the first measurement of the speed of light in 1676.

Like its sister group, l'Académie française, l'Académie des sciences was disbanded at the time of the Revolution, but reemerged as part of the new Institute of France and continued to exert immense influence on French science. One mechanism for doing so was by means of prize competitions, sponsored and judged by the Académie. Precise definition of the problem for a competition was a way of stimulating research into directions that the powerful members of the Académie deemed desirable. The underlying motivation, in a contentious period, was not necessarily always altruistic.

The bottom line here, as with le Jardin, is the strength and survival of the life-blood of science through crisis and national disaster.

Related Place to Visit: Paris (Jardin des Plantes).

The Century of Enlightenment

The French mathematician Jean Lerond d'Alembert called it "the century of philosophy par excellence." Exuberant philosophers like Voltaire, Diderot, Rousseau, and Montesquieu were indeed at the core of the movement, and mathematicians like d'Alembert and Lagrange were in the thick of it, too—

probably believed, in fact, that advances in mathematics were the movement's most forceful component. We describe below some of the early moments of scientific enlightenment—we call them early because of the inevitable continuity with the Napoleonic era that followed.

Newton in French: Voltaire and the Marquise. Voltaire (1694–1778) has been said to personify the Enlightenment. He was without doubt the link between philosophy and the physical sciences, a popularizer who immensely sharpened public awareness of science, and (not the least of his achievements) he was the catalyst in the process that undermined the Cartesian cult. Voltaire was often at odds with the authorities. Some of his books were banned. He was in prison a couple of times and on one such occasion was released only on condition that he leave France to live in England, which he did for about two years. It was there that his eyes were opened to the wonders of Newtonian philosophy. He had left the world a "plenum," he wrote in a letter in 1733, and found it in London to be a "vacuum."

Voltaire's intimacy with the Marquise du Châtelet (1706–1749) began in 1734, when she invited him to her chateau in Cirey-sur-Blaise to escape another possible arrest. Her husband, the Marquis, raised no objection, extramarital relations being an accepted feature in the French aristocracy. The Marquise was in fact an extraordinary woman, passionate both in the expression of her sex and in the pursuit of mathematics, which she had learned by inveigling two of the then most prominent French physicists (Maupertius and Clairault) into giving her lessons. And she had a special passion, it seems, for Newton's mathematics.

The upshot was a painstaking translation of Newton's *Principia* into French, which occupied the Marquise for more than a decade. It was not completed until the year of her death in childbirth and was published posthumously. The translation included comments and, it is said, even some improvements, where Newton's original text had not been entirely clear to her. The book had a huge influence on French science by making the work of Isaac Newton directly accessible. It remains to this day the only French translation of the *Principia*.

After her death Voltaire published a eulogy of his ex-mistress, which speaks not only to her influence as Newton's translator, but sums up an entire period of scientific history in France. "The sublime truths which we owe to Newton were only fully established in France after a whole generation had grown old in the errors of Descartes."

Related Place to Visit: Lunéville.

The Comte de Buffon (1707–1788). Buffon was the most prominent prerevolutionary jardinier, holding the top post of superintendent of the Jardin du Roi for an incredible 50 years, from 1739 until his death. He was born in Burgundy, in the little town of Montbard, and it is said that he never really liked living in the big city of Paris. In any event, he returned to Montbard every summer to administer his extensive estate, which included a working forge where Buffon manufactured iron for the Ministry of War to be used for the making of cannons. This was not done entirely for the money it brought in, for metallurgy was one of Buffon's many scientific interests. In fact, Buffon was a kind of latter day Pliny, an indefatigable writer on everything under the sun, author of the celebrated *Histoire naturelle*, a 44-volume attempt to embrace all of scientific knowledge, both physical and biological. It was an immensely influential and popular work, which has gone through huge numbers of editions and imitations for over 150 years.

Unfortunately, the *Histoire naturelle* has little in the way of enduring or endearing quality. It abounds with errors, untenable speculations, and much that is pure fantasy. Buffon's lasting contribution lies more in the development of the Jardin under his leadership and in the protegés he encouraged and supported, who included Jean-Baptiste Lamarck, arguably the founder of the idea of the evolution of species.

One creditable piece of Buffon's work (one of the few experiments he ever did) was an estimate for the age of the earth. It was really no more than a repetition of something Newton had already done a century earlier, but it attracted much attention among naturalists who would not normally have read Newton and it created healthy controversy. Newton had surmised that the earth might be continually cooling and noted that a globe of iron an inch in diameter, heated to red hot, will take half an hour to lose all its heat. On that basis he calculated that a globe the size of the earth would require more than 50,000 years to cool. Buffon, with larger iron balls close at hand in his foundry, redetermined the rate of cooling and repeated Newton's calculation. The earth must have a history of "74,047 years approximately," he reported in 1778. The result was controversial, of course, because of the still widespread faith in the Biblical age of less than 6,000 years.

Related Places to Visit: Paris (Jardin des Plantes), Montbard.

Geology in the Auvergne. No place on earth has had more importance in the shaping of the science of geology than the rugged mountains of the Auvergne. It began with purely utilitarian projects, the creation of maps to show how the mineral content of the land varies from place to place, to pinpoint areas where mining projects would be profitable. But at least some of the mapmakers used their brains as they worked, and in the Auvergne in particular they realized that rocks and excavations provide evidence that cries out to be interpreted—that there is within them a fascinating history to be discovered. The development of this history consists of two stages—the proposal by Jean Étienne Guettard (1715–1786) that the Auvergne must once have contained active volcanoes (like Vesuvius and Etna in the present), and the later more provocative assertion of a wider global role for volcanic activity by Nicholas Desmarest (1725–1815). The latter fueled a controversy that was to last for almost 100 years, creating two opposing factions in geology, who came to be called Vulcanists and Neptunists.

Basaltic rocks, often in the form of spectacular vertical columns, were at the heart of the controversy. Neptunists claimed that they were formed long ago by precipitation of inorganic salts previously dissolved in sea water and that volcanoes were a more recent unrelated phenomenon. But Desmarest could see the basalt in the Auvergne in intimate association with undeniable relics of volcanic activity (craters retaining their shapes, lava and pumice around them), and he could not accept the idea that strikingly similar formations in different places could have different origins. Other adherents of the Vulcanist school who followed pointed to the absence of fossils as additional evidence for an igneous origin. Vulcanists were accused of blasphemy and atheism because the overall history of the earth as seen by most Neptunists emphasized the reality of Noah's Flood.

A field trip to the Auvergne soon became an obligatory journey for budding geologists from all over Europe. Charles Lyell, for example, came for the first time in 1828 and more than once thereafter.

Related Places to Visit: Auvergne, Giant's Causeway (Ireland), Staffa (Scotland).

The Chemical Revolution: Antoine Lavoisier (1743–1794). We were taught in our generation that he was the greatest chemist who ever lived, who slew the dragon of the phlogiston theory and thereby opened the gates to the modern kingdom of atoms and molecules. That ought to be enough to put Lavoisier right at the top of French scientists, along with Laplace, Cuvier, Pasteur, Madame Curie. Then why does France's celebration of him seem less enthusiastic than it is for some of these others? Is national pride here muted by awareness of national shame at what was done to him?

Born in Paris to a family of importance, Lavoisier evinced an early interest in science, became friendly with geologist Guettard and collaborated with him for a while in the geological mapping of France. The diversity of minerals aroused his interest in chemistry and (not lacking wealth) he was soon on his way in a well-equipped laboratory in his own home. He kept good notebooks; he thought about what he was doing; he published books that were revolutionary for his time. One of his claims was that there is an equal amount of mass at the beginning and at the end of every chemical process—surely a *sine qua non* if one is to make any sense out of chemistry at all—but precisely the point of logic where the phlogiston theory had sowed the seeds of confusion, viewing combustion as *removal* of something from the material being combusted. Lavoisier's careful and quantitative weighings showed instead that it was oxygen being *added,* and after that things began to fall into place. Most important, he discovered the chemical elements (he was able to recognize about 30 of them), out of which all other substances are made, and he proposed that compounds should be named after the elements that they contain. It was a feat of true creative genius, an enormous step forward from the years before him, when every known substance was a unique entity, unrelated by name to any other substance, and when interconversions were a kind of magic.

(The law of definite proportions of elements in a given compound was still some years away, of course, and the equating of elements with atoms and compounds with molecules could only come after that. And Lavoisier, in advocating new nomenclature, didn't have the inspiration to use symbols instead of words for his elements. But it was he who swept away the conceptual fog. The roots of the familiar modern descriptive chemistry are clearly present in his work.)

One of the verities of prerevolutionary France (and a source of wealth for the middle class) was the existence of middle men, who did what government itself does in more modern times, and Antoine Lavoisier was a beneficiary of this system. He was a member of two organizations that subcontracted government functions. One (which Lavoisier entered in 1768) was the *Ferme général*, which collected excise taxes for the government. Another (appointment in 1775) was the *Régie des Poudres*, which undertook the procurement and maintenance of the national supply of gunpowder. Lavoisier found a wife at the *Ferme*, the daughter of the chief *fermier*. She was only fourteen years old when they married (Lavoisier himself was twenty-eight) and came to share her husband's life in every sense, in his work as well as domestically. She translated English papers for him and helped keep his laboratory notebook. At the *Régie des Poudres* Lavoisier quickly became the top man of the organization, with a home in the national arsenal where he and his wife lived until 1792. Lavoisier took both positions very seriously—for example, he proposed reforms in taxes as well as helping to collect them. And he was always a man of honor, putting national interest and his obligations to the country before personal gain, especially in the changed climate that accompanied the Revolution, the noble aspirations of which he fully supported.

After the Revolution, as we all know, came the Terror. Lavoisier was one of its tragic victims. On May 8, 1794, all the still-living members of the long-disbanded tax farm—28 of them, including Lavoisier's father-in-law—were, in the course of a single day, tried, found guilty of former crimes, and executed. Hasty attempts were made to exempt Lavoisier on the basis of his invaluable current services to France (on the Committee of Weights and Measures, to give just one example), but to no avail. "La République n'a pas besoin des savants," was the cynical response. "Il faut que la justice suive son cours." The victims were thrown into nameless graves. The honors and memorials that were Lavoisier's due never came.

Related Places to Visit: Paris (National Technical Museum, Place de la Concorde).

The Age of Napoleon (1795–1815)

It was another Frenchman (Victor Hugo), not Napoleon, who said

On résiste à l'invasion des armées; on ne résiste pas à l'invasion des idées

but they could have been Napoleon's words, for he had an unbounded enthusiasm for new ideas and for science in particular, an acute understanding of the benefits it could furnish to society. No other ruler of any modern country has been anywhere near Napoleon's equal as a patron of science.

The ground had been prepared by revolutionary legislatures before Napoleon's rise to power. They had introduced the metric system of weights and measures and had created new institutions—the Grandes Écoles for professional training; the highly charged First Class of the Institute of France, which replaced the former l'Académie des Sciences; the museum for teaching and research at the Jardin des Plantes. But the new institutions could well have withered in the bud, for much of the distinctive achievement of revolutionary France was reversed when Napoleon took charge. In fact, the opposite happened. Napoleon encouraged the new institutions, took an active interest in all their doings, was an actual participating member in the First Class of the Institute. Science flourished as never before. To give just one example, Napoleon took a team of savants with him when he set out for Egypt in 1798, a uniquely idealistic aspect of his march of conquest. It led to the discovery of the Rosetta stone (the later instrument for deciphering hieroglyphics) and the publication of a masterful and elegant series of books under the title *Description d'Égypte*. A research institute was set up in Egypt, modeled after the reformatted Paris academy.

The members of the Egyptian expedition included physicist Jean-Baptiste Fourier, chemist Claude Berthollet, and biologist Étienne Geoffroy St. Hilaire. Claude Berthollet was a particularly close friend of Napoleon's and instructed him in chemistry. Before going to Egypt he had headed Napoleon's commission to Italy to select art works for expropriation to French national galleries. While in Egypt he was fascinated by the salt-rich Lake Natron at the edge of the desert and made an important discovery: Familiar chemical reactions involving simple salts had clearly not gone to completion at the high concentrations in the lake, as they would have done under ordinary laboratory conditions. This was the first evidence that amount as well as intrinsic affinity can determine chemical composition, the first inkling of reversibility and the laws of chemical equilibrium. Berthollet was showered with honors on his return and was allowed to acquire a country house in Arcueil (suburban Paris) and to set up a private teaching and research institute there. A couple of years later, Pierre Simon Laplace bought the house next door and for about ten years the two of them came close to being czars of French physical science. They dominated the selection of topics for prize competitions at the Institute, for example, thereby helping to steer younger scientists into directions of their choice.

The influence of this group extended far beyond the lifetimes of its principals and beyond the boundaries of France. Berthollet and Laplace had two prominent disciples, Joseph Gay-Lussac in chemistry and Jean Baptiste Biot in physics, and they in turn had students who would later rise to prominence— Louis Pasteur and Justus von Liebig, for example—and they in turn had their students and followers. Germany's explorer and naturalist Alexander von Humboldt lived in Paris during this period and took chemistry lessons from Gay-Lussac, and they did an experiment together to measure the combining volumes of hydrogen and oxygen gas in water, getting the impressive result of 199.9/100.

The two of them traveled to Italy a little later to measure the intensity of the earth's magnetic field as a function of latitude. And Gay-Lussac and Biot made the first recorded balloon ascent with a scientific mission in 1804 to measure magnetic field as a function of altitude, rising to over 13,000 feet (4,000 meters) above sea level. [Gay-Lussac later left Biot behind to lighten the load and attained an altitude of 23,000 feet (7,000 meters)!]

Napoleon himself was fittingly international in his enthusiasm for science. He lionized Alessandro Volta (*see* under "Italy") when he came to Paris from Italy to demonstrate the production of electric currents, and he gave him a gold medal and a pension. Another medal went to Englishman Humphry Davy (*see* under "England") (at a time when England and France were at war!) for installing a giant voltaic pile in London and using it to isolate the metallic elements sodium and potassium. (Napoleon ordered an even larger pile to be constructed in France.) And still another medal was struck in honor of the English physician Edward Jenner and vaccination was made compulsory in the French army.

What a torrent of new ideas!

Pierre-Simon Laplace: Big Step beyond Newton. Pierre-Simon Laplace (1749–1827) was the standard-bearer of the age in theoretical physics and mathematical mechanics. Do present day students (outside France) fully appreciate how crucial the development of new mathematical methods by Laplace and some of his compatriots were for the full expression and acceptance of Newtonian mechanics? (And for the twentieth-century extension to quantum mechanics as well, it should be noted.)

The problem that was solved can be stated quite simply: Though Newton's explanation of celestial motion was reasonably convincing, observed planetary or lunar orbits never agreed exactly with theoretical predictions. Newton himself had been worried that these deviations might indicate some then unrecognized force tending to instability. Would the solar system one day fly apart? The more reasonable explanation was, of course, an oversimplification in the theoretical calculation of the effect of gravity alone. The orbit of a planet around the sun is surely not determined exclusively by the gravitational attraction between planet and sun, but should also be affected (more weakly) by the attractions of more distant planets. Similar considerations would apply to the orbits of moons around planets. But Newton's laws dealt only with the forces between the two bodies at a time.

The development of new analytical methods to overcome this limitation was a French achievement. The foremost names associated with it are those of Joseph-Louis Lagrange (1736–1813) and of Laplace. While both names are equally important for pure mathematics, Laplace was the dominant force in explicit applications to physics. His most important work, *Celestial Mechanics,* was published in five volumes between 1799 and 1825 and claimed to "offer a complete solution of the great mechanical problem presented by the solar system, and bring theory to coincide so closely with observation that empirical equations should no longer find a place is astronomical tables." Celestial orbits could now be predicted correctly, and lingering skepticism about the philosophical correctness of Newtonian mechanics was banished.

Laplace, not known as a modest man, went on from there to make the statement so often cited in introductions to modern physics—with implicit smirks at such naiveté—to the effect that if he were given the location and vectorial velocity of every atom in the universe at the present instant, then he would be able to calculate both the future and the past record of the entire assembly! (Did that raise questions for philosophers on the subject of determinism versus free will? None other than Albert Einstein was shocked a century later by the *antithesis* of Laplace's statement, by Heisenberg's uncertainty principle and other touchstones of modern probabilistic physics. "God does not play dice!" Einstein protested.)

Laplace was born in Beaumont-en-Auge, in the Camembert and apple brandy region of Normandy, the son of an unpretentious farmer. He came to Paris at age eighteen through the sponsorship of the mathematician d'Alembert and he rose rapidly to prominence after that, not only because of his innate ability, but also, one suspects, because he had great talent for promoting himself. He became politically influential, as we have already noted, but was never popular with his colleagues because of his aggressive boosting of his own status, often at their expense.

Related Place to Visit: Beaumont-en-Auge.

Jean Baptiste Fourier: Flow of Heat and Tides of War. It is quite an education to scan modern textbooks of calculus and applied mathematics and to see the names of Lagrange and Laplace appear over and over again in quite diverse contexts. However, an even more broadly recognized mathematical name, for which no textbook index is needed, is that of Jean Baptiste Fourier (1768–1830)—Fourier series, Fourier integrals and Fourier transforms are household words for physicists and engineers, representing indispensable tools of their trade. It is noteworthy then that Fourier's mathematics was quite different in kind from that of Lagrange and Laplace. It was, in fact, quite uncharacteristic of the prevailing trends of French physics. It was developed to *describe* the flow of heat, but to do so empirically, deliberately rejecting physical models to explain what heat might actually be, in contrast to Laplace's emphasis on a particulate model for all matter. Fourier was thus a lesser scientist, one can say, lacking one of the dimensions of intellectual creativity.

But what a life the man had, what an epic of adventure! He is an outstanding example of a child of the Revolution, someone who could not have achieved success without it—would not even have had the opportunity. He was the orphaned son of a tailor in Auxerre in Burgundy. One of his father's friends provided for his education at Auxerre's military school, but Fourier's lowly birth and impoverished status were incompatible with a career in the army. Just twenty-one years old when the Revolution began, Fourier naturally embraced it with enthusiasm, but later got into trouble when he became disgusted with the excesses of the Terror. He was arrested in 1794 and probably was lucky to survive unscathed. (An appeal for clemency to Robespierre played a part. Robespierre rejected it but then Robespierre himself fell victim to the guillotine, and Fourier may have been spared because he was perceived as an intended Robespierre victim.)

Then came war and we find Fourier in high places, a member of the team of savants who went to Egypt and a personal friend of Napoleon's. Fourier was one of the principal organizers of the project to publish the elegant *Description d'Égypte*, and he wrote a historical preface for it, full of enthusiasm for the glories of the ancient Egyptian civilization. On Fourier's return to France in 1801, Napoleon rewarded him with a state administrative position, the prefecture of Isère, which includes the important city of Grenoble. Fourier was to hold this post for 14 years, and it was here, in his spare time and in relative isolation, that all his major scientific work was done.

But the tides of war intervened dramatically again after Napoleon was defeated and banished to Elba in 1814. Fourier managed to hold his job, but when Napoleon returned from exile for a briefly triumphant march on Paris, our hero was in an unenviable position. Grenoble was directly on Napoleon's route and Fourier, as prefect, was forced to order the defense of the city against him, even though he knew perfectly well that the defense would be useless. He managed to avoid an open encounter with his former friend by leaving Grenoble from one side of the city as Napoleon entered from the other. When Napoleon regained power, he bore no grudge and even made Fourier a count and appointed him to the more important prefecture of the department of the Rhône with headquarters in Lyons. Fourier (almost fifty years old by now) of course lost that job after Napoleon's final defeat and the return of the monarchy. He decided to move permanently to Paris—there were no prospects anywhere else—but he had to contend with the stigma of having been one of Napoleon's favorites and had a hard time before he was able to take his rightful place among his peers. A curious postscript, given the diametrically opposed mathematical paradigms of the two men: Fourier succeeded Laplace as perpetual secretary of the French Academy of Sciences and in 1827 he even became one of the "immortals," a member of the Académie française.

A final irony—the tides of war again enveloped Fourier long after he was dead. A bronze statue of Fourier in his home town of Auxerre was requisitioned by the Germans in World War II to be melted down for guns. But they did not get all of it, for the mayor of Auxerre, in a stealthy midnight raid, saved two of the statue's bas-reliefs, which are still proudly exhibited today.

Related Place to Visit: Auxerre.

At the Jardin des Plantes: Fossils, Extinction, and Evolution. A different kind of battle was in progress at the Jardin, apparently little influenced by Napoleon's wars and ultimate defeat, a prototype of the modern debate between evolutionists and creationists. The basic ideas themselves are very old, for people have always wondered where the inanimate world and the living things around us come from. Among the early Greeks, for example, Anaximander of Miletus theorized that "at the birth of this world a germ of hot and cold separated off from the eternal" and all things afterwards came from this single source—but he did not tell us how it happened, how a single germ might have evolved into the multiplicity of forms around us. Later on, Hebrew religious thought asserted the antithesis of Anaximander's idea, stating that earth and the heavens and every plant and every other living thing were created separately by a supreme being. This is the theology of creation that Christianity embraced and enforced as orthodoxy for several centuries. But it was in Paris, after the Muséum National d'Histoire Naturelle was founded as part of the reorganization of the Jardin du Roi, that the debate between these opposing views of origins for the first time took center stage in a modern scientific institution with an eager public following. The most prominent of the advocates were **Jean-Baptiste Lamarck** on the side of evolution and **Georges Cuvier** on the side of creationism.

Lamarck (1744–1829) was already fifty years old, an underappreciated assistant botanist (appointed by the former director Comte de Buffon), when he was given a professorial appointment under the new order. The quaint title of his appointment, Professor of Insects and Worms, has been cited as a measure of his low esteem—it has been suggested that nobody else could be found who was willing to commit himself to study this insignificant class of animals. The new job gave Lamarck a mandate to lecture and, for the first time, to have his own independent views heard. He seized the opportunity and began to make fundamental contributions to science. One achievement was to recognize that worms and insects are not insignificant at all, but an important separate class in the animal kingdom, characterized by lack of a bony skeleton. It was he who invented the modern name *invertebrates* for them. He also coined the word *biology* for the study of all forms of life, both plant and animal, insisting that the sciences of the inert world (physics and chemistry) were not adequate for understanding life, which, it might be mentioned, was another blow against Cartesian doctrine. (And Lamarck thereby launched another celebrated debate of the nineteenth century, that between so-called vitalists and champions of a purely mechanistic approach.)

But it is evolution for which Lamarck is remembered today. The French in fact call Lamarck the founder of evolution, which is an exaggeration because one cannot really identify one individual as the originator of such a natural idea, but it is true that his was the first clearly argued evolutionary theory. Paris was the right place at the right time to propose it, with fossils just becoming accepted then as relics of former living things, similar but not identical to present life-forms. Unfortunately Lamarck had an incorrect and indefensible mechanism for evolution. He seriously proposed that living *individuals* continuously adapt to their environment and that characteristics acquired in this way can be inherited, that antelopes stretching their necks to seek food from high branches on trees will gradually, over many generations, evolve to giraffes. Lamarck's name has become anathema to most modern geneticists for this reason, but the criticism seems harsh. The fact remains that Lamarck was a champion of evolution at a time when most people believed that species were fixed and that existing species were originally created exactly as we see them now.

Cuvier (1769–1832) was a much younger man, who joined the museum staff in 1802 with the more businesslike title, Professor of Comparative Anatomy. He was an opportunist with a modern thirst for success in his chosen field of natural history, who rapidly became Europe's expert on fossils and thereby the authority on origins. He owed an indirect debt to Napoleon, who was in the midst of a massive rebuilding scheme for the city of Paris. The limestone quarries of Montmarte were being used at full steam, exposing layer upon layer of fossil remains—shellfish, reptiles, fish, mammals—and Cuvier seized the opportunity to practice what the title of his museum post decreed, namely comparative anatomy, and, on the basis of fossil finds, he introduced new species and classes into the Linnaean scheme of classification of animals. The bones of elephants and related pachyderms were among his most spectacular finds, and they became evidence for what was then an unpopular notion, the idea that previously abundant species could have become extinct. The frequent lack of correspondence between some species in the fossil record and the existing local fauna was of course quite familiar, but many scientists tried to explain it by supposing that the missing species might have migrated to more favorable climates and might now still be living in poorly explored parts of the earth. But mammoths and other large "disappeared" mammals are too big to be "lost," even in obscure parts of the globe. They must be "extinct."

Ironically, given that extinction and evolution are now so intertwined in our minds, Cuvier believed in fixity of species and categorically denied the possibility of evolution. This was the core of the dispute between Cuvier and Lamarck and others at the Jardin who leaned toward an evolutionary theory. It was of course partly engendered by the way Lamarck defined evolution as a gradual process—extinction, to Cuvier, was clearly incompatible with evolution defined in this way. The overall level of the debate was, however, too vitriolic for many tastes. In retrospect that may be seen as a reflection of the primitive state of the life sciences at the time in comparison with the more sophisticated thinking in physics.

It should be noted that Cuvier has an important place in the history of geology as well as in the field of evolution. His work on fossils and extinction inevitably led to a particular kind of theory for the history of the earth, subsequently called *catastrophism*. What was the underlying cause of successive extinctions? The strata in the Paris geological basin showed a layer rich in freshwater species, followed by a layer with marine deposits, followed by another with freshwater shellfish. A large proportion of the species in all three layers were extinct. The logical explanation lay in successive deluges, sufficient to wipe out much of the existing forms of life. The overall importance of such catastrophes for the history of the earth was subsequently put in question when the uniformitarian theory of Charles Lyell became popular, but arguments actually continue to this day, with meteorite impacts replacing deluge as instruments of catastrophe.

Related Places to Visit: Paris (Jardin des Plantes), Montebéliard.

Post-Napoleonic Physics

André Ampère (1775–1836): Unhappy Electrician. It is a fascinating incongruity—volts and amps are inexorably linked in our daily lives, jointly labeling practically every electrical thing we ever use, but the men after whom they are named, Alessandro Volta (*see* under "Italy") and André-Marie Ampère, were opposites in personality and in how they fared in the French Revolution and its aftermath. Volta was a happy man, confident and high-spirited, and (despite being Italian) he flourished under French rule and was a favorite with Napoleon. Ampère, by contrast, was studious and naive, and his personal life was dogged by misfortune. The first shock came in the aftermath of the French Revolution, when Ampère was still a youth. His father, an honest and compassionate man, was drafted by the people to be a judge in Lyon, and in that position had protested and prevented many excesses of the revolutionaries. When the Republicans captured Lyon in 1793, he was summarily tried for his moral stand and sent to the guillotine. André Ampère was eighteen years old, and it was more than he could bear—for a whole year he retired into himself, unable to cope with the outside world. After he recovered he loved, wooed, and married the lady of his choice, and they had a son, but then his wife became ill and died. Ampère moved to Paris and there married again (and had a daughter), but the family of his new wife swindled him out of his patrimony, and wife and mother-in-law combined to make his life so miserable that he had to seek divorce, probably a traumatic move for a devout Catholic. His son and daughter lived with him, but then his son fell under the spell of a notorious beauty and became a member of her decorative court, and his daughter married an army officer who was always drunk and violent. Poor Ampère himself had some moderate success in academic life, but his meager income was mostly derived from holding the position of inspector for the French national university system. He died in 1836 in Marseille while on an inspection tour, alone and unhappy.

What kept up Ampère's interest in life was his science and philosophy. He was essentially self-educated—encouraged and often tutored by his father, provided access to his father's library, but given complete freedom in the subjects (Latin, mathematics, philosophy) that he chose to pursue. He soon became an intellectual prodigy, but for a long time his interests were too diffuse to produce much published work, and we know about what he was doing only from letters. He devoted much effort to chemistry, for example, and probably anticipated Humphry Davy in correctly identifying what we now call chlorine as an element and not a compound.

It was not till 1820 (by now forty-five years old) that Ampère started to concentrate his work on electromagnetism, stimulated (as so many others were) by Hans Christian Ørsted's remarkable discovery in Denmark demonstrating that a current flowing through a wire will deflect a magnetic needle placed close to the wire (see under "Denmark"). Many who had not seen the experiment at firsthand were skeptical, but Ampère accepted it without question and within one week had produced his own first paper on the phenomenon. He labored prodigiously in this field until 1827, publishing in that year his monumental *Memoir*, which provided both many new detailed experiments on the relationship between moving electric charges and magnetism and Ampère's own theoretical explanation for them. He demonstrated quantitatively that the force on Ørsted's magnetic needle is directly proportional to the length of the wire and the amount of current and inversely proportional to the square of the distance from the wire. His findings made it possible to use magnetism for quantitative measurement of flowing electricity, providing the foundation for the first practical device (ironically called a *galvanometer*) for measuring electric current.

Related Place to Visit: Poleymieux.

The Essence of Light. The branch of physics in which the French particularly excelled was optics. We have not the space to mention all the people who contributed to this subject, but one who demands inclusion is **Auguste Fresnel** (1788–1827). He was trained as an engineer and earned his living building highways for the state, but somehow found time and energy to sort out a major problem in physics. He is responsible for the classical wave theory of light. It was a particularly striking achievement because it had been French science (especially Laplace) that had just recently elevated Newtonian mechanics to its greatest heights (and Newton to the status of an infallible hero), and the wave theory required a turn against Newton who held light to be corpuscular.

Newton himself had been aware of the weakness of his theory. Light often behaves in a most uncorpuscle-like fashion, as when it is *diffracted* by passing through a narrow aperture or when it becomes *polarized* by passing through Iceland spar crystals. Newton was forced to invoke strange and unconvincing interactions to explain these phenomena, and there were always adherents of a rival wave theory of light, originally proposed by Dutchman Christiaan Huygens. But Huygens visualized his waves as longitudinal (like sound waves), where the little motions that carry the energy are in the same direction as the direction of travel of the wave itself, which made the wave symmetrical in the perpendicular direction and unable to explain polarization any better than Newton's theory can. Fresnel carried out decisive optical experiments to render the corpuscular theory untenable, but his truly great contribution was to change the nature of the wave. His model was based on continuous trains of *transverse* waves, with undulatory motions perpendicular to the direction of travel and allowed to take any direction in the 360° circle at right angles to the direction of propagation. (Polarization was then easily explained. When light waves pass through, interact with, certain types of material, the transverse vibrations of the emerging wave are confined to just one perpendicular plane.)

Did Fresnel achieve instant acclaim? He did not, partly because a decisive experiment was deemed necessary as final proof (see the following section), and it was to be nearly 20 years after Fresnel's early death from tuberculosis before it was done, but partly also because the days of Napoleonic enthusiasm for science were gone. Fresnel had to continue to work for the state as an engineer, with only one concession—since he was now an optical expert, they transferred him from highway construction to the Lighthouse Commission!

Related Place to Visit: Broglie.

The Speed of Light. All this excitement about the intrinsic nature of light sparked renewed interest in how fast light travels. What is the speed of light? The difference between the velocities in air and in water became especially important as a potentially definitive test between the corpuscular and wave theories of light. The explanation of refraction according to wave theory requires light to travel faster in air than in water. The corpuscular theory, on the other hand, predicted a faster speed in water.

The first measurement of the speed of light had actually been made in France in 1676, at the Paris observatory, by the Danish astronomer Ole Rømer. Like other determinations made since then, it had been based on the time required for light to reach the earth from heavily bodies (Jupiter's moons in Rømer's case). The results were not very accurate and in any case could not be used for comparison between air and water. **Hippolyte Fizeau** (1819–1896) made the first terrestrial measurement, using light traveling between Montmartre and Suresnes in Paris, with a mirror and a cogwheel to intercept the reflected ray. This method of course still could not be applied to measure the difference between air and water and it was **Jean Bernard Foucault** (1819–1868) who was the first to succeed with that, in measurements made over a 12-year period after 1850. His ingenious apparatus used a rapidly oscillating mirror, which reflected light to two stationary mirrors, one of which was placed at the end of a tube of water. The two light beams, one passing through air and the other through water, were reflected back to the oscillating mirror (which by now had moved a little) and then back to the source. The results showed a displacement of the two beams with that traveling through air moving faster than that passing through water. The wave theory triumphed, the corpuscular theory was dead. But was it? The twentieth century brought more surprises, as we shall soon see.

Numerical Note. The absolute values for the speed of light are of interest here. Fizeau had 313,000 kilometers per second and Foucault (in air) 298,000 kilometers per second. The currently accepted value (in air) is 299,800 kilometers per second, about 186,000 miles per second.

Foucault's Pendulum. Foucault was actually an extremely versatile mechanical genius. The precision gears and perfectly polished mirrors for measuring the speed of light were just one invention. The modern gyroscope was another and his happiest invention of all was his pendulum for demonstrating the rotation of the earth, doing it so simply that an observer is instantly convinced without need for numerical calculation or any other learned skills. It was installed as a public demonstration in the Panthéon in Paris in 1851 and proved to be an enormous success for the popularization of science there and later in other cities.

The device is based on the self-regulation of all pendulums, which Galileo had in principle already recognized, and something that every reader can test for himself. Make your own pendulum with a heavy weight at the end of a long light thread and attach it to a support that can be turned. Set the pendulum swinging in any desired direction. Now turn the support, through 90°, for example. The direction of swing of the pendulum remains unchanged! (More accurately, it would remain unchanged under laboratory conditions. With a crude do-it-yourself pendulum some circular precession will usually be added to the motion.)

Suppose now that we use a huge heavy pendulum in an enormous hall like the Panthéon; suppose that we avoid air currents or other perturbations and use a support that is rigidly attached and cannot itself be rotated. What do we expect to see? What we *seem* to see (despite the fixed support) is a steady change in the direction of swing, 15° per hour, returning to its original orientation in 24 hours. What is going on? There is only one conceivable explanation—the Panthéon itself (with its fixed support) must be turning, making a complete circle every 24 hours!

Related Place to Visit: Paris (National Technical Museum).

Limits on Energy: Sadi Carnot and the Carnot Family. Here we have a most unusual situation. Sadi Carnot (1796–1832) is universally acknowledged as the author of a truly brilliant highlight in the history of physics and chemistry, but he is celebrated very little in his native land and is actually regarded as a lesser member of a family bristling with national celebrities. Sadi's father, Lazare Carnot (1753–1823), is the most important, always referred to as "Organisateur de la Victoire" of the French Revolution. He was originally an engineer and he put his skills to use to organize the logistics of the Revolution, always managing as if by magic to have supplies and men in the right place at the right time. He was a member of the Committee of Safety, who unreservedly voted for the execution of the king and condoned the excesses of the Reign of Terror. Sadi's brother and nephew were also important in national affairs and the latter (also named Sadi) was actually elected president of France in 1887 and died at the hands of an anarchist assassin in 1894. Does it all sound more dramatic than thermodynamics? It isn't, when you come to think of it. Scientist Sadi discovered what is, in effect, the second law of thermodynamics, an absolute limit to our power, and the irreversibility of the arrow of time. That is pretty dramatic stuff, especially for a nineteenth-century society that by and large believed in future progress without foreseeable end.

Sadi Carnot was an engineer by training, like his father, but died at the age of only thirty-six from cholera following an attack of scarlet fever. His fame rests on a single paper, the only one he ever published (in 1824), entitled *Reflections on the Motive Power of Fire and on Machines Fitted to Develop Their Power*. In other words, it dealt with devices like a steam engine, where heat from burning coal or wood provides energy of a kind, and the task of the engine is to convert it to energy of another kind, "motive power," as he called it, or "mechanical work," as we might call it today. Such engines were known to be very inefficient and Carnot (and undoubtedly many other people) wanted to improve the situation. Carnot took the unusual first step of trying to understand the general theory of the transfer of heat into work before he set to work to build apparatus and he did so by means of what is known now as a *Gedankenexperiment*, a thought experiment, using only pencil and paper and already established principles of mathematics, physics, and/or just plain common sense. His is one of the classic examples of such a device, the elucidation of the uncertainty principle by Born and Heisenberg 100 years later being another (see under "Germany").

The *Gedankenexperiment* was very simple: Design an idealized engine, with frictionless pistons and perfect insulation to prevent heat loss; specify exact conditions for all stages in the operation of the engine, such as the temperature and pressure of the steam; finally work out what will happen by applying the known laws of physics. Since it was all on paper, one could (within obvious limits) assign any actual values one wanted to the numerical parameters. Carnot's result was as simple as the experiment itself, but entirely unexpected—sensational, in fact. It showed that conversion of heat into work cannot occur at all unless heat flows from a high temperature to a lower temperature in the course of the process, and even then the efficiency of conversion is theoretically limited by the magnitude of the difference between high and low. The practical possibility of an efficiency anywhere near 100 percent was immediately eliminated, for temperatures way beyond a reasonable range would be required, but the theoretical existence of a limit soon came to be seen as the most important aspect.

As it happened, Sadi Carnot had an entirely false picture of what heat really is. He thought of it as a substance, an element, as Lavoisier had done, and he died too young to see the experiments of Joule (see under "England") and others that would have forced him to change that view. But the beauty of the *Gedankenexperiment* was that it didn't depend on one's picture of molecules and their motion, only the empirical laws of gas expansion were involved. Carnot's result has thus remained a part of the factual baggage of thermodynamics ever afterwards. Lord Kelvin used it as the basis for the creation of an absolute scale of temperature, Clausius used it to define the concept of entropy, and so forth. Carnot's objective was practical—to design a more efficient engine—but what came out of it was one of the great cornerstones of our theoretical understanding of the world around us.

Related Place to Visit: Nolay.

Biology and Medical Science

Claude Bernard: Physiology Breaks Away. Physiology, the science of
how the body really works, seems to have progressed only slowly through the
ages, with less drama and fanfare than most other branches of science. One
reason for this is that bits and pieces of physiology tend to be subsumed under
other names, especially chemistry or medicine. But that is only a partial explanation, for physiology has in truth been a laggard and still is today. We know less
about the inside of the brain, for example, than we do about the inside of the
atom or the coils of DNA in our genes.

Claude Bernard (1813–1878) owes his place in history first and foremost to
his influence in changing people's concepts of medical or biological science as a
whole, concepts that dictated how it should be studied and taught. Before him
physiology was intimately linked to anatomy. Life as a whole was regarded as the
sum of the actions of anatomically distinct organs, each playing its designated
role. Bernard's work demonstrated influences of one anatomical part on another,
generating the realization that the whole is more than the sum of its parts.

Claude Bernard was born in the village of St. Julien, in the heart of the
Beaujolais region of Burgundy. His parents were vineyard workers, but they
apprenticed Claude to an apothecary. Claude himself had aspirations to a
literary career and went off to Paris with a play he had written. (In later life,
referring to his apprenticeship, he said that as a pharmacist "I wrote tragedies
and inscribed the labels of phials in a beautiful script.") In Paris he was soon
convinced that it would be wiser to build on his apothecary training and he
proceeded to obtain an M.D. degree and to start physiological research under
François Magendie at the Collège de France. There he found his vocation. He
remained in Paris the rest of his life, but never forgot his roots, returning to St.
Julien annually for the grape harvest. He was married for 20 years, but his wife
hated Bernard's work (they eventually separated) and neither of his two daughters would have any truck with their father. The vineyard always remained
Bernard's most consuming passion apart from his work.

Among the specific breakthroughs made by Bernard are his discovery of
the role of pancreatic juice in the digestion of fats, the role of the liver in
synthesizing glycogen from sugar and storing it for future use, and the role of the
nervous system as a control mechanism for numerous bodily functions. Though
still ill-defined, these discoveries set the stage for modern physiological chemistry and for "integrative" physiology—the interplay among organs, blood circulation, and the nervous system in complex animals. Equally important is the fact
that he did his experiments using living animals. Cannulae were inserted into
the intestinal tract so that the intestinal fluids could be sampled while an animal
was going through its daily life more or less normally. Anesthetized animals were
used for dissection and control function was studied by cutting selected nerves.
Gone were the days of the classical anatomist's cadavers and animal corpses, and
physiology as a separate discipline emerged.

Related Place to Visit: St. Julien-sous-Montmelas.

Louis Pasteur (1822–1895), a towering figure in history compared to Bernard, was in some ways more than a scientist, but in other ways perhaps a little less. His outstanding contribution was as a crusader, a knight fighting a holy war, exhorting the public to throw off the yoke of centuries of ignorance and complaisance, challenging them to make use of science to help them in their constant battles against disease and against unforeseen commercial disasters. The other side of the same coin, however, is that almost all the hard science behind the substance of his crusades came from others, from less illustrious contemporaries. Yes, Pasteur was the flagbearer for the germ theories of fermentation and disease, but he was not the originator, nor was he the studious researcher who defined what germs are and studied their life cycles. We should also remember that, though seen today as one of the founders of medical science, he was, in fact, a chemist by training. He never immunized anyone by his own hand, for example.

Pasteur's personal triumph was of course immense. Born the son of a humble provincial tanner, he rose to unprecedented heights and became a legend in his own time. The now world-famous Pasteur Institute in Paris was created specifically for him while he was still alive and active. A jubilee was held to celebrate his seventieth birthday in 1892 and was attended by thousands of scholars and statesmen from all over the world. The president of France (none other than the younger Sadi Carnot) led Louis Pasteur on his arm to the stage to receive the accolades of the audience. When Pasteur died in 1895, he was given a state funeral and was buried in a special mausoleum on the grounds of his Institute. For many years afterward the Institute staff went there formally twice a year to mark the anniversaries of his birth and death and to express their devotion to his memory.

Pasteur's scientific life as a chemist began as a student in Paris and as a young faculty member at the University of Strasbourg, where he took a step up the social ladder by marrying the daughter of the Rector—she was to become his lifelong loyal helpmate. The subject of his work was optical activity, the ability of some substances to rotate the direction of the transverse oscillations of polarized light waves. Specifically, he studied solutions of tartrates, asymmetric molecules which exist as what we now call *stereoisomers*, chemically identical, but with atomic structures that are mirror images of one another. Pasteur discovered that optical activity is related to crystalline asymmetry (and thereby, one might surmise, to molecular structure), but he did not pursue this problem in depth for he found quite by accident that mold growing in one of his flasks of tartrate used only one of the two stereoisomers as a nutrient. With this he was off and running on what became a lifelong conviction—that optical activity plays a central role in the chemistry of life!

Pasteur's next professorial appointment was at the University at Lille, where he became involved in trying to solve problems in the production of alcohol by fermentation of beet sugar. "Louis is now up to his neck in beet juice," Madame Pasteur wrote in a letter to her father-in-law. The beet juice proved to be another success story for Pasteur. For one thing it reinforced his conviction about optical activity—beet juice is optically active—but the true milestone discovery concerned the many visible contaminants in the juice, which were suspected to be the cause of production problems, and, indeed, some of them were. But one of the supposed contaminants turned out to be something altogether different, a microbial agent—yeast sprung to life—without which fermentation cannot work at all. The conclusion was devastating: Fermentation cannot be a purely chemical process, but must be a biological one, where beet sugar is first of all food for yeast's metabolism, just as the tartrate in Strasbourg had been food for an infecting mold. The germ theory of fermentation was proclaimed. It was not a new theory, for the function of yeast as a fermentation agent had been demonstrated 20 years earlier by, among others, Theodor Schwann, the originator of the cell theory for all living matter. But the original idea had been squashed by the German chemist Justus von Liebig, who was an adamant antivitalist and would not tolerate any suggestion that a living thing could be involved in what for him was just simple chemistry that he could duplicate in the laboratory.

After this, they could not keep Pasteur in the provinces. He returned to Paris, the center of the French academic world, ultimately as professor at the Sorbonne. Numerous and far-reaching ramifications of the germ theory soon followed. Microorganisms were identified as the causes of diseases of silkworms that threatened the silk industry and of anthrax in farm animals, cholera in chickens, and rabies in beast and man. They could be killed by prolonged heating, which gave rise to the commercial process of pasteurization. Pasteur seized on Edward Jenner's successful use of cowpox infection to protect against smallpox (see under "England") and extended it broadly, always giving proper credit to Jenner's priority. Immunization with altered or attenuated germs was soon found to prevent many infective diseases, and was probably Pasteur's greatest legacy in the eyes of the public.

Scientific footnote. Pasteur's work became the final blow against the theory of spontaneous generation of life, a subject of controversy for hundreds of years. Even the worldly wise chemist Justus Liebig believed till the day of his death (1873) that putrefaction of dead living matter, like fermentation, is a purely chemical process and that living microorganisms found in the rotting soup are *products* of the chemistry—life spontaneously created—and not germs that arrived from without and then took over the direction.

Related Places to Visit: Paris (Pasteur Institute), Dôle, Arbois, Strasbourg.

Human Antiquity

French archaeological sites have played a pivotal role for the growing realization of the antiquity of *homo sapiens* in Europe. The standard textbook terms for successive stages in the art of toolmaking (Mousterian, Perigordian, etc.) are derived from these sites.

Stone Tools in the Sand. The tidal flats of the Somme near Abbéville are a veritable treasure house of fossils and relics of early civilization. **Jacques Boucher de Perthes** (1788–1868), an amateur paleontologist (professionally, a tax collector) found the first evidence here for the existence of man before recorded history. Inspired perhaps by a friend who died young (Casimir Picard), Boucher de Perthes enjoyed poking around the sands as a hobby and began to unearth flints that bore clear signs of human workmanship. Moreover, they were made from a kind of rock not found in the vicinity.

Boucher de Perthes continued to explore the entire region, discovering not only tools but remains of elephant and rhinoceros bones and eventually publishing, between 1847 and 1864, a three-volume monumental work on the subject of "antediluvian man" in the region of the Somme. The scientific establishment was not impressed, in part because Boucher de Perthes's drawing skill was poor; in part because he included questionable objects in his collection—stones claimed to bear hieroglyphics—and, most importantly, because he had found no human remains. Intervention by an English geologist, Joseph Prestwich, saved the day. He inspected the sites near Abbéville and himself discovered a human jaw together with worked flints in a gravel pit at Moulin-Quignon, an Abbéville mill. Early man had indeed lived in Europe, probably as long as a million years ago!

The Cro-Magnon Skeletons. There's no place like the Dordogne for getting an education about the antiquity of man. Even the casual tourist, coming

---

Time Course of Human Evolution

Appearance of first mammals	about 200 million years ago
First primates	about 60 million years ago
First hominids, designated as *Australopithecus*, found mostly in Africa. The name means *southern ape.*	about 3 million years ago
First species designated as *Homo,* again from Africa.	about 2 million years ago
Homo erectus, a truly bipedal ancestor, first specimens from Java and Peking.	about 1 million years ago
Earliest tools, from southern England and from Abbéville in France.	about 1 million years ago
First Neanderthal man	about 100,000 years ago
Cro-Magnon man	about 25,000 years ago

here to camp or occupy a holiday cottage, cannot avoid being made aware of the chronology of human evolution because so much of the evidence comes from right here.

The focus on this area began when human skeletons of considerable antiquity were discovered in the Vézère Valley in 1868. They were named Cro-Magnon man, after the cave where they were found, and it soon became apparent that these skeletons were virtually indistinguishable from modern human remains, quite unlike the fossils of Neanderthal man that had been discovered in Germany in 1856. This is a truly modern being, living about 25,000 years ago. The initial find triggered more exploration, and not only Cro-Magnons but also many specimens of Neanderthal skulls were found, with the characteristic thick brow. In fact, some of the ones from here were more complete than the original specimen from the Neander Valley. Many tools were found associated with the skeletal remains, and then came prehistoric art, cave walls covered with accurate depictions of animals. Vézère Valley for nearly a century became the laboratory par excellence for all anthropological research. In the last few decades, the laboratory has in effect been opened to public view, for the valley has developed into a sort of theme park for anthropology, somewhat more touristy in spots than we might like, but still a place without its equal for learning about the origins of our own species of being.

The science that emerges from studies of relics of the past tends, of course, to be less firm than the texts of physics or biology, and controversy is ever present. Is some particular skeleton on the direct path to yours truly or on a dead-end branch of evolution? Did Neanderthal and Cro-Magnon men coexist and how far apart are they on the evolutionary scale? Is Neanderthal little more than a technically skilled chimpanzee? Or is he effectively H. sapiens, just an early race thereof? We have discussed professional opinion on this question in our story of the original Neanderthal find (under "Germany") but should note here that not all the controversy in this field is equally weighty, and some may actually strike us as amusing, reflecting an influence of currently popular social theories. For example, we used to think of "cavemen" as strong and fierce hunters of wild beasts, ancestors in whom we could feel a certain degree of virile pride. But "man the hunter" was replaced by "man the seed-eater" in the 1970s, following in the footsteps of the flower children of the previous decade, the caveman being pictured now as using his free arms to carry the fruit he had gathered. And still more recently the feminist movement has decreed that it isn't "man" at all, but "woman" who has determined the path of evolution—the free arms of our bipedal posture help to cradle the baby, and social development, too, is dictated by the need to protect and feed our young. Who knows what new interpretation the 1990s will bring?

One thing that seems to be uncontroversial is the weather. We were in the midst of an ice age and the climate here in the south was like that of Scandinavia today. Herds of reindeer roamed the land and provided food and warm skins and bone for tool-making. Successive retreats and advances of the ice cap took place (on a time scale of thousands of years) and were presumably important in generating population movements and transfer of learned skills to and from widely separated areas.

Caveman's Art. The cave paintings in the Vézère Valley and related areas (south to the Pyrenées and into northern Spain) have an extraordinary impact on the visitor. Most of us, conditioned no doubt by the pace of recent technological advances, tend to think that the human race has only recently emerged from a state of barbarism. Some of us have grandparents who could not read or write. We marvel at the Egyptian pyramids, dating from 2500 B.C., and at the stone circles in northern Britain (some from 3000 B.C. and even earlier, see "Scotland"), the latter far from the classical origins of Western culture in the Mediterranean area. Given these prejudices, the prehistoric art we see here is mind-boggling. It is securely dated as deriving from the period between about 40,000 B.C. and 12,000 B.C. It reflects sophisticated talent in drawing, with spectacular attention to fine anatomical detail, and excellent production and use of color. All of these skills must have been passed on from one generation to another, implying the existence of teacher/apprentice relations, and there are obvious similarities in design and technique from one region to another, suggesting that painters traveled long distances to learn from one another. The best studied paintings are in large caves specifically set aside for painting, definitely not used as living quarters. A gathering place for some primitive ritual perhaps? If so, was professional rivalry among the artists superimposed, a contest to exhibit the best decorative skills? Whatever the precise answer may be, the net result is that we must drastically revise our opinion of Stone Age man. He was not brutal but sensitive, a skilled observer, a person with aesthetic appreciation, perhaps in toto not greatly different from what we are today!

Related Places to Visit: Abbéville, Lascaux II, Les Eyzies-de-Tayac, Tarascon-sur-Ariége.

The Twentieth Century

The Curies: Radioactivity. From the turn of the century we have Marie Curie (1867–1934), the undisputed first lady in the history of science. Poland was under Russian occupation at the time and France was the dreamed-of land of liberty. Marie and Bronia Sklodowska, daughters of an impecunious Warsaw physics teacher, yearned to live in Paris and worked out a way for both to be able to do so. Marie should work as a governess to help Bronia establish herself as a Paris doctor, and Marie herself would follow when Bronia's earnings could support her. It came to pass as planned, Marie traveling fourth class on a train, seated on a camp stool. She enrolled in the Sorbonne, taking courses in physics and mathematics, and lived in a cheap rented room where she could be alone and study her books night and day. After two years she took the examination for a certificate in physics and ranked number one among all candidates. A year later she was number two in a similar examination in mathematics.

In 1894 Marie met and married Pierre Curie (1859–1906), eight years her senior and just completing his thesis for a physics doctorate. Unlike Marie, Pierre was born to wealth and privilege, educated by private tutors before he entered the university, but he was intensely serious about his work and completely unconcerned about life's material rewards and comforts; in spite of the glaring difference in background, he was an ideal partner for Marie. Pierre was director of laboratory work at the municipal École de Physique et Chemie while he was working on his doctoral dissertation, which took 12 years to finish, not an unusual length of time because dissertations in those days were supposed to be weighty, major contributions to the candidate's chosen field. (Pierre fulfilled this requirement with flying colors. His thesis work investigated the loss of magnetic properties of ferromagnetic materials when they are heated, and he discovered and defined the critical point of transition now known as the Curie Point. We must never think that Pierre was a lightweight in the partnership with Marie.)

As for the technical story, it begins with the more or less accidental discovery of natural radioactivity by Henri Becquerel, one of the better tales of scientific serendipity. Becquerel, up to that time nothing more than a dabbler in research, was caught up in the excitement generated by Röntgen's discovery of x-rays in 1895 (see under "Germany"). He believed that x-rays might be related to fluorescence or luminescence, to which end he was studying some fluorescent crystals of uranium, triggering the secondary radiation by shining sunlight on the crystals. Initial results had been encouraging, for some kind of penetrating radiation was certainly observed. But then bad weather intervened and heavy clouds obscured the sun. Becquerel shoved all his materials into a drawer until the sun should shine again and that is when the accident took over. There happened to be some photographic plates in the drawer, wrapped in black paper, and, surprisingly, they were found to have been exposed when the drawer was opened. Penetrating radiation indeed, but coming from where? The upshot of it proved to be that uranium itself was the culprit. The rays came from the crystals, but have nothing to do with fluorescence and don't need the stimulation of sunlight, and they are not the same as x-rays; they are a different kind of mysterious ray, a natural attribute of the uranium itself. (Such is the secret of great discoveries—sometimes.)

Marie Curie was just then looking for a physics thesis topic and Becquerel's discovery excited her, partly because it was such a new subject that there was no tedious library research to be done. Only laboratory work could find the answers to the mystery, and Marie soon proved to have unlimited energy and enthusiasm for that. Pierre provided the laboratory space in a wretched basement in the École de Physique et Chemie and soon he became personally involved at Marie's side. A rapid cascade of discoveries followed. They unearthed several mineral samples that proved to be radioactive, not all of them containing uranium. More important, the one that did contain uranium, the crude ore pitchblende, surprisingly had much higher radioactivity than could be accounted for by its uranium content alone, and therefore must contain some other radioactive substance, "hotter" than uranium itself because it could be present in only a tiny amount. The Curies at once set out to isolate and purify the new source of radiation and discovered not one, but two new elements, radium and polonium, the latter named after Marie's native land. It turned out to be a herculean task, because so little of the material was there. Quite literally, tons of the crude ore needed to be processed to obtain enough product for chemical characterization, and the Curies had neither money nor laborers to assist them. The Austrian government generously provided the ore from the state uranium mine at Joachimsthal, Bohemia, but the labor had to come from their own hands. It was not until 1902 that they had purified enough radium to measure its relative atomic weight, but after that reward was swift and the Nobel Prize in physics was awarded jointly to Henri Becquerel and the two Curies in 1903.

In 1904, a year *after* the award of the Nobel Prize, Pierre Curie was appointed professor at the Sorbonne and was finally able to design a decent laboratory. He did not live to enjoy it, for he was tragically killed in an accident in 1906. Marie was able to use it, however, for she was chosen to succeed Pierre as Sorbonne professor, the first time a woman had ever taught at that illustrious institution. She became involved during and after World War I with medical applications of radium and x-rays, leaving the continuing evolution of the physical understanding to others (notably Rutherford, Soddy, and Bohr). She herself became increasingly aware of the powerful effects of radiation on the human body. Given what we know now, she actually had an unexpectedly long life, dying ultimately of leukemia in 1934 at age sixty-six. Her work was continued by one of her daughters, Irène, and her husband, Frédéric Joliot. They studied the artificial production of radioactive substances, and they too won a Nobel Prize for their work. And, like Marie, they too died of cancer.

Related Places to Visit: Paris (several sites), Gif-sur-Yvette.

Count Louis de Broglie: The Dual Nature of Matter. And, finally, we go back to (or close to) optics. A century after the French physicist Auguste Fresnel had dispelled all doubts about the wave nature of light, Albert Einstein came along to upset the apple cart. He became intrigued by the photoelectric effect (the ejection of electrons from metals by light) and in order to explain it, he had to re-invent Newton's corpuscles—here light was certainly behaving like a mass of bullet-like little particles! Now what? It was another Frenchman who took up the challenge. Louis de Broglie, in his dissertation for a doctorate at the University of Paris in 1924, brilliantly used Einstein's own relativity theory to arrive at the dramatic conclusion that all matter had a dual essence—all matter can behave as wavelike in some experiments and particulate in others.

A fascinating aspect of de Broglie himself is that he was a cultural anachronism (at least in France), a gilt-edged nobleman entitled to call himself Prince Louis Victor de Broglie. When he received a Nobel prize in 1929, he was the first "prince" to do so. He is also the only physicist to have received the award for his Ph.D. dissertation.

A strange coincidence occurs in this long search for the nature of light. Fresnel was actually born at the Broglie estate in Normandy because his father had a contract to do construction work for the family. Thus, from this small piece of French soil came both the death of Newton's light corpuscles and the resurrection of particles that sometimes behave like waves.

Related Place to Visit: Broglie.

PRINCIPAL PLACES TO VISIT

Paris and Environs

PARIS IN GENERAL

Paris overtly proclaims its history and honors its many accomplished citizens of former years, including scientists, being quite unlike London (for example) in that regard. Numerous streets are named for scientists and there are official plaques throughout the city to designate the buildings where scientists lived or worked or died. A recent count listed over 1,500 plaques, 129 of them commemorating *les savants*. A plaque in Montmartre (Rue Ronsard), for example, indicates the entrance to the quarries where Georges Cuvier discovered the fossils of extinct animals in 1798; four separate plaques are associated with Pierre and Marie Curie. (But there are no plaques in the Place de la Concorde, where the guillotine once stood and more than a thousand victims met their gruesome fate, among them, on May 8, 1794, Antoine Lavoisier. There is a Rue Lavoisier a few blocks north of the Place de la Concorde, so named much later on the insistence of his widow. It is on land that had belonged to her father, who was executed on the same day as her husband.)

There are some interesting tombs. René Descartes died in Sweden in 1650, but his remains were brought back to Paris and have been moved several times since then; they now reside in the church of St. Germain-des-Prés, in the chapel of St. Peter and St. Paul. (But the memorial inscription is on the opposite side of the church.) The Père Lachaise cemetery on the east side of Paris has the tombs of Claude Bernard and Gay-Lussac, alongside Proust, Bizet, Chopin, and Oscar Wilde. (Tombs of Pasteur and Pascal are mentioned separately.)

Even train stations are named after scientists, notably the station *Laplace* on the RER line just south of the city limits. It commemorates the famous houses in adjacent Arcueil, where physicist Simon Laplace and chemist Claude Berthollet are said to have exerted a dominant influence over French physical science in the Napoleonic era and for a few years thereafter. Berthollet's house became a kind of Institute for Advanced Studies, where Jöns Jakob Berzelius from Sweden and Francophile Alexander von Humboldt from Germany were among the distinguished regulars. John Dalton came here in 1822 to convince the initially skeptical Frenchmen of the validity and importance of his atomic theory.

CITY OF SCIENCE AND INDUSTRY

This is a monstrous "theme park" extolling science and its applications, which must be seen to be believed. Whether one will be any wiser after a visit will be a matter of experience and temperament. It is likely to be most useful as a supplementary resource for school children taking elementary science courses and guided by their teachers. The glossy high-tech approach may appeal especially at that level.

The overall tone is set by what one sees at first entry, the *Géode*, a giant steel globe with a mirror surface and an auditorium *within it*, its tiers of 357 seats suspended from a single pillar. Scientific instructional films are shown here around the clock. Beyond the Géode is the *Explora*, which houses the main exhibits, divided into four sectors: "From the Earth to the Universe," "The Adventure of Life," "Matter and the Work of Man," and "Language and Communication." Headsets can be rented to pick up running commentaries in four different languages as one wanders about, and there are also informative panels, TV sets with instructional video shows, and interactive gadgetry of all kinds. Some items are very good and quite sophisticated—an excellent hands-on apparatus for proof of Pythagoras's theorem and a clear demonstration of symmetry axes, for example, in the mathematics section at Level 1 of "Earth to Universe." Others seem merely tawdry—a winding trail "in the eye of the microscope," for example, in "Adventure of Life," or a huge panel map of the earth that lights up to show where polygamy or polyandry is practiced. Many of the exhibits are geared to familiar modern technology: rockets, jet planes, a submarine, particle accelerators, ecosystems, and so on.

The City is at the northeast edge of Paris and is open all day every day except Monday. Telephone 40.05.72.72. The Métro station is Porte de la Villette. There is said to be a reception team fluent in eighteen languages, including sign language.

GIF-SUR-YVETTE: Purification of Radium

This suburb is where the Curies carried out the first stage in the purification of pitchblende on their way to the isolation of radium. Radium was only a trace component of the pitchblende ore, and the Curies had to use eight tons of the ore to obtain a single gram of pure radium. It was, of course, not possible to carry out such a large-scale process in the Curies' small laboratory in Paris. The early stages in the purification were accordingly carried out on waste land outside Paris, convenient to train tracks for delivery of the ore, in what is today Gif-sur-

Yvette. The name of a street, Rue de Radium, commemorates the site, but it is not explicitly publicized. It is now a residential street, but some gardens have concrete patches in unexpected places. Has residual radioactivity been encased there?

INSTITUT CURIE (Rue Pierre et Marie Curie)

The Institut Curie, 11 Rue Pierre et Marie Curie, just a few hundred meters south of the Panthéon, was initially created explicitly for Marie Curie, with the name of "Institut du Radium." It is today a modern research facility, but Marie's former laboratory and office have been preserved as a kind of museum, which is open to the public by advance appointment. It contains some of Marie's notebooks, instruments, laboratory coats, and a replica of Pierre Curie's device for quantitative measurement of ionizing radiation—the essential tool for the discovery and purification of radium and other radioactive elements, because of the miniscule amounts contained in the native ores. Needless to say, the actual technical artifacts from the Curie period were highly contaminated and had to be subsequently destroyed. Scientific equipment on show in the museum dates from a later period, when Marie's daughter Irène and her husband Frédéric Joliot held sway in the laboratory. There are sculptures of Marie and Pierre in the Institute's courtyard, done by a Polish artist for the celebration of the centenary of Marie's birth in 1967.

It is important to appreciate that the fine institute we see here came to Marie Curie only late in life, at the end of World War I. As anyone even slightly aware of the Curie legend knows, Marie and Pierre's discovery and purification of radium were done in the most wretched, cold laboratory imaginable, in the basement of the École superieure de Physique et de Chimie. The site on the Rue Vauquelin, about 500 yards (500 meters) south of the present Institute, is marked by a commemorative plaque. There is another plaque at 24 Rue de la Glacière (on the other side of the Seine, close to the observatory), to mark the apartment where Marie and Pierre were living at the time and where their daughter Irène was born in 1897. It was not until 1905 that reasonable laboratory space was provided for the Curies in the Sorbonne and Pierre himself never had the chance to use it, for he was run down and killed in 1906 by a horse-drawn carriage in the Rue Dauphine. (Marie's health had begun to decline from the effects of radiation even before the Institut du Radium was opened. For the last 20 years of her life she lived close to her laboratory, at 36 quai de Berthune on the Ile St. Louis—another plaque indicates the place.)

The Institut Curie telephone number is 43.29.12.42. The closest Métro station is Cardinal Lemoine.

JARDIN DES PLANTES

Paris's botanical gardens were founded in 1626 as the Jardin du Roi. Unlike most establishments of this kind, the gardens became a center for all French natural science and remained virtually unruffled by the Revolution, apart from the de-royalization of the name. Buffon, Cuvier, Lamarck, and many other French natural scientists resided on the premises and did most of their work here. Even the physicist Henri Becquerel held a position here (as aide-naturaliste, a post apparently inherited from his father) and had a laboratory for applied physics in the house formerly occupied by Cuvier himself. It was here that Becquerel more or less accidentally discovered radioactivity in 1896 and thereby excited the interest of Marie and Pierre Curie and others. A less familiar name is that of the lipid chemist Marie-Eugénie Chevreul who worked here up to the ripe old age of 103. (He liked to eat his butter, too, and was evidently unaware of the negative effect of lipids on longevity.) Statues of many of these notables are scattered about the gardens, though Becquerel has only a plaque. The statue of Lamarck proudly calls him "founder of the theory of evolution," a label that some would consider controversial. In any event, the intellectual battles between Lamarck

Lamarck, "Founder of the Doctrine of Evolution," in the Jardin des Plantes.

and the much more powerful Georges Cuvier are part of the fascinating history of the Jardin.

Small areas of the gardens now serve special purposes—a menagerie, for example, and an alpine garden. The buildings where research used to be done have become museums. One of them (the original Museum of Natural History) now houses fossils and is likely to be the most interesting of the group for the casual visitor. A mineralogical gallery at the other end of the Rue Buffon is said to have an especially fine collection. Some old trees are noteworthy. One of them, an old Cedar of Lebanon, was planted in 1734 by Bernard de Jussieu, one of the earliest superintendants of the gardens. An oriental plane tree is said to have been planted by Buffon in 1785.

The Gardens are always open; the menagerie is open during daylight hours except on holidays. The museums on the grounds are closed on Tuesdays and holidays. Telephone (Museum of Natural History) 43.36.54.26. Closest Métro station is Gare d'Austerlitz.

NATIONAL TECHNICAL MUSEUM
(in the Conservatoire National des Arts
et Métiers)

Here we have a museum as different from the City of Science and Industry as one can imagine. It was created by an act of the revolutionary Convention in 1794. "Let original models of instruments and machines which have been invented be deposited here," it was decreed, and "let the construction and use of tools be explained." The decree has been followed ever since and as a result we have before us a vast all-encompassing collection of museum pieces. Clocks, watches, trains, bicycles, motor cars, aeroplanes, refrigerators, musical instruments, electrical generators, microscopes, telescopes—you name it and you will find it, although staff tell us that they can actually display at any one time less than one-tenth of their possessions. An extra dividend is the building itself, the former priory of St. Martin-des-Champs, part of which dates back to the twelfth century.

This accumulation of objects would not by itself fall within the scope of this book were it not for the museum's deliberate stress on pure science and its technical instrumentation, with clearly written accompanying explanations. There are several of Pascal's mechanical calculating machines, dating from 1642; Buffon's burning mirrors to focus the rays of the sun (à la Archimedes); electrical devices that trace the history of our understanding of electricity from the two-fluid theory of the Abbé Nollet, through Volta, Coulomb, Ampère, and beyond; optical devices all the way up to early electron microscopes; even an early cyclotron is shown. There is an excellent exhibit on the standardization of weights and measures.

Of particular interest in relation to the highlights of science that we like to stress in this book is an attempt to create a proper tribute to the "father of chemistry," Antoine Lavoisier. Situated prominently at the foot of the main staircase (the former entrance hall of the priory), the display contains both comprehensive educational placards and apparatus that he used in his research. Lavoisier was a crusader for quantitation and the instruments shown are truly impressive—there is nothing of the primitive here. Beautifully engineered beam balances and gasometers are especially striking. Also of interest are several calorimeters. They remind us that heat was considered an element by Lavoisier and by most scientists of his time and that Lavoisier collaborated with physicist Simon Laplace to measure its quantity and properties.

Finally there is a special treat—Foucault's pendulum, suspended from the twelfth-century high vaulting of the priory church, its path of oscillation turning slowly hour by hour to mark the rotation of the earth beneath it. Foucault's original pendulum was installed in the Panthéon in 1851, but popular demand led to the construction of several duplicates. The one in the museum was on display at the 1855 Universal Exposition in Paris.

The museum is open daily except Mondays and holidays. Telephone 40.27.23.75. Métro stations Réaumur Sébastopol or Arts-et-Métiers.

Foucault's pendulum. The first public demonstration was made in the Panthéon in 1851.

OBSERVATORY (near Port Royal, south of the Luxembourg gardens)

The Paris observatory dates back to the ambitious days of Louis XIV and his chief minister Colbert. It was completed in 1672; its four walls are oriented precisely to the four points of the compass; the southern wall defines the nominal latitude of the city and a perpendicular line through the center of the building defines the "Paris meridian." The actual numerical coordinates, relative to other places on earth, were established with the aid of the Danish astronomer Ole Rømer, brought here by Colbert because he had inherited the mantle of Danish expertise that had been established a century earlier by Tycho Brahe (see under "Denmark"). Rømer remained in Paris for several years and it was here that he accomplished his main scientific achievement, the measurement of the speed of propagation of light, in 1676. The event is marked by one of the official city plaques placed on the observatory wall. Christiaan Huygens from the Netherlands was here for several years in the same period and was the first to see the rings about the planet Saturn.

In front of the observatory entrance is a statue of the French astronomer LeVerrier, effectively the discoverer of Neptune, the eighth planet of the solar system. The seventh planet, Uranus, had first been sighted by William Herschel in England in 1781, but irregularities in its orbital motion suggested the existence of a more distant planet beyond. LeVerrier in 1846 predicted its orbit on the basis of mathematical calculations and the prediction, of course, included its "present" location. A German observer (J. C. Galle) found it where predicted on the very next day—the instruments at the Paris observatory lacked the requisite precision. (This was probably the first discovery of an object in sky on the basis of calculation, which has now become commonplace.)

The observatory and its grounds were temporarily closed to the public on our most recent visit, but the building could be admired from the outside. Telephone 43.20.12.10. Métro station Port-Royal.

PASTEUR MUSEUM (Rue du Docteur-Roux)

The Pasteur Institute is today one of the world's foremost medical research institutes, in the forefront of the fight against disease (particularly AIDS) and in the advance of knowledge through basic research. Pasteur lived in a mansion on the institute grounds for the last six years of his life, and this house is now a museum, open to the public. A former guest bedroom has been converted to show items related to Pasteur's work, but the rest of the house has been left mostly as it was when he lived here. There are many paintings and photographs of Pasteur and his family, including a copy of the famous painting that shows the president of France leading Pasteur into the amphitheater for his 1892 jubilee triumph, with the great Scottish surgeon, Joseph Lister, arms extended, waiting there to greet him. In Pasteur's former bedroom are admirable portraits of his parents, which he painted himself in Arbois when he was only fourteen years old. There are also decorations conferred on Pasteur from all over the world, gifts from the grateful and other admirers.

The science room reminds us (even emphasizes) that Pasteur was a chemist with no formal training or experience in medicine. There are flasks and bottles used and labeled by Pasteur himself, polarimeters for measuring the rotation of the plane of polarization of light, microscopes, and so forth. From a later period, when he turned increasingly to what we now call microbiology, there are filters for removing viruses or bacteria (made from porous clay by Pasteur's assistant, Chamberland, who got the idea from the clay pipes smoked by Emil Roux) and the swan-necked flasks designed by Pasteur to disprove the frequent claims for spontaneous generation of living microorganisms from putrifying organic matter. A pamphlet is provided to guide the visitor through the house, and a talking taped commentary can be turned on. Both are available in English if desired.

The highpoint of the visit is undoubtedly the chapel in the basement, built explicitly to house Pasteur's casket and body. (Mme. Pasteur was subsequently buried in the same chapel, but quite unostentatiously.) Pasteur's son Jean-Baptiste was responsible for the design of the chapel. He had been a diplomat in Italy and deliberately intended the Pasteur crypt to be an imitation of the mausoleum of Galla Placidia, the famous Byzantine chapel in Ravenna. The

Pasteur's funeral chapel. The mosaics illustrate highlights of his career. Note the struggle with a rabid dog on the ceiling.

walls and ceiling are completely covered by cheerful mosaics, depicting scenes from Pasteur's life rather than the religious themes of the Ravenna prototype. We have sheep to symbolize Pasteur's work on anthrax, vines and mulberry leaves for his work on fermentation and silkworm disease, and even a mosaic of a rabid dog struggling with the young shepherd Jupille, the second person to be vaccinated against rabies. Pasteur's remains lie in a black marble sarcophagus in the center of the chapel. Over the grave are four great white angels, representing Faith, Hope, Charity, and Science.

The museum is open afternoons on Monday to Friday, closed on holidays and all of August. Telephone 45.68.82.82. The closest Métro station is Pasteur.

ST. JACQUES TOWER and Other Memorials to Pascal

The existence of a vacuum and the associated determination of the density of air were especially controversial in France because the doctrines of Descartes denied the possibility of a vacuum. Blaise Pascal's definitive experiments, demonstrating the effect of altitude on the height of a column of mercury that air pressure could support, may thus have had greater impact than the prototype of such experiments done earlier by Torricelli in Italy. Pascal's most famous trial was carried out in 1648 on Puy-de-Dome (see section on Auvergne), but he did a duplicate experiment (though at much lower altitude) at the Tour St. Jacques on the Place du Châtelet in Paris. The tower (172 feet [52 m] high) was once the belfry of a church and today has some meteorological instruments mounted on its top. A statue of Pascal stands in a vaulted open space at the foot of the tower. There is a barometer at his side and a pile of books behind him.

Pascal died in Paris in 1662 and was buried in one of the city's most beautiful churches, St. Étienne-du-Mont, on the Rue Clovis, just behind the Panthéon. The church is renowned for its magnificent carved roodscreen, unique in Paris. Pascal's remains lie at the base of pillars behind the altar. A separate Latin epitaph is inscribed in a chapel to the right of the roodscreen.

Métro stations are Châtelet for the tower and Cardinal Lemoine for the church.

The Provinces

ABBÉVILLE (Somme)

Abbéville is near the mouth of the Somme on the edge of the vast gravel beds deposited by the river on its way to the sea. Human prehistory, that part of our history based on tools and other evidence found in the ground (not on Bibles, folklore, and the like), was born here, largely due to the efforts of Jacques Boucher de Perthes. He found two kinds of relics. The first were obtained in the 1830s from peat that was uncovered when a canal was dug to divert the Somme waters from the town. Boucher de Perthes attributed these relics to a Celtic people, supposed precursors of the Gauls. (The canal is still there, and the point of diversion is on the south side of the town at la Portelette, near the railway station.) The second kind of relic, more primitive stone axes and flints, came from gravel quarries, one at Menchecourt, one near the Moulin Quignan, another near the hospital. The relics were found by digging to a considerable depth, and they were associated with fossils of extinct animals, like mammoths. They were clearly older and Boucher de Perthes called them antediluvian—from a human society that existed before Noah's Flood. There is a commemorative plaque on the hospital railings on the Boulevard de Vauban, erected in 1949 to celebrate the centenary of the publication of the first volume of Boucher de Perthes's book about his discoveries.

The principal site of interest for today's visitor is the city museum in the center of Abbéville, which is named after Boucher de Perthes. It houses both a collection of art (lower two floors) and an exhibit (on the upper floor) devoted to prehistoric artifacts and other natural history. A great deal of thought has gone into this latter part, which includes detailed explanations of paleontological and geological research. There are aerial views of archaeological sites, photos of modern digs, photos and adjacent drawings of exposed geological cross-sections (stratification). An excellent collection of stone tools found in the Somme valley over the years since Boucher de Perthes's early excavations is displayed. It should be noted that this collection was begun by Casimir Picard (1810–1841), an early explorer of the Somme deposits and a partner of Boucher de Perthes.

A drive west from Abbéville, along the river to the coastal estuary, provides a good view of the tidal basin and the sandy deposits that are still being formed.

The museum is open afternoons only, daily except on Tuesdays. Explanations and guides are in French only. Telephone (Tourist Office) 22.24.27.92.

AMBOISE (Loire Château)

In 1516, Leonardo da Vinci accepted an invitation from the French king François I to settle at Amboise, one of the king's own favorite residences, where he had lived with his mother and sister as a youth. Leonardo was sixty-four years old at the time and remained until his death in 1519, left entirely free to work as he pleased. Notes and drawings from the period indicate his continued preoccupation with what we would today call applied science. His residence, Clos Lucé, was a fifteenth-century manor house a few hundred meters behind the main château; it has been reconstructed so that we get a good idea of what it might have been in Leonardo's time—kitchen, bedchamber, study, and other rooms all contain period furnishings. An essential feature is a small museum, where some of Leonardo's inventions are displayed, by means of models produced by IBM and (regrettably) bearing the stamp of slick twentieth-century salesmanship. "At Clos Lucé Leonardo invents the year 2000," the advertisement tells us, "it is living testimony to an incredible genius." In spite of the ballyhoo, some of the exhibits do give us some appreciation for Leonardo's comprehension of scientific principles, but the official museum in Leonardo's birthplace (at Vinci in Italy) provides a more scholarly view of the great man's accomplishments.

The main château of Amboise is one of the most interesting of all the Loire châteaux, a fortress as well as a residence, standing high above the left bank of the river. Its architectural jewel is the Chapelle St. Hubert, set astride the ramparts, which was at one time the private chapel of the queen. This is where Leonardo was buried after his death. The intervening four centuries of neglect and destruction have obliterated any possibility of individual identity, but all of the chapel's human remains have been transferred together to the north transept and a plaque set in the wall informs us that Leonardo's are among them.

Close Lucé is a popular tourist site, open daily except in January. Telephone 47.57.62.88.

ARBOIS (Jura)

Louis Pasteur's family moved here from Dôle when Louis was only five years old, and this is where he attended school. He later returned almost every summer for his vacation and gradually transformed the house into a bourgeois residence. We can see it now (with home laboratory intact) as it was in his later life. Not far away, on the tree-lined Promenade Pasteur, is a familiar statue of the great man. Outside the town (1.3 miles [2 km] north, to the right of route N83) is the small vineyard where he did some of his experiments on fermentation. It is still in use, its wine reserved for special Pasteurian occasions.

The "Maison de Pasteur" is open from April to October, daily except Tuesdays. Telephone 84.66.11.72.

AUVERGNE

We come here to gain conviction that there is a story of the earth to be told, following in the tracks of early French geologists and of curious tourists ever since.

Puy de Dôme. Puy de Dôme is the highest peak (4,835 feet—1,465m) of the Chaîne des Puys, just 6 miles (10 km) west of Clermont-Ferrand. The Auvergnats used to think it was a giant fortification built by the Romans; its volcanic origin was not recognized until 1751. The view is fantastic. We look down on a chain of younger volcanoes both north and south, the outlines of their craters still intact, though now grass-covered, with cattle or sheep grazing peacefully within. Pascal used Puy de Dôme in 1648 to demonstrate the existence of a vacuum and the weight of air. The Romans had a temple on the

No possible doubt about former volcanoes! In the foreground is Puy de Côme, a few kilometers outside Clermont-Ferrand. Puy de Dôme (background) is where Pascal demonstrated the weight of air and the reality of a vacuum, long before the Vulcanist controversy.

summit; today there is a weather station and observatory instead. There is a toll road to the top for those who don't like to climb on foot.

Just to the north of Puy de Dôme is **Puy de Pariou,** one of the youngest volcanoes in the area, with a perfectly shaped deep crater. One can still see where the lava flowed downhill to the east, toward Orcines on the highway below. Outstanding places on the south side of Puy de Dôme include **Puy de la Vache,** a crater where one side broke away to release a torrent of molten lava that formed a 4 mile (6 km) long ridge. It blocked the stream in the valley below and created the lake, **Lac d'Aydat,** now a popular recreation area.

Volvic, about 13 miles (20 km) north of Clermont-Ferrand, has quarries which are a rich source of a hard black volcanic stone (andésite) that has many uses including plaques on city streets. The *Maison de la Pierre* is a subterranean museum penetrating to the core of a lava flow descending from Puy de la Nugère. Visits are accompanied by a recorded commentary that details the successive phases of a volcanic eruption.

The toll road up Puy de Dôme is closed in winter. Puy de Pariou is accessible on foot from route D941ᴮ, but it lies within a shooting range and access is restricted—inquire locally before you go. The climb to Puy de la Vache is off route D5, not far from the Château de Montlosier, which houses the administrative headquarters of the *Parc naturel régional des Volcans d'Auvergne.* Guided tours of the Maison de la Pierre are provided daily all year, except Tuesdays in winter. Telephone: 73.33.56.92.

Monts Dore. Here, about 28 miles (45 km) south of Clermont-Ferrand, we have the remains of much older volcanoes, the outlines of their craters no longer visible. North of the town of Le Mont Dore is another volcanic lake (Lac de Guéry) and just beyond it Col de Guéry (4,170 feet—1,264 m) with a view upon two basalt rocks, Roche Tuilière and Roche Sanadoire. The former is a fine example of the prismatic basalt columns that were at the center of controversy in the early days of the awakening of the earth sciences—crystalline deposits from a receding sea according to the Neptunists and the frozen cores of volcanoes according to the Vulcanists. When these columns are seen in isolation (Giant's Causeway described under "Ireland"), there may be room for argument, but here there can be none.

Monts du Cantal. About 94 miles (150 km) south of Clermont-Ferrand, between Aurillac and Murat, we have the grandest of the mountains of the Massif Central, but also the oldest. The Cantal volcano was active about five to ten million years ago and was then 9,900 feet (3,000 m) in altitude, with a circumference in excess of 62 miles (100 km)—an Auvergnat Mount Etna. Glaciers and rivers have gradually eroded the peaks and the highest elevation is now 6,120 feet (1,855 m). But the rocks still eloquently proclaim their volcanic origin. (As they also do 63 miles [100 km] further east, around Le Puy, with its famous church on top of the stump of an old volcanic core.)

AUXERRE (Burgundy)

Auxerre stands on the banks of the Yonne, built on a steep hillside and surrounded by broad boulevards that were once fortifications for the town. The narrow, winding streets climbing steeply from the river bank are undoubtedly much as they were at the time of Jean Baptiste Fourier, who was born here in 1758. The Church of St. Étienne (once the cathedral) is a magnificent edifice, much of it dating from as early as the thirteenth century. The old episcopal palace has been restored and is now the seat of the departmental prefecture. The Church of St. Germain was once part of an abbey and is currently being restored. Two lovely adjacent squares occupy the topmost part of the town, flanking the city hall, and in one of them once stood a memorial statue to Fourier.

Fourier had been a teacher at the local military school in the early days of the Revolution, and then became increasingly active in local affairs. He became well known for his bold defense of victims of the Terror, for which "crime" he himself almost became a victim in 1794, saved only by a lucky change in top management in Paris. He later became one of Napoleon's trusted friends, a leader of the Egyptian campaign. He did his best scientific work in middle age, when he was prefect of the department of Isère, centered in Grenoble. He never returned to Auxerre, but the town expressed its pride in its native son with the aforementioned bronze statue, erected in 1849. It would still be there, but for the German occupiers in World War II, who needed metal for their guns and melted

Napoleon and Fourier in Egypt. Fourier is the one in the center, writing things down. (This is one of the tablets rescued from wartime meltdown.)

down the statue. But they did not get all of it, for the mayor in a stealthy midnight raid saved two of the statue's bas-reliefs and they are now mounted on the walls of the municipal museum in the Place du Maréchal Leclerc.

We recommend a stroll through the old town (quite apart from its association with Fourier) to recall the flavor of past centuries when this was a busy center of commerce and major port. A notable characteristic is a relative absence of "tourist trap" shops. This is a real city that has preserved its cultural heritage in a tasteful manner.

BEAUMONT-EN-AUGE (near Lisieux, Normandy)

Pierre Simon Laplace was born here in Beaumont-en-Auge, in the Camembert and apple brandy region of Normandy. Beaumont-en-Auge is a picturesque little town, founded in 1055, perched on a promontory overlooking the valley of the River Touques. Though Laplace's family were unpretentious farmers, they lived in a house on the Place de Verdun, a fine square forming the town center, with one side open for a view into the valley below. The house where Laplace was born is now an apartment building and has a plaque on its side, put up by the community. Its simple inscription is unusually modest for a text that describes the town's one historic figure: "Sous un modeste toit ici naquit Laplace, lui qui sut de Newton à . . . [faire] encore un nouveau pas,"—in other words, he learned his stuff from Newton and took a step beyond. In the center of the square is a more imposing monument, a statue erected in 1932 with the financial aid of the Carnegie Foundation. Here Laplace stands proudly on a high pedestal, with bas-relief medallion profiles of Galileo and of Newton below him.

This is a great spot to bring a picnic lunch, sitting in the park surrounding

Place de Verdun in Beaumont-en-Auge, with a statue of Laplace and (on the left) the house where he was born.

the statue and appreciating the quiet of this small community that produced one of France's most celebrated scientists.

BROGLIE (near Bernay, Normandy)

This busy little town lies at the foot of a hill on which is built the château of the Ducs de Broglie. The town was once called Chambrais, but was renamed in 1742 for the Broglie family (originally from Piedmont in Italy) in return for their mighty military deeds on behalf of France, in Spain and Poland and Austria. Successive generations have continued to serve their adopted country as statesmen at several levels, but around 1900 there was a break in the tradition and two of the family, Maurice and his younger brother Louis, turned to physics instead of politics. Both were highly successful and young Louis de Broglie won a Nobel Prize in physics in 1929 for his brilliant theoretical concept of the duality of matter—all matter can seem to be either particulate or wave-like, depending on what aspect of behavior is being studied. The immense château still belongs to the family. It is not open to the public, but its 800 foot (242 m) façade can be seen from a hill on the opposite side of the Charentonne River, on the road leading to la-Barre-en-Ouche in the general direction toward Paris.

A unique coincidence relates the town of Broglie to the duality of matter in another way. Auguste Fresnel, who (more than any other single individual) was responsible for the universal adoption of the wave theory of light and rejection of the particulate theory, was born in Broglie in 1788, his father having been a construction engineer for the de Broglie family. The twentieth-century de Broglie theory applies to light as much as to weightier matter, and we now know that light too has intrinsically a dual nature. There is a commemorative plaque for Fresnel at the house of his birth, across from the marketplace.

CLERMONT-FERRAND (Auvergne)

This city is the birthplace of Blaise Pascal. Its university is called the Université Blaise Pascal. Its principal museum (Musée du Ranquet) has a Pascal room, which contains one of Pascal's mechanical calculating machines, portraits, documents, and other memorabilia of Pascal and his family. (Another claim to fame is the Michelin factory, giving rise to the nickname "La cité du pneu"—in English, "city of the tire.")

Clermont-Ferrand's skyline is dominated by the mountain Puy de Dôme. It was here that Blaise Pascal demonstrated the effect of altitude on barometer readings, supporting his view that what pushes up the fluid in a barometer is the weight of the air and not a manifestation of nature's abhorrence of a vacuum. Pascal, whose health was always precarious, did not venture the climb himself, but sent his brother-in-law Périer instead.

The museum is open all year, closed Sunday mornings and Mondays. Telephone: 73.91.37.31.

DESCARTES (Touraine, formerly "La Haye")

This bustling market town, just off the main road joining Tours and Poitiers, changed its name only recently to that of its most famous citizen. There is a statue of Descartes in front of the Hotel de Ville, erected in 1849. Around the corner is the *maison natale* on 29 Rue Descartes, which contains a museum with documents related to his life and works. The house is quite plush; Descartes clearly came from a prosperous merchant family.

This is one of those places where the chief attraction is to see where a famous man was born. And, for those who believe that the acclaim for this particular famous man is perhaps a little exaggerated, one might wonder about the Cartesian cult per se. How did it become so intense? Why did it persist? Why did this busy little market town adopt the name of Descartes so recently, almost 400 years after his birth?

The museum is open afternoons except on Tuesdays.

DÔLE (Jura)

Louis Pasteur was born in Dôle on December 27, 1822, the son of a humble tanner who had his workshop on what is now called the Rue Pasteur, a narrow street, the backs of whose houses overlook a canal. All the local tanners had their shops here, presumably using the canal to get rid of their wastes. The *Maison Natale de Pasteur*, at 43 Rue Pasteur, is now a museum. A taped running commentary guides you as you walk through the rooms (available in English on request), and it provides a succinct and well-organized summary of Louis Pasteur's career.

Above all, we get a genuine feeling here for how humble Pasteur's background was. The small size of the rooms contributes to this, as does the little workshop showing tanner's tools. The best testimony came from Louis Pasteur himself, in a little speech he made in 1883, when a commemorative plaque at the *maison natale* was dedicated:

> Oh! my father and mother. Oh! my dear departed ones, who lived so humbly in this little house, it is to you that I owe all!

And it is to his parents that he ascribes the intense patriotism that was so characteristic of him. Their care was "to teach me the greatness of France" and it was their inspiration that led him to associate the greatness of science with the greatness of his country. (The Pasteurs moved from Dôle to nearby Arbois in 1827 and there is another museum there.)

The *maison natale* is open from April to October, daily except Tuesdays. Telephone 84.72.20.61.

LASCAUX II (near Montignac, north end of Vézère valley, Dordogne)

The Vézère valley is a truly grand place to visit, a veritable theme park for anthropology, and Lascaux is its showpiece, one of the marvels of Europe. Lascaux II is a superb replica of two main rooms of the original Lascaux cave. Every detail was meticulously copied, including precise dimensions; even the texture of the rock is faithfully reproduced. (A film at Le Thot explains how it was done.) The paintings, dating from about 15,000 B.C., include a leaping cow and other bovines, horses, bison, deer, and even an odd-looking imaginary animal, with the body of a rhinoceros, a bear-like muzzle and two horns. Many of the friezes show animals on the run, with the sense of movement captured realistically by the artist. The most impressive display of paintings is in the first hall one enters, the *Salle des Taureaux* (Bulls' Hall), containing remarkable pictures of a herd of black bulls. No ordinary tools or utensils were found in the cave, suggesting Lascaux was never used as a dwelling. However, more than 100 lamps have been found (designed to burn animal fat), obvious necessities for artists working in the dark interior of a cave.

Close to Lascaux II is **Le Thot Prehistoric Center**—the two are normally visited together. Le Thot is an outstanding museum, set within a small park containing bison and other live specimens of animals depicted within the caves. Noteworthy are some *Przewalski horses*, a species from Siberia that is much closer to the Stone Age horse than to our common Western horse. To entertain the children, there is an animated model of a mammoth, which roars realistically and takes up water with its trunk, and models of prehistoric huts, with Stone Age men, mammoth bones, and so on. There are some fine views of the countryside, especially from near the animated mammoth.

A great deal of effort has gone into the material exhibited in the museum and explanatory captions are given in English as well as French. All animals found in cave paintings are listed or pictured. Illustrations come from many places, not only from Lascaux, and they include, for example, an excellent giant photograph of the bas-relief sculptured bison from distant Tuc d'Audubert in the Pyrenees. Interesting historical detail is provided—for example, the fact that hyenas existed, but generally avoided the presence of man, so that hyena caves are always separate from caves used by humans. Details of technique are explained—engravings on rocks came before paintings.

An outstanding exhibit is an audio-visual show, displaying cave art from other places. Individual items have been combined into a giant mural and are illuminated in turn by a spotlight, while a recorded tape provides a synchronous spoken commentary (in French). We see the first discovered paintings this way— the superb cave ceiling from Altamira in Spain—and the bisons from Niaux in the Pyrenees and the famous spotted horses from Peche Merle, much further south in the Périgord district. It is almost as good as being there in person.

Combined tickets are issued for admission to Lascaux II and Le Thot, and they are (understandably) quite expensive. Both places are closed in January and on Mondays except in July and August. In the latter months the number of visitors who want to visit the cave may exceed capacity, and reservations are strongly recommended. Telephone 53.51.95.03.

LES EYZIES-DE-TAYAC
(south end of Vézère valley, Dordogne)

Les Eyzies is the normal point of first entry for visitors to the land of prehistory. It has a national museum, the cave where Cro-Magnon man was discovered, and much else—all in the midst of spectacular scenery. A whole group of caves in the rock, once inhabited by a large family or tribe, can be seen at St. Christophe, about halfway between Les Eyzies and Lascaux.

The **National Museum of Prehistory** lies within Les Eyzies, in a structure built into the side of a cliff, with overhanging rock above, which was originally a thirteenth-century fortress. It houses a rich collection of prehistoric items, not only from the Dordogne but also from other French archaeological sites—such as samples of the first arrowheads (*les pointes*) of clearly human manufacture, discovered, as we have noted earlier, at the mouth of the Somme near Abbéville. There are stone tools going back over two million years, bone tools from the more recent Magdalenian period, and examples of primitive art. One showcase has a reproduction of the best preserved human burial from the modern period (about 15,000 years old, coming from near Bordeaux), with the skeleton folded into a fetal position, intentionally, it is thought. The museum may be a little demanding for the casual visitor. All items are well displayed and carefully identified by labels (only in French), but no overall guidance is provided to show how particular items fit into the totality of the archaeological story.

L'Abri de Cro-Magnon (Shelter of Cro-Magnon), near the train station of Les Eyzies, is where the Cro-Magnon skeletons were discovered in 1868 by railway workers cutting into the hillside to make room for the train tracks. They found several human skeletons, stone tools, weapons, and pierced shells, the latter presumably used as ornaments. The rock shelter had been named after a local hermit called Magnon who had lived there. (There is an interesting twelfth century fortified church at Tayac, just beyond the cave on the same lane.)

La Roque St. Christophe, about 6.3 miles (10 km) northeast of Les Eyzies on the road toward Montigny and Lascaux, provides a memorable impression of what it was really like here 20,000 years ago. *La Roque* is a majestic cliff, about 0.6 miles (1 km) in length, rising vertically nearly 330 feet (100 m) above the valley floor. Large numbers of caves can be seen, hollowed out of the rock in five superimposed tiers. Much of what we have listed as being in the National Museum came from here, and excavations are still going on. In more modern times, the cliff terraces have served as foundation for defensive fortifications—against the Normans in the tenth century, for example—and remains of these can also be seen. The cliff terraces are open to the public from April to November.

L'Abri du Moustier (Shelter of Le Moustier) is on the same road as la Roque St. Christophe, on the opposite side of the river. It is a relatively shallow cave in which a human skeleton of the Neanderthal type was discovered in 1909. This and other secondary discoveries of such skeletons silenced the skeptics who had claimed that the original Neanderthal skeleton probably represented a pathologically deformed modern human being and not an intermediate evolutionary form of the human species. Tools from around this area are early and crude and define the *Mousterian* cultural period.

La Madeleine: The site where the Madeleine deposits were found is near Tursac, again on the same road, but closer to Les Eyzies. The tools from here are sophisticated and recent, and gave rise to the definition of the *Magdalenian* cultural period. Most of the items are in the National Museum, and there is no exhibit open to the public at the actual site.

Font-de-Gaume, on the outskirts of Les Eyzies-de-Tayac, is another cave with superb art—multichrome representations of bisons, a parade of female reindeer before a possessive buck, and other kinds of deer. In this case (unlike Lascaux II) we see the original and not a reproduction, but the advantage of that is not really marked, and the disadvantage is that fewer visitors can be admitted because of the sensitivity of the paintings to atmospheric change.

The foregoing represent only a fraction of the places to visit in the vicinity. On the road toward Périgueux, for example, are the upper and lower Laugerie deposits, places that were continuously occupied by man for about

30,000 years, and the *Grotte du Grand Roc*, which has a spectacular display of stalactites, stalagmites, and similar formations. There is a fossil center on the road toward Sarlat, where demonstrations of flint-knapping techniques are given.

The attraction here is immense even for casual tourists and it is probably a good idea to visit outside the peak months of July and August. (But note that most hotels are open only from April to October.) The National Museum is open daily except Tuesdays. Telephone 53.06.97.03. Font-de-Gaume is also closed on Tuesdays and the number of visitors on other days is strictly limited. If possible, arrive at the site before 9 A.M. to queue for tickets. Telephone 53.08.00.94.

LUNÉVILLE (Lorraine)

This garden city (former summer residence of the Dukes of Lorraine) takes pride in claiming the Marquise du Châtelet, translator of Newton's *Principia*. She was Voltaire's mistress, and the two of them were offered refuge here in 1748 (from debt collectors) by one of the most delightful characters of French history, Stanislas Leczinsky, Duke of Lorraine, deposed former King of Poland, father of King Louis XV's wife Marie. Stanislas was a great patron of arts and letters and other intellectual activities, and he generously made his summer château in Lunéville available to the couple. It was here that the translation of *Principia* was completed, and the first volume was sent off to the King's librarian. The Marquise died in childbirth a few days later, and the actual publication of her work was posthumous.

A principal avenue is named after the Marquise and there is also an Avenue Voltaire. The Marquise was buried in Lunéville's principal church, the Église St. Jacques, in an underground tomb beneath an unmarked slab of black marble. The slab can be lifted to give access to the tomb, where the proper memorial inscriptions are to be found.

Don't fail to see the Lunéville château, a majestic structure with a vast courtyard, often called "le petit Versailles," and the adjacent delightful flower gardens. Nancy, 22 miles (35 km) to the west, is the capital of Lorraine, and even richer in ornate splendor than Lunéville—all due to the great Stanislas.

MONTBARD (Burgundy)

Montbard is the birthplace of the Comte de Buffon, the place to which he returned every summer. It lies in picturesque Burgundy country, close to Fontenay Abbey, one of Burgundy's great architectural relics. The town remains to this day a metallurgical center, a heritage of Buffon's foundry.

Buffon's home and gardens (on the site of a former château) are preserved, and the gardens are now a public park with attractive paths and walks. Buffon's study and one of the former château towers constitute a small museum, in which we can see many interesting items, e.g., over 1,000 prints of bird paintings by

F. N. Martinet, who went on many expeditions *pour le roi* to collect specimens, and a lightning rod of the type invented by Benjamin Franklin—Buffon was a Franklin fan and a promoter of Franklin's theory of electricity in France. The park has a statue of the anatomist Louis-Jean-Marie Daubenton, a young Montbard doctor whom Buffon took on as protegé and collaborator, and who became the first director of the Jardin des Plantes after the Revolution. Outside the park, in the Place Buffon is the mansion that Buffon built for himself, joined by a footbridge over intervening alleys to the park and to his study. Also outside the park is the church of St. Urse with an attached memorial chapel, where Buffon's body was taken for burial after he died in Paris in 1788.

For conducted tours (daily), ring the bell at St. Louis Tower.

MONTBÉLIARD (Jura)

Montbéliard is the birthplace of Georges Cuvier. It was an anomalous town at the time. It was a Protestant enclave within an otherwise Catholic land to which many nonconformists had migrated during periods of religious oppression. It was French-speaking, but not actually a part of France, being governed instead (since 1397) by the Dukes of Württemberg. As a result of this situation, Cuvier received his higher education at the Academy in Stuttgart and had to become fluent in the German language to do so—the great German poet Friedrich Schiller had been an Academy student a few years earlier. His atypical background may have been an advantage to Cuvier in the competitive atmosphere of Paris, for he came there at the peak of the post-Revolutionary enthusiasm for novelty.

Montbéliard is much larger today than in Cuvier's time, but it is still very much a Protestant town; the Lutheran church of St. Martin (built in 1604) dominates the central square with the same name. The town hall is on the same square and in front of it, the most prominent position in the square, is a grand bronze statue of Georges Cuvier. The main shopping street of the town is also named after Cuvier. There is at present no museum.

NOLAY (near Beaune, Burgundy)

Nolay is the home of the Carnots. The most famous one was not the thermodynamicist/engineer Sadi, but his father, Lazare Carnot, also an engineer, but better known as the "organizer of the victory" of the French Revolution. Later on another Sadi was President of France. Sadi the thermodynamicist was actually not born in Nolay, but in Paris, for the date was 1796, and his father was still busy in the capital.

The Carnot house has remained in the family to this day. An impressive statue of Lazare stands in front of the house. It shows him with books to his right, dividers (compasses) in his left hand and a hefty sword swinging from his belt.

We can interpret it perhaps as a reflection of the family as a whole—scholarship, engineering, and "hefty" political power—and the books and dividers indicate more similarity between father and son than their places in history suggest.

POLEYMIEUX (near Lyon)

André-Marie Ampère was born in Lyon, but the family moved to nearby Poleymieux shortly afterward, and it was here that André grew up and where he is remembered and honored today. The Maison d'Ampère, created here in 1931, is actually more than a memorial to Ampère—it is a very good museum of electricity in general, going beyond Ampère to Faraday (*see* under "England") and all the way to modern power stations, and backward in time with a poster history of electrostatics from the time of the Greeks to Coulomb. It is all done in a manner comprehensible to school children or laymen, but all of us can undoubtedly profit from an instructive hour or so here.

An important feature is the presence of many well-designed and well-maintained working models, activated by pushing a button, with explanations both in French and in English. One example is a model of Ørsted's experiment, showing that a magnetic needle moves when a current flows (*see* under "Denmark"). Another illustrates *Ampère's rule*, predicting the direction in which the needle moves. We go on from there to other aspects of the magnetism of current-carrying coils and to solenoids, induction coils, electromagnets, and early electric motors. Note that Ampère himself created the word *solenoid*, from the Greek word for a tube or channel. One room in the museum bears on Ampère's own life (books, papers, honors awarded, and so on). There is a huge bronze statue of the man outside the museum, about 200 yards (180 m) away.

The museum is open daily except on Tuesdays. Telephone 78.91.90.77.

ST. JULIEN-SOUS-MONTMELAS
(near Villefranche, Beaujolais)

St. Julien, home of Claude Bernard, is a charming village in the heart of the Beaujolais country. The Bernard museum is on the edge of the village, part of a typical Burgundy farm complex, containing several buildings arranged in a square around a central courtyard. At the back of the complex is the *maison natale*, the modest house where Bernard was born in 1813. At the front is the grand manor house, which Bernard purchased from the owner in 1861. It became his home and now houses the museum. All around are the fields of grapevines and if you come in the summer, they will be heavy with the grapes for the coming Beaujolais crop. Everything is preserved much as it was when he was alive, and there even continues to be a *Cuvée Claude Bernard* vintage on the market.

The museum contains all kinds of Bernard memorabilia, including photo-

Claude Bernard dissecting. A copy of the Lhermite painting is in the museum at St. Julien. (Original held by Académie Nationale de Médecine, Paris.)

graphs, copies of manuscripts, and so on, as well as laboratory equipment (mostly chemical) and surgical tools used for animal experimentation. There are several cannulae of the type that Bernard used to tap fluids from the stomach and intestines. There are also pictures of Bernard's friends and contemporaries and a copy of a famous painting by Lhermite of Bernard in the process of a dissection of what appears to be a rabbit. On the upper floor, there is a useful chronology on the wall, listing Bernard's achievement in parallel with contemporary events in world history.

The museum is open daily, except Mondays and the entire month of March. Telephone 74.67.51.44.

STRASBOURG (Alsace)

Strasbourg now houses the parliament of the European Community, but the Place de la Cathédrale has been a popular meeting place for young and old from all over Europe since long before the EC was formed. Louis Pasteur came to Strasbourg as a young chemistry professor in 1849, fresh from his thesis experiments on optical activity. It was here that he discovered that the growth of mold in one of his samples generated optical activity where none had been before, which led him away from pure chemistry to biological and medicine-related research. Equally important for Pasteur's future was an event in his personal life—it was here that he met and married Marie Laurent, the daughter of the rector of the university.

The present university buildings were not built then—they owe their existence to the Germans, who seized Strasbourg from the French in the War of 1870–1871 and held it until 1918. But the building where Pasteur had his laboratory on the Rue de l'Académie still exists and now houses the *École Maternelle et Primaire de l'Académie*. A prominent inscription in stone over the main door gives the dates Pasteur was here.

TARASCON-SUR-ARIÈGE (Pyrénées)

Just outside this noisy little town, in the deep valley of the River Vicdessos, is the Cave of Niaux, the site of one of the earliest discoveries of Stone Age paintings in France (recognized as prehistoric art in 1906). The setting, close to the border with Andorra, with the often snow-covered peaks of the Pyrénées as a background, is spectacular. The entrance to the cave is on a huge stone porch high up the limestone cliffs that line the valley. Someone familiar with the cliff dwellings of the American Indians would be likely to jump to the conclusion

Cave paintings. This one is from the Salon Noir in the
Niaux Cave near Tarascon.

that the artists here (more than 12,000 years earlier) likewise built their homes on such an easily defended site. All available evidence is against that. Our Magdalenian ancestors appear to have lived and/or hunted on the valley floor and the cave was used solely for some unspecified ceremonial function. The artistic representations themselves are superb, especially the astonishingly accurate pictures of several bison, impaled with arrows accurately pointed at the heart. One disadvantage is that the pictures are far from the cave entrance, in the so-called *Salon Noir*, at the end of a long rugged hike through vast chambers and long narrow passages, on rough and broken stone—the only light coming from heavy battery-powered lanterns issued to all visitors.

As an educational experience, Niaux comes nowhere near being in the same class as Lascaux II and Le Thot, but the small number of paintings actually seen make a truly powerful impact, both because of the brilliance of the artistic perception and also, perhaps, because the viewing of them is a little more intimate. There is also a little fillip here for those who like to wonder for themselves, like to ponder mysteries as yet unsolved. Why did our ancestors find it desirable to hide their precious art so deep inside the rock? How did the artists and the presumed later visitors to the gallery (or temple or whatever it may have been) light their way?

Guided tours of the cave (limited to 20 persons at a time) take place three times daily, more frequently in summer. Reservations are essential. Telephone 61.05.88.37.

9

The Netherlands

The Netherlands had a golden age in science beginning in 1581 when independence from Spain was achieved under the leadership of William of Orange. The country celebrated its new freedom by welcoming religious minorities and new intellectual ideas, and it became a refuge for many who were suffering religious persecution in other parts of Europe, notably Portuguese and Spanish Jews and French Huguenots. Many of the new immigrants were merchants and skilled artisans, and they helped to promote economic prosperity in spite of continuing warfare. (Dutch independence had to be repeatedly defended.) With rare wisdom, the Netherlands used some of its resulting abundance to found centers of learning, and the University of Leiden (founded by William I in 1575) in particular became one of Europe's great academic centers. Smaller universities sprouted throughout the country, in a mood reminiscent of more recent days in England and America, to spread the opportunities for higher education as widely as possible.

An illustration *par excellence* of the Netherlands' seventeenth-century preeminence is provided by the career of the French philosopher, René Descartes (1596–1650), who spent most of his productive years here in preference to his native France. The greater part of Descartes' *Discourse on Method* was written in Utrecht, and the book was published in Leiden in 1637, not in the country of his birth.

Two Giants of the Seventeenth Century

In the seventeenth century the Netherlands gave birth to two giant figures of its own in the history of science, **Christiaan Huygens** and **Antoni van Leeuwenhoek**. It is perhaps characteristic of a liberal and prosperous society that the two men should come from different backgrounds. Huygens was an aristocrat, member of a sophisticated and much traveled family, whereas van Leeuwenhoek

began as a simple artisan, attended no university, and virtually never left his native town of Delft.

Is Light a Wave? The grandfather of Christiaan Huygens (1629–1695) was the secretary of William I of Orange, the creator of national independence; his father Constantijn was likewise prominent in statecraft, but also a humaniṣt, poet, and close acquaintance of Descartes. Christiaan himself never had to earn a living, traveled widely and corresponded with many famous men. In 1664 he moved to Paris to spend 15 years at the Académie Royale des Sciences at the personal invitation of French King Louis XIV and his finance minister, Jean-Baptiste Colbert. He returned to den Haag in 1681, when Louis XIV and his court were becoming increasingly hostile to Protestants, and remained until his death in 1695.

Huygens has been compared to England's Isaac Newton, who was 13 years his junior. Like Newton he was a brilliant mathematician; in physics he anticipated Newton in some of his ideas, worked within the same framework of many of the same problems, often coming to the same conclusions. But unlike Newton, Huygens worked on a broad variety of problems, without Newton's concentration. Newton took 20 years to write *Principia*, and it is impossible to imagine Huygens spending that much time on a single project.

Huygens's best remembered work is on the nature of light and here his ideas were radically different from those of Newton. Newton supposed light to be corpuscular, but Huygens could not conceive a reasonable explanation for many of the properties of light on that basis (especially refraction) and proposed instead that light must be wave-like in nature, like sound waves or the waves that ripple across a pond after a stone has been thrown in. Newton's prestige was too great for Huygens' view to prevail and the corpuscular theory remained scientific orthodoxy for more than 100 years. It was not until the nineteenth century that the phenomenon of light interference forced an about-face, and then Huygens' view became orthodox and Newton's "wrong." A century after that we began to appreciate that both were right in a sense and that light needs to be regarded as having a dual nature, particulate and wave-like at the same time.

(With the wave theory came a troublesome problem. How could one imagine any wave motion without a substance to do the moving? The up-and-down of a water wave is unthinkable without the water, and the traveling compression in a sound wave needs collisions between air particles—sound indeed cannot be transmitted through a vacuum. Thus arose the postulated existence of the space-filling *luminiferous aether*, to provide a medium for the oscillations of a light wave. Huygens did not invent it, but he provided the seemingly invincible logic behind it. It took Einstein—in 1905, 330 years later!—to do away with that problem.)

Huygens (even if he didn't write a *Principia*) must be regarded as having been in the mainstream of the great fundamental ideas of physics, in the same league as Galileo, Newton, Maxwell, and Einstein. Unlike the last three he also had a practical side; he designed and built the first working pendulum clock, and he created an improved telescope with which he made the first recorded observation of the rings of Saturn.

Related Places to Visit: Den Haag, Leiden, Paris (Observatory).

Life under the Microscope. Antoni van Leeuwenhoek (1632–1723) did not come from a wealthy or influential family, never attended a university, spoke no Latin, did not travel at the invitation of kings, and in fact lived all his life (apart from a single foreign trip) in the small town of Delft. Again unlike Huygens, van Leeuwenhoek was first and foremost an observer, with a keen, practical, and logical intellect, but disinclined to formulate grand theories, something he consciously rejected as being an academic occupation and therefore outside his domain. Leeuwenhoek's surname, incidentally, was created by himself: the word means *Lion's Corner* and he chose it because his father owned the corner house near the *Leeuwenpoort* (Lion's Gate) in the town.

Leeuwenhoek's father was a basket maker, and the son was apprenticed to a cloth merchant in Amsterdam. He became a shopkeeper when he returned to his native Delft and then a civil servant, holding successively more important positions, the final one as wine-gauger, which included being general inspector of weights and measures. Leeuwenhoek was about forty years old before he gave any thought to science or to the possibility of doing scientific work himself, but, since he lived to be over ninety, he had plenty of time for a long and successful scientific career, which began with his design of a better microscope. It is generally acknowledged that the Middelburg spectaclemakers built prototypes of both telescopes and microscopes long before Leeuwenhoek, and the latter had undoubtedly used their products in his business to examine the quality of the weave of cloth, but Leeuwenhoek built the first instruments designed for research, with high magnifying power, sufficiently short focus, and versatile adjustable specimen holders.

There was also a streak of genius in the way Leeuwenhoek used his instruments. Others before him had used microscopes (less powerful than his, but that's not relevant here), but only to see better what they had already seen with their unaided eyes—Hooke had discovered cells in cork in that way, for example. Leeuwenhoek did this kind of thing, too, apparently with more success than others. But, most importantly, he also looked where the naked eye could see nothing, where none had bothered to look before—at drops of water, for example. And there he found an entirely new class of living organisms. He saw countless moving objects in drops of water or water-based fluids. He unreservedly (perhaps naively) equated life and motility, and therefore concluded that what he was seeing must be "little animals." He called them *animalcules*, the modern term is *microorganisms*. He developed a system of practical size standards (a hair from his head, for example), by which he could tell exactly how large each of his objects was. He communicated his first results to the Royal Society of London in 1676, where they caused a sensation and, at first, disbelief. Leeuwenhoek was required to produce testimonials from distinguished Delft citizens before the Royal Society would take his claims seriously. Even then they were skeptical, and they instructed the Royal Society's own resident experimenter, Robert Hooke, to see if he could repeat the observations and gave full credence only after he was indeed able to do so.

Through the years Leeuwenhoek unfolded a world previously undreamt of—bacteria, protozoa, red blood cells, the complex structures of lice, mites, and fleas, spermatozoa and insect reproduction, and much, much else—creating one of those moments in history when not only science can leap forward, but popular imagination, too, is inspired to novel vistas. Jonathan Swift, for example, wrote this little poem at about this time:

So, naturalists observe, a flea
Hath smaller fleas that on him prey;
And these have smaller still to bite 'em;
And so proceed *ad infinitum*.

Leeuwenhoek continued for many years to send his results to the Royal Society of London, which published English translations or summaries in its *Philosophical Transactions*. His work thereby received wide dissemination and Leeuwenhoek himself received an uncommon measure of public acclaim. It is said that a steady stream of eminent visitors from all over Europe came to his door—Peter the Great, James II, the Grand Duke of Tuscany—so many that he had to demand introductory letters from lesser folk. Some of these tales may be apocryphal, but a visit from Peter the Great of Russia is plausible, since Peter lived in Holland for a while.

Related Places to Visit: Delft, Leiden.

The University of Leiden—Academics, Eclectic and Electric

The University of Leiden was established in 1575 by William of Orange as a reward to the citizens of Leiden for withstanding successfully two sieges by the Spaniards. The story is that the citizenry were offered a choice of certain tax exemptions or a university, and they chose the latter. And academic they have been every since, with the premier educational institution in Europe for more than 100 years and always one of the best even as the rest of the world caught up.

Leiden was especially popular for its course in medicine, though those who attended were not necessarily physicians. Nicolaus Steno, anatomist and geologist at the Accademia del Cimento in Florence, received an M.D. degree from Leiden in 1664. The Swedish naturalist Linnaeus (also an M.D., received at nearby Harderwijk) spent three years in Leiden from 1735 to 1738, and the first outlines for his *Systema Naturae* were written here. Scottish geologist James Hutton had a Leiden M.D., as did another famous Scotsman, John Pringle. The latter was a practicing doctor (physician to Queen Charlotte of England), but he was a broader scholar as well and a president of the Royal Society. The most famous teacher in the medical course was **Hermann Boerhaave** (1668–1738), who also wrote (in 1732) what many consider to be the earliest proper textbook of chemistry.

In physics the name of Leiden (which until recently was spelled with a y) will always be associated with the **Leyden jar,** or, as Benjamin Franklin called it, "Musschenbroek's wonderful bottle." It is the first example of a working capacitor, capable of storing a huge quantity of electricity and releasing it at will. It was not actually invented in Leiden, but was first championed and publicized in 1746 by Leiden professor Petrus van Musschenbroek, who was almost as famous a teacher as Boerhaave had been a few years before. The effects of the electrical discharge of a Leyden jar could be devastating, and it quickly became a centerpiece for work and fun (serious research as well as spectacular entertainments). Peter Collinson in London sent one of the devices to Philadelphia in 1747, and it became the starting point for Benjamin Franklin's work on electricity and his subsequent identification of lightning as an electrical spark. The Frenchman Abbé Nollet (tutor of the dauphin and a former student at Leiden) used the device for entertainment at the court of King Louis XV. Rows of soldiers or even young priests lined up and joined hands and involuntarily leaped into the air as the shock of the electric discharge passed along the line.

"The most memorable place in science," is what the historian Barthold Niebuhr called Leiden 200 years ago, but the university was actually as famous for law and theology as for science. Hugo Grotius, first advocate of the idea of an international system of law, began his career at Leiden around 1600. Fittingly, today's International Court of Justice is in the Netherlands, in den Haag.

Related Place to Visit: Leiden.

Time and Space

Hendrick Antoon Lorentz (1853–1928) is one of the famous figures from the great transition period of physics, between the end of the nineteenth century and the beginning of the twentieth. Though not as well-known to the general public as, for example, Einstein, Planck, and Bohr, he was, in fact, highly influential. Albert Einstein said of him: "For me personally he meant more than all the others I have met on my life's journey."

Lorentz, professor of theoretical physics at the University of Leiden for over 30 years, was probably the first (earlier than Einstein) to make the fundamental break with traditional mechanical concepts of matter and forces. He was grappling with the problem of how light or electromagnetic waves move through space, but all original ideas he came up with seemed to be blocked by the dogma of the all-pervasive *aether*, espoused by fellow-countryman Christiaan Huygens, and seemingly a most sensible dogma, as we noted earlier. Lorentz, unwilling to discard the aether in name, eventually found himself forced to discard it in effect by stating that it had no mechanical role, no effect on his equations. In Einstein's words, it was an "audacious step" and from it followed the equally audacious "Lorentz transformations," expressing the startling notion that "time" and "length" (as they appeared in his equations) cannot be *absolutes*, but must depend on how fast an observer of events is moving. These ideas are fairly familiar today as components of Einstein's theory of relativity, but their origin as mathematical constructs lies with Lorentz. They must have seemed like extreme fantasies of science fiction at the time.

Lorentz shared a Nobel Prize in physics with his compatriot Pieter Zeeman in 1902, but the award was for something he did later, not for the work just described. Einstein's Nobel Prize in 1921 was also not for relativity. Meddling with traditional concepts of time and space remained controversial for a long time.

Related Place to Visit: Haarlem.

The Road to DNA

Hugo de Vries (1848–1935) was born in Haarlem, scion of a family of several generations of scholars and statesmen. He studied in Würzburg and other places and was one of Amsterdam's earliest professors (the Netherlands' principal city did not have an accredited university until 1877). Charles Darwin's *Origin of Species* was published while de Vries was a student and aroused his interest in the evolution of plant species, which became the lifelong subject of his work. None of his work can fairly be described as revolutionary, but he was in a modest way a truly vital cog in the wheels of progress. He deduced the basic laws of hereditary segregation—Mendel's Laws—from his own experiments and then discovered only accidentally a reprint of Mendel's 34-year-old paper. He was the first of three such rediscoverers of Mendel's work in the year 1900, who between them ignited an interest in the quantitation of the laws of inheritance that led ultimately to the modern molecular mechanism involving DNA.

De Vries also made an independent conceptual contribution. He was really the first to envision evolution as a series of abrupt changes bringing new species into existence in a single leap. He coined the term "mutation" for such a change, as distinct from "variation" within an individual species. He was convinced that there must be a physical entity in each cell that had to change when a mutation occurs, and he called such entities *pangenes*; the modern term *gene* did not come into use until 1913.

Related Place to Visit: Lunteren.

PRINCIPAL PLACES TO VISIT

DELFT

Delft is an attractive town with particularly delightful canals and a worldwide reputation for its blue dishware. Tourists abound in season, most of them frequenting the little shops displaying and selling the famous china and perhaps unaware of the two famous sons born here in the year 1632—Vermeer, the artist, and van Leeuwenhoek, the microscopist.

The house where van Leeuwenhoek was born no longer exists (it was at the place where the Oostportschool now stands), but two of the sites where he lived and worked are marked by bronze memorial plaques. One is at the corner of Oude Delft and Boterbrug—the plaque is attached to a wrought iron fence, but the actual building is gone. The second plaque is at the corner of Nieuwstraat and Hippolytusbuurt, in the wall of what is now a commercial building. Van Leeuwenhoek died at this latter site in 1723 at the ripe old age of 91, and it is here that he is said to have received his many famous visitors. He is buried in the nearby "Old Church" (thirteenth century), and there is a monument to him on the north side of the tower, near the stained glass window representing William the Silent, the Dutch king who was assassinated in Delft in 1584.

The church is no longer in use. It is closed in winter, but open to the public on weekday afternoons from April to October. Telephone (tourist office) 015-126100.

DEN HAAG

Hofwijck, the summer home of the Huygens family, is located in Voorburg, a suburb of den Haag. It was designed by Constantijn Huygens, Christiaan's father, and completed in 1640. Constantijn was an influential member of the Dutch ruling councils and a poet besides, and the elegant house, set beautifully among orchards and canals, fitted his status. It is still lovely today, despite the fact that the main highway and railway line out of den Haag traverse the former gardens and form an ugly lesion on the east side of the formerly secluded park. The quiet canals are still there, inviting a moment's rest for passing pedestrian or cyclist. The building itself still has its old kitchen in the cellar and the original living room at ground level, filled with portraits of Huygens family members. Most of the rest of the building is devoted to memorabilia of Constantijn, but one room on the upper floor commemorates Christiaan and includes what is said to be the first constructed pendulum clock, which had been made for the church at Scheveningen, the seaside resort just north of den Haag. The important thing to note is that Christiaan owned this summer residence after his father died in 1687 and, though he did not like it as well as the year-round house in the city, he spent much time here and even erected a mast in the grounds to which he could attach his telescope and view the skies.

It is fascinating to reflect on the contrast between Huygens and his near-contemporary (and intellectually comparable) English mathematician and physicist, Isaac Newton. The Newtons were not poor—they were country squires and their family home in Woolsthrope was substantial. But the Newton house (see p. 128) was clearly a farmhouse, designed for people who work all day with muddy boots, whereas *Hofwijck* was built for elegant garden parties and musical soirées, attended by well-dressed gentlemen and ladies with long dresses and delicate slippers.

The museum is open afternoons except Mondays and Fridays, but the little park around the house, with its walks and waterways, is accessible at all times. Telephone (tourist office) 070-354-6200.

HAARLEM

Haarlem is in the heart of the Dutch bulb center, and each spring the road from Haarlem to Leiden affords an incredible multi-colored spectacle, unequaled anywhere in the world. The city itself has a history going back to the Middle Ages and counts Frans Hals and other artists among its former citizens. Its interest for our purposes lies in the Teylers Museum, the oldest museum in the Netherlands (founded 1778), dedicated by its founder to serve both science and the arts. Today the museum can hardly be classed as among the most distinguished institutions of its kind, but it has a certain charm and happens to be a good place to focus on two highlights in the history of science, one ancient and one very modern.

The museum's first director, Martinus von Marum, was an indiscriminate collector, and the museum's contents still retain their original haphazard character, including dinosaur skeletons, minerals of all kinds, old telescopes, and ancient air pumps. There is a battery of early Leyden jars and a friction generator for charging them, but little in the way of explanation to indicate how they work. One of the telescopes is a lovely wooden one, built by the Herschels in England.

One unique exhibit, typical of what an indiscriminate collector might acquire, is a skeleton of the famous *Homo diluvii testis*, a supposedly human witness of the biblical deluge. It illustrates one of the more bizarre episodes in the history of paleontology, promoted by an avid fossil collector, Johann Jacob Scheuchzer (1672–1733). Scheuchzer was obsessed with the search for remains of the miserable sinners who perished in Noah's Flood and eventually actually believed that he had found human skeletons to fill the bill in a quarry on the German side of the Rhine, near Schaffhausen. The quarrymen there, aware of his passion, obliged Scheuchzer with a steady supply of the skeletons over the next several years. Scheuchzer enthusiastically broadcast his discovery far and wide, with the warning "Take Heed!" as a preface to his tract. He might have applied this warning to himself, for one of his friends raised a valid objection to his sermonizing, namely that the skeletal vertebrae in his specimens lacked a canal for passage of the spinal cord and therefore could hardly be mammalian, much less human. But Scheuchzer was too full of enthusiasm to listen and at least part of the outside world agreed, for *Homo diluvii testis* became an accepted textbook item.

It was not until 1825 that the record was set straight: France's Georges Cuvier came to Haarlem to examine the specimen there, and pronounced it to be the remains of a large salamander. It was then noted that all the specimens that Scheuchzer had obtained from the obliging German quarrymen contained only the top half of the skeletons—the bottom half, which would have included a long tail, was invariably missing. The visitor will also note that the tailless skeletons are not much more than half a meter long, and it is not easy to understand today how anyone could ever have imagined them to be the remains of human beings, even without the problem of the spinal cord canal. (The skeleton is in Showcase 29 on the main floor. Several samples are provided, together with a Swiss stamp that pictures an uncut giant salamander skeleton, complete with tail.)

In a more recent period, Hendrick Antoon Lorentz was curator of the Teylers Museum for 16 years, a curious choice, given that he was a theoretical physicist. It appears that his teaching duties at the University of Leiden were becoming increasingly burdensome to him (he had been there for 30 years) and the curatorship was made available to him in 1912 to give him more time for his research. (Should we have invited a comment from a typically harried director of a present-day museum?) There is a portrait of Lorentz just by the entrance to the old Teyler library in the museum. His books and notes are kept here and are available for scholars who might need them.

Teylers Museum is open daily except Mondays, only in the afternoon on Sundays. Telephone 023–319010.

LEIDEN

The most interesting building of the present university is at No. 73 Rapenburg, one of the prettiest streets in Leiden, with a canal down the middle. The building contains an *Aula* (or Senate Chamber), the walls of which are lined with handsome portraits of most of its early and some of its more recent professors, and there is a lovely wooden staircase leading up to it. Unfortunately, this chamber is still in use for examinations and other university functions, and it is not open to the public, but the rest of the building can be admired. (The doorway to No. 73 also provides access to the university's botanical garden.)

   Boerhaave Museum. This museum, named after the former professor and physician, has been in existence for many years, but it has recently been completely restructured and installed in brand new quarters on the site of the former Boerhaave hospital. At an artistic level it has been beautifully done—the

An original Leeuwenhoek microscope, on exhibit at the Boerhaave Museum in Leiden. The lens is only about one millimeter across; the screws help center the sample behind it.

renovation retains the original architecture and the exhibit layout is spacious and encourages unhurried perusal. The emphasis is historical rather than didactive, with contents arranged in chronological sequence and not by subject area. We are made acutely aware that the division of science into specialized fields is a recent phenomenon and that in Leiden's heyday the distinction between physics, chemistry, and even medicine was blurred. The museum has a commendable international flavor, less chauvinistic than might be expected, though achievements of Netherlands scientists are of course properly stressed. The Dutch have long been instrument makers for much of the world and a predominance of instruments in the exhibits reflects that—the collections of surgical tools, telescopes, and microscopes are especially noteworthy. Even seasoned specialists will be fascinated by the technical advances that the chronological style of the museum naturally unfolds.

One of the highlights of the museum is a faithful reproduction of Boerhaave's anatomy theater, clearly patterned after the prototype in Padua. Individual instruments include three of van Leeuwenhoek's original microscopes (which prove to have extremely tiny lenses), Leyden jars and batteries, Huygens clocks, as well as more modern items, such as the first artificial kidney (dialysis machine), designed by Dutchman Willem Kolff in 1943, and a prototype electron microscope manufactured by the Philips Co. in 1947. The museum also has a fine archival library, which occupies the site of the cells in which madmen were kept in the old hospital. (Is there a hidden message here?)

The Boerhaave Museum is on Lange Sint Agnietenstraat and is open daily except Mondays. Telephone 071-214224.

LUNTEREN

Lunteren, 44 miles (70 km) east of Amsterdam, is in the region of the Netherlands that lies above sea level. The immaculate little town has none of the canals so characteristic of the western part of the country. Lunteren has another asset, however—it is close to the Netherlands' great national park, Hooge Veluwe. The park has many miles of hiking and cycling trails, and contains the famous Kröller-Müller art museum, particularly strong on van Gogh, a place of pilgrimage for art lovers from all over the world. The botanist/geneticist Hugo de Vries in 1918 chose what was then the "remote village" of Lunteren (where the soil was suitable for an experimental garden) as his place of retirement, and he lived here happily for 17 years, remaining professionally active until his death.

De Vries was a rich man when he retired, and bought three adjacent houses on the main street of Lunteren, with a large park area to the rear. One house served as his laboratory and one of them, a grand mansion, was his residence. It is now preserved more or less intact as the "Park Hotel Hugo de

Vries." A famous picture of de Vries in old age, standing in his garden, hangs in the hotel lounge.

The hotel at present caters only to small conferences and is open from March to October. If the owners are not too busy, they allow visitors to see the house. Telephone: 08388–5141.

MIDDELBURG

The pretty little town of Middelburg, tucked away in the southwest corner of the country away from principal tourist areas, has a completely reconstructed medieval center and some of the most interesting old buildings in all of the Netherlands. The town had on one occasion (in 1609) a truly significant impact on science history. There were spectacle makers in Middelburg and at least one of them, Hans Lipperhey, had devised a crude spyglass to make distant objects appear closer. Either Lipperhey himself or one of his fellow townsmen is said to have tried to peddle the instruments in Italy. Galileo, who was in Venice at the time, was stirred to excitement when he heard about it and set off at once to try to catch up with the peddler in Padua, but the man had left. Galileo stopped to think about the matter and figured out what the principle of design must be. He promptly built a telescope himself, which turned out to be far better than the instruments being offered for sale by the traveling Dutchman. The rest is legend; the telescope catapulted Galileo into national prominence and the observations of the skies that he made with it gave him a kind of public fame that he would never have achieved on the basis of his more intellectual work on motion and mechanics. (And, of course, it ultimately led to his conflict with the Catholic Church.) Galileo was already forty-five years old when this happened and there is no evidence that he had ever deliberately planned to engage in astronomical observations. Three cheers for Middelburg!

It is often asserted that one Zacharias Jansen invented the telescope or microscope or both in 1590, and Middelburg has a street named after this famous citizen. Jansen, however, was born in 1588 and therefore rather too young to have invented anything in 1590. It is probably true that he was an accomplished lens polisher and he is thought to have constructed a telescope in 1604, but he never claimed to have *invented* it—that claim was actually made by his son in 1655, long after his father was dead. (To compound the problem, it is not even certain that Zacharias Jansen's local fame at the time rested on his optical skills. He was an expert counterfeiter of Spanish coins, which was considered a patriotic activity, for the former oppressors of the Dutch people had not yet given up all hope of regaining their dominance.)

"MITTELEUROPA"

10

Germany

Most of Germany's vaunted achievements in science date from a relatively narrow period. German science was in the doldrums in the eighteenth century and through the reign of Napoleon, at a time when French science was preeminent. When Germany's turn came, it coincided with the heady rise of the Prussian state and the subsequent forging of a single nation. But it didn't last long, for two destructive wars and the insanity of the Hitler years all but destroyed the intellectual enterprise.

For this reason we cannot realistically look at German science in terms of a chronological sequence of highlights, as we have done for some other countries. Germany had its isolated shining stars in the earliest days of our history—as did Italy, England, France, Poland, Denmark and the Netherlands, but afterwards there was little of outstanding merit until that one century-long spurt. Everything seemed to flower together and the active participants all overlapped with each other. The major part of this chapter—the first section excepted—thus consists of a selection of individual topics, confined areas of science where German influence was indeed mighty, all dating roughly from the fall of Napoleon until around 1930.

Early Days

The Protestant Reformation of the sixteenth century and the resultant Counter-Reformation of the Roman church caused years of strife in all of continental Europe, and not least in Germany. Some hope of religious toleration and relative tranquility was sought by the so-called Peace of Augsburg in 1555, but the unfortunate effect of this agreement was not peace but further and more devastating wars. In an attempt to put Romanists and Lutherans on an equal footing, it had been decided that each ruling prince would determine the religion to be practiced on his lands and would have the right to eject from his area any who

225

did not conform to his religious persuasion. The ultimate result of this brilliant piece of political negotiation was to divide the country into small fiefdoms that had not only the usual earthly antagonisms, but were now saddled with deep religious divisions as well. Matters became even worse in 1618, when local strife escalated into full scale war, the Thirty Years' War, a battle for land and political power as much as religious principle. France and other neighboring countries joined in, but most of the fighting was in Germany. Its countryside was laid waste, its cities were ravaged, its economy was ruined.

Surely a situation unconducive to peaceful intellectual affairs, one would think? History proves otherwise!

Trailblazer of Astronomy: Johannes Kepler (1571–1630). In the midst of this religious and political chaos appeared Johannes Kepler, a man with an insistent drive to seek order and harmony in the universe, in which task he succeeded, although his own everyday life was the very opposite, a mirror of the turbulence of the times.

Kepler was born in Weil-der-Stadt in the Duchy of Württemberg. His family seems to have been an unpleasant lot, his mother described by Kepler himself as "small, thin, swarthy, gossiping and quarrelsome, of a bad disposition," his father as "vicious, inflexible, quarrelsome, and doomed to a bad end." Indeed, the father abandoned his family forever in 1588 when Kepler was sixteen years old. (The mother in old age was tried for being a witch, and Kepler spent many months between 1617 and 1620 to save her from being burned at the stake.) In spite of this bad start, Kepler received an excellent education and a state scholarship to the University of Tübingen, where he went to study with the faculty of theology. Then, unexpectedly, came an offer of the post of mathematics teacher in the Lutheran school in Graz, which, had he been more prudent, he might have turned down because Graz was the capital of the Roman Catholic province of Styria, whereas Kepler was a committed Protestant. Kepler was indeed eventually expelled from Graz because of his religious association, but not before he had become quite famous—from Graz came the first of his inspired solutions to the mysteries of the cosmos, a fantastical construct of nested spheres and polyhedra, a model of symmetry and harmony, though (it must be said) lacking much connection to reality.

As it happened, the banishment from Graz proved to be a blessing in disguise, for the year was 1600 and Tycho Brahe, the astronomer, (see under "Denmark"), had just recently moved to Prague, bringing with him the huge volume of precise astronomical observations that he had made in Denmark. Kepler became Brahe's assistant and, when the latter died soon after, he inherited Brahe's job of imperial mathematician. More important, by the deathbed wish of Brahe himself, he inherited the treasure of his data, which up to then had been jealously guarded.

It is still easy today to feel the sense of revolution in what followed, as Kepler grappled with the problem of finding his imperative order in the cosmos, no longer free to fantasize, but constrained by the need to remain within the strict confines of Brahe's observations. A further restriction was that Kepler was an enthusiastic supporter of the Copernican heliocentric model of the universe, and insisted that the data must fit it—Brahe himself had still had the sun circling the earth in the models he built. Kepler daringly abandoned perfect circular orbits in favor of elliptical ones, forced to do so by the data. He found his order in mathematical terms and formulated the laws that seemed to govern the movement of the planets. It was all published in 1627 in the celebrated *Tabulae Rudolphinae*, a complete compilation of past and future positions of moon and planets, dedicated (posthumously) to Emperor Rudolf II, who had been both Brahe's and Kepler's patron and protector.

Kepler himself never lost his sense of divine inspiration, the notion of a God-given design that everyone but himself seemed too blind to perceive. He was ecstatic when he discovered his "third law," for example, the one that makes the profound statement that the squares of the periods of revolution of the planets are proportional to the cubes of their mean distances from the sun, a statement that he could prove with real numbers. "The die is cast, and I am writing the book," he said. "It can wait a century for a reader, as God himself has waited six thousand years for a witness."

But the turbulence of Kepler's life continued unabated. Rudolf died in 1612 and Kepler left Prague to live in Linz, where he became involved in more religious battles, this time a painful schism within the Protestant ranks. His mother's witchcraft trial interrupted his work. Five of the seven children of his second marriage died in infancy or at birth. The Thirty Years' War broke out in 1618, and Kepler thereafter had trouble collecting his salary and money due to him for publication of the *Tabulae*. He had gone to Regensburg to petition the Emperor for some of the money that was owed when he fell ill and died in 1630. He was buried in the Protestant cemetery there, but the cruelty of religious strife still pursued him after death—the churchyard was demolished in one of the battles and his bones were scattered.

Related Places to Visit: Weil-der-Stadt, Regensburg, and Prague (Czechoslovakia).

Much Ado about Nothing. Otto von Guericke (1602–1686), mayor of Magdeburg, designed and carried out a famous experiment, which had the effect of dispelling the age-old doctrine that "nature abhors a vacuum." He thereby opened up the science that used to be called *pneumatics*—in modern terms, the physics of gases. But his experiment was also a grand spectacle, a public attraction like a circus or (150 years later) a balloon ascent. Thousands of people must have seen it in Madgeburg or in other towns where it was reenacted, and pictures of it circulated throughout Europe.

Guericke came from a patrician family with a long record of public office in Magdeburg. His education was good and included a stint at the University of Leiden in the Netherlands. He served as mayor of Magdeburg for 30 years (1646–1676). Like Kepler, he had to cope with religious strife (the Thirty Years' War only ended in 1648), but (unlike Kepler) he mostly coped well. He, too, went to Regensburg to attend the imperial diets, but he attended as a delegate, a representative of his city, not (as Kepler did) in the role of petitioner.

It was in fact at one of the Regensburg meetings that Guericke first heard about the vacuum pump designed in Florence by Torricelli and decided to build something similar for his own use, for he was an ardent advocate of Copernicus and the question of what lies between the heavenly bodies fascinated him. A vacuum seemed a plausible answer, but there were adamant opponents to that idea, including Guericke's celebrated contemporary René Descartes (see under "France"). Space without matter was an absurdity in their view. A pump to expel air from a vessel should be able to settle the controversy and Guericke, when he could spare the time from more important duties, applied himself to design an appropriate apparatus. After several tries he came up with the ideal design: two large metal hemispheres, joined at their open ends (and crudely sealed off from the outside) by closely fitting flanges. Ports at the surface were used to attach pumps and to remove most of the air, creating a partial vacuum inside. The ports were sealed and teams of horses were harnessed to the hemispheres, pulling in opposite directions to try to separate them. But the vacuum held. Even six or eight horses to a side, straining with all their might, could not pull the hemispheres apart—only when the valves were opened and air was readmitted did that happen. The readmission of air was, of course, an essential part of the demonstration, the convincing proof that "nothing" had been there before to counter the pressure of outside air.

(Another aspect of the apparatus illustrates the prevailing confusion about air that needed to be overcome. Guericke intitially thought of air as a fluid that would behave like a liquid and would fall to the bottom of a partly evacuated vessel; in his first designs, the outlets for the pump were always *at the bottom* of the apparatus. When he found that pump ports placed anywhere on his spheres would work equally well, he was actually making a discovery, namely that air and other gases are elastic and normally fill all the space of any container in which they are placed.)

Related Place to Visit: Magdeburg.

Lean Years and Philosophers. The Thirty Years' War was followed by lean years, when little happened in Germany that can be said to represent roots of the sciences as we now know them. Two noteworthy philosophers, however, graced the scene during this period.

One of them was **Gottfried Leibniz** (1646–1716), acknowledged to be one of the great intellects of his day. Scientists know him best in the role of mathematician, as co-inventor of the calculus, but this was only one facet of his many-sided career. The greatest demands on him probably came from his service to the rulers of Mainz and Hanover, for whom he acted as legal advisor and traveling emissary. It was during a business trip to Paris that he met and studied with Christiaan Huygens (see under "Netherlands") and began to develop the ideas of the calculus, an achievement that has given him posthumous fame but led to decades of dispute with Isaac Newton during his lifetime—a dispute that still flares up from time to time in our own day. (It is Leibniz's nomenclature that we use today when we write "dy/dx" for a first derivative.) Leibniz was worn down by this dispute and what he saw as a general lack of appreciation for his many contributions to philosophy and mathematics. At his funeral in Hanover only his secretary was present, and his death went unnoticed in all countries except France.

Leibniz's fate was hardly an encouragement for bright young men to turn to philosophy or science, and there was a gap of nearly a century before the appearance of **Immanuel Kant** (1724–1804), who wrote fanciful works on such varied subjects as physical geography and theories of the heavens before settling down to philosophy. He spent almost his entire life at Königsberg and simply by his presence gave Königsberg University (founded in 1544) a stature it had never had before. Several later German scientists acknowledge their intellectual debt to Kant's philosophy, and his influence on European science as a whole is said to have been great. Just how he did this is, however, not easy to discover, for his writing is convoluted and often contradictory. Did he inspire some of his followers by his noble definition of what constitutes proper science? Only that which can be "proven irrefutably," he claimed. Who among us does not long for knowledge of how such level of certainty might be attained?

The Bergakademie

Toward the end of the eighteenth century, in the mountains of eastern Saxony, appeared an institution that became a genuine international center and may be taken as a beacon for the end of Germany's lean years. It was the Bergakademie in Freiberg (established in 1765), the world's first and most influential school of mining. The man who made Freiberg more than just a trade school was **Abraham Gottlob Werner** (1750–1817), professor at the academy from 1775 to 1816. He came from a local family that had been connected with mining for three centuries, and at first he taught only mineralogy—how to recognize what's what among the rocks, how to classify, how to separate the precious from the dross. But he soon added a course on the history of the rocks as well, inspired perhaps by whiffs of enlightened speculation from further west. "Rocks are not dispersed at random," he told them, "but follow each other in definite order," and went on to give his ideas on how they got to be there.

Ironically, given Freiberg's land-locked location, Werner's theory invokes the ocean and became known as the Neptunic theory. In the beginning, Werner said, the Earth was completely enveloped by a primeval ocean, in which all the solids of present day lands were present in suspension. Then the waters started to recede and primitive rocks (granite, then basalt) began to crystallize out. As the ocean retreated, crests of mountains appeared, detritus mingled with earlier chemical deposit, life began. Then, as the ocean level fell even further, detritus (plus organic matter) became the dominant solid matter, deposited as limestones, sandstones, and so forth, in the familiar geological strata—with fossils as evidence of the appearance of ever more advanced forms of life. It was not a profound theory, nor even particularly original, for similar ideas had been expressed by the philosopher Leibniz many years before, and to modern eyes (and perhaps to some of the brighter students at the time?) it has a serious flaw, an unstated problem ignored. Where did all the water go? As the ocean level fell, did the water evaporate and vanish into outer space? Or was it absorbed into some crevice within the earth and, if so, where is it now?

Werner's theory, despite its naiveté, filled a void and became incredibly influential. It was one of those fortuitous coincidences. People suddenly realized how little they knew about the world they inhabit and eagerly wanted to learn more, and just at that point in time an oracle appeared, who had the answers in his regular course of student lectures. In the words of the French geologist/paleontologist, Georges Cuvier,

> At the little academy, founded for the purpose of training mining engineers and mine captains for the mines of Saxony, there was renewed the spectacle presented

by the universities of the Middle Ages, for students flocked thither from every civilized country. One saw men from the most remote countries, already well advanced in years, men of education holding important positions, engaged with all diligence in the study of the German language, so as to fit themselves to sit at the feet of this "Great Oracle of the Sciences of the Earth."

Alexander von Humboldt, German explorer and naturalist, was Werner's most famous student and provides eloquent testimony to the powerful attraction that Freiberg (and mining and/or geology) must have held at the time. For Humboldt came from the privileged class—town house in Berlin, hunting lodge nearby, private tutors in his youth—yet he chose to leave his studies at the University of Göttingen and to come to Freiberg instead, staying here for eight months of study.

Werner's influence was particularly strong in Britain. George Bellas Greenough, first president of the Geological Society of London (founded in 1807) had studied under Werner and was a disciple of his view of geology. William Buckland, first professor of geology at Oxford (and Charles Lyell's teacher there) rushed off to Freiberg as soon as the end of the Napoleonic wars made it possible to do so, to gather pearls of wisdom from the great oracle at his home. And from Scotland came Robert Jameson, professor of natural history in Edinburgh, to study at Freiberg in 1800. He became perhaps the most forceful Neptunist anywhere, with a famous book in its advocacy published in 1804. (It is a curious paradox that James Hutton was also from Edinburgh and that his *Theory of the Earth*, diametrically opposite to Werner's ideas, had been published there in 1795. Thus Jameson might have been expected to be one of the first to realize the faults of Neptunism, but in fact he was one of the last of the disciples to abandon it.)

Related Place to Visit: Freiberg.

Göttingen University: Gauss and Weber

A more traditional seat of learning with more enduring influence emerged at Göttingen. It was a new university (founded 1736), but the older ones had disappeared or become ineffectual. The University of Heidelberg, for example, which had been founded in 1386, was virtually demolished during the Thirty Years' War, its library sent off to the Vatican and later to Paris. Restoration did not begin until 1815.

Göttingen had a seemingly modern breadth of scholarship. There was J. F. Blumenbach (1752–1840), for example, a kind of embryo anthropologist, one of the first persons ever to view man as an object of study for Natural History, who divided humans into five races and tried to establish the relationships between them by anatomical studies. Other forerunners of now popular academic subjects were the Grimm brothers, Jakob (1785–1863) and Wilhelm (1786–1859), best known to us for *Grimm's Fairy Tales*, but actually renowned scholars, considered the founders of comparative linguistics. They were responsible for the basic

Grimm's Law, stating the principle that consonant sounds undergo regular transitions in the evolution of languages from one another—V or F in place of P, for example, as in "Vater" and "pater." They also produced the first comprehensive dictionary of the German language.

In the physical sciences, the early Göttingen stars were **Carl Friedrich Gauss** (1777–1855) and **Wilhelm Weber** (1804–1891). Gauss was a brilliant mathematician who applied his skills in the service of physics. He was born in Braunschweig, the offspring of several generations of humble laborers who worked as gardeners and handymen and who thought little of any form of education. It is quite remarkable (given the times) that Gauss's precocious abilities were brought to the attention of the Duke of Braunschweig, who was so impressed after an initial interview that he subsidized a proper education for him in Braunschweig and later at the University of Göttingen and continued to support him even after he received his degree. Gauss's early work was entirely mathematical. We commemorate his name in the Gaussian distribution (also known as normal distibution), the simplest and most symmetrical formulation of the statistical distribution of a variable parameter about its mean, but his derivation of this function is just a small fraction of his mathematical output. In 1801 he calculated the orbit of the first discovered asteroid (Ceres) in the solar system and correctly predicted when and where it would next be visible (a year later). That led to his appointment in 1807 as director of the Göttingen observatory and professor of astronomy, positions he held until his death. The university appointment required little in the way of lectures or student contact, which was probably a good thing since Gauss is reported to have had little patience with those less gifted than himself.

Weber, much younger than Gauss, came to Göttingen as physics professor in 1828. He and Gauss became friends and began a long scientific collaboration. Their major contribution was to quantify the measurement of magnetic force and to make precise measurements of terrestial magnetism. Again we commemorate by means of a word (a household word for any physics student), namely the unit *gauss* by which magnetic field strength is designated. They also showed how to relate the quantity of electricity to more common physical units and in fact the unit now known as *coulomb* was at one time called the *weber*. While making their magnetic measurements, Gauss and Weber made an important invention— the first electromagnetic telegraph—which enabled them to communicate between the Göttingen observatory and the physics laboratory by means of a wire strung between the two.

It might be noted in conclusion that the Göttingen renascence did not go all that smoothly. In 1837 the elector Ernest Augustus of Hanover revoked a liberal constitution that had been granted only four years previously. Seven professors protested and were promptly expelled. The "Göttingen Seven" included Wilhem Weber and the Grimm brothers. Reinstatement did not come until 1849 when more moderate political thought returned.

Related Places to Visit: Göttingen, Braunschweig.

The Rise of German Chemistry

There is no question about German leadership in the meteoric rise of chemistry in the second half of the nineteenth century and for some decades beyond. The role of Germany was comprehensive, covering not only descriptive and synthetic chemistry, but also the new field of physical chemistry, which sought to apply the laws of physics to chemistry so as to isolate general principles, independent of the specific atoms or molecules that might be involved in a particular reaction. The laws of thermodynamics (discussed below) are the prime examples. They are as much (or even more) a part of chemistry as they are of physics.

Justus von Liebig (1803–1873) was the dominant figure. He founded the science of organic chemistry and saw it grow from birth to maturity within his own lifetime. He thought about chemistry in the grand manner, always linking the details of what went on at the laboratory bench to the broader picture. What is an acid? Are "radicals" a reality? Where do plants get their carbon? He had the knack of harnessing the efforts of eager students and coworkers in pursuit of his ideas. He argued ceaselessly and often maliciously with rivals in the field— contemporaries, youngsters, senior citizens such as Jakob Berzelius (see under "Sweden"), it seemed to make no difference who they were. He founded and edited the great journal of chemistry, *Annalen der Chemie*, which became the vehicle for the dissemination of important new work from all over Europe—but Liebig also considered it his God-given duty to use the *Annalen* to point out the error of their ways to many scientists with whom he disagreed. He was a great and influential scientist, but he was not a pleasant man.

Liebig was born in Darmstadt and was fascinated by chemistry from his earliest days. He was apprenticed at age sixteen to an apothecary not far away in Heppenheim, but his apprenticeship was not a success, and he strove for a broader education. At the time he could not get it in Germany and went to Paris to study with Gay-Lussac and others. There he met and made a favorable impression on Alexander von Humboldt, who had earlier worked with Gay-Lussac. Humboldt recommended Liebig for a professorship in chemistry at the University of Giessen and Liebig (aged twenty-two at the time) got the job and remained for 27 years. Here he set up his laboratory, which he used for teaching as well as research. In fact, he was probably the most influential teacher that chemistry has ever known. Three hundred pharmacists and 451 chemists were students here while Liebig was professor and 60 of the latter went on to become professors all over in Europe. (In 1852 he moved to the big city of Munich, which gave him a higher status and a grander laboratory, but nothing he did there ever equalled his achievements in Giessen.)

Scientific high points in Liebig's career include the development of quantitative analytical methods for carbon and hydrogen, essential prerequisites for the quantification of organic chemistry. He also extended the theory of radicals which had been proposed by Berzelius—the idea that small groups of atoms may stick together in chemical reactions, to create individual entities with a certain degree of permanence. Without this concept, organic chemistry would become incredibly complex, all but impossible to understand. Liebig and his coworkers recognized ethyl and benzoyl radicals, for example, and this was more of a feat than we can now appreciate, for the problem of atomic weights had not yet been solved at the time so that the formulas for these entities were uncertain—it makes the genius and imagination involved in their recognition all the greater.

Mention should also be made of Liebig's texbook *Organic Chemistry in its Applications to Agriculture and Physiology*, first published in 1840. The title epitomizes his need to take the broad view, spilling even beyond his immediate scientific field. The influence on agriculture is usually regarded as good. Liebig's book was, for example, the first to state forcefully that all carbon in plants is derived from atmospheric CO_2, none from the soil, and had an immediate effect on those who were working on the production of commercial fertilizers. On the other hand, Liebig's views on physiology, biochemistry, and medicine were not at all beneficial—we shall give one example in the story of Theodor Schwann.

Related Places to Visit: Giessen, Munich, Darmstadt, Heppenheim.

The most brilliant of Liebig's students was **August Kekulé** (1829–1896). By chance he happened to be born in Darmstadt, as Liebig was, but (unlike Liebig) he came from a noble family, of Bohemian origin, who could trace their ancestry back to the fourteenth century. Kekulé's full name was properly Friedrich August Kekulé von Stradonitz (Stradonice being a village near Prague). The accent on the terminal 'é' was a Napoleonic addition, dating from the years when the French emperor briefly ruled Hesse-Darmstadt.

Kekulé is often regarded as more brilliant and more original than Liebig himself, but, of course, he could not have achieved what he did except in the context of the already existing framework that Liebig had created. He was, however, far ahead of Liebig and of most chemists of the day in his ability to visualize the three-dimensional spatial organization of complicated organic molecules containing multiple carbon atoms. He is personally responsible for the two most basic structural concepts in all of organic chemistry. The first is that carbon atoms must be tetravalent, i.e., they must each have effectively four arms for forming bonds to neighboring atoms and *all must be used.* Sometimes, to satisfy this condition, two or three arms must combine to form double or triple bonds between adjacent atoms. The second basic fact is the division of all organic chemistry into two branches, *aliphatic* and *aromatic.* This came about because the benzene molecule and related molecules derived from it did not seem to fit into the tetravalent carbon formulation even with allowance for double or triple bonds. In 1861, while on the faculty of the University of Ghent in Belgium, Kekulé, in a moment of inspiration, got the answer to the problem: The benzene molecule must be a *closed ring* of six carbon atoms. Indeed that is what it is, and this ring is the nucleus of all organic molecules in the aromatic category.

In 1867 Kekulé returned to his native country to become a professor at the University of Bonn and to set up a chemical institute there. He continued to do important work there and was much honored. In 1886 they held a celebration in Bonn to mark the twenty-fifth anniversary of the benzene formula, and Kekulé gave an address explaining how the inspiration had come to him—in a dream-like vision, in which a chain of carbon atoms seemed to resemble a snake biting its own tail. (Needless to say, there are historians who doubt the authenticity of this tale.)

In conclusion, another credit due to Kekulé should be mentioned. It was he in 1860 who convened the first International Chemical Congress in Karlsruhe for the purpose of resolving conflicting views about absolute atomic weights and systematizing the writing of formulae for organic compounds. It was at this meeting that Cannizaro revived the 50-year old ideas of Avogadro (see under "Italy") and put to rest the almost universal confusion that had reigned for so many years.

Related Places to Visit: Bonn, Darmstadt.

Finally we come to the negative side of Liebig, the victims of his merciless intolerance. The most famous of them is **Theodor Schwann** (1810–1882) who is generally credited with establishing the cell theory as accepted biological doctrine, i.e., the notion that living organisms are built up from tiny cells, somewhat the way that molecules are made from atoms. In 1839 he published his famous "Microscopical researches on the similarity in structure and growth of animals and plants," based in part on his own careful observations of cell division and the like. All living matter is made of cells, he stated, or of substance thrown off by cells. The cells have a life that is to some extent their own but subject to regulation by the organism as a whole. All cells share characteristic features: They have a nucleus, protoplasm, and cell membrane. "The great barrier between the animal and vegetable kingdoms, viz. diversity of ultimate structure, thus vanishes. Cells, cell membrane, cell contents, nuclei, in the former are analogous to the parts with similar names in plants." These tenets have remained unaltered to the present day.

Theodor Schwann has other credits to his name, all gained while still a very young man. He coined the term *metabolism*, meaning subject to change, for the chemical reactions that go on inside a cell for synthesis and energy production. He did pioneering work on muscle contraction. He observed that fermenting sugars were teeming with microorganisms (yeast) and correctly inferred that the microorganisms were the cause of fermentation, anticipating Louis Pasteur by 20 years. Schwann was an altogether brilliant man, surely destined, one would think, for fame and fortune.

Alas, no! Schwann's career as a scientist did not continue beyond age thirty. The contention that alcohol fermentation is caused by a living organism (made not only by Schwann, but also by a Frenchman, Cagniard de la Tour) ran afoul of the mainstream of contemporary chemical opinion, which championed the cause of "pure" organic chemistry against "vitalism." Liebig, in particular, sneered at the possible intervention of a living creature in fermentation, and his associate Friedrich Wöhler published a vicious caricature in the famous *Annalen der Chemie*. This satire—report of an imaginary microscopic investigation— described yeast as a tiny animal with exactly the same shape as a distilling flask that one would use for the laboratory production of alcohol. It had a funnel-like mouth; the body of the flask was imagined as a stomach; there was a little tube to represent the anus (for excretion of alcohol) and another tube for the escape of carbon dioxide. Elsewhere in the same journal were more serious papers on purely chemical fermentation, pure test tube production of alcohol, as carried out in Liebig's laboratory.

It is generally believed that Liebig's ridicule caused a timid appointments committee to deny Schwann a professorship at the University of Bonn that he had otherwise every reason to expect. Schwann was sufficiently discouraged (or disgusted) to decide then and there to give up science altogether. He devoted the rest of his life to mysticism and theology, with professorships in theology at Louvain from 1839 till 1848, and at Liège from 1848 to 1879. Microbes and the germ theory of fermentation eventually became accepted through the championship of Louis Pasteur.

Light from the Sky

A new era in astronomy begins! Attention shifts from the planets to the stars, and from the stars themselves to the light that they emit. And here in Germany there is a healthy intrusion of chemistry into the subject, which would have been less likely in other countries, where chemistry was not as much in the forefront.

To begin with the stars themselves: Tycho Brahe in the sixteenth century, using only his eyes, unaided by any magnifying device, had catalogued the positions of 777 fixed stars; by the early eighteenth century, with the help of the telescope, this number had grown to the tens of thousands. But how far away are they? No meaningful estimates of actual distance were available. How this information could be obtained was clear—it was the traditional method of triangulation with the diameter of the earth's orbit as a base, i.e., the apparent change in position of a star at six-month intervals (called the measurement of *parallax* by astronomers). But the distance to the stars was clearly immense and the angular change so small as to be virtually immeasurable. It was **Friedrich Bessel** (1784–1846), appointed by the King of Prussia to direct a new observatory at Königsberg, who first achieved the requisite precision and gave us an actual distance. It was for one of the closest stars, known as 61 Cygni in the star catalog, and the result of the measurement was 350,000 times the earth's orbital diameter, about 10^{14} kilometers! It is a truly mind-boggling number. (It corresponds to 10.9 light-years in the units we now use.)

Another Bessel achievement came from watching the brightest of all our stars, Sirius A. He discovered an anomalous slow oscillation in its position from which he concluded that Sirius must be a binary star, its companion as massive as itself, but *invisible*. He had the kind of mind that could accept this at first shocking conclusion with equanimity—why should luminosity be an essential quality of cosmic bodies? (The companion star Sirius B was eventually discovered just where Bessel said it had to be and turns out to be very dim, not invisible. But the twentieth century has given us "black holes," which do in fact lack any luminosity.)

Finally, a contribution to mathematics should be mentioned. Bessel put great effort into devising new mathematical methods for dealing with planetary and stellar motions, and from this work emerged Bessel functions, mathematical expressions which turn out to be useful in a multitude of applications. Bessel was a small and delicate man with a disorder that always made him look prematurely old, but all who met him report a transformation when he began to talk and revealed the youth and brilliance of his mind. He died of cancer in 1846 and was buried near his observatory.

Bessel's telescope was built, not in Königsberg, but at the opposite end of Germany, by the firm of Utzschneider, Reichenbach und Fraunhofer in the little town of Benediktbeuern in Bavaria. The guiding genius of this company was **Josef von Fraunhofer** (1787–1826), the son of a Bavarian glazier, who was apprenticed at an early age to another of the same ilk, but taught himself mathematics and theoretical optics in his spare time and (quite apart from his skilled craftsmanship) went on to make his own remarkable observations and measurements of the heavens. It is said that a stroke of good luck for his career was the collapse in 1801 of the workshop where he served as apprentice. The rubble fell on him, but he was rescued and given 18 ducats by the elector of Bavaria to celebrate his miraculous escape. With this money he was able to buy his release from the apprenticeship, to purchase his own glass polishing machine, and thereby to attain professional status.

Fraunhofer did not restrict himself to producing commercial glass products and telescopes for observatories. He became himself an active researcher, and in 1813 he used a diamond point and his remarkable manual skills to produce an optical diffraction grating with 310 lines ruled per inch! With such gratings it is possible to produce spectra with unprecedented resolution (far better than with a glass prism), and Fraunhofer used them to record the spectra of the sun and the stars. He found that the light emitted from the sun differs from the light of distant stars, which was the first demonstration that stars emit their own light, unlike the planets, which merely reflect the sun's rays. But his most remarkable discovery was the detection of a pattern of thin black lines in the spectrum of the sun, known ever after as the *Fraunhofer lines*. They were an unsolved mystery to him and his contemporaries. What were black lines doing in the midst of the blue, green, and red of the normal spectrum? Fraunhofer noted at the time that they seemed in some cases to correspond to the wavelengths emitted by materials heated to very high temperatures, but speculation was not in his nature and the true significance of the lines was not discovered until much later.

Fraunhofer transferred his optical workshop from Benediktbeuern to Munich in 1819 and died there of tuberculosis in 1826, a mere thirty-nine years old. Biographers tell of an epitaph inscribed on his tombstone: *Approximavit Sidera*—"He brought the stars nearer." It seems to have weathered away; at least we did not see it when we visited the cemetery.

Analytical Spectroscopy. The explanation of Fraunhofer's lines—a unique blend of chemistry and physics—came from the University of Heidelberg, a result of the collaboration between **Robert Bunsen** (1811–1899) and **Gustav Kirchhoff** (1824–1887). Bunsen (the chemist) was the son of a professor of modern languages at the University of Göttingen. He studied chemistry there and held several academic posts before settling down as professor of chemistry at Heidelberg in 1852. Kirchhoff (the physicist) was the son of a Prussian state official in Königsberg and began his career in academic physics at the university there. He and Bunsen had briefly been colleagues on the faculty of the University of Breslau and Bunsen successfully proposed Kirchhoff to fill a vacancy on the Heidelberg physics faculty in 1854.

One of Bunsen's interests was in the preparation and characterization of pure elements from their compounds. The famous Bunsen burner was invented by him specifically for the purpose of chemical analysis, to produce an intense nonluminous flame in which salts and metals could be heated to sufficiently high temperature to produce the colors that had become recognized in many cases as distinctive. The collaboration with Kirchhoff began when the latter suggested to Bunsen that color could be given a far more precise quantitative definition by means of a spectroscope, such as Fraunhofer had used. The results were spectacular. It was the birth of a truly new science, chemical spectroscopy, which has grown to become the mainstay of all chemical identification analysis today.

(Bunsen's high temperature colors are what we now call atomic emission spectra. Characteristic spectral lines for all metal atoms were quickly established. A systematic study of purified alkali metals produced spectral lines that could not be identified with any known metals, and they proved to arise from two hitherto unknown elements, rubidium and cesium. The number of elements in the alkali metal class, which includes sodium and potassium, was thereby increased from three to five. The striking similarities between them were an important factor in the evolution of the Periodic Table of Elements. Dmitri Mendeléev, chiefly responsible for the latter, was a student at Heidelberg about this time.)

Fraunhofer's lines were investigated as part of this project and their explanation proved to be spectacular in its own right. Kirchhoff interposed a sodium flame between the incident sunlight beam and the spectroscope, and this enabled him to verify that the yellow lines characteristic of sodium were at exactly the same wavelength as some of Fraunhofer's mysterious black lines. (Yellow superseded black in dim sunlight.) But he made an unexpected observation when the intensity of the sunlight became very high—now the sodium flame made the dark lines even blacker than before. He quickly arrived at the explanation: A substance capable of emitting light at a certain wavelength can also absorb light at the same wavelength. The Fraunhofer dark lines themselves can be ascribed to absorption that had occurred in the solar atmosphere! Which in turn means that there must be vaporized sodium in the solar atmosphere and the other Fraunhofer lines must represent absorption by other elements.

Immense prospects were opened up for the astronomer. The chemical composition of the sun and the stars could be ascertained from optical measurements on earth. One new element (helium) was discovered in the solar spectrum in 1868, but that was the only one—even the most distant stars are evidently composed of precisely the same kinds of atoms that we have here on earth. This was surely a momentous discovery, the final deathblow for advocates of a difference between the heavens and the earth.

Related Places to Visit: Benediktbeuern, Heidelberg, Munich.

The Laws of Thermodynamics

There is a popular way to express the meaning of the two great laws of thermodynamics. The first law, the law of conservation of energy, tells us "You cannot win!" and the second law, the law of increasing entropy, makes it even grimmer, with the message, "You can't even break even!" As first formulated, these laws were macroscopic, empirical, unifying concepts based on everything we see all around us, but making no reference to (and therefore not dependent on) any microscopic particulate theories of matter. Their consistency with the physics of atoms and molecules has, of course, since been established, but that came much later than the time of which we write, when many people were not yet convinced that atoms and molecules really exist.

Hermann Helmholtz (1821–1894) was a giant of nineteenth-century science, perhaps one of the last with a romantic yearning for grand unifying principles. He himself became famous for one of the greatest of all unifying principles, the first law of thermodynamics, the law of conservation of energy. This law grew gradually from diverse observations by many different people, and one cannot point to a single moment when one individual stood up and said, "I announce a new universal law of physics." But Helmholtz came close to filling that bill in 1847, with the publication of a creative work, *Ueber die Erhaltung der Kraft.*

Helmholtz's father was a schoolteacher and an ardent lover of philosophy, but the family was not wealthy and young Hermann (who really wanted to be a physicist/philosopher) had to find a way to earn a living. Accordingly, he enrolled in a medical program that gave him free education in return for eight years of service as a doctor in the Prussian army. He combined his medical education with related research in physiology (with a great Berlin teacher,

Johannes Müller) and proved to be so good that he was relieved of part of his military service, and (in 1848) was able to accept the offer of an academic position at the University of Königsberg. In 1855 he became professor of anatomy and physiology at the University of Bonn and in 1857 the government of Baden, then a quite separate state from Prussia, offered Helmholtz the chair of physiology at Heidelberg, which he accepted. He remained there for 13 productive years, but in 1871 was finally able to reassert his original love for physics and philosophy when he was invited to the University of Berlin to become professor of physics and to supervise the construction of a new institute of physics, which was to be entirely under his control. (They moved around a lot in those days in German academia. Helmholtz was no exception.)

Helmholtz's specific contributions to science are numerous and extraordinarily varied. In Heidelberg, for example, he wrote a book on the *physiological* foundation of music appreciation, a work that combined knowledge of the anatomy of the ear, the physics of sound, the physiology of hearing, and the mathematics of harmonics. But the very breadth of his interests diminishes the sharpness with which his specific contributions can be defined. He was still a junior physiologist in Müller's group in Berlin when he published *Ueber die Erhaltung der Kraft*. It was intended in part to support the group's conviction that life itself contributes no mystic vital force to the actions of living things—in this case by the assertion that the huge force capacity of muscle movements can be entirely accounted for by the energy derived from food intake. Being related in this way to biological phenomena, Helmholtz's supporting data could not come close in quantitation to Joule's data (ten years later) on the equivalence of heat with other forms of energy. But, as it happened, Joule did not philosophize and did not proclaim the general principle that his results asserted. Whereas Helmholtz did. In fact his experiments and his paper may be said to have done more than that, for conservation of energy in the biological context has overtones that go beyond the physical law.

Entropy and Its Unrelenting Increase. There is no ambiguity in assigning credit for the second law. In its initial empirical form, it is the work of **Rudolf Clausius** (1822–1888) alone. Clausius, a nearly exact contemporary of Helmholtz, was much more narrowly focused, concentrating almost exclusively on the subject of heat and thermodynamics. He was also more of a loner and more argumentative, often to the point of becoming objectionable. Like Helmholtz, he moved several times from one institution to another, but settled eventually in Bonn. He was actually in Switzerland when he published his great papers. He was one of the first professors at the newly created technical institution, the ETH in Zürich, but he moved back to his native country after 12 years, as soon as a good opportunity presented itself. He was in fact a very patriotic German and took an active part in the Franco-Prussian War of 1870 as leader of an ambulance corps. He was wounded and never fully recovered from the injury, which may account in part for his quarrelsome attitudes late in life.

His second law was a brilliant creation based on Sadi Carnot's studies (in 1824) of the efficiency of engines and the unidirectional nature of the flow of heat. He invented the concept of *entropy* to encompass the seemingly inexplicable form of energy that cannot be used to perform work and he gave it the symbol S, which we still use. The second law is the conclusion of a tightly reasoned 50-page paper published in 1865. The famous summary, "Die Energie der Welt ist constant. Die Entropie der Welt strebt einem Maximum zu," constitutes the final two sentences in his paper. The first part expresses the maxim of the conservation of energy. The second extends the unidirectionality of the flow of heat to all spontaneous processes known to man.

Clausius's work was read avidly throughout the world and was the cornerstone of later developments in molecular kinetics and thermodynamics by the likes of Maxwell in Scotland, Boltzmann in Austria, and Gibbs in the United States. (Gibbs *begins* his celebrated 1871 treatise on thermodynamics by quoting Clausius's two sentences.) It is strange and perhaps tragic that Clausius gave no sign of interest in these developments, which were utterly dependent on his own work. He argued petulantly in print with Maxwell and seems to have been altogether indifferent to the other two.

Related Places to Visit: Bonn, Zürich.

Neanderthal: The World's Most Famous Skeleton

In 1856, in a cave in the Neanderthal Valley, a skeleton was found by workmen. Johann Karl Fuhlrott, a teacher from nearby Elberfeld, was called in to examine the find, and he correctly identified the skeleton as human. But he noted that the skull was different, with thick prominent cranial ridges, and concluded that this was an important discovery, the remains of a prehistoric kind of man. Modern dating methods confirm Fuhlrott's surmise and place the age of the Neanderthal skeleton at 60,000 years.

Where did schoolteacher Fuhlrott get the wisdom to reach his conclusion, three years before publication of Darwin's *Origin of Species*, at a time when the very idea of evolution of man was still anathema to most people? We cannot guess, but we certainly know that the German scientific establishment was not impressed. They had a good laugh about the naive schoolteacher and his crazy interpretation. This was just a recent specimen, they decreed, but pathological, an idiot as evidenced by the cranial deformity, ravaged by rickets in youth and by arthritis in old age. The chief detractor, Rudolf Virchow, was Germany's leading pathologist, and one could hardly argue with him.

Reception in England was more enthusiastic. Thomas Huxley, for example, champion of evolution and Darwinism, unequivocally welcomed Neanderthal into the human family and included a detailed description of the remains in his essays on man's history, published in 1863. And soon after that the *antiquity* of Neanderthal man was unequivocally established by discovery of almost identical specimens in other parts of Europe, all with the same prominent cranial ridge and bowed legs. Which, of course, did not require acceptance of Neanderthal's propinquity to modern man—most people, in fact, did not accept that. One renowned English anthropologist found the notion repulsive as late as 1921. "Neanderthal man is revealed as an uncouth race," he said and went on to express his pride in modern *H. sapiens* and his success in competing for living space with so brutal a species.

The subject of the humanity of Neanderthal man remains a topic for intense dispute to the present time. Neanderthal skeletons have recently been found in artificial positions and in apparent association with deliberately placed ceremonial objects (flower offerings, circles of goat horns, etc.). That has suggested to many anthropologists that the Neanderthal people may have buried their dead, and therefore that they may have had deep spiritual values, rendering them so close to *H. sapiens* that they don't merit a separate species designation. Some anthropologists now regard denial of fully human anatomical and behavioral status to the Neanderthals as "reactionary and essentially racist."

Others dispute the evidence for ceremonial burials, saying that association with goat horns and such may be entirely accidental. They point, for example, to the common feature of the thick protuding ridge of the brow in all Neanderthal skulls as undeniably different from the essentially modern race of Cro-Magnon, that lived near the same period and, at least in France, on the same patch of territory.

Research continues and opinions shift right up to the very present. A paper published in 1989 deals with the controversy of whether or not Neanderthal man had the gift of human speech, related to the finding of an intact hyoid bone in a new Neanderthal skeleton from Israel. This small U-shaped bone is associated with the speech apparatus of modern man and the authors infer from this and related evidence that the speech capability of Neanderthal man may have been fully developed. Does that mean he actually talked and told bedtime stories to his kiddies? An editorial comment on the article stresses the huge gap between morphology and behavior and suggests that the question of actual speech may not be solved until "we discover a deep-frozen Neanderthal who is susceptible to resuscitation." How teacher Fuhlrott would have enjoyed the arguments!

Related Places to Visit: Neanderthal, Bonn.

Microbes, Nerves, and Psychology

Rudolf Virchow (1821–1902), the derisive critic of Neanderthal man, exerted a dominant force over German biological science for nearly half a century. He was even a member of the Reichstag for part of that time, able to argue his views at the highest level of government. He must be credited with creation of the concept of cellular pathology (the recognition of disease at the cellular level) and with the promotion of sanitary reforms in urban life. But he was also a typical Prussian, dogmatic and inflexible. He tried to elevate science to the level of a quasi-religious dogma. He opposed not only Neanderthal man, but also the blossoming science of bacteriology—there can be no single cause of disease, he insisted.

An overall more wholesome influence on matters pathological came from **Robert Koch** (1843–1910), often regarded as one of the chief founders of bacteriology, a claim with some legitimacy. Louis Pasteur's name is, of course, irrevocably associated with the advancement and public acceptance of the germ theory of disease, the identification of microbes as causative agents. But Koch was the one who first studied them scientifically. He was the first to isolate a bacillus and culture it in a nutrient medium outside its animal host. He studied bacterial life cycles and identified bacterial spores that can lie dormant until they find a suitable victim. He began with the anthrax bacillus, obtained from the blood of sheep that had died of the disease, cultured in drops of blood on the stage of his microscope, but he moved quickly to human diseases and isolated and observed the tubercle bacillus (1882) and the cholera bacillus (1883). In 1885 he was given a chair in Berlin University and made director of the Institute of Health and in 1905 was awarded the Nobel Prize for Medicine for his development of tuberculin as a test for tuberculosis.

Koch began his career as a country doctor (in what is now a part of Poland) and entered the scientific stage relatively late in life. By 1900 he was back in practical medicine, this time as a "world" doctor, traveling to distant countries to identify the causative agents of epidemics and helping the local authorities to keep them in check. In his own country, Koch's work naturally involved him in confrontation with Virchow, whose lectures in pathology had been part of his training. But Koch was younger and just as dogmatic and aggressive (and often just as unpleasant) as the latter and came to no harm. His ability to actually keep people alive was worth more than reams of polemic.

The Birth of Experimental Psychology. Moving from pathology to the study of human perception we come to a field where German science was uniquely innovative. German physiologists began to interest themselves in sensory phenomenon, one of the most prominent being **Hermann Helmholtz,** whom we have already met as the expounder of the first law of thermodynamics. Helmholtz had always retained an interest in philosophy inspired by his father, especially in epistemology, the question of how knowledge is acquired. He saw this problem as a physical one and studied acoustics and vision, thereby focusing on the initial receptors for signals that ultimately become part of knowledge. In the course of this project, Helmholtz experimentally determined the rate of conduction of a signal along a nerve. He also invented the opthalmoscope, the instrument still used today to obtain a magnified image of the retina of the human eye.

The great breakthrough to scientific respectability for psychology came in 1875 when the University of Leipzig saw fit to establish what it actually called an Institute of Experimental Psychology and appointed **Wilhelm Max Wundt** (1832–1920) to be professor of this new subject, with the mandate to investigate human response to various stimuli and the ability to learn and retain information. The stage had been set earlier, not only by Helmholtz and other physiologists, but even more directly at the University of Leipzig, by two former professors. One was Gustav Fechner, who had invented a discipline called psychophysics and had written a textbook on the subject in 1860. The other was Ernst Weber, who gave his name to Weber's Law, which states that the quantitative sensitivity to stimulus depends on the strength of the preceding stimulus, or, in mathematical terms, that the intensity of sensation increases approximately as the logarithm of the stimulus. Weber was a brother of the physicist Wilhelm Weber in Göttingen and the two wrote a joint paper on acoustics and wave motion. (The law is sometimes ascribed to Fechner more than Weber.)

As it turned out, Wundt himself never added any original contribution to what his predecessors did—no fundamental measurement like that of the rate of nerve conduction, no new mathematical laws, no problem freshly defined. But he bound his predecessors' work together, with, in the words of one historian, "a systematic logic that he himself contributed." Many present-day psychologists regard Wundt as the father of experimental psychology, a title that he may be said to merit by virtue of the enormous influence of his laboratory through the students it produced. Young men came from all over the world to conduct psychological experiments under Wundt's direction and carried away with them a unique view of how psychological research should be conducted. Americans were especially conspicuous: Wundt's former students were responsible for the creation of dozens of new laboratories in the United States.

Wundt was born not far from Heidelberg, was trained as a physiologist, and spent 17 years as a member of the Heidelberg physiology faculty—including a stint as assistant to Helmholtz, which is where he presumably picked up what would become his vocation. But he was passed over in the selection of a successor to Helmholtz when the latter left for Berlin in 1871. His stature within the European scientific community, never as high as it was in America, diminished further in his final years, when he became an ardent supporter of Germany's aggressions in World War I and (in 1915) wrote a paper, "Die Nationen und ihre Philosophen," eulogizing German thought and culture while belittling those of England and France, Germany's enemies.

Related Places to Visit: Leipzig, Berlin (Koch Museum).

Ushering in the New Age of Physics

There was a peaking of talent in physics late in the nineteenth century and on into the twentieth. The so-called "new physics" came in no small measure from German scientists.

Perhaps surprisingly, we begin again with Hermann Helmholtz. Don't sell him short as a physicist because he straddled the boundary between physiology and physics and even gave some thought to human psychology—for we meet him here as a teacher of genuine physics students, for whom he set difficult problems that dealt unerringly with truly fundamental problems. One of them was **Heinrich Hertz** (1857–1894), whom he steered to the problem of proving experimentally that the *purely theoretical* concepts of Maxwell's theory of electromagnetism are demonstrably real. Hertz accomplished the task brilliantly. He devised means to generate and detect electromagnetic waves, transmitted them from source to detector, showed that their speed of transmission is the same as the speed of light, and that the waves can be reflected, refracted, and polarized just as light waves can. These discoveries invited a host of applications, such as the use of electromagnetic waves for signal transmission. We now call it radio and appropriately designate the intrinsic frequencies of radio waves in units of kiloHertz or megaHertz.

In the course of this work Hertz accidentally observed an enigmatic phenomenon, namely that light falling on certain materials can give rise to a stream of small charged particles (later shown to be electrons), whose number is proportional to the intensity of the incident light, but whose energy (the speed with which they travel) is unaffected, contrary to what classical physics would predict. This is the photoelectric effect, one of the gateways to the quantum theory, and Albert Einstein won a Nobel Prize a generation later for explaining how it happened.

Hertz sadly did not live to see the long-range fruits of his experimental genius, for he died at the early age of thirty-six after a long period of poor health. He is the only prominent scientist we know whose biography was written (in 1901) by his mother!

Related Place to Visit: Bonn.

Another famous usherer-in was **Wilhelm Conrad Röntgen** (1845–1923), who was not one of the intellectual giants of physics (as Hertz was), but whose accidental discovery of x-rays in 1895 was one of the grand spectacular events in the history of science. News of it spread almost instantly around the world, and the discovery was appreciated as heralding the dawn of a new age by scientist and layman alike.

Röntgen was the son of a cloth merchant from the Rhine province, and he had a typically mobile Germanic career. He earned a doctor's degree from the Polytechnic Institute in Zürich in 1869, became an assistant to a physics professor there, moved with him to the University of Würzburg in 1871, and shortly thereafter to Strasbourg, which had become German territory after the Franco-Prussian War, and where a new German university was being organized. Röntgen was given his own chair at the University of Giessen in 1879, and in 1888 he moved back to Würzburg as professor of physics and director of the Physical Institute. In 1894 he became rector of the university, an administrative post which appears not to have interrupted his research, because the discovery of x-rays came the following year. (In 1900 Röntgen moved again, at the request of the Bavarian government, to become director of the Physical Institute in Munich.)

Röntgen was one of many physicists studying the conduction of electricity through rarefied gases, and it was just luck that there was a coated screen nearby that fluoresced whenever his apparatus was turned on, pointing unmistakably to the emission of invisible rays from his apparatus. But his reaction was truly professional, in the sense that he recognized the significance of the phenomenon and the need for meticulous documentation before announcing his discovery, which he did on December 28, 1895. So careful were his studies that nearly all of the basic properties of x-rays were accurately described in this first paper. Röntgen was almost immediately summoned to Berlin to demonstrate the effects of x-rays to the Kaiser and on January 13, 1896 he was awarded the Prussian Order of the Crown. Newspapers and magazines all over the world carried x-ray pictures within a few weeks and Röntgen received a Nobel Prize for his discovery in 1901, the very first such award to be made.

Röntgen did not keep the prize money, but donated it to the University of Würzburg. He was a retiring and unassuming man, who worked at different times on diverse problems in the realm of physics, built most of his own apparatus and invariably worked alone in his laboratory to avoid distractions. He himself played no part in the worldwide spurt of efforts to discover the physical meaning and origin of x-rays.

Related Places to Visit: Würzburg, Munich.

Quanta of Energy. The quantum theory—or, at least, the *need* for such a theory—is an easy part of the new physics to understand. It begins very simply with the conversion of heat into light, as seen for instance in the glow of the embers from a wood or coal fire. The scientific name is *black body radiation* and it had become a well-known puzzle by 1900 because the spectrum of the emitted light is not what conventional (Newtonian) physics would predict. To be precise, the emission diminishes sharply (anomalously) at short wavelengths. In 1900 a forty-two-year-old physicist, **Max Planck** (1858–1947), presented a paper at the German Physical Society proposing a simple solution to the puzzle, which, he showed, could mathematically account for the anomaly. The gist of it is that we must drop our preconceived notion that energy is continuously variable and imagine instead that, at least in its conversion to light, it moves as discrete packets or *quanta*.

And so it proves it to be. The energy per quantum is related to the wavelength of the light, the exact relation being $\epsilon = h\nu$, where h is known as Planck's constant and ν is the frequency of the light, inversely proportional to the wavelength. The observed emission drops off at low wavelength (high frequency) because new probability rules enter into the picture when energy is packaged this way. Quanta of very high energy become less probable than those of lower energy.

The revolution seemed immense at the time because the idea of energy continuity was so deeply entrenched, but in retrospect there was no compelling logic behind the prejudice. We accept that matter is atomic. Why not energy as well? In any event, Planck was showered with honors and was appointed director of the prestigious Kaiser Wilhelm Institute for physics. After World War I Kaiser Wilhelm ceased to exist, and after World War II all his former institutes were renamed Max Planck Institute in Planck's honor. They are among the leading research institutes in Europe today. Planck, incidentally, was afflicted with blind patriotism and supported Germany with unqualified enthusiasm through both world wars.

Related Places to Visit: Berlin, Göttingen.

The Battle over Determinism. Planck's quantum theory not only explained black body radiation, but it was also used by Albert Einstein to solve the puzzle of Hertz's photoelectric effect (see under "Switzerland") and by Niels Bohr to explain why electrons and a positive nucleus can coexist in the inside of an atom (see under "Denmark"). But it also necessitated the invention of a new kind of mechanics (non-Newtonian) to describe these no longer continuous motions. It was called *quantum mechanics* and was developed independently in the 1920s by an Austrian, **Erwin Schrödinger** (1887–1961), and by a German, **Werner Heisenberg** (1901–1976), a student of **Max Born** (1882–1970) in Göttingen. In Schrödinger's hands, the resulting equations resembled those for a wave, which made Born very unhappy, because particles such as electrons mostly behave like corpuscles and not like waves. In 1926, Born made a proposal which (for him) resolved the contradiction—the wave must be a probability wave, the square of the amplitude in the wave equation at any point giving the probability of finding an electron (or other particle) at that point. That may have satisfied Born, but it didn't go down well with many other physicists, who found it hard to swallow the concept that a particle has a probability instead of a fixed position. Heisenberg and Born together then shocked everybody even more with the *uncertainty principle,* which showed that for very small bodies, it is experimentally impossible (even if one doesn't think explicitly in terms of waves) to exactly determine both location and momentum at the same time. By thus throwing determinism out the window, the whole philosophy of physics was altered, and some of those most influential in the development of the original quantum theory (Planck and Einstein among them) never accepted such a limitation on the powers of human observation or understanding.

The pace of German achievement, of course, crashed with the advent of Adolf Hitler. Max Born (who had Jewish blood in him according to German racial dogma) fled to England in 1933 but retired back to Germany some 20 years later. Erwin Schrödinger left in 1933 in protest over racial persecution, though he himself was not affected. He went to live in exile in Ireland until 1956, when he returned to Vienna, the city of his birth. Einstein (who was a naturalized Swiss, but had gone back to his native Germany) moved to the United States.

Werner Heisenberg and Max Planck remained in their homeland and continued to work actively for the state. A personal tragedy befell Max Planck when his younger son was executed in 1944 for complicity in the plot to assassinate the Führer.

Related Place to Visit: Göttingen.

Atomic Power Is Unleashed

Official histories have until quite recently told us that the atomic age began on December 17, 1938, when Otto Hahn and his assistant Fritz Strassman at the Kaiser Wilhelm Institute in Berlin bombarded uranium with slow neutrons, splitting the uranium nucleus into smaller fragments, a process accompanied by the release of previously unimaginable amounts of energy. The true story is a little more complicated. First, we recognize retrospectively that others had split the atom before Hahn and Strassman did it—Enrico Fermi in Italy and the Joliot-Curies in France—but they did not realize what they had done. Second, understanding of the significance of Hahn and Strassman's experiment owes as much to Hahn's former collaborator, Lise Meitner, as to the experimenters themselves. Her role has been obscured by the fact that she was a Jew, exiled from Germany just a few months before the experiment was done.

Otto Hahn (1879–1968) and **Lise Meitner** (1878–1968) had collaborated for several years in investigating the products of atomic reactions with neutrons, repeating experiments done elsewhere in Europe, searching for an explanation of just what was going on. They were a good combination: Hahn was an expert chemist, skilled in the analysis for trace amounts of radioactive atoms, and Meitner was an experienced physicist, head of the nuclear physics group in Berlin. They were both by this time rather more elderly than the typical discoverer of new truths. Meitner, being Jewish, had already been excluded from the teaching faculty of the University of Berlin in 1933, but was permitted to continue her research, and it was not until 1938 that her personal safety became so insecure that escape (to Sweden) became mandatory. It was shortly after her departure that Hahn and Strassman made the unexpected discovery that bombardment of uranium with neutrons leads to the appearance of barium as one of the products, with a nucleus about half the mass of uranium.

Why was it unexpected? The reason is that previously known nuclear transformations had come from bombardment of various atoms by alpha particles and had always involved capture of the latter and ejection of a smaller proton, with overall addition of mass to the target nucleus. The idea that the target could be split to yield lighter nuclei had not been seriously considered. Hahn was puzzled and naturally turned (by letter) to his recently departed physicist colleague for advice. Meitner and her nephew (Otto Frisch) rapidly grasped what must have happened. They were the ones who called it nuclear fission and had the know-how to calculate the enormous energy release that must accompany such a process. Early in 1939 Hahn published his results in the German journal *Naturwissenschaften,* and Meitner and Frisch sent their interpretive findings from exile in Scandinavia to the English journal *Nature.*

The rest of the story is part of modern legend. All physicists realized the danger if the German military could capitalize on the discovery. Albert Einstein was persuaded to write his famous letter to President Roosevelt, explaining the situation. Roosevelt understood and that is how America came to build the atom bomb. Germany, it turned out later, had tried to do the same, but had not succeeded. Otto Hahn *alone* was awarded a Nobel Prize in chemistry in 1944.

Epilogue. For many years the Deutsches Museum in Munich displayed a laboratory table labeled "Worktable of Otto Hahn" containing an apparatus for neutron irradiation. The apparatus was, in fact, designed by Lise Meitner in the physics section of the Kaiser Wilhelm Institute. In February of 1989, the museum's administrators, under pressure to remedy the error, decided to add Meitner's name to the caption, but they identified her as a "Mitarbeiter," which is the Germanic equivalent of assistant and not the equal coworker that a literal translation of the word might suggest. Later that year (as a result of a paper given by historian Ruth Sime on Lise Meitner and her work) the inscription was changed again to give Meitner full credit. As a final apology, a bust of Lise Meitner has now been included in the Hall of Fame of German scientists in the museum.

Related Places to Visit: Berlin, Munich.

PRINCIPAL PLACES TO VISIT

The last war was terribly destructive and much that we might expect to find in the way of cherished old buildings and other memorials is simply not there, being lost in the rubble. Königsberg, for instance, Prussian center of learning for a thousand years—associated with Kant, Bessel, Kirchhoff, and others—was demolished in the Russian advance toward Berlin. It became Russian territory after the war and is now called Kaliningrad.

Western Germany

BENEDIKTBEUERN (Bavaria)

Benediktbeuern is a popular stop for tourists, not because of its association with Fraunhofer, but as the site of an ancient Benedictine monastery and an eighteenth-century Rococo chapel. As it happens, the shop used by Josef Fraunhofer and his associates to make optical glass and fine telescopes—called the Fraunhofer Glashütte—is right behind the monastery, in a former laundry building. It contains two huge furnaces used by Fraunhofer for glass making, a few very small telescopes, pictures, and other memorials to the town's most famous former citizen. There is a 12-minute recorded commentary in German.

The museum is open daily, except Wednesdays. The key must be collected from a house across the street. Telephone (tourist office): 08857–248.

BONN (Nordrhein-Westfalen)

Bonn is the birthplace of Ludwig van Beethoven and Germany's formal capital city. A visit here should include a stroll along the Rhein, watching the barges and other commercial traffic on the river.

The **University of Bonn** was an important nucleus for the growth of German science in the nineteenth century. Its first building took over the residence of the Elector, an imposing baroque structure with charming surrounding lawns. The principal science buildings were put up about 1,000 yards (1 km) away, around the Poppelsdorfer Schloss. Some of the departments have moved to the outskirts of the city and many of the original buildings are in a decrepit state, but an exception is the old chemistry building, currently being remodeled to house microbiology. It was designed explicitly for August Kekulé, who was professor of chemistry at the university for nearly 30 years, and whose statue, guarded on two sides by lions with human faces, stands in front of the building. The most noted physics professors were Rudolf Clausius and Heinrich Hertz. The latter found Clausius's house on the market when he moved to Bonn in 1889 and bought it for his own residence. The house is at Quantiusstrasse 13 (behind the railway station) and is marked by a plaque.

The **Rheinisches Landesmuseum,** located one block from the railway station, focuses on the history of the area, including mock scenes of what prehistoric as well as historic (Roman) settlements were like. It contains the original roof of the skull from the Neanderthal skeleton (50,000 B.C.). Various other bones from the same skeleton are stored and not on public display. Inevitably, there is a statue showing an artist's impression of what this prehistoric man must have looked like.

The museum is open daily except Mondays. Telephone: 0228–632–158.

BRAUNSCHWEIG (Lower Saxony)

Carl Friedrich Gauss was born in Braunschweig in 1777. He received much of his education here and had the extraordinary privilege of generous patronage from Duke Carl Wilhelm Ferdinand, which made him financially independent for most of his life. Gauss returned to live here for a while after his student days at Göttingen and much of his early mathematical work (including the calculation of the orbit of the asteroid Ceres) dates from that time. The local citizens raised a subscription for a commemorative statue on the 100th anniversary of his birth, which can be seen in the city today in a little square named *Am Gaussberg.* There used to be a Gauss museum, too, but it was destroyed during World War II.

Braunschweig is also the native city of **Agnes Pockels** (1862–1935), a Cinderella of the world of science, heroine of a heart-warming success story. She was denied an education by the rules of the day, but undertook to learn physics on her own with the help of her younger brother, who (perhaps inspired by Agnes) did become a professional physicist and a professor at the University of Göttingen. She was fascinated by the films of oil in the pans in her kitchen and, dissatisfied by what the textbooks had to say on the subject, developed new methods for measuring surface tension and began to acquire a better understanding of the underlying physics of this rather esoteric subject than anybody else had. But how was she to know? Her brother's field was electromagnetism—who could tell her whether her work had any value or was even publishable?

Then her brother noticed an article by the famous Lord Rayleigh in England, which seemed to address the same problem that she was working on, and Agnes (twenty-eight years old at the time) wrote him a letter, describing her own studies. The letter was of course in German, which Rayleigh was not good at, and it came from someone with no credentials or institutional affiliation. Moreover, Rayleigh was just then a very busy man, even secretary of the Royal Society, which added enormously to his customary duties. Most people in his position would have thanked Agnes Pockels politely for her interesting letter and done no more about it. But Rayleigh was a man of unusual public spirit and chivalry. He had the letter translated, studied it carefully enough to appreciate its significance, and personally sponsored immediate publication in the British journal *Nature.* The Pockels method of measurement was quickly adopted throughout the world (it is the basis for the Langmuir trough used for surface studies today) and the importance of her work has been fully recognized in Britain and the United States. But not as much so, it seems, in her native country.

There is a postscript. We had some correspondence with a faculty member at the Technical University in Braunschweig and, lo and behold, the postal address was "Pockelsstrasse." Could it actually be a token of municipal recognition? No such thing, it turned out. The street name commemorates Wilhelm Pockels, a dutiful mayor of the city, who served in that position for 25 years. We wrote a letter to the Oberstadtdirektor, advancing Agnes's claim for recognition (not the first to have done so), but evoked little sympathy. Let the academics take care of their own, he suggested. Why don't they name a building after her at the university? The fact that Agnes was never at a university—and wasn't even allowed because of her sex to attend the senior high school (Gymnasium)—would presumably not make much difference to city officials.

Pockelsstrasse runs through the middle of the university campus.

DARMSTADT (Hessen)

Justus von Liebig and August Kekulé were born in Darmstadt, 26 years apart. The fact that the former was later the teacher of the latter is pure coincidence.

A statue of Liebig stands in the central Luisenplatz of Darmstadt and a small room in the Technische Hochschule (Department of Organic Chemistry) on the outskirts of the city serves as a kind of Kekulé museum, which is open only by appointment. It contains a desk that once belonged to Kekulé, many portraits, original papers, letters, awards, and so on. One truly distinctive item — which makes the Kekulé room worthy of a visit, at least for chemists — is a magnificently bound book, given to Kekulé on his sixtieth birthday by friends, admirers, and students. It consists of 134 photographs of the donors and their signatures and many now well-known names are included: Bunsen, Erlenmeyer, Beilstein, Landoldt, for example.

The Kekulé collection has a negligible endowment, and only two of the staff of the Chemistry Institute could grant access when we visited. Telephone numbers 06151-162176 or 162876.

GIESSEN (Hessen)

Justus von Liebig came to Giessen as professor in 1824, appointed by the Grand Duke of Hesse on the basis of an enthusiastic recommendation from Alexander von Humboldt. He remained until 1852; the intervening years are said by many to have been the most important ever in the history of chemistry.

Liebig's laboratory was originally built for him in what used to be the guardhouse of a military barracks and it was restored as a museum in 1920. In its present form it houses his former office and laboratories as well as a set of rooms specifically designed for chemical experiments and teaching. There is a lecture hall with built-in facilities for lecture demonstrations, probably a novelty in Liebig's day. There is chemical apparatus of all kinds, including the prototype of the great workhorse of organic chemistry, still called the Liebig condenser, and an impressive analytical balance, capable of weighing up to 100 grams with an accuracy of ± 1 milligram. There are many stoves for burning wood and coal — there was no gas in those days — and there is even a sand bath heater (used when close contact with fire might be dangerous) quite like one actually used by us in our youth. The museum also retains a valuable collection of books and papers. The most interesting items in this category are the student notebooks, neat beyond a professor's wildest dreams, everything done in pen with sharp line drawings, all in perfect order. They could well be finished pieces of work, ready as they stand for publication in some scientific journal.

A taped lecture, illustrated with slides, in German, English, or French, is turned on for visitors by the museum attendant. This gives a good summary of Liebig's career and principal scientific accomplishments, but is not designed to provide a broad view of chemistry in his time. Controversies, for example, are mentioned several times, but opposing views are not presented. An amusing aspect (for chemists trained before World War II) is a portentous voice proclaiming the primitive conditions under which Liebig had to labor. In fact, the laboratory rooms resemble typical university laboratories from as late as the 1930s and 1940s, wooden benches and all.

Giessen formerly had a statue to commemorate Liebig, but it was destroyed in a 1944 bombing raid. The museum has a picture of it, which shows it to have been a baroque monstrosity whose loss need not be mourned.

The Liebig Museum is open daily except Mondays. Telephone: 0641-73692.

GÖTTINGEN (Lower Saxony)

The most conspicuous memorial site in Göttingen is a cemetery, the **Stadt-friedhof,** located on the road to Kassel. There is a scientists' corner here, where many famous scientists who worked or studied in Göttingen are buried close together. They include Max Planck, the original discoverer of the need for energy quantization; Otto Hahn, one of the authors of the famous paper on the splitting of the atom; Walther Nernst and his entire family; and several more. Hahn's tombstone bears an enigmatic, perhaps ominous inscription:

$$^{92}U + {}^0n$$

The top line is standard chemical language for the reaction of an atom of uranium (isotope of mass 92) with a neutron. But how are we to interpret the down-pointing arrow? The end of the world or maybe descent into hell?

Max Born is buried with his wife in a totally different part of the cemetery, the family plot of his wife and her forebears. His epitaph, too, is in the form of an equation, a mathematical formula in this case: $pq - qp = h/2\pi i,$ and what will strike the layman about it is the fact that $pq - qp$ is not zero, as he would expect. It turns out that p and q stand respectively for the momentum and the position of a particle in space and the significance of the inequality of their forward and reverse products is the underlying basis for Heisenberg's uncertainty principle. This may be Born's claim to posterity for at least an equal share of the credit.

There is an amusing anecdote about the interment of Walther Nernst, a none too popular physical chemist (but sufficiently proficient to have won a

Göttingen tombstones.

Nobel Prize in 1920). He died in 1945 on his estate in East Prussia and was buried there, with two colleagues, Karl Bonhoeffer and Max Bodenstein, serving as pallbearers. When the Russians annexed East Prussia, the remains were removed to German soil (to Berlin) and there was another ceremony with Bonhoeffer and Bodenstein again in attendance. Some years later the family thought he should really lie in Göttingen, where he had been professor for most of his career, and so the body was moved once more, still with the same honorary escort. "I'm getting tired of this," Bodenstein is reported to have remarked to his partner, who, however, responded more cheerfully: "You can't bury Nernst too often" was his reported reply.

Physicist Carl Friedrich Gauss, who of course belongs to an earlier era, is buried in the small Albani Friedhof within the old city of Göttingen. It is a large tomb, easily found along the principal footpath. A more prominent memorial to him is the **Sternwarte,** the original astronomical observatory specifically built for Gauss between 1803 and 1816. It is now a museum, but it is not open to the general public. The building has a plaque that jointly memorializes Gauss and his colleague Wilhelm Weber for their invention of the first electric telegraph. A few blocks from the Sternwarte is a statue that again shows Gauss and Weber together.

There are 250 memorial marble tablets scattered throughout the city to indicate where and when Gauss and other famous professors and students had their homes. Famous Americans seem to be conspicuously absent. Willard Gibbs studied in Göttingen, for example, and Irving Langmuir received his Ph.D. degree under Nernst, but there are no tablets for either one.

Old astronomical instruments and Gauss memorabilia in the Sternwarte museum will be shown to interested individuals if sufficient notice is given. Telephone: 0551-39-5042.

HEIDELBERG (Baden-Württemberg)

Heidelberg is one of the major tourist attractions in Germany, not so much for its historical or architectural importance, but more for its magnificent setting along the banks of the Neckar River. Its university is the oldest in Germany (first founded in 1385) and the most romantic (the model for Sigmund Romberg's *Student Prince*), but it has had a checkered history. The period from 1850 to 1875 is perhaps its only period of real eminence. Kirchhoff, Bunsen, and Helmholtz were among the senior faculty during this period. Wundt and the chemist Lothar Meyer were among the junior faculty, and Dmitri Mendeléev (1860) and the American Willard Gibbs (1868) were among the transient scholars.

The only memorial is a plaque to show where Kirchhoff and Bunsen did their research, in a house (built in 1707) at the corner of Hauptstrasse and Akademiestrasse. The inscription reads "In this house Kirchhoff and Bunsen applied their spectral analysis to sun and stars and thereby opened up the chemistry of the universe." A statue of Bunsen stands across the street in front of the Friedrichsbau, now housing the Psychology Institute of the University.

Visitors might enjoy a walk along the Philosophenweg high on the hillside above the right bank of the Neckar, with good views of the town. It commemorates no known philosophers, but everybody in town goes there for evening strolls and their own philosophizing. Undoubtedly Bunsen, Kirchhoff, and all the others did so, too.

HEPPENHEIM on the BERGSTRASSE (north of Heidelberg, Baden-Württemberg)

The Bergstrasse at the foot of the Odenwald Mountains is a popular drive between Heidelberg and Darmstadt. The slopes of the hills are covered with orchards and vineyards, and the road passes through numerous picturesque villages. The Marktplatz in Heppenheim is particularly pleasant with its sixteenth-century wooden buildings and town hall. Justus Liebig was apprenticed to the apothecary in Heppenheim in 1818 at age sixteen, and the pharmacy where he worked is preserved in the Marktplatz. Here Liebig experimented on his own with silver fulminate, had an explosion, took off part of the roof, and was (not surprisingly) fired. The former pharmacy is now a Bierstube. The front room contains a few apothecary trappings and the association with Liebig is marked by a plaque on the outside.

MUNICH (Bavaria)

Munich is a kind of capital city, the center of everything for southern Germany. Liebig, Fraunhofer, and Röentgen are among the scientists who established their reputations elsewhere, but moved to Munich toward the end of their careers.

The former Pirsch pharmacy on the old Market Place in Heppenheim, where Liebig served as an apprentice. It is now a Bierstube.

The **Deutches Museum** is one of the city's great attractions, beautifully situated on an island in the Isar River and one of the largest museums in Europe devoted to science and technology. It has the best educational displays on fundamental physics and chemistry that we have seen anywhere. The principles of the various branches of physics—mechanics, optics, sound, fluid dynamics, and so on—are presented by means of simple, working models with excellent explanations for laymen or students. All these exhibits are in the appropriate historical context and provide information about the scientists of earlier years who made the great discoveries. A separate building houses an exhaustive library and photographic archives, both open to the public. (There are of course also more conventional kinds of technological exhibits—early motor cars, the first camera, and even a section on technical toys. But the museum's unique excellence is in the category of pure physical science.)

An entire room is devoted to Josef von Fraunhofer, who was a Bavarian by birth. It produces spectra on the spot for the visitor (comparing glass prisms and Fraunhofer's gratings), shows both continuous and line spectra, and includes a reproduction of Fraunhofer's original solar spectrum with its famous dark lines. There is even a contemporary cartoon of Fraunhofer being rescued from the ruins of the workshop that almost buried him in 1801.

The chemistry exhibits include a laboratory "of the time of Lavoisier" and a reproduction of one of Justus von Liebig's laboratories, but the latter is not as effective in its impact as the Liebig Museum in Giessen. A highlight of the

Fraunhofer remembered, at the German Museum in Munich.

chemistry section is the display of the apparatus used for the discovery of atomic fission, which was actually set up for the museum by Otto Hahn himself. No space age technology here—just ordinary laboratory apparatus! (The pieces shown are the original equipment, arranged so as to fit onto a single table. They were spread over three rooms at the time the experiments were actually done.)

Other noteworthy features include an alcove devoted to the great pioneer of polymer chemistry, Hermann Staudinger. He has not (in our opinion) generally received the public recognition he merits. On the negative side, one should mention the virtual absence of exhibits related to biology or even to biochemistry, which in part must reflect the fact that Germany's nineteenth-century prominence in science was heavily biased toward physics and chemistry.

A perhaps amusing component of the museum is its **Hall of Fame,** an earnest attempt to honor the "greatest" German scientists and inventors by means of paintings, busts, or stone reliefs. Among the honorees are Copernicus, whose inclusion as a German would surely be disputed by the Poles, and Albert Einstein, who might himself have regarded his inclusion as a dubious honor, given that he and his theories were despised in his native land for most of his life. Two recent additions (since the current official guide to the museum was published) are busts of Lise Meitner and Werner Heisenberg, both rather controversial—Meitner because the German establishment dragged its feet for many years in recognizing her central role in the discovery of atomic fission, Heisenberg because of questions about possible close relations with the Nazi leadership in World War II.

Other places of interest in Munich include the **Municipal Museum,** which is mostly devoted to Munich's general cultural history but also contains a reproduction of Josef Fraunhofer's laboratory benches and equipment, and the **Südliche Friedhof,** where Liebig and Fraunhofer are buried. Liebig's grave is somewhat ostentatious, with his bust on top of the gravestone. Fraunhofer's tomb is next to the outer wall, and we found it (in 1991) nearly overgrown with shrubs and clearly uncared for. A telescope and the sun are carved on the memorial, but erosion seems to have removed all trace of the inscription ("Approximavit Sidera") which is reported to have been there originally.

The German Museum is open daily all year, except for certain holidays. Telephone: 089–21791. The Municipal Museum (housed in a fifteenth-century building) is closed on Mondays. Telephone: 089-233-2370.

NEANDERTAL
(east of Düsseldorf, Nordrhein-Westfalen)

Neandertal (modern spelling of the more familiar Neanderthal) is a valley, which used to be deep and narrow, cut through limestone rock by a little stream, the Düssel, as it plied its course to the nearby city of Düsseldorf. The name of the valley recalls the Calvinist theologian and poet Joachim Neander (1650–1680), writer of many Protestant hymns, some of which are still sung today, who used to come to this valley to contemplate in solitude when the place was still remote from the world. The valley remained remote until about 1830, when the limestone from its steep walls was needed for expanding construction and industrialization in the surrounding area. The valley then became a giant quarry, its walls systematically sliced away and loaded onto wagons. Many natural caves (typical of limestone rocks) were discovered in the course of this operation, and it is one of these caves, the Kleine Feldhofer Grotte, that yielded the famous skeleton.

Neandertal today is an amusing place to visit. It is a nature preserve, a mixture of forest and meadows in a now wide expanse (no residue of rock or caves), with many broad hiking trails, where German families can take their weekend outings in the woods. At the main entrance, there is an inn where you can buy beer or the local specialty, gooseberry wine. There is a small hotel next door, a popular place for local weddings, where the bride and groom can go outside after the ceremony and have their picture taken alongside a squat stocky stone Neanderthaler—wielding a club, but somehow not at all menacing—with a benign look on his face.

There is a museum in the preserve, which tells the story of the initial discovery and contains a replica of the skeleton—the original skull can be seen in the Rheinisches Landesmuseum in Bonn. There is also a naively conceived meadow in the preserve, with live "Stone Age" animals. Bison are there, legitimate holdovers from times gone by, but the others are simply variants of

Neanderthal Man. Monument at the entrance
to the park.

modern horses and cattle, ludicrously labeled "forerunners" and said to have
been obtained by "selective retrograde breeding."

Neandertal can be reached by public transportation from Düsseldorf. The closest town
signposted on motorways is Mettmann, about two miles (three km) away. The museum is
open daily except Mondays, closed in December and January.

REGENSBURG (Bavaria)

Regensburg has a strategic location on the river Danube which made it for many
centuries an ideal city for meetings between the kings and princes of German
states. It served as such in the days of conflict between Protestants and Catholics, in the troubled era that led to the Thirty Years' War. After that war (in
1663) its position as a kind of center for the Holy Roman Empire was formalized
and a perpetual diet, forerunner of the German Reichstag, met here regularly.
Neither the Empire nor its presumptive capital city were ever effective overt
political entities, but discreet talk and planning undoubtedly took place all the
time until Napoleon dissolved the Empire altogether in 1806.

Regensburg has a fine old town center, spared the bombardments of the
last war. Keplerstrasse is just a few meters from the Danube and the house where
Kepler lived from 1626 to 1628 is number 2 and backs onto the river. The house

is still there and marked by a plaque. The house where Kepler died in 1630 is number 5 across the street and contains a small museum. A few minutes' walk away, behind the Altes Rathaus, is the Haidplatz, a lovely triangular square with buildings going back to the thirteenth century. Otto von Guericke is reputed to have carried out a public demonstration of a vacuum here for the benefit of all the visiting dignitaries. (But the story is declared untrue by the city archivist.)

Guided tours of the Kepler memorial house are provided daily except Mondays. For times, telephone 0941–507–2957.

ULM (Baden-Württemberg)

Ulm is a famous old city on the Danube, with what is considered to be an architecturally outstanding cathedral, the Münster. It is famous in the history of science as the place where (in 1879) Albert Einstein was born, but the city is strangely ambiguous about this distinction. It does not proclaim itself as the city where this genius came into being. It does not include his birthdate among the official important dates, whereas a mere visit by Kepler in 1626 is recorded. Ulm has some monuments to Einstein, but they are not listed in the literature put out by the city for the guidance of tourists. The Einstein family, of course, lived here for only a short time after Albert was born, but most places don't consider such brevity of residence as an excuse for ignoring a native son.

The chief Einstein monument is in the civic center (Behörden Zentrum) a few blocks north of the Münster. It is an often reproduced sculpture of the physicist, with his head emerging from a snail shell and his tongue sticking out—at the world, presumably, sneering at it for holding on to obsolete theories? We found it a rather disrespectful memorial to a man who loved all mankind as well as he loved physics.

An even more obscure monument stands just outside the train station. It is an ugly abstract sculpture which one would never associate with Einstein without reading the inscription, "Hier stand das Haus in dem am 14. März 1879 Albert Einstein zur Welt kam." A few meters away is the only tribute that strikes a note of genuine respect, a modest free-standing stone slab, with Einstein's head carved on it. It turns out to be a gift to the city of Ulm from the people of India!

WEIL DER STADT (Baden-Württemberg)

We have here an immaculately well-preserved town, the birthplace of Johannes Kepler, and what a difference from Ulm! Kepler (like Einstein) remained but briefly in his native city, but that has not prevented Weil der Stadt from boasting its pride. A grand monument to Kepler stands in the middle of the marketplace, dominating the old town hall (1582) and two fountains. The Kepler statue shows the scientist seated on an octagonal base, one arm resting on a pedestal-mounted globe, dividers for measuring distance in the other hand.

Four sides of the base declare Kepler's fields of science "Astronomica–Physica–Mathematica–Optica." The other four sides resemble a famous Luther Statue in the city of Worms by paying tribute to antecedents–niches on these sides contain smaller statues of Copernicus, Tycho Brahe, Jobst Byrg, and Michael Maestlin. (The last two names may not be familiar: Byrg, sometimes spelled Bürgi, was a mathematician and astronomer in Kassel. Maestlin was Kepler's teacher at the University of Tübingen and his faithful supporter thereafter.)

Just off the market place is Kepler's birth house, now the **Kepler Museum.** We know of no other that so thoroughly and faithfully details the life of an individual scientist and at the same time places his work in the context of his time. There is lucid exposition, for example, of the different explanations for the apparently retrograde motions of Mars and other planets, as offered by Ptolemy, Copernicus, Brahe, and Kepler. Precision models show that any of them might in principle account for the observed motions. Kepler's own models were made by another Tübingen professor, Wilhelm Schickard, and they are shown, as are mechanical calculating machines designed by Schickard. We see reproductions of the frontispieces of the Rudolphine Tables and other Kepler publications, copies of correspondence with Galileo and others, sketches of all the houses where Kepler lived, documentation of the witchcraft trial of Kepler's mother, and much more. This museum is well worth a journey. There is a richly illustrated guide book for sale, which describes pretty well everything that is in the museum, and tape-recorded commentaries are provided in every room.

The Kepler Museum is open seven days a week, except some Sundays. Telephone: 01049-703-32197.

WÜRZBURG (Bavaria)

The Institute of Physics at the University of Würzburg was in the town center, close to the railway station, when Wilhelm Röntgen discovered x-rays there in 1895. Most of the university has since moved to new quarters on the outskirts of the city and the buildings of the former institute now house a high school, the Fachhochschule Würzburg-Schweinfurt. The rooms actually used by Röntgen have, however, been set aside to create the **Röntgen-Gedächnitsstätte** in his memory. It is essentially a small museum containing replicas of original equipment, such as the Crookes tube from which the x-rays emanated, and examples of x-ray pictures. There are also a replica of Röntgen's Nobel medal and copies of associated documents. All the material is clearly and thoughtfully presented.

Being here makes us think about the tremendous benefits that x-rays have brought to medicine and the never-ending arguments about the merits of basic versus specifically targeted research. As F. K. Richtmeyer and E. H. Kennard said it many years ago, in a textbook now probably out of print: "Had Röntgen deliberately set about to discover some means of assisting surgeons in reducing fractures, it is almost certain that he would never have been working with

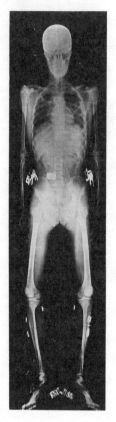

First x-ray photograph of an entire person, made in 1925.
x-ray pictures of *parts* of a human body were disseminated
worldwide within days of Röntgen's first announcement in
1896.

the evacuated tubes, induction coils, and the like, which led to his famous
discovery."

The former institute is on what is now called the Röntgenring. There is a pleasant little
park with a duck pond across the street, where kiddies can play while their parents visit
the museum. Telephone (tourist office): 0931-37436.

Berlin and East

BERLIN

The last time we visited Berlin, the Wall was still there and one had to pass
through checkpoints to go from West to East. That impediment is now gone.

Pergamon Museum. This is one of the most fascinating museums in all of
Europe—a marvellous reconstruction (within the museum halls) of parts of the
ancient city of Pergamon ("Pergamum" in English) and a gate from nearby
Miletus. Pergamum was an important place in the late period of Greek science.

The anatomist/physicist Galen was born there in 129 A.D., when the city was part of the Roman empire.

Koch Museum. A museum in honor of Robert Koch is located within the Institute for Medical Microbiology of Charité, the clinical segment of Humboldt University (Berlin's *prewar* university). The museum has preserved the old reading room in which Koch first announced his discovery of the tuberculosis bacillus on March 24, 1882. Adjacent rooms contain a microscope used by Koch, the certificate of his 1905 Nobel Prize, and other memorabilia. Outside the Charité is a white marble statue of the great man. Across the River Spee (at Hermann-Matern-Strasse 57) is the house in which Koch lived and had his laboratory, the place where all his work on the isolation and growth of bacteria was actually done. The house is marked by a plaque.

Splitting the Atom. The western suburb of Dahlem, about six miles (10 km) from mid-Berlin, is best known for its superb art museums. It is also a scientific center and the home of the Free University of Berlin.

In 1911, at a time when Dahlem was still nothing but fields and meadows, the first Kaiser Wilhelm Institutes for science were built here. The very first one was the Institute for Chemistry, and Otto Hahn was one of the original members of the staff. Lise Meitner joined soon after, first as part of Hahn's section, but soon director of her own research group in nuclear physics. The culmination of their collaboration was the first properly documented fission of an atom in 1938, which led in a few years to the development of the atomic bomb in the United States and subsequently to the use of nuclear power as an energy source throughout the world. Meitner, being Jewish, was forced to leave Berlin shortly before the critical experiment was done, and it was a young assistant, Fritz Strassman, who actually fired the fateful neutrons. The event is commemorated by a large bronze plaque on the old Institute building at Thielgasse 63/67, now part of the Free University, a modern institution dating from the days when the city was divided.

The Pergamon Museum (on "Museum Island") is open daily all year. The Koch Museum is on Clara-Zetkin-Strasse 96, just a few steps from the Brandenburg Gate. It is open on Wednesdays only; visits on other weekdays are possible by appointment. Telephone: 030–21234 (tourist office), 220–2411, extension 252 (Koch Museum).

FREIBERG (Saxony)

Freiberg, where the historic Bergakademie was founded in 1765, is a pleasant town with an unspoilt *Altstatt* in the center and a surrounding green park with a peaceful river and walking paths. The present Bergakademie campus is in modern buildings on the Leipziger Strasse, the main road into the town from the north, but basic science appears to be not as integral to the academy as it once was, for the scientific section (*Sektion Geowissenschafter*) remains in the old town, behind the Gothic cathedral. The building is appropriately named the **Abraham Gottlob Werner Building** and has Werner's head in bas-relief on the outside. It contains a fine mineral collection, which is open to the public. There is another memorial to Werner in the park area to the northwest of the town center. From here there is a pleasant walk along the banks of the Mulde River.

Near the Werner building is a memorial to another famous professor at the Bergakademie, the chemist **Clemens Winkler,** who discovered the element germanium here in 1886 and named it patriotically for his fatherland. (Germanium and its near relative silicon are essential constituents of semiconductors and computer chips.)

In one of the two old marketplaces, the Untermarkt, is the **Stadt-und-Bergbaumuseum.** It has a three-dimensional mock-up of the walled town of Freiberg as it was in the seventeenth century and a room devoted to organ building—Freiberg is famous for that as well as for mining and geology. The top floor is devoted to the mining industry, but mostly to its practical aspects. Apart from a framed paper with the signatures of all the former professors at the Bergakademie, there is nothing specific about Werner or the historic period when he was in Freiberg. A more unusual attraction for tourists is an old mine shaft used in the Academy's teaching program, the *Lehrgrube Alte Elisabeth.* Its opening times are severely limited, but the atmosphere is there even when it is closed.

The mineral collection in the Werner Building is open to the public on Monday, Wednesday and Friday mornings and on Monday and Wednesday afternoons. The museum is open daily except Mondays. Conducted tours of the Alte Elisabeth mine are given on Saturday mornings in the summer. Telephone (tourist office): 0762–3602.

LEIPZIG (Saxony)

Leipzig is famous for its biannual trade fair (the Leipziger Messe), which has a history going back to the Middle Ages. It is famous among musicians as the home of Johann Sebastian Bach, who served as organist and "Thomaskantor" at the Thomaskirche from 1723 to 1750. Its university, where Wundt and his colleagues worked, is one of the oldest in central Europe, founded in 1409 by 400 disgruntled German students who had been enrolled at the University of Prague and were frustrated by what they took to be discrimination against Germans by the indigent Czechs. The philosopher Gottfried Leibniz was born in Leipzig and attended the university. His statue stands in front of the entrance to the main building of the present university complex.

The historic university was destroyed by bombing in World War II and the structure we now see was built in the postwar years of Communist rule. It is a spectacular skyscraper (34 stories) in the midst of a huge plaza, with an excellent public restaurant (Panorama Café) on the top floor. It was intended as a showpiece, a center for Marxist-Leninist scholarship. Despite its size, there was no room in the original plans for chemistry, physics, and biology or even for psychology in its traditional investigative form. All these subjects were relegated to the periphery.

Wundt and colleagues in Leipzig. One of the instruments on the table (enlarged at right) is a *chronoskop* for measuring reaction times with millisecond precision.

We therefore have to go far from the central plaza to find the progeny of the institute for experimental psychology that Wilhelm Wundt created here in 1875—the "Sektion für Psychologie" and the associated Wundt Institute for Counselling, housed in an old bourgeois villa. It has a "Wundt Gedenkzimmer" on the second floor, which contains the desk where he worked and some of the apparatus he used in his experiments—acoustical signal generators, chronometers, and the sliding-gauge calipers used for accurate measurement of the distance between simultaneous skin pricks. This room is normally kept locked and arrangements must be made in advance to get permission to see it, but there is an open anteroom with photographs of the most important treasures within, and this should be enough for most casual visitors. The anteroom also has a photograph of the venerable Professor Wundt himself, with long white beard and spectacles, sitting at a laboratory table with four of his younger colleagues and his assistant, Hartmann. Other photographs show Wundt's Leipzig predecessors, Ernst Heinrich Weber and Gustav Theodor Fechner, and modern men from abroad, holders of the Wilhelm Wundt visiting professorship created in his memory.

The Wundt Institute is on Tieckstrasse, off Kurt-Eisner-Strasse, about 1.5 miles (2.5 km) from the center. Telephone ("Sekretariat"): 041–393–214.

MAGDEBURG (Saxony)

Otto von Guericke is Magdeburg's most famous personage. The city's technical high school and a major street are named after him, and there is an impressive monument (incorporating a fountain) next to the Rathaus. A side panel on the monument shows an embossed relief of the hemisphere experiment, and the opposite side has another panel showing the old city of Magdeburg, in profile along the River Elbe, before its destruction in 1631 in the Thirty Years' War. Guericke's house was among the buildings destroyed, but he rebuilt it in 1634. This house survived until the nineteenth century, but has now been replaced by a savings bank. The site (on the Münzstrasse) is marked by a plaque.

The **Kultur-historisches Museum,** Magdeburg's major museum, devotes a section on the ground floor to the former mayor. It contains replicas of the hemispheres (the originals being in the science museum in Munich) as well as some do-it-yourself working apparatus. One device provides an alternative way of demonstrating the force of air pressure against an evacuated space—in this one the effect of evacuation is to raise a very heavy weight. There are pictures of von Guericke and of Magdeburg in his time and of the hemisphere experiment. Other do-it-yourself demonstrations of apparatus designed by von Guericke include an ingenious thermometer and various electrical contraptions. Overall, the technical section of the museum (as opposed to the cultural) is quite small, most of it devoted to practical devices such as steam engines.

The museum is open daily except Mondays. All explanations are in German and no booklets are provided. Telephone (tourist office): 091–35352.

Otto von Guericke's experiment in Magdeburg in 1660, from an engraving made in 1664.

11

Austria

Österreich, "land to the east" in literal translation, is actually more of a center in political history, a sort of focal point of Mitteleuropa, if such a region can be defined at all. It might not seem so today, appearing peripheral to the heart of Europe, not even a member of the European Economic Community, but that is the way of life, a story of ups and downs. Austria's heyday was the reign of Habsburg king Charles V, who ruled over a huge part of Europe, all the way to Spain, from 1519 until his voluntary abdication in 1555. But the country was a dominant force as often as not even under the lesser Habsburgs who followed, and in fact remained so until Bismarck and a newly vigorous Prussian state finally sent them packing in mid-nineteenth century. The lowest point in Austrian history came not too long after that, when Hitler's Anschluss absorbed the entire country into his Greater Germany in 1938.

Perhaps surprisingly, Austria did not play a conspicuous role in the story of science in the time of its political prominence, despite the fact that the University of Vienna is one of the oldest in Europe, founded in 1365. The Habsburgs probably did little to encourage original thinking by the professors. There was actually an opportunity at one point to create a scientific tradition, for the German astronomer Johannes Kepler, full of new and sweeping ideas, held his first professional position in Austria, at the Protestant school in Graz. But this was the time of religious upheavals in the wake of the Reformation, and Kepler was driven out in 1599, when Habsburg Archduke Ferdinand vowed to cleanse Austria of the Lutheran heresy—and who could care less about the stars! (Later in life, Kepler held a position at the University of Linz and that institution now goes officially by the name of "Kepler Universität," but there is little indication of affection at the time, neither Linz for Kepler nor vice versa.)

Some of the later Habsburgs became famous for their elegant courts and their patronage of the arts, especially music. Was there ever the equal of the Vienna of Haydn, Mozart, Beethoven, Schubert? But science did not come into

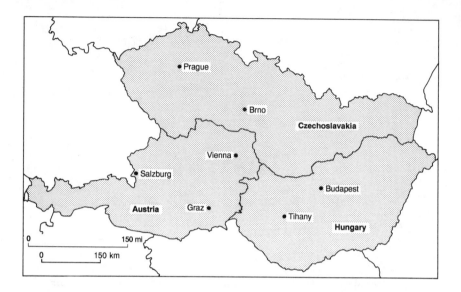

its own until after the Habsburg dynasty had seriously begun to fade and its universities began to enter into the mainstream of Germanic culture. It is then, in the nineteenth century, that we begin to find familiar names in the roster of Austrian scientists, though their number remained small. There is Christian Doppler, for example, known to us for his explanation of the Doppler effect, the changes in frequency of sound from a moving source. Later came the philosopher/scientist Ernest Mach, for whom the Mach number for supersonic speeds is named. Mach unfortunately was an uncompromising advocate of the positivist school of philosophy, the overall effect of which was painfully destructive, for it denied any value to the use of imaginative models in the interpretation of experimental data. Even atoms and molecules were included in Mach's catalog of contempt, and even Albert Einstein (at a meeting between the two men as late as 1912) failed to budge Mach from his position.

Thermodynamics and Molecules: Paradox Resolved

There was a bridge to be built between the abstract notions of thermodynamics and the material atomic/molecular picture of matter, and it is perhaps surprising that the bridge was built in Austria and not in England, which was tops at the time in these esoteric subjects. (Cambridge University's James Clerk Maxwell, had even been the pioneering founder of molecular statistics, which was one of the essential tools for the work.) But it was **Ludwig Boltzmann** (1844–1906), unaided by foreign influence as far as one knows, who solved the problem. He was born and educated in Vienna, although much of his work was carried out in the provincial city of Graz. He is acknowledged by the experts today to have been one of the geniuses of late nineteenth-century physics, yet he was not widely appreciated in his own time and even today his name is not as well-known to the general public as it ought to be.

The gap to be bridged was huge. On the one hand we have the molecular picture—myriads of molecules in helter-skelter motion, as yet unseen, but revealed in the manifestations of gas pressure, heat capacity, and so forth. The molecules were assumed to collide according to Newton's laws, the collisions being reversible in the sense that directions of molecular motion are all equivalent. The events in any single collision could just as well have happened backwards. On the other hand, we have the second law of thermodynamics, the unidirectionality of all spontaneous natural events, the inexorable increase in entropy, the "arrow of time," as it is sometimes called. At least on a macroscopic scale one direction is allowed, the opposite is forbidden. How can the two be reconciled?

The problem can be stated more cogently in terms of energy. If entropy is multiplied by temperature, we get a quantity with units of energy, and the sense of the second law of thermodynamics then becomes that this form of energy cannot be usefully applied, cannot be employed to drive the wheels of vehicles or industry. What is this mysterious *unusable* portion of the energy around us? Can we account for it without violating Newton's laws? If not, then surely the imagined but unseen molecules of matter, whose forceful motion contributes part of the energy, cannot in reality exist.

Boltzmann solved this problem in a sustained effort beginning with a seminal paper published in 1877. The reconciling concept is *randomness*, a property intrinsic to a collection of small particles moving around willy-nilly within a defined space—"randomized" energy cannot do useful work. It was a truly virgin concept, a radically new idea that nobody else had thought of.

Boltzmann's work has affected much of theoretical physics and a new fundamental constant of physics has emerged from it. It is a kind of scaling factor between the energy units that we use in everyday life and the energies of molecular motions. It is called the Boltzmann constant, usually designated by the single letter k. It is a component of many basic laws of physics, including Boltzmann's famous equation for the molecular interpretation of entropy,

$$\text{entropy} = k \log W$$

in which W is a statistical factor giving the number of different ways energy (or position) can be distributed among multitudinous molecules without affecting observable bulk properties, a factor that Boltzmann showed must always increase in irreversible processes, and which in effect is a quantitation of the concept of randomness.

Boltzmann's genius was not generally recognized by his contemporaries. Some did not fully understand statistical analysis, but even those who did had legitimate cause for some skepticism because the kinetic molecular model for matter could not yet explain everything about the measurable properties of matter. Entropy had undoubtedly been the most challenging, the seemingly insurmountable paradox, but lesser problems remained, resolution of some of which had to wait for the advent of the quantum theory in 1900. Some critics, like Wilhelm Ostwald, *de facto* leader of German-speaking physical chemists, were self-righteous phenomenologists, who on principle opposed any model building, but presumably were especially adamant about models they didn't really understand. Boltzmann's Austrian contemporaries were among the hostile, which must have hurt badly—especially the repeated taunt of Boltzmann's former teacher, Ernst Mach, who asked at every opportunity, whenever atoms and molecules were mentioned: "But who has ever seen one?" By 1900 Boltzmann began to suffer severe depression and in 1906 he committed suicide. The contribution of scientific controversy to his unfortunate end is unknown.

Related Places to Visit: Graz, Vienna (cemetery), Duino (Italy).

Scientist or Quack?

Sigmund Freud (1856–1939) is a name we all recognize. He invented much of the popular image of what goes on in the mind and originated many intrinsically poorly defined terms that have become household words—the unconscious, for example, and psychoanalysis, Oedipus complex, and the ego. And all of us have surely been embarrassed more than once by making "Freudian slips." Whether any of it can legitimately be called science is, however, open to question. Freud's evidence was based in part on introspection and on the interpretation of dreams and in part on his ability to cure hysteria by hypnosis in his medical practice. All his theorizing was done without a glimmer of recognition that controlled experiments might be desirable. Is this the stuff that science is made of?

In our opinion, the question is perhaps irrelevant, for, like it or not, Freud's influence on the subsequent course of the science of the mind has been enormous. The influence was indirect, but nevertheless real. The very problems that acknowledged legitimate scientists have posed post-Freud, and some of the vocabulary they use, were shaped by Freud's writings and theories.

Freud was actually born in Freiburg, Moravia (now Pribor, Czechoslovakia) but spent nearly his entire life in Vienna. He was trained as a physician and neurologist but early in his career became fascinated with what he was to term the human *psyche*. He introduced the concepts of conscious and unconscious mind, and speculated about the effects of repression and the driving force of human sexuality upon the dark recesses of the unconscious part. He never received an appointment at the university in then strongly anti-Semitic Viennese society, but he acquired some fervent disciples during the long years of his practice of psychoanalysis, and these spread his gospel far and wide. At the academic level, however, during Freud's lifetime and since, there has never been a lack of determined opposition, from highly qualified neuroscientists and psychiatrists, and also from sociologists, who were eager to promote their own fancy theories of cultural determinism in which individual innate factors, conscious or otherwise, had no place.

Freud's ideas also met (especially during his lifetime) with fierce opposition from many humanists. His emphasis of sexual drive as a prime instinct, particularly in young children, was not a popular stance. Even later and more tolerant commentators often view Freud's influence on public perception of human emotions as negative—Matt Cartmill, for example, has characterized Freud's message as "to be human is to be mentally ill." But Freud himself remained undaunted by criticism, and patients continued to come to his door until 1938 when the Anschluss swallowed Austria into Nazi Germany and Freud was forced to escape. He found refuge in England, where he died the following year. As a condition for being allowed to leave the new Greater Germany with some dignity, Freud had to sign a statement saying that he was leaving of his own free will and that he and his family had been well-treated. Freud did so and added a little remark of his own: "Ich kann die Gestapo jedermann auf das beste empfehlen" (I can highly recommend the Gestapo to everyone). Under the circumstances that is the ultimate chutzpah.

Related Place to Visit: Vienna.

PRINCIPAL PLACES TO VISIT

GRAZ

The old city of Graz is situated on the River Mur and dominated by the Schlossberg rising above the left bank. The atmosphere of an ancient town is still pervasive despite the installation of modern shops in old buildings and throngs of shoppers on the street. The city prides itself on being the place where Johannes Kepler got his professional start as a teacher at the Protestant Academy that existed in the city from 1568 to 1599. The school was closed by the fervent Catholic archduke in 1599 (becoming a convent), and Kepler and other Protestants were driven out. The buildings, among the loveliest in Graz, are now part of a shopping arena at the end of Paradiesgasse and their historic significance is marked by a plaque. The house where the astronomer lived is also preserved, at the back of the courtyard of the Keplerkeller, a lively taproom at Stempfergasse 6.

Graz University was originally founded in the sixteenth century (and was, of course, Catholic in Kepler's time), but no ancient buildings remain. Its most famous scholar in recent times was the physicist Ludwig Boltzmann, who was a professor here from 1876 to 1890, which was his most productive period. He is commemorated by a plaque on the staircase of the **Physics Institute** on Universitätsplatz 5.

Boltzmann is known for his work as a theoretical physicist, creator of the link between the laws of thermodynamics and the atomic/molecular theory of matter. It happens that he was also fascinated by experimental apparatus, not so much for research as for the demonstration of fundamental principles of physics, and a multitude of instruments dating from Boltzmann's time has recently been unearthed from storage space in the basement of the Physics Institute. Some were built by Boltzmann himself, others were designed by equally famous physicists from other countries. The instruments have been beautifully restored and form a superb collection, one of the best of its kind in the world. What is particularly impressive about them is the huge effort that evidently went into the design of equipment for purely didactic motives, to promote the better understanding of physics lectures—a practice that assuredly does not exist today in most European or American universities. A few items of the collection are displayed in the ground floor hallway of the building, but most are held in a closed room, awaiting the opening of a museum that will house them.

The collection of instruments will be shown to anyone with a professional interest in them. Contact the Arbeitsgruppe für Physikgeschichte at the Institute. Telephone: 0316–380–5193.

SALZBURG

Salzburg is the picture postcard city of Austria, nestled among mountains, lakes, and châteaux. It is the home of Mozart (and the present renowned Mozart music festival) and of the Trapp singers, heroes of the heart-warming musical show, *The Sound of Music*. It was also the scene of a heart-warming incident in the history of science. The Swiss iconoclast Paracelsus (see under "Switzerland")—also known as Philippus Theophrastus von Hohenheim—hounded from one city to another as an undesirable troublemaker—was given protection in Salzburg by the tolerant Archbishop Ernst. He died here in 1541 and was buried in St. Sebastian church. A monument was erected for him a couple of centuries later and still stands in the church precincts. It bears a noble inscription: "Here is buried Phillipus Theophrastus, distinguished Doctor of Medicine, who with wonderful art cured dire wounds, leprosy, gout, dropsy and other contagious diseases of the body, and wished his goods to be distributed to the poor."

VIENNA

The Zentralfriedhof (cemetery) on the edge of the city is a place of pilgrimage for many visitors to Vienna. It has a special section of Ehrengraben (honor graves) where Beethoven, Schubert, Brahms, Strauss, and many Viennese Bürgermeister are buried. There is a scientist among them, however, Ludwig Boltzmann, interred in Section 14C. Being placed in this company is a singular tribute, considering that his peer group in Austria did not seem to like him too much for most of the time when he was alive. The tombstone itself bears the inscription "$S = k \log W$," Boltzmann's famous equation linking entropy to the world of atoms and molecules. (How many tombstones in the world carry equations?) Other members of Boltzmann's family are buried with him, up to his grandson, his last male descendant, who was killed in the war in 1943 in Smolensk.

Another place of pilgrimage, for the many admirers of Sigmund Freud from all over the world, is the old Freud house on Berggasse 19, which was both his home and the seat of his practice. It has now been converted into a museum, which contains Freud's consultation room, restored to its erstwhile state. In the entrance hall we find his familiar walking stick and hat, and throughout the building much original furniture, photographs, documents—altogether a well-designed panorama of his life. Individual items are numbered, and corresponding text and commentary is provided by mimeographed guidebooks (available in all major languages), which one can borrow as one walks through the rooms of the house. A printed book with much the same text and copies of some of the photographs is available for purchase.

Part of the exhibit deals with the revolting events of Freud's last years. There are photos of brown-shirted Nazis burning Freud's books, a picture of his house defaced with paint, to label the occupant a Jew, and, finally, photos of him as a frail old man, over eighty years old, forced to flee for his life. Four of his sisters, it might be noted, did not leave when he did and died in the holocaust of the concentration camps. This view of the unspeakable depravity of the Nazis is particularly chilling because we know the victim almost as if we had met him in person and we know him to have been innocent of any evil intent. Probably unintentionally, the exhibit focuses on how little we really understand about human psychology, the very field with which Freud was clumsily attempting to grapple. The holocaust was engineered by the legitimate rulers of supposedly civilized countries, and most of the German and Austrian populations unquestionably acquiesced to some degree. How could that happen? Freud would not have been able to explain it, but neither can the professional psychologists of today. We can only hope that it won't happen again, but no scientific evidence exists to buttress that hope.

Just a few steps away from Berggasse 19, adjacent to Roosevelt Platz, is Sigmund Freud Park, with a statue of Freud. Another monument, erected in 1977, is in the outskirts of the city, in a place called Bellevue, where Freud used to like to take walks. It bears an inscription, which declares: "Here, on July 24th 1895, the secret of dreams revealed itself to Dr. Sigm. Freud." It is strange to think that we can here identify (so, at least, they tell us) the very instant when the inspiration came that would soon radically alter the popular image of men and women of themselves.

The Freud Haus is open daily, mornings only from Monday to Friday. Telephone 01-311596.

12

Czechoslovakia

Good King Wenceslas looked out
On the Feast of Stephen,
When the snow lay round about,
Deep and crisp and even. —J. M. Neale

The fabled good king ruled Bohemia for a short period in the tenth century, but was caught up in the warfare between the Germans to the west and the Slavs to the east; he was assassinated in 929 by his brother Boleslav. Isn't that the story of Czechoslovakia in a nutshell, seemingly forever? Czechs and Slovaks and Germans, attempting to live side by side, sometimes in harmony, often in discord. One must not be fooled by the fact that Czechoslovakia per se, as a name for a country, did not come into existence until 1918, after World War I, for that was simply a cosmetic act, a formal declaration of the end of the Habsburg empire, which made Bohemia and its neighbors independent of Austrian domination. All else would continue as before. Czechoslovakia is now again independent, but whether internal conflicts have totally subsided remains to be seen.

Once in this tale of a thousand years the capital city of Prague had a moment of scientific glory. It was in the reign of King Rudolph II, a melancholy man by all accounts, who was Holy Roman Emperor at the same time as he ruled as King of Bohemia. In 1599 Rudolph hired the boisterous Danish astronomer Tycho Brahe to be his Imperial *Mathematicus* and gave him first a castle in the country and then a villa in Prague to pursue his observations of the skies. Brahe died in 1601—from a surfeit of good living, it is said—but he had in the meantime hired poor tormented Johannes Kepler to be his assistant, and Rudolph made the fortunate decision to keep Kepler on as Brahe's successor. The eventual result was the publication of one of the momentous works of astronomy, a tabulation of the positions of all the known planets on any given date, then or in the future. It was dedicated to Rudolph and is known as the *Rudolphine Tables*. It was based on Brahe's huge volume of accurate observations, but was in fact much more than a mere tabulation, for it incorporated Kepler's proclaimed laws governing Brahe's observations. Planetary orbits are not circles, for example, is what the first law stated—they are ellipses with one focus on the sun. What a blow to medieval notions of perfection! (See under "Germany" for more on the subject.)

The Laws of Inheritance

Gregor Mendel (1822–1884) is Czechoslovakia's most notable figure in the relatively modern era. He was a farmer's son from a German-speaking village in Moravia, but chose to leave the farm to become a monk at the Augustinian monastery in the Moravian capital of Brno. There he set up a garden, in which he studied the heredity of peas. The results were not at all what was expected and led him to propose an entirely new mechanism for the process of inheritance. Other botanists read his work (published in 1865), but did not seem to grasp its significance—no scholar shouted "Eureka." It was 1900 before three other botanists independently did the same type of experiments and reached the same conclusions. They soon rediscovered the work of what they considered an obscure Moravian priest and acknowledged his priority. The basic principles of inheritance have been known as Mendel's Laws ever since. They are the foundation on which all modern genetics is based.

The foregoing romantic tale is common knowledge, but actually quite misleading. First, the monks in Brno were not recluses living a Spartan life of contemplation, their minds fixed on the good book and the afterlife, but were active teachers and scholars, committed to educating the sons of local citizens; they were the local intelligentsia. (The now popular Czech composer Leos Janaçek worked at the monastery for some years before establishing a music conservatory. He played the organ at Mendel's funeral.) Second, Mendel was by no means unprepared for the work he was to do, for the monks had sent young Gregor to the University of Vienna when he first joined them. Here he studied physics and natural sciences and even statistics. He was supposed to obtain a teaching diploma as well, but failed in his examinations. Third, there was nothing unworldly about Mendel's garden. Being ineligible for teaching, he was expected to do something else that would be useful and chose to study plant breeding for its potential commercial benefits. (He became well known among pomologists for his improved varieties of apples and pears.)

None of this detracts from the grandeur of Mendel's work, seemingly so simple, yet so profound in its interpretation. Mendel studied the cross-fertilization of different pure strains of peas, peas that had bred true for certain specific characteristics through many generations. He chose seven easily observed pairs of characteristics—short versus long stems, round versus wrinkled seeds, and so on—and then examined these characteristics in succeeding hybrid generations of his plants. The results of literally thousands of such experiments (and their proper statistical analysis) led to a startling conclusion. Each parent plant must contribute one (and only one) version of a character to the offspring, so that the latter carries two versions. But only one of them is actually expressed as a visible physical attribute. Mendel saw no intermediate forms in his hybrids—either a plant had long stems or it had short stems. Thus, one parental character must be *dominant* and the other *recessive*, the latter being expressed only when both constituent versions are the same. This was heredity in an all or none fashion and refuted popular views of the day that progeny were some sort of average of their parents. It was just as much a blow to traditional dogma as Kepler's elliptical orbits had been for astronomy more than two centuries before.

The lack of immediate impact should not surprise us, for Mendel published his papers in 1865, when the chromosome and its role in heredity had not yet been discovered. It is not till after this discovery that Mendel's magic number of two (one from each parent) begins to make sense in terms of visible attributes of a living cell. The double helix of DNA, of course, provides the crowning explanation.

Related place to visit: Brno.

PRINCIPAL PLACES TO VISIT

BRNO

Brno, the capital of Moravia, is a commercial city, containing the Augustinian monastery where Gregor Mendel discovered the laws of inheritance named after him. Part of the monastery is now a museum in his memory, called the Mendelianum. A patch of garden in front of the entrance is said to be Mendel's actual experimental plot, where he did the thousands of hybridization experiments that were the basis for his results.

The number "2" is the magic number here. The statistics of Mendel's results are the same as the statistics of tossing two coins simultaneously, and it made good sense to Mendel, for there are two sexes, allowing each metaphorical coin to be derived from one parent. It makes sense in modern terms, too, for chromosomes (not yet discovered in Mendel's day) are generally paired. These basic principles emerge clearly from a visit to the museum, presented by means of detailed posters. Flowers planted in Mendel's garden patch are also intended to help, but they are merely floral representations of numbers (three red and one white in the second generation, for example), unrelated to anything to do with hybridization. They may even cause confusion by obscuring the statistical nature of actual hybridization experiments.

The former refectory of the monastery now contains a sequence of show-cases and posters to display the facts of Mendel's life, education, and work, and they go on from there to a few highlights of modern genetics, such as the discovery of chromosomes and the role of DNA. Another room (a former chapter hall) is now a conference room, with contemporary furniture and a fine portrait of monk Gregor. There is also a good photograph of Mendel with some of his monastic colleagues, which shows them as anything but unworldly monks—it's more like the annual group picture of a present-day departmental faculty.

On the whole the museum fails to provide a sense of the enormous achievement of the man. A giant wall poster, for example, gives us a synthesis of Mendel's ideas from elements derived from the works of many predecessors: Laplace, Galileo, Newton, Lamarck, and even Aristotle. A quotation from one of Mendel's teachers (C. F. Napp) shows that the latter already asked critical questions about plant breeding ("Was vererbt und wie?") 30 years before Mendel. What is not said is that dozens of others must have asked the same questions and that the whole world had access to the same elements—but Mendel alone and no one else provided the answers. Contemporary botanical opinion did not even grant both sexes a role in inheritance; the male alone was commonly thought to be responsible for inherited characteristics!

The *Mendelianum* is open all day Mondays to Fridays. Ring the bell for admission if necessary.

PRAGUE

The city has undergone a face-lift, after decades of lamentable neglect, presumably to help pack in the tourists. The effects are impressive. Prague has an abundance of old buildings, ornately adorned, brightly painted, more Viennese than Vienna itself. And the concrete block monstrosities that blight the landscape of many eastern European cities are fortunately out of sight in central Prague, relegated to the southern side of the city.

Prague had the first university in Mitteleuropa, founded in 1348 by scholars escaping from plague-infested Italy and named Charles University for Charles IV, king of Germany and king of Bohemia. Not surprisingly, faculty and students organized themselves right from the start into four so-called nations— Czech, Saxon, Bavarian, and Polish. The present university still occupies the original site (the Carolinum on Zelezna Street), but there is little left to remind one of its origins or former national divisions.

The great days for science here were the days of Tycho Brahe and Johannes Kepler (around 1600), which culminated in the publication of the *Rudolphine Tables* of astronomical positions. Remains of the old summer palace, which King Rudolph gave to his astronomers for a residence and observatory, were unearthed in the 1950s in the courtyard of a modern school (now called the Jana Kaplera Gymnasium). Brahe and Kepler are commemorated by a plaque and by a marvellous statue of the two of them, standing side by side, their facial expressions and body stance defiant, suggesting that they may be about to start a

TYCHO BRAHE
JOHANNES KEPLER

Hilltop statue in Prague, where the observatory stood in 1600.

duel with some opponent of their work. The site (corner of Parlerova and Keplerova streets) is high up on the Hradcany hill, even higher than the castle itself, quite appropriate for a former observatory. It is a somewhat strenuous climb from the turreted Charles Bridge across the river below.

Tycho Brahe is buried in the historic church of Our Lady before Tyn, on the Old Town Square. An impressive memorial tablet stands just beyond the new altar railing on the right side of the nave and the actual tombstone is just below it. Kepler outlived Brahe by 30 years and left Prague after King Rudolph died. A plaque marks the house where he lived from 1609 to 1612, at 4 Karlova, across the street from the Clementinum, a former Jesuit college.

13

Hungary

Buffoons of the world, that's how one lamenting Hungarian poet described his own people. "Shall we always be defeated?" is a refrain repeated over and over in Magyar literature. Suleiman the Magnificent of Turkey crushed the Hungarians in battle in 1526 and the country was dominated by the Ottoman empire for the next 150 years. Then came centuries of subservience to the Austrian Habsburgs and more recently there have been the Russians. Hungary boasts many national heroes, such as Francis II Rákóczy, celebrated by the stirring *Rákóczy March*. But who was he? A gallant loser, leader of a failed revolt against the Austrians. It is not just ancient history, for the unsuccessful 1956 attempt at liberation from the Russians repeats the pattern. Just weeks ago as we are writing, a new attempt at liberation. Will this one last?

There is a strong Hungarian cultural identity despite the lack of political freedom, perhaps because of the Magyar language, rooted in the East and lacking cognate links to the main European language families. And the time-honored Mitteleuropa trick of solidifying military victories by moving settlers into conquered lands (stolid German-speaking farmers and shopkeepers in this case) did not work very well here—many settlers liked it better in Hungary than where they came from. And, though Hungarian culture is strongest in music and the arts, it does not lack a scientific component. We cite two nineteenth-century scientists here who have earned honorable places in the history books. It is not without irony that one of them came from among the German-speaking settlers, but he appears to have been seduced by the Magyar spirit and exceptionally defiant of Viennese authority, which (in keeping with tradition) did him little good in his career.

Physician, Wash Thy Hands

The name of **Ignaz Semmelweiss** (1818–1865) is relatively unfamiliar, but how well he mirrors the politics and culture of place and time—Budapest and Vienna in this case and the early nineteenth century. He is a minor figure in our history and he had but one flash of genius, but that's one more than most of us can claim, and he should at least have been recognized by his colleagues. That he was actually ignored (even despised) can partly be blamed on his origin in Budapest, at a time when only a Viennese was allowed the luxury of genius. But the career of Semmelweiss is also an example of how stupidity and entrenched prejudice can impede the flow of reason, a regrettably ubiquitous theme in the history of science, not confined to any one age or arena—the story has value as a lesson even for today.

Semmelweiss belonged to one of the Germanic families, and like many other Hungarian young men with the financial means, he was sent to Vienna for his higher education. He acquired a degree in medicine and took a position in the maternity department at the University of Vienna. In those years deaths from puerperal fever contracted in childbirth were appalling in number—sometimes as many as 30 to 40 percent of the mothers died—but there was a strange statistic in the hospital in which Semmelweiss worked. The hospital had two obstetric wards, one in which midwives were trained and one in which medical students practiced, and the mortality rate from puerperal fever was a factor of ten less in the midwives' ward than in the students' ward. (And women who delivered their babies at home did even better than that.) It was Semmelweiss who by chance discovered the connection between the infectious disease and the site of delivery. An associate had died of septicemia after cutting himself with a dissection knife, and the symptoms of his septicemia were so similar to those of the women suffering from puerperal fever that it did not take a Sherlock Holmes to find the culprit for the childbirth deaths. Medical students spent a lot of time dissecting cadavers and often went directly from the dissecting room to the obstetric ward. On the other hand, midwives never had contact with cadavers. The obvious answer was that the students were somehow infected with septicemia from their handling of cadavers and carried this dread disease to their patients. In Semmelweiss's own words: "The death of a colleague from a dissection wound unveiled to my mind an identity with the fatal puerperal cases." Semmelweiss's solution was to insist that all students wash their hands in chloride of lime before attending any maternity cases. Not surprisingly, the incidence of puerperal fever in the students' ward dropped by a factor of ten.

One might imagine that such a feat of life-saving would have brought fame and fortune to Semmelweiss, but it did not. Most scientists still rejected the idea that diseases were related to the small animalcules discovered by Leeuwenhoek 200 years earlier. The biomedical scene was dominated by the likes of Liebig and Virchow in Germany, who proclaimed a fashionable mechanical view of life, in which a living cell was simply a small mechanical and chemical engine. Illness reflected an intrinsic malfunction of that engine—invasion by some other (microscopic) living thing as a cause of malfunction was unthinkable. Semmelweiss's medical director and many of his colleagues first scoffed and later became openly antagonistic. Finally, after an ill-judged participation in a popular revolution (the one that deposed the imperial advisor, Metternich), Semmelweiss was dismissed from the hospital and denied any further appointments in Vienna.

Semmelweiss returned to Hungary and became professor of obstetrics at the University of Pest. He imposed his strict washing procedure on the students and physicians and again the incidence of puerperal fever dropped dramatically. There is evidence that his message was beginning to be heard in some places, for the University of Zürich tried unsuccessfully to get him to accept a position there in 1857. But by and large the powers in science continued to reject the germ theory of disease, and the medical profession continued to ignore Semmelweiss. It was not till a generation later, at the opposite end of Europe, that the Scottish surgeon Joseph Lister preached the same sermon as Semmelweiss had done. This time the message was slowly accepted, for Louis Pasteur in France was by then convincing the world with irrefutable proof that microbes cause and spread disease. The die-hards in the hospitals were forced to capitulate.

The circumstances of Semmelweiss's death in 1865 are ironic. He appears to have shown signs of mental deterioration and was committed to an institution for the insane. At the time of his admittance he had a small dissection wound on his hand (a consequence of failing concentration?), which became septicemic, and he died from the very disease he had done so much to prevent.

Related Place to Visit: Budapest.

Physics and Mathematics

Lorand Eötvös (1848–1919) was the son of a very famous man, József Eötvös, writer and Hungarian patriot, better known in his native land than his son would ever be. But Lorand became a physicist and did an experiment, still cited in nearly all basic textbooks today, that made his name known worldwide, albeit to a more specialized audience. What Eötvös did was to measure the force of gravity with great precision for many different substances and masses at many different latitudes on the earth's surface. His results demonstrated that inertial mass—the mass involved when an arbitrary central force changes the state of motion of a body—is the same as the mass that determines gravitational attraction between one body and another. Further, the proportionality between the force of gravity and the mass of a body is identical, regardless of the material of which a body is made.

Why did Eötvös put so much effort into this work? Why are his results still considered so important? The reason is that Newton's law of gravitation, which states that the attractive force between two bodies is proportional to the product of their masses and inversely proportional to the square of the distance between them, is a purely *empirical* law, based on no prior principle of physical theory. Newton himself emphasized this and is often quoted for his vigorous disclaimer of any hypothesis about the physical basis for gravitational attraction. Such empiricism, powerful in the sense that it rests on undeniable data, is weak in another sense in that it cannot address questions that the data themselves do not cover. For example, is the proportionality in the gravity law precisely the same for chemically different substances? If the moon had the same mass but were made of gold or silver, would its orbit be exactly the same? Eötvös answered these questions in the affirmative, to within the best experimental accuracy he could produce, but it was by no means intuitively obvious that it would come out that way.

There is even an extension to modern physics. Minute anomalies in the orbit of the planet Mercury around the sun were beginning to be recognized in Eötvös's time. Eötvös's results exclude the possibility that the anomaly can be ascribed to a compositional difference between Mercury and other planets. Some other factor must be involved—this proved to be one of the experimental supports for Einstein's theory of general relativity. (Einstein himself did not know about Eötvös's work at the time, but was convinced of the invariance of the gravitational constant for other reasons. He had many critics who would have been delighted to prove him wrong.)

After Eötvös. Lorand Eötvös, like his father, achieved fame working within his own homeland, not on foreign soil. Since his time there have been several more world-renowned Hungarian physicists and/or mathematicians, but they all left Hungary early in their careers and practiced their professions abroad, mostly in the United States. The list includes the celebrated applied mathematician, John von Neumann; Eugene Wigner, 1963 Nobel laureate in physics; Edward Teller, central figure in the development of nuclear weapons for the United States and (especially) proponent of the H-bomb; and Leo Szilard, another important figure in the U.S. nuclear program, but strenuously opposed at the time to the development of the H-bomb.

Related Places to Visit: Budapest, Tihany.

PRINCIPAL PLACES TO VISIT

BUDAPEST

Budapest straddles the Danube, with the Buda hills on the right bank and Pest, the administrative and commercial center, on the left. The view from Castle Hill across the broad sweep of the river to the parliament building on the other side is unforgettable.

The museum to commemorate Ignaz Semmelweiss—in the house in which he was born—is in Buda at 1 Apród Street. It is actually an excellent general medical history museum with only a little space devoted to Semmelweiss himself. It goes back to early man, the Egyptians, the Greeks, and then, more broadly, from medieval to relatively modern Europe. A fine collection of early surgical and obstetrical instruments is especially noteworthy, and there is a reconstructed pharmacy with lovely porcelain jars and bottles.

The room devoted to Semmelweiss memorabilia contains his desk, portraits of the family, and so forth. One cabinet has a copy of his book and open letters he published to refute his detractors. There is an interesting copy of a German textbook that Semmelweiss used as a student in Vienna in which his notes are written in Magyar—more testimony to the fact that he was Hungarian, not German. Semmelweiss's remains are interred in the courtyard of the house and their history reflects the slow appreciation of the man's worth. He died in Vienna in 1865 and was originally buried there. Thirty years later his bones were transferred to Budapest's honor cemetery; finally, in 1965, they were moved here to the house where he was born and is remembered.

Another monument to Semmelweiss is a statue of the good doctor, with a mother and babies sitting at his feet, placed in front of the old St. Roch Hospital in Pest, which is where he practiced medicine. This used to be the site of isolation barracks in the old days because it was outside the city. There is a pretty little church (St. Roch Chapel) next door.

Budapest's other celebrated scientist, Lorand Eötvös, has no individual monument, but is honored by having the city's university named for him. The oldest buildings (housing the present law faculty) are in the inner city at the end of Eötvös Lorand Street. The University Church next door is one of the most impressive pieces of baroque architecture in the city and well worth a visit.

The Semmelweiss Museum is open daily except Mondays. Telephone: 1-753-533.

Ignaz Semmelweiss, savior of mothers and babies.
The statue is outside the hospital where he worked.

TIHANY (Lake Balaton)

Lake Balaton, the largest lake in central Europe, is Hungary's favorite recreation area. The south shore is sandy, perfect for bathing; the north shore is wooded and hilly. The lake is shallow and freezes in winter. Its smooth and level surface was considered ideal by Lorand Eötvös for perfecting the torsion balance he designed for precision measurement of gravitational force, and he erected a tent on the ice here in the 1890s and stayed several months to obtain experimental data.

Eötvös made his headquarters at Tihany on the northern shore, a village of great historical interest. There is a fine museum on the top of the hill in the village center, situated in a former fifteenth-century Carthusian monastery. Its exhibits include Roman and medieval remains unearthed in the vicinity and some very fine tapestries and glass sculptures. The museum used to have a memorial room for Eötvös, but it had been removed when we visited in 1991. We were told that a new museum for "geophysical things" was in the making, but it was not clear when this would happen, nor whether it would be within the same building.

The present museum is open only in the summer.

14

Switzerland

The Swiss confederation of heterogeneous cantons was first formed in the thirteenth and fourteenth centuries (mostly from bits of Germany, Italy, and Burgundy) as a military alliance against a common enemy, the Habsburgs. It has clung sturdily to independence ever since, in the center of Europe, but a little aloof from its neighbors, its daunting mountain ranges perhaps encouraging a degree of isolation. Scientific highlights are few in number, but Switzerland did provide fertile soil for Albert Einstein, which his native Germany had failed to do.

Home-Grown Talent

Aureolus Philippus Theophrastus Bombastus von Hohenheim (1493–1541), who called himself **Paracelsus,** is not a truly shining light in the history of science. No lasting discoveries or intellectual insights can be ascribed to him. But he is worth brief mention as an iconoclast, whose crude and often irrational efforts to sweep away the stranglehold of authoritarian teaching gained him notoriety throughout central Europe and may well have helped pave the way for (weaken resistance to) the more constructive revolution that was to come.

Paracelsus is thought to have been born in Einsiedeln, an ancient site of pilgrimage in the canton of Schwyz. He practiced medicine without any formal training, and had the good fortune to be called to Basel to treat the famous printer, Johann Froben, who was seriously ill. He restored Froben's health, and also appears to have impressed the philosopher Erasmus, then a resident of Basel. The two of them secured his appointment (in 1527) as city physician and professor at the university. Paracelsus used these positions as a platform for blasting the established teachings and practices of physicians and apothecaries. He refused to take the traditional Hippocratic oath. He lectured in the local version of German instead of in Latin. He ranted and raved against the "humor"

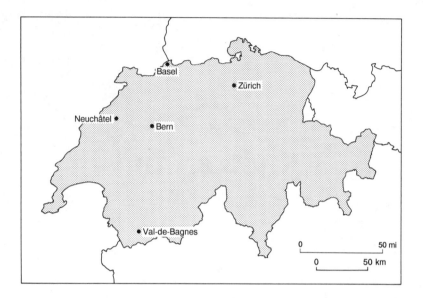

theory of well-being and disease and burned the works of Galen and Avicenna at a public bonfire. Paracelsus boasted that his teaching would be based on *experience* and not on the sacred texts of old and that good health must be defined in terms of chemicals instead of humors. He prescribed chemicals for the treatment of disease (mercury and sulfur, for example) instead of blood-letting or traditional herbs, and that may have had an indirect beneficial effect, for it encouraged alchemists to expand their horizons. Producing drugs became an alternative to the transmutation of elements to gold in the alchemist's quest for wealth.

Paracelsus did not remain long in Basel. He antagonized far too many people and was soon forced to leave. He became an impoverished wanderer, never welcome for long in any one place as his shrill truculence increased with the years. He was finally given refuge in Salzburg (Austria), where he died and was buried.

Science in the Family.   In Basel some time later there lived an extraordinary scientific family, the Bernoullis. Spanning three generations, as many as eight members of the family merit biographical sketches in the *Dictionary of Scientific Biography*. The oldest (Jakob) was born in 1654, the youngest, a great-nephew, died in 1807. No other family in the history of science can match this record. The family of Charles Darwin and the Struve family (relatively modern astronomers) come closest, each with six biographies in the *Dictionary*.

The Bernoullis (who had originally come from the Netherlands) were primarily mathematicians, but they lived at a time when mathematics had a broad influence on other sciences. The calculus invented by Newton and Leibniz provided a powerful new tool for mathematical analysis of a host of problems, previously inaccessible, although many of them may be judged elementary today. Jakob Bernoulli, for example, in 1691 solved the problem of the precise geometrical form taken by a rope suspended from supports at its two ends. It turns out to be a curve described by a simple equation and now called a catenary. Bernoulli's analysis of this problem laid the foundation for building suspension bridges.

The most famous member of the family is Daniel Bernoulli (1700–1782). He was one of the first people to apply calculus and Newtonian mechanics to the flow of fluids (as distinct from solid particles). He derived "Bernoulli's Equation," an early special case of what we now know as conservation of energy, relating flow velocity, gravitational potential and pressure. The equation is the theoretical basis for all fluid dynamics. The shape of the standard airplane wing, curved above and flat below, is a familiar practical application. When air is intercepted by the forward moving wing, it must flow faster over the longer curved surface above than the shorter flat surface below, and Bernoulli's equation then predicts that the pressure must be higher below, providing lift to the wing. (Other applications include the curve of a properly thrown baseball and the change of rate of flow of water in rivers as a function of the depth.)

A generally unappreciated aspect of Bernoulli's book, *Hydrodynamica*, is the astonishing anticipation of the kinetic molecular theory of gases over 100 years before its normally recognized inception. He viewed gases as composed of "corpuscles, which are driven hither and thither with a very rapid motion" and by use of statistical methods he derived Boyle's Law (relation between volume and pressure) on that basis. This work was largely ignored until Rudolf Clausius revived the idea in the mid-nineteenth century.

Related Places to Visit: Basel, Salzburg (Austria).

The Ice Ages

Twenty thousand years ago, almost yesterday in the history of the earth and its inhabitants, much of the Northern Hemisphere was buried under huge sheets of ice, in places more than a mile thick. In Europe the ice extended from the North Pole to the shores of the Mediterranean. In America it covered the northern third of what is now the United States. Huge amounts of water were drawn from the oceans to create this ice cover, so that sea levels fell to more than a hundred meters below present levels. This created land areas now buried by water, including the corridor between Asia and Alaska, probably the route by which Stone Age hunters first reached the American continent. There has been a warming trend since then. The great glaciers (e.g., those of Switzerland) are residues of this Ice Age and most of them are still receding.

This well-known piece of Earth history was first brought to public attention on July 24, 1837, at a historic meeting of the Swiss Society of Natural History in Neuchâtel. The harbinger of the news was a brash and aggressive young man, **Louis Agassiz** (1807–1873). Though only thirty years old, he was already quite well-known for his research on fossil fishes, and was for that year the president of the Natural History Society. Expected to present a scholarly paper on the subject of his research, he launched instead into a passionate (and, to most of his audience, shocking) exposition of the Ice Age idea and the evidence for it. It was by no means his own idea, for it had been proposed before in various guises (even by another Swiss naturalist, Jean de Charpentier), but Agassiz was the first person of stature who endorsed it, with a captive audience of professional colleagues.

The evidence that pointed inexorably to a huge former ice cover comes from what are called *erratic boulders*, boulders, some as big as houses, that clearly don't belong where they are—granite rocks, for example, in valleys lined by limestone hills. Such boulders are common in the Jura mountains near Neuchâtel and in the valleys south of the Rhone (e.g., Val de Bagnes), and the only logical origin would seem to be the granite bedrock of the Berner Oberland. How did they get from there to their present locations? Noah's Flood was the popular explanation, but granite doesn't float on water. Besides which, some of the boulders are found near the tops of mountains, and a flood that high is scarcely credible, given that water (as distinct from ice) rapidly attains nearly the same level everywhere. On the other hand, the ability of slowly flowing glacier fronts to move rocks, and to leave them behind when the glacier retreats, is familiar to everyone, especially in Switzerland where advancing and retreating glaciers are a common feature of the landscape.

Agassiz did not immediately persuade his audience, and colleagues from other countries, often unfamiliar with glaciers and skeptical about the flow of ice central to the idea, were even less easy to convince. But Agassiz continued to press his own conviction, by means of papers and a book, *Etudes sur les glaciers*, published in 1840, and eventually the doubters dwindled to insignificance. Agassiz himself traveled widely to lecture and to make geological observations, and in 1848 settled permanently in the United States, as professor at Harvard University. He was one of the charter members of the U.S. National Academy of Sciences, founded in 1863 to aid the government in the prosecution of the Civil War. It is interesting that Agassiz, though himself a champion for geological evolution, opposed Darwinism later in life and firmly adhered to the belief that only God could create new species.

The Ice Age theory, apart from its intrinsic importance, is interesting as an illustration of the method by which scientific ideas become accepted. Already by 1840 this was sufficiently sophisticated so that facts alone were no longer sufficient, and a theoretical explanation for them was necessary for general acceptance. In the case of the Ice Age theory, why did the earth grow colder 20,000 years ago? Will the present warming trend reverse itself, and will another Ice Age beset us? Are the answers related to evolutionary processes within the Earth or to astronomical events? Theoretical analysis to bear upon these questions involves almost all the apparatus of mathematical physics. The outstanding work on the subject was done by a Serbian astronomer, Milutin Milankovitsch, and his theory and its subsequent elaborations show that the Earth's climate undergoes regular cyclical changes as a result of subtle variations in its motion in the solar system. Barring interference by modern social forces (the greenhouse effect), another cooling trend should begin soon and give us another Ice Age in perhaps 20,000 years.

Related Places to Visit: Neuchâtel, Val de Bagnes.

Mostly Germans

The ETH. Founded in 1855, the Polytechnicum in Zürich (Eidgenössige technische Hochschule) is one of only a handful of Swiss federal (as contrasted to cantonal) universities. A number of its most renowned scholars (either as students or faculty members) came from Germany during the time of German domination of physics and chemistry. Rudolf Clausius, for example, was one of ETH's charter members, professor from 1855 to 1867, and his paper defining entropy and the second law of thermodynamics dates from this period. Wilhelm Röntgen was a student here, receiving a diploma in mechanical engineering in 1868 and a Ph.D. a year later. And, of course, this is the *alma mater* of Albert Einstein.

A relatively modern pioneer was Hermann Staudinger, chemistry professor at ETH from 1912 to 1925. During this period he founded the science of polymer chemistry and therewith created the seed for today's huge synthetic polymer industry. He showed that the huge quasi-molecular particles of some natural substances (particularly rubber) are in fact true molecules like any other—macromolecules is what they and their synthetic cousins are called today. He had to fight much opposition, for the then current view was that these were aggregates of smaller molecules and highly sophisticated theories were being proposed for how they were held together. (Staudinger returned to Germany in 1925. The reason for his long sojourn at the ETH was that he had denounced Germany's use of poison gas in World War I and was considered *persona non grata* until he publicly modified his stand.)

Albert Einstein (1879–1955) was different from the others. For one thing he may arguably be called the outstanding scientist of the twentieth century. (It has even been suggested that this century might in future histories be named "The Age of Einstein.") For another, though born in Germany, he had no reason to love it, whereas he did love Switzerland. He did the core of his work in Switzerland, and acquired Swiss citizenship, retaining it to the end of his life. (He later also became an American citizen, but did not have to give up his Swiss passport to do so.)

Einstein was born in Ulm in southern Germany and went to high school in Munich, but was never able to adapt to the formalized, rote-memory training that was practiced there. He became, in fact, a dropout, a discard of the system. In 1914, after he had acquired international repute, the Germans made amends in a sense by appointing Einstein as director of the Kaiser Wilhelm Institute for Theoretical Physics in Berlin, but that proved to be short-lived, to be reversed when Hitler came to the fore. Einstein's theories became reviled for being "Jewish"; his bank account, apartment, and summer home were confiscated; and he and his family fled, first to Belgium and then to the United States, where Einstein became director of the Institute for Advanced Studies at Princeton. And there, as we all know, he wrote the famous 1939 letter to President Roosevelt that led to the development of the atomic bomb by the Allies, when it could have been done by the Germans instead.

The contrast between Switzerland and Germany was enormous, in spite of the close relations between German and Swiss universities, and nothing illustrates it better than Einstein's life and career. It was not that any special favors were done for him, but simply that the Swiss had room within their system for an independent spirit. Einstein applied for admission to the ETH in Zürich in 1896, but failed the entrance examination. He was not deterred, and it was not subsequently held against him. He went back to high school for a year, to the cantonal school in Aarau (far more congenial than Munich). There he made up his deficiencies, passed the ETH exam the following year and went on to get his diploma. Getting a job proved a little harder, but he eventually found one with the federal patent office in Bern, where he remained for seven years, reading and evaluating patent applications by day and continuing his studies and his theoretical research during off-hours. It was during this period, within a single year (1905), that he produced not only a dissertation for his Ph.D. degree, but also his four greatest papers.

It is a point to be made and remembered: Einstein was not at the center of things when he changed the face of physics, not in Berlin, nor at an Institute for Advanced Studies, nor even in Zürich; he never sat at the feet of older scholars who could give him sage advice. Einstein was in the academic hinterland in Bern, kept busy all day by a demanding job; doing his physics in his rooms and in coffee-houses at night, with two young friends as his only intellectual companions—they called themselves the "Akademie Olympia" and (as Einstein described them later) dedicated themselves "with childlike delight to anything that was clear and clever."

What were the four papers, all in Volume 17 of the *Annalen der Physik?* The first, in March 1905, was on the photoelectric effect, the quantum-based explanation of Hertz's enigmatic observations on the emission of electrons from a metal bombarded by light. (This paper was the basis for Einstein's rather belated Nobel Prize in 1921.) The second paper, entirely unrelated, was his theory of Brownian Motion, a brilliant and simple explanation of how random motions of molecules lead to unidirectional diffusion from high to low concentrations. (This paper removed lingering doubts about the actual existence of molecules in the minds of many physicists.) The third paper (June 1905) was the *Theory of Relativity*, the most fundamental revolution in physics since the days of Newton. The fourth (a consequence of the preceding one) was on the interconversion of mass and energy and contained the portentous formula $E = mc^2$. A true *annus mirabilis!*

(The 1905 theory of relativity pronounced the speed of light as beyond the conventional rules of relative motion and thereby dealt a mortal blow to conventional ideas of time and space. It has become known as the special theory of relativity, to distinguish it from the broader general theory of relativity, which came later. Among other things, the latter predicted the now well-documented expansion of the universe.)

Related Places to Visit: Bern, Zürich, Ulm (Germany).

PRINCIPAL PLACES TO VISIT

BASEL

Basel is Switzerland's "City on the Rhine," and the old city on the river bank is a popular tourist area. The fabulous Bernoullis made their mark here. Jakob Bernoulli is buried in the transept of the ancient Münster, his tomb marked with a spiral in memory of one of his geometric equations. A few blocks away is the Peterskirche, the burial place of Daniel Bernoulli, within walking distance of the apartment in which he lived on Kleine Engelhof. On Klingelbergstrasse one finds the University lecture hall, the *Bernouillianum*, with busts of three of the Bernoullis at the entrance. The old auditorium of the main university building has portraits of the family.

As for Paracelsus, Basel's earlier scientist of note (or notoriety), the embers of his bonfires are dead, and he himself is buried in Austria. Curiously (since Paracelsus initiated the change in medical practice that necessitates synthetic remedies) Basel is today a world center of the pharmaceutical industry, the basis for much of the city's wealth. Three giants of the industry, Ciba-Geigy, Roche, and Sandoz, are based here and we can see their huge factories along the banks of the Rhine. The city also has a pharmacy museum, on Totengässlein, a small street off the Marktplatz. A bust of Paracelsus has recently been placed there by the Paracelsus Gesellschaft, an organization dedicated to his memory. The city has a marked pedestrian itinerary called the *Paracelsus Rundgang*—no particular association with the man, but it requires some exertion, which contributes to our good health, which is what Paracelsus was trying to promote.

BERN

Albert Einstein arrived in Bern in February 1902, in rumpled clothes, with all his belongings in a single suitcase. He had come to apply for an academic job, which he didn't get, but in June, with the help of the father of a former Zürich

The heart of Old Bern, with its famous mechanical clock and the Zähringen fountain with its warrior bear. The Einstein Haus, where Einstein worked out his theory of relativity, is on the same street, just a few doors down.

fellow-student, he was appointed (probationally) to a lowly post in the federal patent office. He was promoted to second rank in 1906 and remained in that position until October 1909, when he left Bern for a teaching position at the University of Zürich. During his seven and a half years in the city, Einstein married Mileva Maric and had his first child by her, and published the papers that would prove to be among the greatest in the history of theoretical physics. This city of Bern, as provincial a place as one can find in Europe, is where Einstein's genius came to flower. (One has to have some familiarity with the Swiss to see how the federal capital can be "provincial," but there is no question that it is. Zürich, Basel, and Geneva are the Swiss cities for people with portmanteaus and foreign connections.)

We can still see most of Einstein's Bern today, a piece of good fortune that we could hardly expect in a more progressive city. The principal tourist trail through the old city, from the train station to the bend in the river and the bear pit on the other side, passing en route the great clock with all its moving figures and the many brightly painted fountains built in 1545—this is precisely where Einstein lived and worked and where he and his three-man "Akademie Olympia" talked, walked the streets, and ate their frugal meals. Almost all the ancient buildings and the arcades that shield you from rain or sun are exactly as they have been for centuries. The Gerechtigkeitsgasse, for example, where Einstein had a furnished room when he first came to Bern, is part of the tourist trail. So is the Kramgasse, where he lived in an apartment during the crucial years from 1903 to 1905. It's just a few steps from the little Zähringen Fountain, with the bear in full armor rearing up on its hind legs, and just a few steps from the great mechanical clock, which was going through its motions in his day just as it does for us. The patent office (never more than a handful of rooms in an office building) was for a while at the corner of Genfergasse and Speichergasse, in a building now housing post office adminis-tration. (It moved later to the street called Bollwerk, to a building since demolished to make way for an expansion of the Bahnhof.) The Hotel Storchen, where the Bern Science Society used to meet, was on Spitalgasse and is no longer a hotel, but the lane named Storchengässchen tells us which of the houses it occupied. One should presumably see all this on a Sunday morning or a snowy day in winter to get a feel for the quiet atmosphere of a century ago, for the ground floors of all the buildings now serve the consumer society and the arcades tend to be thronged with shoppers. But upstairs it's probably not too different on any day of the week, and students and young researchers still live in the cramped apartments.

Wonder of wonders, the Kramgasse apartment was converted to an official museum in 1979. Two flights up from the street, it succeeds in evoking both Albert Einsteins, the man and the scientist. We can see the stand-up worktable that Einstein used at the patent office and numerous photographs, books, and quotations from his writings. We especially liked the photograph of the three members of the "Akademie," who called themselves by that name to poke fun at the self-important national academies that every country possesses, but who were in fact Einstein's only "university," meeting every night to argue physics old and new, to learn and to dissect and to initiate thereby (knowingly or not) the building of a new world. We were at the museum on a Saturday morning and were impressed by the number of visitors who made their way up the steep spiral staircase (upper portion clearly part of the old house) to pay their tribute or absorb some wisdom. We need more places like this in the world.

The Albert Einstein Haus is at Kramgasse 49 and is open Tuesdays through Saturdays except in December and January. Telephone (tourist office) 031–227676.

NEUCHÂTEL

Louis Agassiz, the leading figure in persuading geologists that a recent Ice Age had engulfed Europe, was one of the first professors to be appointed to the University of Neuchâtel in 1840. He is honored by a bust and plaque in the principal administrative building at the corner of Avenue du Premier Mars and Rue P. L Culon, but, sadly, the local natural history museum at the present time has no exhibits related to Agassiz or even to geology in general.

For dedicated mountaineers there is an *Agassizjoch* at 12,700 feet (3850 m) on the approach route to the summit of the Finsteraarhorn in the Berner Oberland. We don't know if there is a direct connection with Louis Agassiz.

Switzerland abounds with glaciers pushing rocks. It is the logical place to conceive a former Ice Age as the cause of erratic boulders.

VAL DE BAGNES
(near Martigny and Verbier)

This spectacular and desolate valley carries the stream bed of one of the branches of the River Drance; another branch comes off the col of Grand St. Bernard. At the head of the Bagnes branch is the Mauvoisin Dam, one of the highest arched type dams in the world. This valley is the site at which the Swiss mountaineer, Jean Pierre Perraudin, found in 1815 unmistakable signs that glaciers had once filled the entire valley—evidence of an earlier Ice Age unknown to the geologists of the time. He communicated his ideas to the scientific establishment without much success until Agassiz took up the cause in 1840.

There are plans afoot to open a small regional museum in Lourtier (about halfway up the valley), in the house where Perraudin was born. It will have an exhibit specifically related to the Ice Age and another about alpine climbs and expeditions in the area. Another small museum already exists at Le Châble, where the road down the Val de Bagnes branches off from the main road to Verbier, but this museum is opened only three or four times a year for temporary exhibits.

The telephone number of the "bureau" of the present museum is 026–361525.

ZÜRICH

There is a notable absence of glorification of the past in the city of Zürich— Zürchers boast that they erect neither monuments for geniuses nor build pyres for heretics. But they do manage a small plaque to designate the house on Unionstrasse 4 where Albert Einstein lived when he was at the ETH.

The ETH itself is a fine mid-nineteenth century building, situated on Rämistrasse, steeply uphill from the Limmat-Quai. The north side is decorated with the names of famous scientists of the past (i.e., before 1855), but there is no tribute to the ETH's own greats, apart from Rudolf Clausius, for whom a street and steps rising from it have been named. "Rudolf Clausius 1822–1888, Professor der Physik an der ETH," a small plaque proclaims.

However, the great banks of Zürich are impressive and so are the luxury shops in the Bahnhofstrasse.

SCANDINAVIA AND THE BALTIC

15

Denmark

Denmark was once a nation of fierce warriors, Vikings in long boats, armed to the teeth, bent on conquest of every land they could reach by sea. By the time of the birth of western European science, they had settled down, still sporadically skirmishing with their close neighbor Sweden, but mostly peaceful and stable. For so small a country they have played an exceptionally consistent part in scientific progress ever since King Frederick II set up Tycho Brahe as his royal astronomer in the sixteenth century and built him a grand observatory, 100 years ahead of similar actions by England's King Charles II or Louis XIV in France. Later monarchs were less generous, but the Danish tradition for original ideas has lived on.

Early Astronomy

In the late sixteenth century astronomers still believed in a motionless earth at the center of the universe—the sun, moon, planets, and stars all revolving in (sometimes complicated) pathways around it. True, Copernicus had 50 years earlier proposed the heretical idea that the sun is actually at the center, but few people took him seriously. Then, however, accurate measurements of celestial positions and movements began to play a role, converting star gazing into an objective science, where myth and prejudice had to give way to the cold logic of the factual record. Accurate observations have led the way in astronomy ever since, tied to the building of increasingly powerful telescopes. Now we even send them into outer space to avoid atmospheric distortion. As is common knowledge, it all began with Tycho Brahe and Johannes Kepler, and it may therefore come as a shock to realize that neither of them had a telescope at all—it had not yet been invented!

Tycho Brahe (1546–1601) came from a wealthy family and attended no less than three German universities. He would have been exposed there to the

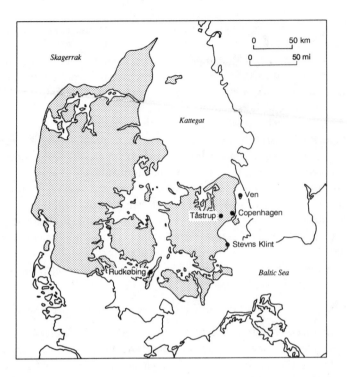

prevailing fashion for philosophical speculation, about the night sky as well as other (perhaps more weighty) matters. What inspired his passion for making his own observations we do not know (perhaps it was the observation of a solar eclipse in his youth), but passion he certainly had. He communicated some of his enthusiasm to King Frederick II of Denmark, who gave Brahe the island of Ven on which to build a house and observatory and who provided him with a handsome income on which to live. Uraniborg ("heavenly castle") is what Brahe called the place, and there he worked for 20 years on building ever better instruments with which to measure what he saw in the skies. He left Denmark when Frederick's successor cut off his funds, and he spent the last few years of his life in Prague. Johannes Kepler came to work for him there as his assistant and ultimate heir.

What were Brahe's specific contributions? One of them was certainly the very idea that experiment should take pride of place before philosophical speculation. (A "tremendous idea" is what Richard Feynman called it, and remember that he was a theoretical physicist.) Secondly there was the huge effort he expended on instrumentation. There is much more to observational astronomy than the sighting of the image, regardless of whether the naked eye or a telescope is used. Brahe designed more accurately graduated scales, smoother rotation of the sighting line in the horizontal and vertical planes, and similar mechnical aids. Most of his contribution came, however, from the prodigious amount of his data, which plotted planetary movement, gave the positions of nearly one thousand stars, recorded the courses of comets—the latter passing through the then presumably impenetrable spheres on which the planets were supposed to be mounted. Subsequently, in the hands of young Johannes Kepler, these data led to Kepler's laws of planetary motion and his confirmation of the Copernican heliocentric system.

Although a modernist in his approach to experimental astronomy, Brahe was still very much in the medieval tradition in his personal life. As a student at the University of Rostock, attending a Christmas dance, he and another student quarreled over which was the better mathematician. They fought it out in a duel next morning in which the front of Tycho Brahe's nose was sliced from his face. (Did that prove him the inferior mathematician?) A silversmith made a replacement for the nose out of gold and silver, which Brahe wore for the rest of his life. Brahe's medieval lifestyle continued after he occupied his "heavenly castle" at Ven. He gave gargantuan, hard-drinking banquets and had a jester in his retinue, a dwarf who sat at his feet and whose babbles were supposed to contain profound gems of wisdom.

Related Places to Visit: Island of Ven (now in Sweden), Prague (Czechoslovakia).

The Speed of Light. A century later came **Ole C. Rømer** (1644–1710), a more sober man than Brahe. He holds a renowned place in the history of science because he was the first person (in 1676) to measure the speed of light, obtaining the value of 225,000 km/s as against the now accepted 300,000 km/s. His feat was actually more than a measurement, that is, more than just the determination of a number for some familiar quantity, for it had been widely assumed since antiquity that light transmission is instantaneous, with no lapse of time between the departure of a signal from one point (the sun, for example) and its arrival somewhere else (such as the earth). Even such famous figures as Johannes Kepler and René Descartes believed that, into the early part of the seventeenth century. Thus Rømer's result established a crucial principle, much more important than the number itself.

Rømer attended the University of Copenhagen under the tutelage of the brothers Bartholin, one of whom had been the discoverer of double refraction of light in Iceland spar crystals. Rømer lived in their house and studied astronomy and mathematics. He impressed them so well that they gave him the task of editing unpublished manuscripts of Tycho Brahe's which they had been assigned to work on. About this time Louis XIV of France had just founded his *Académie des Sciences* and sent emissaries to Denmark to establish the exact longitude of Brahe's Uraniborg laboratory, information that was needed to correct Brahe's precise measurements and predictions to a location in Paris. Louis' emissaries took Rømer home to Paris with them where he was given an official appointment at the Royal Observatory and made tutor to the dauphin as well.

At the Royal Observatory, Rømer's work centered on the observation of eclipses of the moons of Jupiter, for the French were hoping to use predicted times of the eclipses (which depend on the terrestial coordinates of the observer) as an aid to navigation. Rømer soon recognized unexpected discrepancies in the observed eclipses (as seen from Paris), depending on the season of the year, i.e., on the separation between Jupiter and the earth. He found that the results could be explained and future eclipses could be accurately predicted if it was assumed that light has a finite velocity, such that about 20 minutes is required for light to traverse the full diameter of the earth's orbit around the sun. After nine years in France, Rømer returned to Denmark and a professorship at the University of Copenhagen. King Christian V, greatly impressed with Rømer's achievement abroad, appointed him to be his royal astronomer and created a new observatory for him near Copenhagen, where Rømer went on to record many more new astronomical observations.

King Christian also made extensive use of Rømer in other technical and advisory capacities—master of the mint (as Newton was in England), surveyor of harbors, inspector of highways. In 1694 he was made chief tax assessor and is said to have devised an efficient and equitable system of taxation. After the king's death, Rømer became mayor of the city of Copenhagen and subsequently chief of police as well. In 1707 he even became head of the state council for the entire kingdom of Denmark. A noble servant of society, indeed!

Related Places to Visit: Tåstrup; in France, Paris (Observatory).

The Birth of Electromagnetism

Another notable figure is **Hans Christian Ørsted** (1777–1851), who, on a spring evening in Copenhagen in 1820, transformed the separate subjects of electricity and magnetism into the new science of electromagnetism. It was a most unusual event, for the telling blow came in the course of a lecture for the general public. Some accident had prevented a test of the experiment in advance of the lecture, so that the very first observation of the result was made in full view of the audience. The repercussions were swift. Ørsted's experiment jolted a lot of people out of whatever they were comfortably doing at the time and redirected their interests in quite new directions. In fewer than a dozen years Michael Faraday went on to open the gates for exploitation of electromagnetism for the production of electric power.

Ørsted was born on the island of Langeland, one of two sons of an apothecary. He served for some time as his father's assistant in the shop and then went to the University of Copenhagen for a pharmaceutical degree. There he was exposed to and became enamored of philosophy and went on to get a doctorate with a thesis in metaphysics. His subsequent first plunge into original work was marred by misplaced enthusiasm for some wild theories of chemistry and he was not held in high regard, but he found he had a flair for popular lectures—mixing science with abstruse metaphysics—and on that basis was appointed an extraordinary professor at the University of Copenhagen in 1806.

(The term *extraordinary* was in use at the time in Germany and Scandinavia to designate a second-class member of the academic community, not worthy of an ordinary professorship.)

Ørsted's experiment itself was very simple—a magnetic needle is deflected when brought close to a wire in which an electric current is flowing, the needle moving perpendicular to the wire. (The observation had actually been reported once before, from Italy in 1802, but had somehow escaped notice.) It was not just a prelude for practical exploitation, but also a most disturbing result for any serious thinking scientist, for it appeared to deviate fundamentally from familiar Newtonian concepts: (1) The action between electric current and the magnet was developed by electricity *in motion*. Static electric charge exerts no force on magnets. (2) The force between wire and magnet was not simple attraction or repulsion, was not even acting along the intuitive line of force between them, but had a *perpendicular* effect instead. Who had ever seen such a thing before? That's what triggered the swift reaction. And the experiment was so simple that anybody could set it up in their own laboratory in a matter of minutes and confirm that Ørsted was right.

Ørsted himself was actually less interested in the scientific or practical aspects of his discovery than in the philosophy behind it—a rare instance when those who like to relate scientific achievement to other factors in life can make a valid claim. Ørsted, as part of his unorthodox mixing of metaphysics with natural science, was a passionate devotee of Kantian philosophy, which held that all forces of nature are somehow expressions of only two basic forces. That is what convinced him that electricity and magnetism should be related and gave him the motive to search for the relationship, and finding it was for him primarily a satisfying vindication of his philosophical beliefs. Ørsted did not follow up his discovery, nor did he ever again make another lasting contribution to pure science. In keeping with the general spirit of his career, he founded a society devoted to the spread of scientific knowlege among the general public—the society still exists and has been giving an appropriate annual award since 1908. Late in life he wrote a book, *The Soul in Nature*, about the harmony between beauty in art and music and the natural world as seen by science.

Related Places to Visit: Rudkøbing, Copenhagen.

Twentieth Century

Beer and Biochemistry. Carlsberg beer from Copenhagen is famous all over the world, but it comes as a surprise to most visitors to learn that the brewery houses one of the great world centers for biochemical research. The brewery's founder, Jacob Christian Jacobsen, was inspired by Louis Pasteur's scientific studies on fermentation to create the Carlsberg Laboratory on the brewery grounds in 1876, with the intent that it should provide the expert advice needed to manufacture an outstanding product and to maintain its quality. Jacobsen wisely did not seek to control the laboratory, but put its direction into the hands of a foundation, the trustees of which are elected by the Royal Danish Academy of Sciences and Letters. The laboratory has often been in the forefront of general biochemical and physiological research without direct relation to brewing.

One important contribution from the Carlsberg Laboratory has had a worldwide impact. The pH scale we all use today as a measure of acidity, familiar alike to gardeners, environmentalists, sanitary engineers, chemists, and biologists, is a Carlsberg product. It was first introduced in 1909 by S. P. L. Sørensen, who was director of the laboratory from 1901 to 1938 and whose long-range research objective was to gain an understanding of the influence of acidity on proteins and biochemical processes. Sørensen was the first to appreciate the pervasive influence of acidity on everything biological and to develop reliable methods for the routine measurement of the concentration of hydrogen ions— which is what acidity is, in chemical language. It turns out that the practically important levels of hydrogen ion concentration cover an enormously wide range, and this led Sørensen to propose a logarithmic scale for it. The letter "p" in "pH" stands for the *negative logarithm* of the actual concentration.

Niels Bohr. Emulating his countryman Tycho Brahe 350 years earlier, Niels Bohr (1885–1962) was instrumental in creating a dramatic break with the past, this time the break between classical physics—far from its Newtonian origins, but still Newtonian in essence—and what has come to be called modern physics. One aspect of the latter was easy to understand at the time and eagerly accepted, namely, the notion that atoms are not the indestructible ultimate corpuscles of matter that everybody used to think they were but can be broken down to even smaller particles. This idea makes no special demands on the imagination, and one can even draw pictures of it, with the dense nucleus at the center and the much lighter electrons circling around happily in their orbits. This model (in fact proposed by Rutherford in 1911—see under "England") is quite like the familiar solar system with its planets circling around the sun.

Other chapters of the new physics, however, were more abstruse and less easy to accept, one of these being the quantum theory proposed by Max Planck (see under "Germany"). Its central thesis, that energy can be gained or lost only in discrete quanta, i.e., chunks, was thoroughly non-Newtonian in spirit, contrary to intuitive feelings of continuity in the flow of heat, light, and other familiar energy forms. The achievement of Niels Bohr was to fuse the new ideas of quantum theory with the Rutherford model for atomic structure. By the rules of classical physics, the nice planetary model of the atom *won't work.* Bohr showed that only the added constraints of the quantum theory can make it physically acceptable.

Why is that? What about the analogy to the solar system? It turns out that the analogy is false. One of several reasons is that the atomic attractive force is electrical—the nucleus has a positive charge and the circling electrons are negative. Unlike neutral gravitational masses, moving electrical charges should (according to classical electromagnetic theory) continuously radiate energy and thereby lose it. As a consequence the electrons would inevitably spiral gradually inwards toward the center, like an earth satellite that hasn't been given enough energy to stay in orbit. However, if electron energies (within the tiny space of an atom) can be gained or lost only in chunks, then continuous energy loss is impossible. Large changes (e.g., knocking the electron out altogether) are possible, but gradual spiraling is not allowed. (Bohr, of course, supported this argument with immaculate mathematics. He left no doubt about the feasibility of the sort of atomic structure that Rutherford had visualized, though the details had to be modified, not only by Bohr, but also by later work stemming from refinements in the quantum theory.)

Niels Bohr was raised in a tightly knit family where intellectual pursuits were not only encouraged but enjoyed. (His brother, Harald, became a well-known mathematician.) Bohr's wife, Margarethe, was of the same ilk and an active participant in all aspects of his life. After receiving his Ph.D. in 1911, Bohr went to Cambridge for further study with J. J. Thomson, but did not stay long. He was inspired by a lecture given in Cambridge by Rutherford and soon went to work with him in Manchester on the problem of the structure and stability of the atom. The work was completed only after he returned to Denmark, but Bohr and Rutherford remained in touch by correspondence, and there was never a sense of rivalry between them—their friendship and association was to last a lifetime.

Bohr, of course, was soon recognized worldwide for his own genius. He was appointed professor of theoretical physics at the University of Copenhagen and director of the Institute for Theoretical Physics. He received the Nobel Prize for physics in 1922 but did not rest on his laurels after that. He remained in the forefront of atomic research, not only through his own contributions, but also as a catalyst whose guidance influenced many of his peers. His institute became the mecca for theoretical physicists, both young and old. It was unique in the world in being open without restriction to anyone who wanted to work there and in its positive encouragement of new ideas, even if they conflicted with the director's. To name only one beneficiary: Werner Heisenberg formulated his famous *uncertainty principle* here, while on leave from his regular position in Göttingen.

Fascism Resisted. In World War II, Denmark was the first European country (after Poland) to be helplessly overrun by German forces, but it distinguished itself from that point on by its flaunting resistance to German domination and especially by its ceaseless efforts to hamper the Nazi program to exterminate all Jews. When Danish Jews were required to wear yellow armbands with Star of David insignia, King Christian X himself donned the symbol as he rode around Copenhagen on his bicycle and large numbers of other Danes followed suit.

Niels Bohr was a prominent figure in this resistance movement and he helped many scientific refugees to escape to freedom, including fellow physicist

Enrico Fermi whose wife was Jewish. Bohr was able to arrange a truly spectacular escape for Fermi and his wife when Fermi was awarded the Nobel Prize for physics in 1938. The two of them came to collect the prize with all the blessings of the Italian authorities and simply did not return—Bohr whisked them away to his home in Copenhagen immediately after the award ceremony in Stockholm and arranged for them to move to the United States. Bohr himself remained in Denmark during most of the Nazi occupation, but he and his family also became refugees in 1943, when they received a warning from the Danish underground that the Germans were about to arrest Bohr and deport him to Germany. The family fled to nearby Sweden, disguised as fishermen in a little boat. Soon after that, Bohr agreed to help the Allies in their project to construct the atomic bomb. Because Sweden was a neutral country, an unarmed RAF plane had to fly secretly to Sweden to pick up Bohr and to spirit him away to England. (Bohr returned to Copenhagen as soon as the war was over.)

PRINCIPAL PLACES TO VISIT

COPENHAGEN

The Carlsberg Laboratory. The historic laboratory, built in 1897 and the principal place of research until 1976, is at 10 Gamle ("old") Carlsbergvej. It is still in active operation, joined by a covered passageway to the modern research center next door. Neither building is normally open to the general public and a bell must be rung to gain admission to the old building. Inside it there is an impressive staircase rising from the entrance hall, with flanking busts of Louis Pasteur and the German chemist Justus von Liebig. Pasteur paid a visit to the laboratory in 1884.

The Carlsberg Brewery is open to the public. Its entrance is on Ny ("new") Carlsbergvej, around the corner from the research center; the portal is framed by massive granite elephants, which actually support a cooling tower. Guided tours take the visitor through all parts of the brewery and provide him with a taste of the Carlsberg product. The very earliest research laboratory (1876–1897) was a part of the main brewery complex. It is now a museum and is visited as part of the guided tour.

The house in which the brewery founder J. C. Jacobsen resided (built in 1876) is on the brewery grounds, separated only by tall trees and gardens from the railway tracks on one side and the main brewery buildings on the other. It is now the "Mansion of Honor," given as a lifelong residence to a distinguished Danish scholar. Scientists and humanists alternate as occupants. The most celebrated occupant was Niels Bohr, who lived in the house (except for his brief wartime absence) from 1932 until his death in 1962.

Guided tours of the Carlsberg Brewery are provided Monday to Friday at 9, 11, and 2:30.

Entrance to the Carslberg Brewery. Sales of "Elephant Beer" help support basic research.

The Niels Bohr Institute, founded in 1920 explicitly for Niels Bohr, is at Blegdamsvej 15–19, adjacent to the National Hospital. Today it is a thriving institution with ongoing work in many branches of theoretical physics, but it also permits itself the luxury of a Niels Bohr Archives. A small historical room is preserved, containing Bohr's desk and chair and a few other items; the Institute's auditorium is still much as it was in Bohr's later years and contains a few historical pictures.

An appointment with a staff member is normally necessary for admission to the Institute, but a member of the Archives staff can be contacted if the purpose of your visit is purely historical. Telephone: 31 42 16 16.

Other Places. The main building of the old university is on Nørregade near the center of the city. Busts of some half dozen distinguished former scholars, Niels Bohr among them, are installed outside its entrance. Nearby is the Round Tower, built as an astronomical observatory in 1642. Ole Rømer found it to be inadequate for his purposes when he returned to Copenhagen from France, which is why he eventually built his own observatory at Vridsløsemagle (see "Tåstrup"). A grand view of the city is obtained from the top of the tower—a 660-foot (200 meter) spiral ramp makes it easy to climb. A place to relax near the city center is Ørsteds Park, a large park with two ponds, many trees, some sculptures, and a huge impressive statue of H. C. Ørsted.

RUDKØBING (Island of Langeland)

Langeland is one of the smaller of the Danish islands, about 30 miles (50 km) long and about 3 miles (5 km) wide, with beautiful beaches and some forested areas, popular for family vacations. Until 1967 it could be reached only by sea, but then a causeway and two bridges were built to join Langeland and the neighboring small isle of Tøsinge directly to the central island of Funen. Langeland's capital, Rudkøbing, is a picturesque small town (population about 4,000), with many very old houses, much of it beautifully preserved. It is fascinating that Hans Christian Ørsted, a native of this remote (at the time) and unpretentious place should have become a popular lecturer at the University of Copenhagen and should have carried out one of the most significant experiments in the history of physics.

Today we can see a large statue of Ørsted, which was erected in 1920 on the anniversary of the celebrated experiment. It stands on a little square opposite the Old Apothecary Shop, the house where Ørsted was born. Part of the building still houses a modern pharmacy, but another part has been converted to a small museum with a collection of pharmaceutical equipment from three centuries. Adjacent to the museum is an old hotel (Skandinavien Hotel) permeated with the atmosphere of old Rudkøbing. From the square, one can walk down Ramsherred ("Street of the Poor," though now tastefully and expensively renovated) and on through the old town to a small city park, where there is a memorial to the two brothers—Hans Christian Ørsted and his younger brother Anders, the latter a prominent lawyer and writer. The two brothers attended university together, after minimal formal education in Rudkøbing itself.

The pharmacy museum is open afternoons in the summer.

STEVNS KLINT
(16 miles [25km] southeast of Køge)

Here is an easily accessible, beautifully exposed cliff, where even the inexperienced observer can readily identify sharply demarcated geological strata. Analysis of the composition of the strata was an important factor in recent research on the massive extinction of many of the world's animal species 65 million years ago.

The cliffs are 7.5 miles (12 km) long and between 66 and 135 feet (20 and 41 m) high. They were described in the scientific literature as long ago as 1759. The very top layer in the sequence represents glacial deposits from the last Ice Age, only about 15,000 years old, but most of what we see was deposited from the sea millions of years ago, when the area we are looking at was periodically covered by ocean water. The prominent horizontal dividing line about halfway down the cliff is one of the best existing examples of the so-called *cretaceous/ tertiary* boundary, which divides older cretaceous (chalky) deposits from more recent limestone rock rich in mollusk fossils. Both principal parts of the rock face contain dark intrusions, easily seen as we look at the cliff from the observation point. These intrusions are made of flint, the material used by primitive humans to make tools.

The most fascinating part of the cliff are bands of clay within the cretaceous/tertiary boundary itself, called fiskeler (fish clay) because of their distinctive fossil content. This material was used as evidence for the recent hypothesis that the extinction of dinosaurs and many other forms of life about 65 million years ago was the result of a collision between the earth and a small meteorite. The hypothesis was first proposed on the basis of data from Italy (see under "Italy"), showing an anomalously high content of the element iridium, most likely derived from a nonterrestial source. The scientists who did the work needed to verify that they were looking at a worldwide phenomenon, not simply some local Italian peculiarity, and they came here to Stevns Klint because it is a classical example of the cretaceous/tertiary boundary. Their results were even more striking than in Italy. They found an iridium content of 42 parts per billion in the fiskeler, and less than 1 part per billion everywhere else. The confirmation of the predicted anomaly makes it highly probable that much of the fish clay layer (which we can see to be laid down with exceptional uniformity) consists of debris from the meteorite collision which circulated around the earth for many years and was gradually deposited all over the global surface.

The most accessible view of the cliff is obtained at Højerup church, an official state scenic site. This is also where the iridium data cited above were collected. Højerup church itself dates from 1357. According to legend it was built by a fisherman who had been rescued at sea, and the building is said to move backward a little each New Year's night (by supernatural agency) to compensate for gradual erosion of the cliff surface.

There is an information tablet at the site to define the layers one can see.

TASTRUP
(about 13 miles [20 km] west of Copenhagen)

Ole Rømer was born in Århus (in Jutland), where a street is named after him, but the most important memorial is a national one at Vridsløsemagle, just north of the town of Tåstrup, where the remains of Rømer's old observatory were uncovered in 1978. The site has been converted into a monument, with a fine statue of the astronomer, his eyes raised proudly to the skies. There is a museum about 1,000 feet (300 m) away. It is an impressive place despite operating on a shoestring budget, with good explanations of the instruments Rømer devised and why some of them were better than Tycho Brahe's a hundred years earlier and why they are not as good as instruments we have today. Some modern astronomical devices are shown as a basis for comparison. Star gazing evenings open to the public are held here once a week during the winter.

The most spectacular items in the museum are replicas of the "Planetarium" and the "Eclipsareon," two instruments designed by Rømer during his stay in Paris and constructed for him by the Paris clockmaker Isaac Thuret. The planetarium is the first device of its kind that was built according to the Copernican heliocentric system, with the earth as one of the planets circling the sun. The eclipsareon shows the motions of the moon, earth, and sun. Its

Ole Rømer scans the skies at Vridsløsemagle.

unique feature is that it includes offset cams, by means of which the elliptical path of the moon and the varying speed of its motion can be represented. Both models are in perfect mechanical order and can be put in motion by the visitor, by turning a handle in one case and by means of an electric motor in the other.

The two machines were immensely popular in Rømer's lifetime and many copies were made. Jesuit missionaries took copies in the 1680s to the shah of Persia, the king of Siam and the emperor of China. They were especially appreciated in China, where lunar and solar eclipses were central to religious festivals and the ability of the eclipsareon to predict them accurately was thus a great boon. Rømer's original planetary engines fell into disuse after his death. Their mechanism rusted, their metal was vandalized, and they were moved to the Round Tower in Copenhagen, where they were destroyed by Copenhagen's great fire of 1728, when one third of the city went up in flames.

The Vridsløsemagle site was picked out by Rømer himself in 1704, and it is still obvious today why one would want to put an observatory here. The ground is slightly elevated (by Danish standards), with picturesque farmland on all sides. The sky in good weather is crisply clear, and in 1704 sky is all you would have seen at night for miles around. Today, of course, the lights of Copenhagen blot out the stars toward the east. (It should be noted that the observatory foundations were built below ground level for optimal stability and were lost for more than 200 years. It proved no easy task to locate the remains in 1978.)

The site is in open country, but clearly signposted. The Rømer Museum is open daily, afternoons only on Saturdays and Sundays. Telephone 42 52 95 85. Note that Tåstrup is about halfway from Copenhagen to the old town of Roskilde. We strongly recommend a visit to the Viking Ship Museum there.

VEN (Island in the Øresund)

The island of Ven was part of Denmark when King Christian II gave it as a feudal fief to Tycho Brahe for the location and support of his observatory. It became Swedish territory in 1658 after the peace treaty of Roskilde and is most easily reached by ferry from the Swedish mainland. We have therefore listed details about the island and its Brahe memorial site under "Sweden." Access from Denmark is possible in the summer by ferry from Havnegade.

16

Sweden

Industry, commerce, and social concerns are the hallmark of Sweden—they manufacture big and powerful Volvos and Saabs and then insist you drive them most discreetly. But there is also an undercurrent of serious scholarship, a zeal for learning. We see it already in the sixteenth century in Queen Christina (queen since the age of six, still a teenager when she assumed full power), who brought scholars and artists from all over Europe to her court, including René Descartes. (Poor Descartes unfortunately could not stand the Swedish climate and died in Stockholm in 1650.) In the eighteenth century Uppsala was an academic center of excellence, with Carl Linnaeus among the local talent and Anders Celsius, who devised the temperature scale that bears his name. Then came another zealous king, Gustavus III, who founded the Swedish Academy of Science and built an opera house, and even wrote plays to be performed there. (He was too extravagant for some tastes and was assassinated at a masked ball in 1792.) Even in modern times there has been royal participation: Gustavus VI (1882–1973) was an archaeologist and botanist of note.

Sweden, however, also has a unique place in the world of science that is unrelated to discoveries made in its institutes or laboratories. The will of Alfred Nobel has made it, for better or worse, the quasi-official judge of who shall be deemed "best in the world" each year in physics, chemistry, medicine, and even literature. The Nobel Prizes were first awarded in 1901 and have retained their luster. Only the most cantankerous of scientists would not treasure a royal summons to Stockholm above any other honor.

The System of Nature

The system of scientific names we use for all living things is called the *Linnaean binomial system*. It was devised in essence by the Swedish botanist **Carl Linnaeus** (1707–1778), called **Linné** in his home country. Its distinguishing feature is the

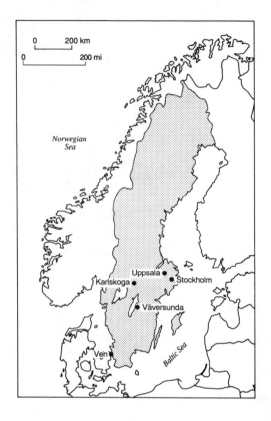

use of two words to describe each species, one giving the genus to which it belongs and the other designating the individual species itself. In the overall system (as used today), related genera are grouped together to define a family; related families define an order, related orders a class and so on to the top, to the three kingdoms, animal, vegetable and *protista*. The details have changed over the centuries (e.g., Linnaeus went straight from genus to order, lacking the intermediate level of family), but the essence remains the same, in particular the practical wisdom that two Latin words suffice for unambiguous identification in worldwide communication between scientists.

Linnaeus was a botanist and the kingdom of plants was his bailiwick. This brings a subplot into the story: What do we use as the basis for classifying plants? The possibilities seem endless. Linnaeus made a brilliant choice—he classified on the basis of the sexual parts of plants. In retrospect that seems sensible, focusing on the very point of reproduction and genetic specification, but it was by no means obvious at the time, when the very idea of sexuality in plants was still novel and controversial. Linnaeus's choice had a peripheral advantage, allowing him to use picturesque language in his descriptions of plants, which may have contributed to the public appeal of his work. The flowering plants, for example, were described as "public lovers," their "nuptials celebrated openly before the whole world," and descriptions of individual orders were consistent with this. For example, *Octandria* (eight stamens and one pistil) was described as having "eight males in the same bridal chamber with one female."

Linnaeus was born in southern Sweden and had acquired his enthusiasm for gardens and botany before he first came to Uppsala in 1728. The formerly grand but by then rather neglected botanical garden in Uppsala stimulated his enthusiasm and so did the patronage of the learned Olof Celsius, who was the leading expert in the local flora. Linnaeus was sent on a trip to Lapland to take inventory of its unfamiliar natural resources and produced a hugely successful report. In 1735 he went to the Netherlands (at the time the center of the scientific world) to obtain an M.D. degree and to learn more about the care of gardens and the nurture of plants. He published numerous works while in Leiden, most notably the first outlines of the *Systema Naturae*, the exposition of his system, which he was to revise and update several times thereafter.

In comparison with other figures in the history of biology, Linnaeus appears somewhat unsophisticated, even unscientific in the sense that he had no desire to learn about plant anatomy or physiology. He fully accepted the Biblical story of creation and believed that nothing then created had ever been destroyed. "There are just as many species as there were created at the beginning," he wrote, and—in reference to his own work—"I followed (God's) footsteps over nature's fields and saw everywhere an eternal wisdom and power, an inscrutable perfection." To this simple outlook he added a winning way with people, innocent charm, an unerring instinct for public relations. His students loved his lectures, given at the university or in the gardens, and the popular excursions he led into the surrounding countryside, which ended in ritual fashion with all the participants marching in closed formation to the music of French horns and drums. Linnaeus himself beat a "troll drum" made of reindeer skin, a souvenir of his Lapland expedition.

Peter Artedi (1705–1735). Many authorities believe that Peter Artedi might well merit a share of the credit for the Linnaean system of classification. He had come to Uppsala a few years earlier than Linnaeus, equally dedicated to the study of natural history but leaning more to the animal world, and the two men became very close friends. Artedi preceded Linnaeus in going abroad to extend his horizons (to England and the Netherlands) and in 1735 settled in Amsterdam. There, after a convivial evening with friends, he regrettably fell into a canal and drowned. He had completed a manuscript on the taxonomy of fishes, which Linnaeus saw through to publication without making any changes and which has an underlying philosophy much like Linnaeus's own. Who had the greater influence on whom must remain a matter of conjecture.

Related Places to Visit: Uppsala, London (Natural History Museum).

Chemistry and the Elements

Sweden has an exceptional record of excellence in the field of chemistry. For example, more of the chemical elements have been discovered here and identified as distinct elements than anywhere else in the world. Many of the so-called rare earth elements (they turn out to be not as rare as was originally thought) were first recognized in a single mine at Ytterby, just outside of Stockholm—hence the names yttrium, ytterbium, erbium, and holmium, the latter derived from the Latin name for Stockholm.

Above all is the Swedish origin of the now standard chemical system of nomenclature, which was devised by **Jacob Jöns Berzelius** (1779–1848). John Dalton, the father of the atomic theory (see under "England"), originated the idea that specific molecules are composed of fixed numbers of constituent atoms and drew pictures of the molecules in which the atoms are represented by circles. He used lines, dots, or letters within the circles to designate the different kinds of atoms. Berzelius substituted the much less clumsy letter symbols based on the first one or two letters of the Latin name of each element; 49 elements were known at the time and his symbols are the ones we still use for them.

Berzelius was, in fact, the most influential chemist of his time. He himself discovered several elements (titanium, selenium, thorium, silicon). He measured thousands of combining weights and hence produced a table of atomic weights, assigning values for 45 of the 49 known atoms. Many of them are now recognized as wrong, but that was often not due to error in the measured weights, but rather to the still unsolved problem of deciding the numbers of atoms involved in particular combinations.

Berzelius did organic chemistry as well as inorganic. He recognized that groups of atoms can sometimes act as a unit, maintaining their identity in different molecules, and he gave them the name *radicals*, which we still use. From the latter notion it was an obvious step to *isomers*. Other words in the Berzelius vocabulary included *catalysis* and *protein*. The Greek roots of the latter mean "to stand in front," and Berzelius suggested the word because he thought of protein as the "principal substance of animal nutrition that plants prepare for the herbivores, and which the latter then furnish to the carnivores."

Berzelius also had a theory about what holds the atoms in molecules together, a theory which he advanced and defended vehemently. The essence of it was that molecules are held together by electrical attraction, individual atoms being intrinsically either positive or negative. This doctrine had immense support, even long after Berzelius was dead, and had far-reaching consequences that were not beneficial. For example, it interfered with acceptance of Avogadro's hypothesis for half a century (see under "Italy"), not because there were objections to the hypothesis per se, but because a consequence of its application was that some gaseous molecules (O_2 and H_2, for example) would need to be diatomic adducts of *identical* atoms.

More recently we have **Svante Arrhenius** (1859–1927), who presents us with a paradox. He is responsible for one of the great discoveries of physical chemistry, the effects of which cut across all other branches of chemistry (and biology to boot!), yet he seems to have been regarded with ambivalence in his native land. His doctoral dissertation in 1884 was accepted by the University of Uppsala with such a low classification ("non sine laude," meaning "not without praise") that he became automatically ineligible for a faculty position. In 1901, after most of his significant papers had been published, he was elected to the Swedish Academy of Sciences, but only in the face of strong opposition. In 1903 he was awarded one of the earliest Nobel Prizes in chemistry (with a highly laudatory citation), which attests to some division in Swedish opinion, for there must have been overlap in membership between the Nobel committee and the Academy judges. The prize seems to have had no lasting effect, for Arrhenius is still not held in the esteem he merits—no statues in public places, no museums or institutes named for him.

Arrhenius came from a farming family, but his father was employed by the University of Uppsala as a ground staff supervisor, and Arrhenius received his scientific education at that institution. However, he chose to do his doctoral research in the laboratory of a Stockholm physicist, thereby probably making enemies at Uppsala, which might have contributed to his lowly degree. Arrhenius then spent four years in the laboratories of some of the most eminent physical chemists in Europe, where he received more encouragement than at home. During these travel years he published his great work (present in embryonic form in his dissertation), which was his theory of the dissociation of electrolytes in aqueous solution. The gist of it is that strong "electrolytes"—the common salts and strong acids and bases—dissociate into their constituent ions when dissolved in water. Common table salt, for example, exists in solution as separate Na^+ and Cl^- ions and not to any appreciable extent as molecules of neutral $NaCl$. The theory was the result of precise measurements of electrical conductivity and other properties of the solutions and their dependence on concentration, and the conclusion was all but inescapable on the basis of analysis of the results. But at the time it was a very radical proposal, seemingly in conflict with the *certainty* that positive and negative charge attract one another, and probably especially so in Sweden because of the legacy of Berzelius's emphasis on that attraction. In the words of one of his Uppsala critics, "It is nonsense to accept . . . that in a solution of potassium-chloride, chlorine and potassium are separated from each other."

Today, of course, it is far from nonsense. Free ions in aqueous solution are elementary facts of chemical science, known to be within the rules of electrical attraction because water molecules, though neutral overall, are highly polar, positive at one end and negative at the other, so that combination of a free ion with the right ends of several water molecules more than compensates for disruption of direct $+/-$ bonds. And in neurophysiology, ions are now actually recognized as the star actors. Nerve impulses are electrical signals produced by the movement of Na^+ and K^+ in and out of the nerve axon. (Calcium ions play a role, too, especially in regulation of the heartbeat.) Our judgment of Arrhenius today is emphatically "summa cum laude."

Related Places to Visit: Stockholm, Uppsala, Väversunda.

Alfred Nobel and the Prize

Each year on December 10, the anniversary of Alfred Nobel's death, the King of Sweden throws a party, highly publicized by the media. The occasion is the award, with much pomp and circumstance, of that year's Nobel Prizes. Have these prizes contributed directly to scientific progress? Has the lure of the prize spurred individuals to an intensity of effort beyond what they might have attempted without it? Probably not, or only rarely, for research is too unpredictable and the judgment of "the best" by an award committee is surely fallible. But the Nobel prizes have unquestionably increased public awareness of science—pure science, as distinct from spectacular technological applications—and they have thereby had an immense indirect benefit.

The man behind the prize, Alfred Nobel (1833–1896), is known as a powerful industrialist, who made a vast fortune out of the manufacture and sale of dynamite and (spurred by misgivings about the potential destructive use of his invention) willed everything he owned to an endowment for the annual awards. At the time of his death he owned 80 factories all over the world and all of them had to be liquidated under the terms of his will to swell the endowment for the prizes.

But there is actually more to Nobel's life than his success in industry, for he was basically a laboratory man. He himself *invented* dynamite. It happened when he was working in Paris in a laboratory where the explosive properties of nitroglycerine had been investigated, with often disastrous results because of the capricious properties of the material. He worked long and hard to tame it, eventually doing so by mixing the nitroglycerine with the porous mineral kieselguhr. It was the first new practical explosive since the arrival of gunpowder in the thirteenth century, and it was the right time for it, a time of huge construction projects, railroads, tunnels, harbors, and the like—everyone needed to blast through the land to clear the way. But dynamite, while the basis for his wealth, was only one of many achievements. Nobel acquired more than 300 patents for a variety of mechanical and chemical inventions, most of them unrelated to explosion. He also built laboratories for himself wherever he lived and worked in them on many different problems.

Nobel spent much of his time outside Sweden, and in fact he died in his favorite villa in San Remo in Italy. He left no widow or children, but there were other relatives who contested his will. It took several years of litigation before the will was declared valid, and one of the factors in the matter was establishment of a legal residence in Sweden.

Related Places to Visit: Karslkoga, Stockholm.

PRINCIPAL PLACES TO VISIT

KARSLKOGA (Värmland)

This town of 35,000 inhabitants can be said to be the place where the Nobel Foundation and its annual prizes were created. Alfred Nobel acquired the huge Bofors ironworks and munitions factory in 1894, just two years before he died; it was then and still is Karslkoga's largest industry, and the factory buildings dominate the town. With the factory Nobel acquired the splendid manor house Björkborn Herrgard, on the north side of the town, which is now a museum, with residential rooms, study, and laboratory, furnished much as they were at the time.

It was while he lived here that Alfred Nobel wrote his will and appointed his good friend Ragnar Sohlman as executor. Sohlman worked here for several years to implement the terms of the will and to formulate the rules for the administration of the awards. It was not as easy a task as might be supposed, for Nobel's family bitterly contested the will. It was in the Karslkoga district court that the ensuing legal battles took place and Nobel's residence here and his salaried position as Bofors director were important in the court's decision, for the establishment of where Nobel belonged was a major element in the legal arguments.

The museum is open every afternoon from June to September. Telephone 0586–81894 (museum) or 0586–61474 (tourist office).

STOCKHOLM

The principal site of interest in Stockholm (especially for chemists) is the **Berzelius Museum** in the Royal Swedish Academy of Sciences. It was founded in 1898 on the fiftieth anniversary of Berzelius's death and has been periodically and sympathetically improved several times since then. It now occupies two or three rooms in a former gardener's house; the space is small, but the presentation is skillful.

Among the exhibits are hundreds of vials and jars containing chemicals (including many purified elements) that Berzelius himself prepared in his laboratory, most of them with labels in his own handwriting—they are eloquent testimony to his interest and labors in both organic and inorganic chemistry. Equipment he used is also on display, such as balances and the blowpipes that used to be the chemist's stethoscope, tools for simple and rapid identification of minerals and other solid substances. We were particularly interested in a glass case containing metal crucibles, some of them quite large. They are actually replicas, for the originals were made of platinum and would carry a huge price today. Wall posters alongside the exhibits tell us about some of Berzelius's achievements. Not all of them are well-known—for example, the fact that his extensive work on preparation of the elements and measurement of their atomic weights was accompanied by a kind of revolution in mineralogy, discarding the historical method of classification on the basis of external experience in favor of a method based on chemical analysis. One small room represents Berzelius's study—desk, chair, copies of books by him and about him. It includes several editions of his six-volume textbook, used as a reference by students for nearly half a century.

In addition to the museum, there is a memorial to Berzelius in the center of Stockholm, in the form of a little park (Berzelii Park) near the Royal Theater, with a huge and imposing statue of the chemist.

The Academy is on the University campus on the north side of Stockholm. (Follow signs to *Vetenskapakademie* from the University underground station.) The museum does not get enough visitors to have its doors regularly open, and it is advisable to call in advance (Monday to Friday) to see it. Telephone: 08-150-430.

The Nobel Prize Banquet. The annual award of the Nobel prizes is Stockholm's great social occasion and includes a sumptuous banquet held in the city hall, the *Stadshuset* at the water's edge, facing the old city. The good news is that it is not necessary to be a Nobel laureate to enjoy the food that is served. It won't be in the magnificent Blue Hall, the site of the banquet on the great occasion itself, but in the public restaurant in the cellar of the city hall, called the *Stadshuskällaren*, where staff are prepared to serve the menus of past banquets if given a few days advance notice. A minimum of four in the party is required; formal attire is not expected.

UPPSALA

Linnaeus Garden. Linnaeus was appointed Professor of Medicine at the University of Uppsala in 1741, after some rather undignified infighting among several candidates for the position. Botany was academically a part of medicine at the time because plant extracts were the most common form of medication, and renovation of the university's neglected botanical garden (originally founded in 1655) was one of the new professor's assigned tasks. A house adjacent to the garden came with the appointment and served as Linnaeus's residence. Classically proportioned, with a red brick façade, it now serves as the garden museum, laid out and furnished much as it must have been in Linnaeus's day.

The garden area itself has been beautifully restored—the layout is nearly the same as the original, modeled according to the prevailing style, with narrow parallel formal beds and three pools and an orangery at the back. Two symmetrical sections (parterres) contain beds for perennial and annual (or biennial) plants, respectively. Arrangement within the perennial parterre is strictly in the order of the Linnaeus classification, but there are 44 beds for the 24 classes, allowing more than one bed for some classes. The annual plants are also grouped together by class, but the order varies from year to year. The path between the two sections is bordered by showy ornamental plants, and the pools beyond have water plants. The orangery used to be divided into *frigidarium*, *caldarium*, and *tepidarium*, to provide for a range of indoor environments, but it is less elaborate

Linnaeus in Lapland costume, from a 1737 painting. The flower fastened to his tunic is the twinflower, *Linnaea borealis*, shown here in a separate photograph. It blooms only briefly, close to midsummer, so you may not see it in the garden when you visit.

today. Parts of it now have nonbotanical uses, such as choir practice for a local group. Two little shelters on top of high poles near the entrance used to house chained monkeys. Linnaeus was very fond of the monkeys and is reported as having been unashamedly grieved when one of his favorites died.

Linnaeus died at his garden residence and was buried in **Uppsala Cathedral.** There is a monument with a medallion portrait in a chapel off the north aisle. The tomb slab itself is in the floor, a little closer to the main entrance. The cathedral is the largest church in Scandinavia and parts of it date back to the thirteenth century.

In the outskirts of Uppsala we have **Linnés Hammarby** (6 miles [10 km] southeast), Linnaeus's former summer residence, now a small state park. Linnaeus sometimes lectured here to students and large crowds of visitors. A little further out, toward the southwest, is **Wiks Slott** (Wik Castle), a fifteenth-century fortress with a fine park at the edge of a lake. Svante Arrhenius was born here in 1859, his father having been overseer of the estate at the same time as he was working for the university. (The university salary improved a year later, and the family was able to move into the city.) **Gamla Uppsala** (Old Uppsala), just north of the modern city, is also worth a visit. It was the royal capital of the Svea kingdom 1,500 years ago and contains burial mounds and other antiquities.

The Linnaeus Gardens (entered from Svartbäcksgatan) are open daily, but the museum is open only in the afternoon. A good historical and descriptive booklet (several languages) is for sale in the museum. Telephone 018-136-540. (Remember that flowers are seasonal and often last only a few days. There may not be many in full bloom on your day of visit.)

VÄVERSUNDA (Östergötland, 38 miles [60 km] west of Linköping)

Jacob Berzelius was born here in 1779, in a house that still stands, externally not greatly altered. It is a private residence, but there is a small monument to Berzelius on one side. A beautiful twelfth-century church stands next door, with a front door decorated with wrought iron and mural paintings on the inside. The surroundings are idyllic, Swedish countryside at its best. Lake Takern is close by on one side, and the dark forest of Omberg not far away on the other, providing a perfect location to inspire the love of nature that Berzelius had, but it should be kept in mind that he became an orphan at the age of nine and moved away to live with an uncle.

Väversunda is just a few kilometers north of Ödeshög. Signposts designate the historic church.

VEN (Island in the Øresund, Reached by Ferry from Landskrona)

The island of Ven is an extraordinary place to visit. It is only about 3 miles (5 km) from end to end, with a resident population (in 1991) of 332, swelled on summer weekends, to be sure, by cycling and picnicking families from the mainland. But 400 years ago (when Ven belonged to Denmark), this little island was the scene of Europe's most important scientific measurements. In the midst of its green fields and grazing sheep and cattle stood the observatory of Tycho Brahe, where the motions of the planets were observed with unprecedented accuracy. Brahe moved from Denmark to Prague near the end of his life and bequeathed his voluminous data to Johannes Kepler, who published them and used them as the basis for his famous three laws of planetary motion. And then Isaac Newton, partly egged on by Edmund Halley to explain Kepler's laws, gave us his own laws of motion and the law of gravitation. Without King Christian's gift of Ven to Tycho, would there have been no Kepler's laws? Would Newton's have been a more obscure career? Would Cartesian doctrines have prevailed longer than they did—ten years, twenty years, even more? Common sense tells us to avoid such hypothetical questions, but we can nevertheless imbibe a profound sense of history when we visit here. It was indeed a vital spot in the sequence of how physics actually developed.

Tycho Brahe erected his castle and observatory on the highest spot on the island, 150 feet (45 m) above sea level. He called it Uraniborg (meaning "heavenly castle"). It was by all accounts a showplace, built in Dutch Renaissance style and surrounded by a walled park, with a gate at each corner. All that we see today is a hole in the ground where the castle once stood; but pictures enable us to imagine how it must have looked. Tycho soon found the castle too small (and too unsteady) for his needs and built a separate observatory across the road, called Stjerneborg, meaning "castle of the stars." It is a lot smaller than the name might lead one to expect; the secret of its success is that most of the structure—five circular crypts around a central warming shelter—was built underground to provide firm solid foundations for Brahe's instruments. The idea was new in Europe at the time, which explains why Brahe's data were so much more precise than anybody else's even though everybody alike had to rely on observations with the naked eye. The observatory site was uncovered in 1951 and the superstructure (cupolas and towers) was restored to what is said to be similar to the original appearance.

The small Brahe Museum was established in 1930. It houses finds made during the excavations of the site and gives us pictures (but no models) of the precision instruments he built, together with a large amount of related historical

Uraniborg on the Island of Ven—a model of how it looked in Brahe's time. All we see today is a hole in the ground, where the foundations used to be.

information. We learn, for example, that Tycho Brahe had a sister named Sophie, who was married to an alchemist and was herself a proficient chemist. But her greatest fame was as an astrologer! She cast horoscopes on the basis of her brother's planetary positions. (We are told that a new museum will be built soon, to open in 1993 or 1994.)

Frequent ferries operate between Landskrona and Ven. It is a 20-minute walk from the Ven ferry landing to the Brahe site. Rental bicycles are in good supply, and the "official" advice is to use them instead of walking—we make no recommendation. The museum is open only in the summer, but all other parts of the site are outdoors and accessible at all times. Telephone: 0418–720–58 (museum) or 0418–169–80 (Landskrona tourist office).

17

Poland and Russia

Neither Poland nor Russia can properly be considered part of any long-lasting grouping of European states and Poland for much of our period of history was not a state at all but a partitioned territory, its segments absorbed by power-hungry neighbors. But both countries had periods when they were at the periphery of European culture and society, and they then produced (as we have come to expect) their share of native sons who were avid to participate in the adventure of scientific discovery. Each country has, in fact, contributed indelible names to the European heritage—the great Nicolaus Copernicus in the case of Poland and Dmitri Mendeléev in the case of Russia.

The Heliocentric Universe

There was a golden age for Poland during the Jagiello dynasty, from late in the fourteenth century until 1572, when Poland and its neighbor Lithuania ruled the land in friendly partnership. The grasping Knights of the Teutonic Order were driven out, arts and sciences flourished, the University of Cracow (founded in 1364) became a center of learning on a par with Prague and Vienna.

It was during this period that the towering figure of **Nicolaus Copernicus** (1473–1543) appeared on the scene. He was born in Torun into a well-to-do mercantile family and received the best education that money could buy, first at the University of Cracow and then at several Italian universities, including Padua, which was already a center of scientific excellence, though Galileo was still a century in the future. Copernicus had a powerful uncle (also his guardian), who was bishop of Warmia and who secured for Copernicus the position of canon of the Cathedral of Frombork (Frauenburg in German). This was as much a political appointment as a religious one, with administrative and fiscal responsibilities; it involved Copernicus in matters of war and peace—the Teutonic knights attempted a resurgence in 1520—and in such mundane problems as

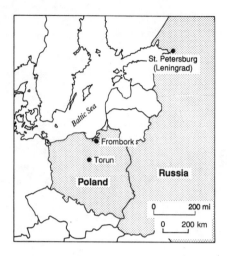

monetary reform. The once popular picture of Copernicus as a monkish recluse, poring over ancient tomes in a remote tower of the cathedral, is utterly false. He was a sophisticated man, applying his obviously brilliant analytical mind to worldly affairs as well as to celestial motions.

What was the origin of his revolutionary ideas about the universe? Some have claimed that they may have arisen from his exposure to Pythagorean thinking while in Italy, the Pythagoreans being noted for their fascination with numbers as the basis for all natural phenomena. Whatever the source of his inspiration, he uncompromisingly rejected the ancient Ptolemaic cosmology in favor of his own heliocentric system, with the earth and other planets in orbit around the sun, and the earth rotating daily on its own axis. And the basis for this terribly disconcerting idea (as it must then have been) unquestionably had to do with numbers. Copernicus showed that a heliocentric system had greater simplicity, requiring far fewer equations to describe planetary motion than the traditional geocentric system with its multiple epicycles. The idea of a helio-centric system had been proposed before, by Aristarchus in the third century B.C., but that was just a clever unsupported hypothesis. Copernicus provided evidence, and that was itself a part of his revolution.

Copernicus's first presentation of the concepts that the sun is the center of the universe and that the earth is in constant rotation came in 1514 in a short manuscript circulated among astronomers in Europe. But it took 30 more years before the final masterpiece, *De revolutionibus orbium coelestium*, was published and Copernicus was literally on his death bed when the book finally left the printer. This monumental work might, in fact, not have been published at all were it not for the efforts of a German mathematician, Georg Joachim (Rhe-ticus), who had become friendly with Copernicus and spent years urging the completion and publication of the book. There has been much speculation about the reason for the delay, but it would be inappropriate to dwell on this subject here, except to say that fear of causing offense to the Church was certainly not a factor. Those were still the days when one could say that "mathematics is for mathematicians," without conceivable relevance to spiritual matters—De revolutionibus was in fact dedicated to Pope Paul III.

(To complicate the matter, it should be mentioned that Rheticus was a Protestant, a follower of Martin Luther. As it happened, he had other irons in the fire by 1540 and the actual task of seeing De revolutionibus through the printing process was entrusted to another vigorous Lutheran, Andreas Osiander. The latter added a gratuitous introduction to the book, in which the reality of the proposals was denied! The authorship was not stated, so that the denial could have been wrongly attributed to Copernicus himself were it not for vigorous intervention by Rheticus and others.)

The Copernican theory found no great immediate support among astronomers. It was Kepler and Galileo in the early seventeenth century who catapulted it into fame. Today, we like to speak of the "Copernican Revolution," but it was surely one of the most prolonged revolutions in history.

Related Places to Visit: Frombork, Torun.

Under the Czars

In the days of Copernicus, Russia was still in many ways a barbaric land, under the oppressive rule of the likes of Ivan the Terrible. But in the eighteenth century (the worst of all times for Poland) Russia turned westward for inspiration—led initially by Peter the Great—and became a respected outpost of the stimulating Age of Enlightenment.

Retrospection. Russian history books today refer to **Mikhail V. Lomonosov** (1711–1765) as Russia's greatest scientist. They also recognize him as a great poet and public servant; a town on the Gulf of Finland, about 30 miles (48 km) west of St. Petersburg, is called Lomonosov in his honor—he once owned a glass factory there. But his name is not familiar to most of us today, nor was it in his own lifetime (even in his own country).

In fact, this fisherman's son from an island near Archangel did some remarkable things in his life. He founded the Russian Academy of Science; he wrote a Russian grammar. In chemistry he published a strong denunciation of the phlogiston theory as early as 1750 in the *New Commentaries of the St. Petersburg Academy*, a journal that was known to Lavoisier, though the latter made no reference to his predecessor when he later came to the same conclusion. Even more startling, perhaps, is the existence of a clear statement by Lomonsov of the principle of conservation of matter, again years before Lavoisier (see under "France"). We are somewhat accustomed today to a small number of forgotten works of genius, retrospectively rediscovered, and we ascribe it to the sheer volume of the scientific literature. But it is hard to see why Lomonosov should have been consigned to near obscurity in the eighteenth century, when the world of science was so much smaller and when Russia was certainly beginning to be a recognized member of the Western intellectual scene. It is an enigma.

The Periodic Table. The periodic table of the elements, hanging in the front of every chemistry lecture room in the world, is the work of the Russian chemist, **Dmitri Ivanovich Mendeléev** (1834–1907). He was born in Tobolsk, Siberia, the youngest of 14 children, and educated at St. Petersburg and Heidelberg. He was in many ways a product of his times, recipient of Tsarist orders of merit, but also an activist for change, one of many who foreshadowed the Communist Revolution that was soon to come. He was actually forced to resign his appointment at the University of St. Petersburg in 1890, after more than 30 years on the faculty, because he supported student demands for change and held so-called democratic tendencies that caused him problems with colleagues. (He received an appointment as supervisor of weights and measures in 1893, which gave less scope for troublesome political activism.)

Mendeléev's great achievement in recognizing periodicity in the relationship between atomic weights and chemical properties reportedly came about while he was writing a massive textbook on the principles of chemistry, a book that proved to be very popular and subsequently went through many editions and translations. He wanted to do more than present the facts, to devise a useful way of grouping similar elements together, and in the course of these attempts, he discovered the crucial correlation with atomic weights. (Which, it should be noted, would not have been possible just a few years earlier, for the values of the atomic weights were in a chaotic state until the 1860s.) As it turned out, the elements did not actually line up perfectly if one stolidly arranged all the ones that were known in the order of their mass, but Mendeléev had sufficient imagination to see that they would do so if three gaps were left in his table— elements not yet known, which would eventually be found, he firmly believed. This necessary contrivance to make things work did not inspire much confidence in Mendeléev's idea, but it ultimately became the decisive evidence in his favor, for the missing elements soon appeared, exactly where predicted, discovered moreover by chemists who had until then paid little attention to ideas about possible order in chemistry. (Gallium was one of the new elements, with the weight and chemical properties expected for the gap adjacent to aluminum; germanium was another, filling the hole next to silicon.)

Mendeléev was not the genius that Copernicus was (and perhaps Lomonosov, too) and did not exactly distinguish himself by his later work. He had already, as a student, decided that mass should be the determining factor for chemical identity and had opposed theories of chemical attraction based on electrical forces (such as Berzelius had held). His periodic table reinforced his prejudice, and he subsequently rejected the existence of the subatomic particles such as electrons that would ultimately explain the periodicity he had discovered. He likewise disputed disintegration of atoms as an explanation for radioactivity and thus remained outside the mainstream of the new atomic physics that was sweeping the rest of Europe near the end of his life. He nevertheless received copious honors, such as honorary doctorates from Oxford and Cambridge and membership in the French Legion of Honor. A mass of students marched in his funeral procession in St. Petersburg, carrying a poster of the periodic table high above their heads.

Related Place to Visit: St. Petersburg.

PRINCIPAL PLACES TO VISIT

Poland

NORTHEAST POLAND:
Land of a Thousand Lakes

This region of Poland was the home of Copernicus for 30 years, during which period the astronomer did all of his scientific work and at the same time executed his duties as the temporal representative of the Bishop. In more recent times the area was part of East Prussia and most of the towns had German names, but World War II restored the land to Poland. The towns on the Baltic coast are now popular summer resorts for the native population, and the many inland lakes attract bathers and sailboats. There are also huge forests teeming with birds and wild animals, where more rugged Poles go camping and mushroom-hunting. The region is still largely neglected by the foreign tourist.

Frombork (the former Frauenburg, east of Gdansk) was home base for Copernicus. It is the city in which he held the position of Canon of the Cathedral. The old, fortified cathedral still stands on a hilltop, surrounded by stone walls from the fourteenth and fifteenth centuries, and it has a remembrance tablet (from 1735) to the famous astronomer in the nave. The tower in the northwest part of the courtyard, built in the late fourteenth century, is named for Copernicus, and the sixteenth-century Bishop's Palace in the southwest corner contains the Copernicus Museum. Here one finds old copies of *De Revolutionibus* and other memorabilia of both the man and the times.

Copernicus traveled extensively in the execution of his canonical duties, and the Polish Tourist Office publishes a map and guide to the region around Frombork listing nearly every village and town that Copernicus ever had occasion to visit. Making a circuit of 125 miles (200 km), we are directed to Braniewo (once Braunsberg and an important city of the Order of Teutonic Knights), then to Pieniezno, the village that used to be the seat of the religious Chapter of the See of Warmia—Copernicus lived here for two years. We then proceed to Orneta, where Copernicus was sent to receive oaths of loyalty (and taxes!) from the local serfs and from there to Lidzbark Warminski, where his uncle, the Bishop, had his home—Copernicus, among his other activities, served as the

Bishop's secretary and medical advisor. Lidzbark Warminski has a fine medieval Gothic castle, well-preserved and now housing a museum. Finally we are led to Olsztyn, a city with a popular folk museum, where Copernicus is said to have been put in charge of the defenses against one of the invaders of the early sixteenth century. Our "monk" emerges as versatile man!

TORUN

The birthplace of Copernicus is a picturesque town on the Vistula River and provides some of the best examples of Gothic urban architecture in Central Europe. (And it's famous for its gingerbread, too.) The tower on the Town Hall dates from 1274 and is the oldest in Poland. The house in which Copernicus was born is now a museum, devoted to his life and work.

Museums in Poland are usually open daily, except Mondays and days following holidays. Telephone (Torun Museum) 267–48.

Russia

ST. PETERSBURG (Leningrad)

St. Petersburg is one of the most beautiful cities in the world. Founded by Peter the Great in the early eighteenth century, it is not very old and lacks the ancient ruins that most European cities prize, but its broad embankments and magnificent buildings alongside the Neva River create a splendid sight. Peter the Great and later Catherine the Great made the city the artistic and intellectual center of Russia, which it remained until the Communist Revolution. Many scientists have made their home here, including the Swiss mathematician Leonhard Euler (1707–1783) and three of the Bernoulli clan from Basel (see under "Switzerland"). Daniel, the most famous of the latter, worked at the St. Petersburg Academy from 1725 to 1733 and probably did most of his work on hydrodynamics here. His nephew Jakob II followed in his footsteps a generation later and married a granddaughter of Euler—he drowned in the Neva while swimming when he was only thirty years old.

The eighteenth-century center of activities was the eastern tip of Vasilyesky island, where the Neva splits in two. The old *Kunstkammer* on the University Embankment was erected around 1730 and the St. Petersburg Academy of Sciences was located here when first founded, moving to its present building next door when larger quarters became necessary around 1785. Mikhail Lomonosov, Bernoulli, and Euler all worked in the old building, which today houses several institutes and a museum dedicated to Lomonosov and containing some of his scientific equipment and books. A major attraction in the museum is the Great Academic Globe constructed in 1754, a map of the world on the outside and a crude kind of planetarium within—a dozen people could stand inside at a time and watch the stars rotate. (A statue of the poet/scientist stands at the head of Mendeléev Row, just beyond the main building of the present academy.)

Leningrad State University on Mendeléev Row is one of the oldest buildings in the city. It originally housed Peter the Great's government offices, but was taken over by the university in 1819. Mendeléev lived and worked here from 1866 to about 1890. The apartment where he lived is now a museum. His study, desk, inkstand, and so on, are preserved unchanged. Instruments from his laboratory are on display and the history of the discovery of the periodic table of the elements is given in detail. In another part of the city (on the mainland across the river) is the Institute of Metrology on Moscow Avenue, which is devoted to definition and measurement of length, mass, and time. Mendeléev founded the institute and worked there from 1893 until his death in 1907. A statue of the scientist stands in the garden of the institute and the wall of an adjacent house is adorned by a huge Periodic Table of the Elements.

Another former residence converted to a museum honors **Ivan Pavlov** (1849–1936), who won a Nobel Prize in 1904 for his research on the physiology of digestion and is best known today for his studies of conditioned reflexes. The location is at No. 1 Lt. Schmidt Embankment, a continuation of University Embankment.

Alexander Nevsky Monastery and Cemeteries. The entrance to the former monastery (founded in 1716) faces Alexander Nevsky Square. Behind it we have St. Petersburg's most famous burial ground, divided into two separate cemeteries. To the left of the main entrance is Lazarevskoye Cemetery, where Lomonosov and Euler are buried. To the right is Tikhvinskoye Cemetery, with the tombs of Fyodor Dostoyevsky and many of Russia's most celebrated musicians: Glinka, Tchaikovsky, Moussorgsky, Rimsky-Korsakov, Borodin, and others. (Borodin, famous for his opera *Prince Igor*, was actually only an amateur musician with little formal training, his principal profession being chemistry, which he taught at the St. Petersburg Institute of Medicine.)

Postscript. Ironically, we have been writing the above on the very day that the Russian Parliament has voted to permit the city of Leningrad to restore its former name of St. Petersburg. It reminds us that the paramount tourist site here is the Finland Railway Station, where Lenin's train arrived late at night on April 3, 1917, to trigger the momentous social experiment that has just concluded and been declared a failure. It is perhaps fitting to end this book with the thought that social sciences *might* at some time in the future attain a level of credibility commensurate with that of the natural sciences. But how does one cope with the fact that a single experiment in a social laboratory must last over 70 years to run its course?

Name Index

Boldface references are to principal *Places to Visit* in relation to the named scientist. Names in italics represent political or literary figures.

Subject Index

References are predominantly to what we consider the "didactic" sections of this book, where we give the background information for the indexed subjects. Related *Places to Visit* are usually listed at the end of individual text segments.

Index of Places